"This book offers extraordinary insights into how long-term, embedded peacemakers make sense of what a just peace requires in the Palestinian-Israeli landscape. These dialogues open a portal into the experience of how narratives emerge and respond to a context of cross-generational loss, exasperation, and lived madness. A must-read if we are to better understand both the challenge and the hope for descriptions and prescriptions about the peace process."

John Paul Lederach, *Professor Emeritus of International Peacebuilding, University of Notre Dame*

"Prof. Hostetter offers us, for the first time, a synthesis of activism and scholarship in the search for peace and reconciliation between Israel and the Palestinians. The most progressive voices are juxtaposed in this excellent book and offer food for thought for anyone wishing to bring peace and justice to historical Palestine. This is the first time that these progressive voices make a synergic appearance, in this incredible book."

Ilan Pappe, *professor in the College of Social Sciences and International Studies, University of Exeter (U.K.), director of the European Centre for Palestine Studies, and codirector of the Exeter Centre for Ethno-Political Studies*

"*Peacemakers in Israel-Palestine* is a wonderful ethnography of Israeli and Palestinian peacemakers and a much-needed and illuminating contribution to the literature on ... Track Two diplomacy and the still unrealized potential it contains for nonviolent transformative change. These voices are essential and must continue to be heard."

Sara Roy, *senior research scholar, Center for Middle Eastern Studies, Harvard University, U.S.*

"Dr. Hostetter's book, *Peacemakers in Israel-Palestine,* is a well-written and well-researched contribution to the study of peacemaking in general and to the Israeli-Palestinian conflict in particular. Of special interest is the way Hostetter has brought the conflict to life by allowing Israeli and Palestinian peacemakers to speak in their own voices, thereby revealing the complexity, variety, and richness of their experiences. I highly recommend it."

Jonathan Kuttab, *executive director, Friends of Sabeel North America (FOSNA), and an international human rights attorney*

Peacemakers in Israel-Palestine

Peacemakers in Israel-Palestine: Dialogues for a Just Peace offers an analysis of the major sources of the Israeli-Palestinian conflict and suggests principles and processes for building a peacemaking platform. The primary aim of this book is to analyze the crucial roles and capacities of mid-level, nongovernmental peacemakers as they provide unique approaches to transforming the Israel-Palestinian conflict. It also aims to analyze and experience dialogue as the primary mode of peacemaking communication. The two-part format of this book creates a structural dialogue. Part I provides an academic introduction to the Israeli-Palestinian conflict, why it matters, the role of identities, and strategies for transforming the conflict based on international law and human rights. Part II is presented in a dialogue format, providing further conflict analysis through storytelling and dialogues with peacemakers. This book will be of great interest to anyone engaged with dialogue and performance studies, peace and conflict transformation, ethnography, social justice, communication studies, and human rights and international law.

Robert D. Hostetter is an academic, peace activist, playwright, and co-founder and director of the Conflict Transformation Program at North Park University in Chicago. For more than 35 years he has worked at the intersection of the arts and peacemaking. In 1998, the Center for Middle Eastern Studies at North Park University invited him to record the stories of older Palestinians who lost homes and villages in 1948 when Israel became a state. He adapted those stories for a play, *The Longing* (2001). For the National Communication Association, he has served as chair of the Peace and Conflict Communication Division.

Routledge Studies in Peace and Conflict Resolution

Series Editors: Tom Woodhouse and Oliver Ramsbotham
University of Bradford

The field of peace and conflict research has grown enormously as an academic pursuit in recent years, gaining credibility and relevance amongst policymakers and in the international humanitarian and NGO sector. The Routledge Studies in Peace and Conflict Resolution series aims to provide an outlet for some of the most significant new work emerging from this academic community, and to establish itself as a leading platform for innovative work at the point where peace and conflict research impacts on International Relations theory and processes.

Neighborhood Resilience and Urban Conflict
The Four Loops Model
Karina V. Korostelina

Reconciling Divided States
Peace Processes in Ireland and Korea
Edited by Dong Jin Kim and David Mitchell

Interactive Peacemaking
A People-Centered Approach
Susan H. Allen

Racial Justice and Nonviolence Education
Building the Beloved Community, One Block at a Time
Arthur Romano

Peacemakers in Israel-Palestine
Dialogues for a Just Peace
Robert D. Hostetter

For more information about this series, please visit: https://www.routledge.com/Routledge-Studies-in-Peace-and-Conflict-Resolution/book-series/RSPCR

Peacemakers in Israel-Palestine

Dialogues for a Just Peace

Robert D. Hostetter

LONDON AND NEW YORK

First published 2023
by Routledge
4 Park Square, Milton Park, Abingdon, Oxon OX14 4RN

and by Routledge
605 Third Avenue, New York, NY 10158

Routledge is an imprint of the Taylor & Francis Group, an informa business

British Library Cataloguing-in-Publication Data
A catalogue record for this book is available from the British Library

Library of Congress Cataloging-in-Publication Data
Names: Hostetter, Robert, 1946- author.
Title: Peacemakers in Israel-Palestine : dialogues for a just peace / Robert Hostetter.
Description: Abingdon, Oxon ; New York, NY : Routledge, 2022. | Includes bibliographical references and index.
Identifiers: LCCN 2022010593 (print) | LCCN 2022010594 (ebook) | ISBN 9781032202341 (hardback) | ISBN 9781032202402 (paperback) | ISBN 9781003262817 (ebook)
Subjects: LCSH: Arab-Israeli conflict--1993---Peace. | Arab-Israeli conflict--Peace. | Jewish-Arab relations. | Peace-building--Israel. | Peace-building--Palestine. | Political activists--Israel--Interviews. | Political activists--Palestine--Interviews.
Classification: LCC DS119.76 .H68 2022 (print) | LCC DS119.76 (ebook) | DDC 956.9405/4--dc23/eng/20220506
LC record available at https://lccn.loc.gov/2022010593
LC ebook record available at https://lccn.loc.gov/2022010594

ISBN: 978-1-032-20234-1 (hbk)
ISBN: 978-1-032-20240-2 (pbk)
ISBN: 978-1-003-26281-7 (ebk)

DOI: 10.4324/9781003262817

Typeset in Times New Roman
by MPS Limited, Dehradun

To Don, who invited me to bear witness to the Israeli-Palestinian conflict, and to join the struggle for a just peace.

To Nancy, who sustained this calling with faith, hope, love, and a shared commitment to the work. Thanks for the outstanding editing and proofreading.

To the family members—Susanna, Hector, and Molly—who participated in various parts of this journey.

Contents

Acknowledgments xi

PART I
Analysis for a Just Peace 1

1 Orientations: An Introduction 3

2 Coming to Terms 17

3 A Conflict of Identities 31

4 Peacemaker Identities 46

5 Dialogues for a Just Peace 61

6 A Platform for a Just Peace 75

PART II
Dialogues with Peacemakers 89

7 The Arts as Beautiful Resistance 91
ABDELFATTAH ABUSROUR

8 The Lessons of Engagement 102
GHASSAN ANDONI

9 Jewish Tradition and Human Rights 113
ARIK ASCHERMAN

10 Peacemaking and Nation-building 125
HANAN ASHRAWI

11 A Journey for Justice and Peace 133
NAIM ATEEK

12 Changing Public Opinion in Israel 145
URI AVNERY

13 The Power of Nonviolence 158
SAMI AWAD

14 The Business of Peacemaking 171
SAM BAHOUR

15 What Reconciliation Requires 182
EITAN BRONSTEIN

16 *5 Broken Cameras:* A Film for Peace 192
EMAD BURNAT

17 Get Up, Move Ahead, Make Peace 195
ELIAS CHACOUR

18 A Comprehensive Solution 203
MONA EL-FARRA

19 Struggles for a Just Peace 214
JEFF HALPER

20 Universal Principles, International Law 233
JONATHAN KUTTAB

21 Telling the Whole Truth 245
GIDEON LEVY

22 A Mandate for Human Rights 253
JESSICA MONTELL

23 The Only Nonviolent Alternative 264
ILAN PAPPE

24 The Infrastructure of Hope 276
MITRI RAHEB

25 Work for the Common Good 289
ESTEPHAN SALAMEH

26 Three Sails for Gaza 302
YONATAN SHAPIRA

27 A Better World for All of Us 314
GILA SVIRSKY

References 321
Index 330

Acknowledgments

Numerous individuals and groups have made this book possible. First of all, I am grateful to the dialogue participants presented in this book. They gave their valuable time to meet with me, to share their experiences and conflict analyses, and they honored my role as an informed listener. Some of them risked harassment and punishment by one or both sets of government officials. All of the peacemakers in this book have given permission to include our dialogues. For some peacemakers, time, distance, and the challenges of the Israeli occupation limited our efforts to a single dialogue. For others, multiple dialogues became possible during eight research trips between 2003 and 2018. Altogether, I recorded and transcribed some 60 peacemaker dialogues.

Seven or eight transcribers completed an enormous amount of work, figuring out people's names, place names, and concepts in Arabic, Hebrew, and English. These transcribers made possible two-thirds of this book, presented here as Part II.

Outstanding editors helped to make this presentable. Linda Kateeb turned a first draft into something readable. Nancy McCann Hostetter combined the patience of a spouse with editing the final drafts. Without their efforts, this book would not have been possible. Though the editors have been scrupulous, I accept responsibility for any mistakes and misunderstandings that remain. I welcome corrections.

Dwight Conquergood, one of my academic advisors, urged me to combine research with ethics, performance, ethnography, and dialogue. John Paul Lederach provided a vision for conflict transformation. Jeff Halper, a public intellectual and peace activist, shared many dialogues about strategic peacemaking. J.D. Mininger supported my interdisciplinary approach.

North Park University provided several faculty development grants. Omar Haramy and the Sabeel Ecumenical Liberation Theology Center in Jerusalem provided friendship and spiritual support. Mark and Susanne Brown and The Lutheran World Federation provided hospitality and included me in weekly volleyball games on the Mount of Olives. Thanks to the Peace and Conflict Communication Division of the National Communication Association for ongoing dialogues.

Thanks also to all the others who made this book possible by providing encouragement, financial support, reading chapters, offering corrections and prophetic insights, and demonstrating *sumud* (steadfastness, resilience, and models of nonviolent resistance): Ilsup Ahn, Sami Awad, Kathy Bergen, Pauline Coffman, Angela Godrey-Goldstein, Kathy Kamphoefner and Paul Pierce, Leona Mirza, Paul and Kate Myers, David and Kathy Neely, Mary Trujillo, Adel Yahya, Rich Lessor and the Oak Park Men's Group, and the Hyde Park Men's Group.

Thanks to Maya Durham Rayner for adapting the illustrations in Chapters 1 and 2. And thanks to Oxford University Press and John Paul Lederach for permission to adapt the "Pyramid of Peacebuilding" (Fig. 1.1) from *The Moral Imagination: The Art and Soul of Building Peace* (2005). Thanks to Mazin Qumsiyeh for permission to adapt "Palestinian Loss of Land" (Fig. 2.1), adapted from *Sharing the Land of Canaan* (2004).

Robert D. Hostetter
Chicago, August 2022

Part I

Analysis for a Just Peace

1 Orientations: An Introduction

A teaching colleague suggests that we should "skip the point and get to the story." But another colleague, a historian, declares that an introduction is crucial for understanding the Israeli-Palestinian conflict. This book offers the opportunity to accomplish both. To engage with the challenging material in this book, begin with this introduction to understanding the background of the conflict, key terms, methods, and the challenges of building a platform for a just peace; then read the verbatim dialogues that follow in Part II. Or begin with the compelling peacemaker dialogues in Part II, then read this introduction.

For more than 70 years, political elites have failed to create a just peace in Israel-Palestine. So, the primary aim of this book is *to analyze the roles and capacities of mid-level, nongovernmental peacemakers* who live in Israel-Palestine. Other aims include analyzing and experiencing dialogue as the primary mode of peacemaking communication, examining the convergence of critical ethnography and conflict transformation, analyzing struggles to end the Israeli control of the Occupied Palestinian Territories (OPT), and efforts to imagine and implement a just peace.

The two-part format of this book creates a structural dialogue: the analyses in Part I are based on a close reading of the dialogues in Part II, and Part II serves as an extension of Part I. This two-part structure provides an introduction to the abundant scholarship about the Israeli-Palestinian conflict as well as the lived experience of peacemakers. This format demonstrates the capacities of mid-level peacemakers to articulate their own analyses and strategies for a just and sustainable peace. Part I provides an academic, ethnographic analysis of how nearly two dozen Palestinian and Israeli peacemakers, through dialogue, narrate their experiences of the conflict and how they became peacemakers. They analyze the sources of the conflict and their strategic responses for transforming it.

Part II provides the primary material, some 40 verbatim dialogues with nearly two dozen peacemakers, on which Part I is based. These nongovernmental Israeli and Palestinian peacemakers work "from the middle" to access political elites and give leadership to grass-roots communities. They engage in a wide range of peacemaking and peacebuilding strategies: to

DOI: 10.4324/9781003262817-2

hold government officials accountable to international law, to advocate for nonviolent change, to build educational institutions, to support healing through the arts and restorative justice, to end the occupation, and to imagine and implement a just peace.

Chapter 1 provides multiple orientations for understanding this conflict: a historical context; why this conflict matters—locally, regionally, and globally; failures of official diplomacy (Track One) to achieve a just peace; consequently, the need for nongovernmental peacemaking (Track Two), including the need for an ethnographic, experiential approach to understanding this conflict; and peacemaking as theory, method, and practice. Chapter 2 defines key terms used in this conflict, and the existential role of peacemakers in Israel-Palestine. Chapter 3 follows from John Paul Lederach's (2003) premise that identities are at the heart of most conflicts, and it examines the major identities in this conflict: national identities, victimhood, demographics, Zionism, land, and various Palestinian orientations. Chapter 4 explores both Israeli and Palestinian peacemaker identities. Chapter 5 examines the possibilities and challenges of engaging in meaningful dialogue—between peacemakers, and between peacemakers and their own ethnic groups. Chapter 6 documents the emerging consensus that the "two-state solution" and the "land for peace" paradigm have died. Among peacemakers, a new paradigm is emerging: One Democratic State (ODS), based on human rights and international law. This chapter concludes with principles, processes, and a platform for a just peace.

1.1 Why This Conflict Matters

For more than 70 years, Jews and Palestinians in the Middle East have engaged in cycles of violence, war, contests over land, and other conflicts (Khalidi, 2020). A longtime leader in the Israeli peace movement, journalist Uri Avnery says that Palestinians and Israelis have been living in a "perpetual state of war" (Part II, p.) for five generations (Part II, p. 149). Both Palestinian and Israeli communities have suffered extensively in this conflict. Even though Israelis wield a huge imbalance of financial resources and military power, Rabbi Arik Ascherman, a human-rights activist, believes that the ongoing conflict has brought major psychological, spiritual, and political costs to Israeli Jews as well as to Palestinians.

This conflict has local, regional, and global significance. In one of our dialogues, Jeff Halper, an activist, public intellectual, and cofounder of the Israeli Committee Against Home Demolitions, calls this an "iconic conflict," at the geographical crossroads of Europe, Asia, and Africa, and the epicenter of conflict between East and West. From 1947 until the present, this conflict has been a central concern of the United Nations (UN). Phyllis Bennis (2002) writes that "Palestine today stands at the symbolic center of Arab consciousness, giving it a regional and indeed international significance far beyond its size" (p. 21). This small territory is the focus of a profound religious consciousness; it is the home of three world religions, with a long legacy of "holy wars"—the Christian Crusades, Eretz Israel, and Islamic jihad (Armstrong, 2001).

It is important, though, to stress that the Israeli-Palestinian conflict is not primarily a religious conflict, but a conflict over land, control, and human rights. The Israeli government has perpetuated more than 50 years of military occupation over Palestine, that is, the West Bank, Gaza and East Jerusalem—"the longest military occupation in modern history" (Khalidi, 2017). Jonathan Kuttab identifies the Israeli-Palestinian conflict as one of the last colonial situations. At every level—as a local, regional, and international conflict—this situation influences global perceptions of democracy, justice, human rights, and international law. In *One Land, Two Peoples* (1994), Deborah Gerner writes that the Israeli-Palestinian conflict provides an opportunity to examine a host of concepts important to international relations—national identity and self-determination, the increasing importance of nonstate actors, the role of natural resources, great power involvement in the Third World, the role of religion in international politics, global militarization, the relative impotence of international law and international organizations like the UN, dealing with very complicated conflicts, and forms of violent and nonviolent conflict resolution.

During my research for this book, Israel launched a war against Hezbollah in southern Lebanon (2006) and engaged in four brutal wars with Gaza—Operation Cast Lead (2008 - 09), Operation Pillar of Defense (2012), Operation Protective Edge (2014), and the 11-day war of 2021. At this writing, the Israeli blockade of Gaza has persisted for more than a dozen years. The possibility of armed conflict between Israel and Gaza remains high. The Israeli-Palestinian conflict also fuels international tensions over nuclear weapons—both Israel's unacknowledged possession of hundreds of these weapons as well as Iran's pursuit of these weapons. The dialogues in this book describe the burdens of military occupation on Palestinians as well as the emotional, religious, and political costs to Israelis. In our dialogue, Israeli journalist Gideon Levy speaks of "the next Israeli war," even an Israeli "need for war and the rituals of war" (Part II, p. 250). Sam Bahour speaks of the "next *intifada* or something worse" if the Israeli-Palestinian conflict is not transformed into a just peace (Part II, p. 117).

1.2 The Failure of Track One Diplomacy

The Arab-Israeli conflict emerged through both military and diplomatic battles. For more than a century, political and governmental elites have failed to achieve a just and sustainable peace between Jews and Palestinians in historic Palestine. During the Second World War, the British asked Palestinians to help defeat the Ottoman Empire, and they suggested that the British would help Palestinians create a state of their own. But in the Sykes-Picot Agreement (1916), the British and the French carved up control of the Middle East for themselves. The British took control of Palestine and Transjordan. In the Balfour Declaration of 1917, the British promised to assist the Jewish people to achieve a state on land that was 94% owned by Palestinians. Lord Arthur Balfour announced that the British government favored "the establishment in Palestine of a national home for the Jewish people … [and] nothing shall be done which may prejudice the civil and religious rights of existing non-Jewish communities in Palestine" (in Pappe, 2006, p. 264). Balfour failed to mention Palestinians by name, or that they were the majority population. During the British Mandate over Palestine (1922–1947), the British generally oppressed the Palestinian majority and supported the emigration of Jews to Palestine.

At the end of the British Mandate, Jews conducted a successful "war of liberation" against the British, and the British referred the Jewish-Palestinian conflict to the UN. The UN proposed a division of Palestine into two states, assigning 55% of Palestine to the Jewish community, which constituted 45% of the population (and owned only 7% of the land), and 45% of the land to the Arab majority, which comprised 55% of the population (Khalidi, 2017, p. 4). Jewish leaders accepted this proposal; Palestinian leaders did not. The UN partition plan (UN Resolution 181) became one of the greatest sources of conflict between Jews and Palestinians and a primary source of the 1948 war (Khalidi, 1997).

In the war of 1948, Jewish forces destroyed more than 400 Palestinian villages, and forced some 750,000 Palestinians to become refugees (Khalidi, 1992). According to Avnery, David Ben-Gurion, Israel's first prime minister, "did not believe in peace with the Arabs. It was Ben-Gurion who decided to drive the Arabs out in the second half of the war" (Part II, p. 149). Avnery says that the Jewish armies changed from espousing survival to "ethnic cleansing" because "we were winning, and we could afford to. If you want to really know what happened, … read the books by Benny Morris, who now says it is a pity we did not drive out more [Palestinians]" (Part II, p. 149).

In *The Ethnic Cleansing of Palestine* (2006), Ilan Pappe documents Ben-Gurion's determination to rid Palestine of Palestinians. By March 1948, the Jewish army, the Haganah, had developed Plan Dalet, "the Zionist master plan for the ethnic cleansing of Palestine" (p. 81). In May 1948, when Ben-Gurion declared Israel a Jewish state, removing "Arab peasants" was one of his deepest concerns (Pappe, 2006, p. 87). Avnery says, "Ben-Gurion was convinced that the Arabs would not make peace with us. Not in our generation. Not in the remote future. Because we had taken their land and driven them out, they would not make peace with us. So, we must live in a perpetual state of war" (Part II, p. 149). Avnery, a soldier in 1948, came to the opposite conclusion.

> After everything I'd seen, I came out of the war completely convinced of several very unorthodox ideas. One, there exists a Palestinian nation. The Palestinians must get a state of their own, and we shall never have peace if such a state is not created. Two, the state of Israel must find a place in a unified Semitic region…. (Part II, p. 148)

Into his early 90s, Avnery still struggled to persuade other Israelis to accept these ideas.

In the 1967 war, the Israeli army occupied the rest of the Palestinian territories—the West Bank, the Gaza Strip, and East Jerusalem—a military occupation that persists to this day. In November 1967, the UN passed Resolution 242, calling for "secure borders" and "a return of occupied land taken in the war." As Rashid Khalidi writes, "The original conflict in Palestine was a colonial one between the indigenous Palestinian majority and the Zionist movement as that minority tried to achieve sovereignty over the country at the expense of, and ultimately in place of the majority" (2010, pp. 4–5).

In the 1990s, in response to the first *intifada*, a "peace process" emerged, including Oslo (1993), Oslo II (1995), Camp David (2000), Taba (2001), Annapolis (2007), Washington (2010), the 2013–14 peace process led by U.S. Secretary of State John Kerry, and Trump's "Deal of the Century" (2020). The scholarship on these diplomatic failures is extensive and diverse (Ashrawi, 1995; Bunton, 2013; Chomsky, 2016; Halper, 2014; Khalidi, 2013; Pappe, 2004).

The Oslo process began with the secret meeting of Norwegian academics and governmental officials functioning in a nongovernmental capacity. Over time, Israeli and Palestinian political leaders took ownership of the process, which culminated on the White House lawn with the famous handshake between Yasser Arafat, the Palestinian president, and Yitzhak Rabin, the Israeli prime minister. This was widely perceived as a breakthrough peace agreement, which would lead to a Palestinian state alongside the state of Israel. The postmortems on this agreement are numerous. For example, Cheryl Rubenberg (2003) contends that Israel never intended to withdraw from the Occupied Territories, based on UN Security Council Resolution 242, or to permit the emergence of a territorially contiguous, genuinely independent state. In "The Morning After," Edward Said called the Oslo Accords "an instrument of Palestinian surrender" (in Wildangel et al., 2013, p. 16).

In the peacemaker dialogues in Part II, Palestinian and Israeli peacemakers reach a similar conclusion. Ghassan Andoni says:

GA: I personally took a very strong stand against Oslo from the beginning.
RH: Really, you were able to see—
GA: Yes. So many friends accused me of being radical, not actually working for peace, disguised as a peacemaker ... because I couldn't fake [support for] Oslo. Nevertheless, during the Oslo period, I spared no effort in trying to develop Palestinian society.... I was so disappointed, but I stayed very engaged. (Part II, p. 109)

In September 2000, as a direct result of the failure of the Oslo Peace process, the second *intifada*, or the Al-Aqsa *intifada*, erupted (Rubenberg, 2003, p. xii).

Another longtime peace activist says the international community must apply more pressure on the Israelis to pursue justice; they're doing the opposite. "They're buying into the Israeli myth that this is all about security. So, they're doing everything they can to try to make Israel feel more secure, in the hope that then she'll make peace. But it's not working that way; it's just like giving drugs to an addict" (Godfrey-Goldstein, 2014). Both the U.S. and other major powers have attempted to serve as third-party negotiators in this conflict. These Track One efforts have mostly failed. See, for example, Pappe (1994), Ashrawi (1995), Bennis (2002), and Chomsky (2016).

1.3 The Failure of U.S. Diplomacy

Since 1948, the U.S. has played crucial diplomatic and military roles in the Middle East. When Prime Minister David Ben-Gurion announced the new state of Israel on May 15, 1948, as a Jewish state, he received immediate recognition from U.S. President Harry Truman. From then until now, the U.S. has provided the leading political and military support for Israel. According to the Congressional Research Service, "Israel is the largest cumulative recipient of U.S. foreign assistance since World War II" (Sharp, 2016, p. 1). In 2016, the U.S. and Israel signed a new 10-year Memorandum of Understanding (MOU) for military aid for 2019 to 2028. The U.S. replaced a previous 10-year pledge of $30 billion with a new 10-year pledge of $38 billion—almost $4 billion per year—in military aid and missile defense.

The connections of the U.S. to the Israeli government have global implications. Israel consistently receives political cover from the U.S. through vetoes in the United Nations Security Council. Since 1967, Israel's military occupation of the Palestinian territories has been made possible by successive American administrations. Khalidi writes, "[There is] not solely an Israeli occupation: Since the very beginning, it has in fact been a joint undertaking, an Israeli-American condominium" (2017), p.1. From the early 1990s until now, the U.S. has been a leading participant in the official "peace process" within the Israeli-Palestinian conflict.

Israel receives enormous bipartisan political support from the U.S., no matter which party holds the presidency. In one of our dialogues, Jeff Halper said that the U.S.-Israel connection has less to do with the U.S. presidency and is much more dependent on the U.S. Senate. The Senate generally supports right-wing Israeli policies, with votes of 90 to 10 or even as high as 98 to 2. For Halper, the U.S.-Israel relationship is both significant and complicated.

> If the [U.S.] Road Map fails and ... the occupation is permanent, you're never going to get Israel out of the Occupied Territories ... and there's no will on the part of the international community to force Israel out.... The whole struggle is going to change into an anti-apartheid struggle, a struggle for one state. (Part II, p. 215)

Israel rejects having an "occupation," since "you can't occupy your own county." So, for Israel,

> they are "disputed territories." That's the way Israel rejects international law and accountability, and the United States goes along with it.... Trying to create a society that violates human rights, violates international law ... based on power and domination and conflict [and] supported artificially by the U.S. is not a recipe for long-term success. (Halper, Part II, p. 217)

Hanan Ashrawi, a frequent spokesperson for the Palestinian Liberation Organization (PLO), says, "There is a lack of political will and a fear of confronting Israel, of using any type of accountability, whether legal, human, or moral.... Israel feels that it can ... do whatever it wants to the Palestinians [because of] the strategic alliance with the U.S., and Israel being a domestic factor in the U.S." (Part II, p. 128).

Gideon Levy underscores this unique Israeli-U.S. relationship. He declares that "any U.S. president, [of] either party, could pick up a phone and quickly end the Israeli occupation of Palestine. I truly believe that an American president could bring an end to the Israeli occupation within months ... but we lack that leadership" (Part II, p. 249). In fact, U.S. presidents have consistently rejected a just peace. Former President Donald Trump boldly supported Israeli policies and interests, recognizing Jerusalem as the capital of Israel, moving the U.S. Embassy to Jerusalem, and proposing his "Deal of the Century." When the UN Security Council, including U.S. allies England and France, condemned the U.S. support for Jerusalem as sole capital for Israel only, the U.S. blocked this resolution with a veto (December 18, 2017). The president of the Palestinian Authority (PA) immediately announced that the PA would no longer consider the U.S. to be an honest broker in any future peace talks.

1.4 "Peace Process" as Deception

Government officials inside and outside Israel and Palestine, as well as in the UN, the U.S., and mainstream Western media, continue to use the term "peace process" as though it is an honest and viable term. But among nongovernmental peacemakers, it is considered a cynical, dishonest, and thoroughly discredited term. For example, Eitan Bronstein says that in Israel-Palestine, the term "peace" became "a very bad word because of the official peace process" (Part II, p. 190). This so-called peace process has served, both for the Israeli government and for the U.S. government, as a rhetorical cover for extending and deepening the military occupation of the West Bank and Gaza. Ilan Pappe (2007) declares, "The facts on the ground are crystal clear: the two-state solution has dismally failed, and we have no spare time to waste in futile anticipation of another illusory round of diplomatic efforts that would lead to nowhere" (p. 1). There is a consensus among Israeli and Palestinian peacemakers that negotiations are useless, even dangerous, if one of the parties is not interested in a fair agreement. Negotiations, then, are a waste of time and create a false impression of progress toward peace.

In this conflict, negotiations have become a substitute for peacemaking, a means to delay and obstruct peace. Negotiations are an instrument used by successive Israeli governments to gain time and to enlarge the settlements and entrench the occupation. The authors of the Kairos Palestine document (2009) state that political elites are committed to "managing" rather than resolving the Israeli-Palestinian conflict. One must look elsewhere for an authentic peacemaking discourse.

1.5 Interdisciplinary Approaches

To engage Israeli and Palestinian peacemakers in dialogue is to be engaged with exemplary human beings. To understand their situation requires interdisciplinary concepts and informed listening, drawn from the fields of peace and conflict, ethnography, communication, and Middle East studies. Over the last 30 years, there has been a flowering of interdisciplinary, qualitative research on interpreting people's lives (Cole & Knowles, 2001), narrative inquiry (Daiute, 2014), "narrative mediation" in conflict resolution (Winslade & Monk, 2001), conflict dialogue (Kellett, 2007), dialogue in Arab-Jewish encounters (Abu-Nimer, 1999), and critical ethnography (Madison, 2020).

In *Composing Ethnography* (1996), Carolyn Ellis and Arthur Bochner celebrate interdisciplinary work, and demonstrate new forms available for composing ethnographic and other qualitative writing:

> **Art:** We're trying to reach across the disciplinary boundaries of sociology, anthropology, communication, cultural studies, race and gender studies, aging, education, nursing, and medicine….
>
> **Carolyn:** Boundaries between academic disciplines have been dissolving for a long time…. Some of the most interesting dialogues about "culture" now take place outside anthropology, among scholars focusing on media, technology, history, literature, pedagogy, and politics. (1996, pp. 15–16)

In this spirit, I have employed theories, methods, and practices of dialogue as they appear in the diverse fields of communication, peace studies, ethnography, and performance studies.

1.6 Dialogue, Ethnography, and Peacemaking

This book explores the crucial role of dialogue as ethnographic and peacemaking theory, method, and practice. Following D. Soyini Madison,

I affirm that "ethnography adheres to a cross section of methods. Ethnography is generally defined by its aim to engage, interpret, and record the social meanings, values, structures, and embodiments within a particular domain, setting, or field of human interaction" (2020, p. 3). This case study is focused on the context and contested domain of Israel-Palestine. As Madison suggests, doing critical ethnography means "we are interlocutors in dialogue with others.... *Critical* ethnography is always a meeting of multiple sides in an encounter with and among others, one in which there is negotiation and dialogue toward substantial and viable meanings that make a difference in others' worlds" (p. 9).

Dialogue is an essential part of doing critical ethnography and peacemaking. Lederach, a proponent of conflict transformation, declares that dialogue is "essential" for promoting justice and peace at all levels—from interpersonal to structural levels. While dialogue "is not the only mechanism, it is an essential one" (2003, p. 21). For Madison, dialogue is lively, creative, and exploratory. "Dialogue emphasizes the living communion of a felt-sensing, embodied interplay and engagement between human beings" (p. 23). For Julia Wood (2004), dialogue is a tensive process: "Dialogue is emergent (rather than performed), fluid (rather than static), keenly dependent on process (... as much as content), performative (more than representational), and never fully finished (rather than completed).... Tension is inherent in and integral to dialogue" (p. xvii). Wood writes that when we engage in dialogue, we and our interlocutors bring to the process our beliefs, values, assumptions, and interests. These dynamics are central for the peacemakers in this study.

Like dialogue, ethnography encompasses theory, methods, and practice (Madison, 2020, p. 13). Ethnographic analysis includes participant observation of and with a particular group of people, in a particular time and place. Ethnographic work, especially "critical ethnography" has an ethical commitment to resist oppression, contribute to greater equity and freedom, and help move unjust situations *from what is to what could be*. Critical ethnography begins with an ethical commitment to address "unfairness or injustice within a particular *lived domain*" (Madison, 2020, p. 4). This responsibility summons a passion for justice and peace in conflict situations. This "positionality" informs my research and advocacy for a just peace in Israel-Palestine. Madison writes, "Positionality is vital because it forces us to acknowledge our own power, privilege, and biases just as we are denouncing the power structures that surround our interlocutors" (2020, p. 6).

Madison (2020) describes critical ethnography, as "critical theory in action" (pp. 23–24). It combines theories—about personal, cultural, and systemic power, social justice and social transformation—with methods of engaging peacemakers as activists and advocates for a just peace in Israel-Palestine. For Dwight Conquergood, ethnographic, performative dialogue is "the quintessential encounter with others" (in Madison, 2020, p. 17). In Chapter 2, I will provide further discussion of my own "positionality" and advocacy for a just peace.

Taken together, the analysis of peacemaker dialogues in Part I and the recorded dialogues in Part II constitute a critical ethnography of and with Israeli and Palestinian peacemakers. The dialogue format demonstrates that genuine dialogue is both possible and very hard work. These dialogues demonstrate the intersection of peacebuilders' personal experience with conflict analysis and strategic action in the real world. While thousands of people all over the world engage in efforts to build a just peace in Palestine-Israel, this book focuses on peacemakers who live, or have lived, in the epicenter of the Israeli-Palestinian conflict.

1.7 Models of Conflict and Peacemaking

Conflict is commonly perceived as a negative, undesirable, and painful condition. But unjust situations usually require some form of resistance or creative conflict in order to generate transformative change. To the extent that conflict is painful and unwanted, it evokes a desire for conflict resolution, an end to the conflict. Analysts recognize that conflict terminology is often confusing, and that it is used in different ways in general usage and among academics. Oliver Ramsbotham, Tom Woodhouse, and Hugh Miall (2011) provide a viable definition for *political conflict*: "By *conflict* we mean the pursuit of incompatible goals by different groups. This suggests a broader span of time and a wider class of struggle than only armed conflict. We intend our usage here to apply to any political conflict, whether it is pursued by peaceful means or by the use of force" (p. 30). Consequently, many writers resort to adjectives to further delineate types of conflict: armed conflict, violent conflict, nonviolent conflict, conflict management, and more. Ramsbotham et al. (2011) contend that *conflict resolution* is a comprehensive term, which implies that the deep-rooted sources of conflict are addressed and transformed, behavior is no longer violent, attitudes are no longer hostile, and the structure of the conflict has been changed. "It is difficult to avoid ambiguity, since the term is used to refer both to the process … and the completion of the process…. Nevertheless, these two senses of the term are tending to merge" (p. 31). Conflict is normal, inevitable, and often necessary for the pursuit of justice. So, a more robust understanding of conflict is necessary.

A growing body of analysts sees conflict transformation as a qualitatively deeper, more comprehensive, and more positive concept than conflict resolution. Conflict transformation is anchored in relationships at all levels—from the interpersonal to the cultural and structural levels. For Lederach (2003), conflict transformation engages a set of relationships across time; it envisions and responds to "the ebb and flow of social conflict as life-giving opportunities for creating constructive change processes that reduce violence, increase justice in direct interaction and social structures, and respond to real-life problems in human relationships" (p. 14).

From this perspective, transforming a conflict is more than a "resolution." It is creative, proactive, and utterly necessary for survival and for generating justice. While attempting to respond to an immediate conflict, a transformational approach creates a framework to address the content, the context, and the structure of the relationship across time. For Lederach, a transformational approach aspires to create constructive change processes *through* conflict, and is deeply connected to truth-telling about the root causes of conflict, efforts to increase justice, and efforts at reconciliation (2003, p. 12). Further, conflicts are not necessarily incompatible if properly understood. Strongly held *positions* may be incompatible, but deeply shared *interests*, such as security and love of family, provide a common ground where those in conflict can meet. This insight is crucial for understanding this conflict, since security is deeply connected to both Israeli and Palestinian concerns.

While Ramsbotham et al. (2011) prefer *conflict resolution* as an umbrella term, they do suggest that *conflict transformation* represents the "deepest level" of conflict resolution (p. 31). Indeed, their analysis of conflict is filled with transformative terms, including "five generic transformers" in protracted conflicts: context transformation, structural transformation, actor transformation, issue transformation, and personal and group transformation (pp. 175–176). Examples of these transformations will appear in Chapter 6 and in the peacemaker dialogues in Part II.

Those "actors" who pursue some form of nonviolent conflict transformation are typically called peacemakers or peacebuilders. While UN peacekeepers may use force to defend themselves or in defense of their mandate, peacemaking typically involves nonuse of military means to prevent or reduce violence and enhance justice (Lederach, 2005). *Peacebuilding* generally refers to longer-term efforts for building civil society, and the preservation of human rights. Peacemaking and peacebuilding are not necessarily sequential, though. As I suggest in Chapter 6, they may be simultaneous.

Peacebuilding in Israel-Palestine has generally been focused on conflict resolution, short-term "negotiations," and third-party, outside, official negotiators. The focus in the present dialogues is on insider, engaged, and indigenous peacemakers. As Ramsbotham et al. (2011) write, "Instead of outsiders offering the fora for addressing conflicts in one-shot mediation efforts, the emphasis is on the need to build constituencies and capacity within societies and to learn from domestic cultures how to manage conflicts in a sustained way over time" (p. 28). This perspective informs the dialogues with indigenous peacemakers in Israel-Palestine.

Since the early 1980s, practitioners and scholars have articulated various models for understanding the official and unofficial types of peacemakers, peacebuilders, mediators, arbitrators, diplomats, and others engaged in conflict resolution and transformation. In the 1980s, Joseph Montville named official, governmental diplomacy Track One diplomacy. Peacemaking outside of official channels he called Track Two diplomacy. In the early 1990s, Louise Diamond and John McDonald (1993) articulated the concept and practices of "multitrack diplomacy." They analyzed the interconnections of Track One diplomacy with eight types of Track Two diplomacy—through business; by private citizens; through education, research, and information; activism and advocacy; religious movements and faith in action; funding; and through media (pp. 2-3).

I have generally followed the model of a three-tiered, interactive concept of peacemakers. This includes Track One diplomacy (political and governmental elites), Track Two diplomacy (nongovernmental leaders), and a third group comprised of grassroots activists. (See Fig. 1.1.) Nongovernmental peacemakers, working "from the middle out," have some access to Track One political leaders as well as access to grassroots movements. Since the Israeli-Palestinian conflict is what Ramsbotham et al. (2011) call both a local and an international conflict, it is important to note that some Track Two peacemakers, such as Uri Avnery, work primarily with their own local ethnic group. Many others, such as Jeff Halper, Elias Chacour, and Naim Ateek, work extensively with international solidarity groups. Variations on the three-tiered peacemaker model appear in Lederach (2005), Ramsbotham et al. (2011), and Salem and Kaufman (2006).

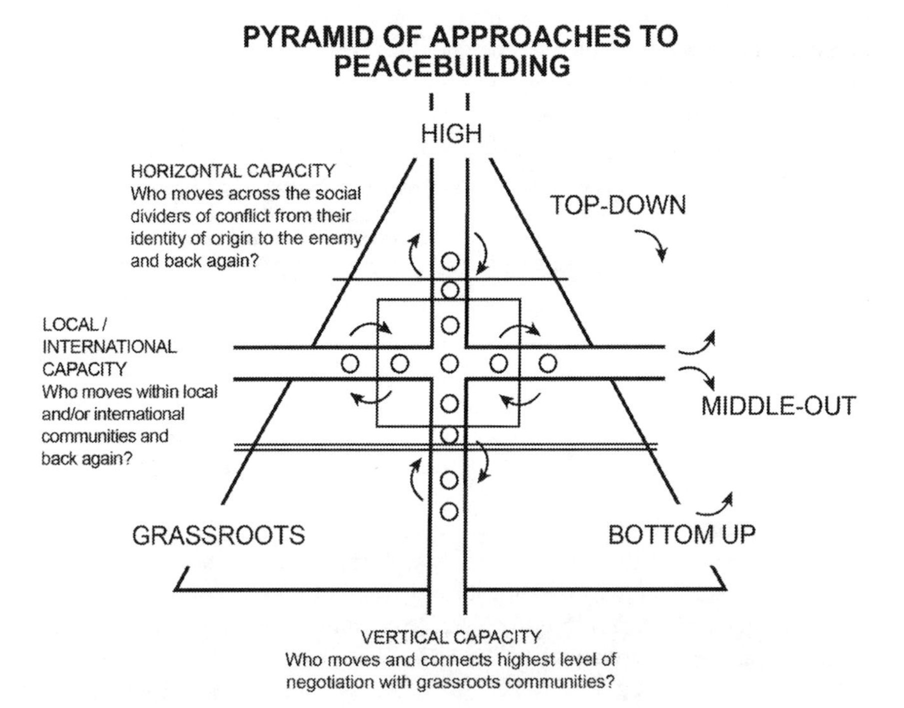

Figure 1.1 Pyramid of Approaches to Peacebuilding.

Source: Oxford University Press.

There are many analyses of the failures of the official, Track One peace processes. According to Halper, the Israeli government removed international law as the basis of the Oslo Accords. If Israel had followed international law, "the whole occupation would resolve itself. That's why Israel wouldn't allow international law to be the basis of the Oslo negotiations" (2003, p. 3). In our dialogue, Ghassan Andoni describes how fervently he opposed the Oslo Accords. For this conflict, analyses of Track One diplomacy failures are exhaustive. (See, for example, Bunton, 2013; Chomsky, 2016; Khalidi, 2013; Pacheco, 2001).

At the grassroots level, Mazin Qumsiyeh provides a very compelling history of the Palestinian philosophy and practice of "popular resistance" (2011), a "movement of direct action," including strikes, demonstrations, resistance to injustice, self-sufficiency, and strengthening community (p. 30). These forms of popular resistance are rooted in hundreds of years of community experience. A small group of oral history collections includes Jewish and Palestinian peacemaker stories of refugees, occupation, and resistance experiences. (See, for example, Hostetter, 2001; Carey & Shainin, 2002; Pearlman, 2003; Farber, 2005).

For Diamond and MacDonald (1993), Track Two "refers to nongovernmental, informal and unofficial contacts and activities between private citizens or groups of individuals, sometimes called 'nonstate actors'" (p. 1), and "to reduce or resolve conflict, improve communication and understanding, lower tension and misunderstanding, and to affect the thinking and actions of Track One by addressing root causes of the conflict" (p. 2). Further, "The basic premise of Track Two diplomacy ... is that the expertise for dealing successfully with conflict and peacemaking does not reside solely within government personnel or procedures. Rather, ... citizens from a variety of backgrounds and with a variety of skills have something to offer and make a difference" (1993, p. 2). In Chapter 2, I will identify additional types of Track Two diplomacy that appear in this study.

In contrast to the preponderance of attention given to official, Track One diplomacy, much less attention has been given to peacemaking "from the middle," or Track Two diplomacy, the efforts of nongovernmental individuals and organizations—variously called civil society, peace movements or peace camps—that devote their efforts to the struggle for a just and sustainable peace. *Refusing to Be Enemies* (2010) provides an excellent collection of essays on Palestinian and Israeli nonviolence as philosophy and strategy. Maia Hallward and Julie Norman (2011) focus their analysis on nonviolent peacemaking during the very violent second *intifada*.

In *Bridging the Divide: Peacebuilding in the Israeli-Palestinian Conflict*, Hanna Siniora writes that "the past century has seen nothing but conflict and spilled blood. Yet, in the past four decades, a minority on both sides has worked relentlessly for peace" (in Kaufman et al., 2006, p. ix). Siniora adds: "Many more publications are needed to describe, analyze, and disseminate information on conflict prevention and peacebuilding activities in our region. This book is an important pioneering effort to illustrate the agony, the pitfalls, and the achievements" of Track Two diplomacy (p. x). However, "there is no concise overview of NGO peacebuilding efforts with a focus on prevention, resolution and transformation.... We need new diagnostic tools" (Kaufman et al., 2006, p. 3).

In that spirit, the following chapters will explore ethnographic and dialogical approaches for understanding conflict transformation and nongovernmental peacemaking. For example, images of the Palestinian loss of land over time suggest an evolving discourse concerning ethnic identity, justice, strategic dialogue, and the requisite principles for a just peace, including human rights, international law, prophetic mourning, imagination, and collective transformation.

1.8 Conclusion

This chapter presents a broad introduction to the Israeli-Palestine conflict. It matters for multiple reasons: it has persisted for more than 70 years; it is one of the epicenters of conflict in the Middle East; and it represents the failure of democratic governments, the United Nations, and other official institutions to develop a just and sustainable peace. Israelis have waged four brutal wars with the Palestinians in Gaza since 2007, and they have stockpiled hundreds of nuclear weapons. This conflict has serious implications for the global world order. To approach understanding the Israeli-Palestinian conflict, this chapter introduces interdisciplinary theories, methods, and concepts of critical ethnography, peacemaking, conflict transformation, and multitrack diplomacy. Israeli and Palestinian government officials (Track One diplomacy) refuse to be accountable to international law and a genuine "peace process." Consequently, this book focuses on the crucial work of mid-level, nongovernmental peacemakers (Track Two diplomacy), and the central role of in-depth dialogue in peacemaking.

2 Coming to Terms

A serious engagement with the Israeli-Palestinian conflict may trigger a wrestling match. Even struggles with angels can be rough. For example, a mysterious being—an angel?—intervenes in the longest family conflict in Hebrew Scripture. In the Genesis account, Jacob and Esau are twins born a few minutes apart. Years later, their father, Isaac, prepares to die, and he wants to give Esau his birthright, which could only be given to the firstborn. But Jacob and his mother deceive Isaac; Jacob receives the birthright, and runs away to save his life. Twenty years later, Jacob comes to terms with Esau, sending him hundreds of animals and servants as an act of restorative justice. On the way to meet his brother, Jacob wrestles all night with a stranger who dislocates Jacob's thigh bone, gives him a permanent limp, and changes his name to Israel, he who strives with God (Genesis 25-32).

2.1 Existential Terms

Like Jacob's crisis, the Israeli-Palestinian conflict also contains broken promises, broken bones, blessings, name changes, questions of restorative justice, and other forms of *coming to terms.* "Coming to terms" suggests an existential situation that requires struggle—perhaps accepted, perhaps blessed, perhaps wrestled to the ground. One might have to come to terms with any major challenge to identity—a loved one's death, financial loss, a heart attack, a betrayal, or losing one's village, even a large change of fortune considered to be "good news." Such challenges require change, often personal and systemic change. Consider the Holocaust, the Nakba, and global pandemics, combined with the fires and floods of climate change.

To examine the Israeli-Palestinian conflict, it is necessary to name the existential core of the conflict. Pappe writes that every book about Israel confronts a "complex and ambiguous reality," and "the result will always be both subjective and limited. Nevertheless, the subjectivity and relativity does not invalidate moral and ethical discussion about that representation.... Versions of reality in Israel are numerous and contradictory, and rarely do they share any consensual ground" (2014, p. 3). For both ethnic groups, this situation presents existential dilemmas. For many Palestinians, to give up a

DOI: 10.4324/9781003262817-3

national liberation struggle and to start a civil-rights struggle is an existential threat (Halper, Part II, p. 223). For many Israelis, giving up a "Jewish state" is also an existential threat.

Coming to terms suggests negotiating a contract or agreement, and "counting the cost." The failed Oslo Accords have generated wounds so deep they help to sustain the conflict. A third meaning literally denotes bringing something into language, the ways in which human beings define terms, tell stories, develop relationships, and construct meaning. These struggles—wrestling with the language of justice and peace—appear in many of the dialogues with peacemakers. They wrestle with competing narratives about land, ancient promises, recent histories, future goals, and strategies for achieving a just peace.

2.2 Positionality and Critical Ethnography

Entering the Israeli-Palestinian conflict involves "coming to terms" with my own "positionality," my own identity, values, and experiences; with the lived experiences of peacemakers in Israel-Palestine; with words and images freighted with intellectual, emotional, cultural, historical, and political implications, including the Holocaust and the Nakba. Even in academic circles, the discourse about this conflict often implies a zero-sum game, a binary framework of being pro-Palestinian or being pro-Israeli, but not both. Jews who are progressive on every other front often support the right-wing policies of successive Israeli governments. I have engaged in challenging dialogues with both Israeli and Palestinian peacemakers who are coming to terms with their own existential quandaries. For me, the biblical prophets provide difficult but important processes for both deconstructing injustice, and for constructing truth and justice. For example, God says to the prophet Jeremiah, "I have this day set thee over the nations and over the kingdoms, to root out, and to pull down, and to destroy, to throw down, to build and to plant" (Jeremiah 1:10). This dual process of tearing down and rebuilding is amply reflected in this book. Halper illustrates this challenge: "We're all against the occupation, but ending the occupation is half the story. Where do we go after that?" (Part II, p. 247).

As an interpretive framework, I have followed D. Soyini Madison's argument that critical ethnography serves as both theory and method; and ethnographic dialogues begin with an ethical commitment to address "unfairness or injustice within a particular lived domain" (2020, p. 5). This ethical positionality informs my advocacy for a just peace in Israel-Palestine. My hybrid positionality includes what Michelle Fine defines as a "positionality of *voices*": the subjects are the focus, "and their voices carry forward indigenous meanings and experiences that are in opposition to dominant discourses and practices" (in Madison, 2020, p. 6). However, Fine's statement that "The position of the ethnographer is vaguely present but not addressed" is not true here. My introductions and my dialogues employ Fine's "*activism* stance, in which the ethnographer takes a clear position," resisting "hegemonic practices," and advocating for justice for marginalized and oppressed people (in Madison, 2020, p. 6). I intend, through dialogue, to present marginalized voices *and* to advocate for a just peace in Israel-Palestine.

My positionality includes coming to terms with being a teacher, researcher, playwright, peace activist, family person, and a Christian by birth and affirmation. My engagement with conflict transformation and nonviolent social change has been filled with delight, discovery, and occasional despair as I ponder questions of my "power, privilege, and biases" (Madison, 2020, p. 6). Engaging with the Israeli-Palestinian conflict is daunting. After graduate school, I had the opportunity to teach a class on "the rhetoric of war and peace." I worked diligently to convey the complexity of the Israeli-Palestinian conflict. But one course evaluation stunned me: "I get it. It's hopeless." I brooded over this comment and began to search for a more transformative approach.

Years later, in 1998, a colleague invited me to go to Palestine to record stories of Palestinians who had lost homes and villages during the Nakba or "catastrophe" of 1948. I recorded more than 50 stories of people who had lived through the trauma of 1948. I adapted 15 of those stories for a full-length play, *The Longing* (2001). We presented the play 20 times, including at the National Communication Association meeting in Atlanta (2003). Both Jewish and non-Jewish friends asked me why I had not told the "other side," the narratives of Jewish experience. I said, Jewish narratives constitute the dominant narrative, and that they most likely knew that story already.

Pondering the question of presenting "both sides" led me to this project of presenting the stories, analyses, and strategic responses of both Israeli and Palestinian peacemakers. As Jeff Halper suggests, there are two sides in the Israeli-Palestinian conflict—those who want to make peace, and those who do not. So, in 2003, I began recording dialogues with Palestinians and Israelis working toward a just peace. Since 2003, I have made eight research trips to Israel-Palestine and experienced some of the challenges of life under military occupation—military checkpoints, Israeli settlements and bypass roads, Palestinian refugee camps, tear gas, curfews in Hebron, hospitals in Gaza and Ramallah, and Israeli sharpshooters high above a peaceful demonstration in Bethlehem.

I have also experienced abundant hospitality from Jews, Muslims, Quakers, Catholics, Lutherans, Mennonites, and Orthodox Christians. Laughter, too. One day, the owner of a restaurant asked why I was in East Jerusalem. When I said I was recording stories of Palestinian and Israeli peacemakers, he burst into laughter at this most absurd joke. These experiences compel me to come to terms with being an American citizen whose taxes help to pay for illegal settlements in the West Bank; to believe that every human being is a child of God; and to practice what Karen Armstrong calls the "triple consciousness" of Jewish, Muslim, and Christian identities (2001), basing my ethics in the Hebrew prophets, the Sermon on the Mount, and international law.

2.3 Situated Knowledge

The dialogues in this book confirm complex relationships among personal experiences, context, and advocacy for justice and peace. The analyses and actions of peacemakers in this book are based on a type of knowledge that "is neither objective nor relativistic. It is built on the struggle of people's everyday lives" (Roach, 1993, p. xxii). As P. Parajuli suggests: "Situated knowledge is a knowledge that is accountable to the knower.... It is always a marked knowledge ... born of resistance" (in Roach, 1993, pp. xii–xiii). Both Israeli and Palestinian dialogue partners describe discoveries and experiences that have prompted acts of resistance. Participants in this book are quite aware of their positionality, their "marked knowledge," knowledge that is accountable to the knower, and learned from the complex processes of resistance and cultural negotiations.

2.4 Informed Listening

Doing critical ethnography involves multiple dialogical roles. In Part I, I provide an academic analysis of the dialogues in Part II. In Part II, my role is entirely dialogical—questioning, listening, participating in analysis, and building relationships. Part II follows Dutta's approach of reversing who is the "expert" and who is the "learner." This approach

> centers itself on the role of listening to subaltern voices, ... creating spaces of change through the voices of subaltern agendas.... For the academic or expert engaging in social change research and praxis, a dialogic engagement with the margins begins with humility, reflexivity, and openness to learning through engagement, thus shifting the traditional role of the expert from a producer of knowledge situated at the centers of power to a listener who works in solidarity with the subaltern sectors to create spaces of structural transformation. (2011, p. 169)

My goal is to minimize the distortions and clarify the points of view of peacemakers, since they differ from each other in terms of goals, strategies, and cultural frameworks. To underscore the importance of dialogue within this conflict, I have retained a dialogical format in Part II. This enables peacemakers to present themselves directly to readers. My questions generally move from personal and cultural contexts to an analysis of the conflict and specific efforts to transform it. I have focused on the positionality and situated knowledge of each peacemaker by asking:

- Where were you born and what were your family and cultural identities?
- What was your early experience of the Israeli-Palestinian conflict?
- Which experiences became turning points, leading you into peace and justice work?

- What is your current analysis of the Israeli-Palestinian conflict?
- What peacemaking approaches have you developed? What are the prospects for dialogue, transformation, and a just peace?

These questions elicit dialogues about identity, conflict, suffering, activism, victimhood, and prophetic imagination. For example, journalist Gideon Levy thinks of his work as "shining a light on Israel's backyard," but he worries that he is only "writing for the archives" (Part II, p. 231). Historian Ilan Pappe describes his experience of changing his identity and moving his family from Israel to England because of death threats. Dr. Mona El-Farra, from Gaza, and Yonatan Shapira, from an Israeli military family, both speak of their efforts to break the siege of Gaza, which began in 2006. Eitan Bronstein moved from Argentina to Israel, discovering years later that his kibbutz was built on top of three demolished Palestinian villages. After graduate work in France, Abdelfattah Abusrour returned to Aida Refugee Camp in Bethlehem, where he grew up, and developed a program of "beautiful resistance" through theatre and nonviolent activism.

Some of the most compelling dialogues demonstrate that one's family of origin does not determine how one comes to terms with this conflict. Pappe describes how he and Benny Morris, as graduate students at Oxford, examined the same archives but chose different ethical responses.

> Benny and I worked in the archives at the same time and we were both shocked … by what we saw compared to what we knew…. We both were the first ones to bring the full picture to the Israeli public of the ethnic cleansing of 1948…. He coped [by] saying that what [Israel] did [in 1948] was the right thing to do. As the years went by, I said this was even more horrible and more despicable than what I thought…. I decided to devote my life to [offering] restitution and compensation, true reconciliation. (Part II, p. 265)

Pappe illustrates a central argument of this book: one's cultural roots have a profound influence, but they are not determinative. The dialogues demonstrate people's capacities for radical change and peacemaking. These dialogues are deeply personal, transformational, and broadly political.

The dialogues in Part II provide compelling insights into numerous ways that peacemakers achieve transformational experience and situated knowledge. For example, when he was six years old, Ghassan Andoni's family moved from Bethlehem to Jordan for his father's work.

> I moved also from being in private Christian schools into public schools…. I got the opportunity … to be raised among Muslims, among refugees, among real kids in a diverse community…. In 1967, when the war happened, … [that was] my first shock of the real conflict between

> Israel and Palestinians ... my first scenes of bombardment, of the [Israeli] army taking over, curfews imposed, and fear. (Part II, p. 103)

As a young person, Jonathan Kuttab embraced nonviolent resistance to the Israelis rather than violent resistance. Later, he became a human-rights lawyer, and learned Hebrew so he could understand and resist the oppressive Israeli legal system. Yonatan Shapira narrates an Israeli example of situated knowledge. He grew up on Israeli air force bases, and aspired to become an air force pilot like his father.

> I totally [identified] with the state [of Israel], ... the typical Zionist poster boy ... in the center of the Zionist narrative, of beautiful peace and bereavement songs ... telling of the first year of the country ... or the beloved son that died in the war. Everything is [woven] together, penetrating your heart and recruiting you to the culture ... to the Zionist narrative, and eventually, in my case, recruiting me to be a fighter pilot. (Part II, p. 303)

This compelling narrative reveals how Shapira's family, education, social class, and professional status positioned him for a thoroughly Zionist identity.

Jeff Halper also analyzes how his work with the Israeli Committee Against Home Demolitions (ICAHD) achieves "situated knowledge," that is, knowledge born of resistance.

> We're an Israeli group that works with Palestinian organizations to resist the occupation.... [We resist] the fallacy of house demolitions. We get in front of bulldozers. With Palestinians, we rebuild demolished houses, which is illegal, so that's an act of political resistance.... It's a way of expressing solidarity with families that are really traumatized, but it also gets to the essence of the conflict, which is displacement.... When we build, we acknowledge to Palestinians that ... you have a right to be here with us.... The building effort gets at the deepest level of conflict between us. We take what we learned on the ground ... to the international community. (Part II, p. 216)

There are many similar stories, situating the conflict and the peacemakers in the context of time and place. These stories inform meaningful dialogues about identity and peacemaking.

2.5 Peacemaking Terms

Definitions of conflict, peace, peacemakers, peacebuilders, and related terms abound. For example, Ramsbotham et al. (2011) write: "*Conflict* is the pursuit of incompatible goals by different groups"; *conflict resolution* is a comprehensive term, "which implies that the deep-rooted sources of conflict are addressed and transformed"; *conflict transformation* represents the deepest level of conflict resolution; *negotiation* is the process in which "parties seek to settle or resolve their conflicts"; *mediation* "involves the intervention of a third party"; *peacemaking* moves toward the "settlement of armed conflict"; and *peacebuilding* "underpins the work of peacemaking ... by addressing structural issues and long-term relationships between conflictants" (pp. 30–32). I concur with Lederach that *conflict transformation* avoids the implications of a singular, one-time solution to a protracted conflict, and implies ongoing relationships and changes at all levels—from interpersonal to social, cultural, and structural levels (2003, pp. 14–22).

In the context of the Israeli-Palestinian conflict, I have mostly used the terms peacemaking and peacemakers to suggest the ongoing, unresolved conflict. However, I have not tried to draw a clear distinction between peacemakers and peacebuilders, since both terms are process-oriented, and because my dialogue partners suggest that peacemaking and peacebuilding may be simultaneous. For example, Hanan Ashrawi said to me, "We are enslaved by the occupation. So, we have to work on freedom while we work on peace simultaneously.... Ending the occupation is crucial. But we are not saying, Give us a peace process; we are not working on nation-building [only]. No ... help us do both" (Part II, p. 131).

In an excellent collection of essays about peacebuilding in the Israeli-Palestine conflict, Edy Kaufman, Walid Salem, and Juliette Verhoeven (2006) employ many related terms for mid-level peacemaking: conflict resolution, civil society, human-rights work, and reconciliation. They include dozens of organizations, such as Ashrawi's Palestinian Initiative for the Promotion of Global Dialogue and Democracy (MIFTAH), and Halper's Israeli Committee Against Home Demolitions (ICAHD) (Kaufman et al. 2006, pp. 223–302). These writers analyze the ideologies and effectiveness of these groups through the time of the second *intifada* (2000–2005). They generally support the goal of a two-state solution. At this writing, however, more than 700,000 Jewish Israelis live in illegal settlements in the West Bank. Trying to move them would be catastrophic.

In Part II, all of the Palestinians and some Jewish peacemakers reject Zionism altogether as incompatible with being peacemakers. Some Jewish peacemakers try to reconcile peacemaking with liberal Zionism. For example, Pappe criticizes Peace Now. "They had no idea what the occupation really meant, and suggested solutions which were not really leading to the end of the occupation. We have now a much clearer group" (Part II, p. 267).

For Lederach and Appleby, the terms peacemaking and peacebuilding overlap, since "peacebuilding addresses every stage of the conflict cycle rather than merely the postaccord, coming-out-of-violence period.... Activities that constitute peace run the gamut of conflict transformation, violence prevention, mediation, and healing in the aftermath of armed conflict" (in Philpott and Powers, 2010, p. 23). So, peacebuilding is an inclusive rather than an exclusive field:

> A multiplicity of actors, originating from and working at all levels of society, with different capacities and areas of expertise, constitutes the reality of peacebuilding today. None of these actors, considered in isolation from the others, has provided the conditions for a sustainable and comprehensive peace in societies divided or threatened by violence. Their efficacy increases, however, when they work together.
>
> (Lederach & Appleby, 2010, p. 35)

In this way, I construe peacemaking and peacebuilding as deeply related terms, and I use both terms as they appear in the context of the dialogues in Part II. However, I use the term peacemaker most often, because it most accurately reflects the current stage of the conflict.

Halper advocates for a political definition of peacemakers as (1) peace and justice workers who promote some combination of intention, effectiveness, outcome, and justice; (2) activists who often lack these elements; (3) members of political parties, NGOs, or churches that have a peace and justice agenda; and (4) fellow travelers, who advocate for and comment on peace issues but are not directly involved (2020). Halper emphasizes focused political work with an endgame (intention), and organization and strategy (effectiveness), leading to a genuinely just outcome. I endorse all of these elements, especially intentionality and dialogues for a just peace. I affirm my solidarity with all of the nonviolent peacemakers, even when I think their strategies are incomplete. For example, I include Uri Avnery, who describes himself as a Zionist-turned-post-Zionist, determined to have a two-state solution, with only a symbolic number of Palestinians able to fulfill the right of return. I include our dialogues because they reveal the boundaries of comprehensive peacemaking. In later chapters, I will say more about both secular and religious forms of prophetic peacemaking as I find them in dialogues with Levy, Awad, Halper, and Pappe.

Peacemakers, working from the middle, offer the best hope for generating truth, justice, and a viable vision for a just peace in Israel-Palestine. Consequently, the goal of the present book is to engage with a diverse group of peacemakers in Israel-Palestine, with their compelling storytelling, their "grounded analyses," and their passion for a just peace. However, analyses are often contested, and the situation is constantly changing. El-Farra, Bahour, Raheb, and Halper all warn of what will happen if the status quo devolves into a third *intifada*, or "something worse."

Coming to terms with this conflict involves coming to terms with "truth and mercy, justice and peace" (Lederach, 2002, pp. 39–40). These concepts apply to this conflict. Principles of truth and justice are central to the dynamics of situated knowledge and knowledge born of resistance. Multiple concepts of justice are crucial for peacebuilding—greater fairness, equity, access, opportunity, distributive justice, and restorative justice. The need for justice permeates the dialogues of both Israeli and Palestinian peacemakers. And yet, there is a passionate, ongoing struggle about what justice means and how it will be accomplished. For Jews, there is a legacy of centuries of anti-Semitic discrimination in Europe, the horrors of the Holocaust, followed by terrorism and regional hostility in the Middle East. For Palestinians, there are centuries of occupation, the Balfour Declaration, betrayal during the British Mandate, an unjust two-state solution proposed by the United Nations (UN Resolution 181), the failure of the international community to enforce UN Resolutions 242 (1967) and 338 (1973), the failure of the Oslo Accords (1993; 1995), and more than 70 years of military domination (1948 to the present).

Pappe asserts deep connections among ideas, truth-telling, and justice. He says, "Israel is still a very indoctrinating state.... If you want to challenge it from within, it is difficult. If you want to challenge it from without, it is difficult" (Part II, p. 267). In *The Idea of Israel*, Pappe locates the central root of the Israeli-Palestinian conflict in contradictory notions of justice. He declares the need for an ethical evaluation of those notions of justice. What he challenges is not Israel, per se, but the dominant *idea* of Israel (2014, p. 3). As Pappe stresses, different versions of reality directly relate to issues of life and death. Consequently, ethical rigor is required.

Pappe argues that to evaluate the idea of Israel is "ethically, morally, and politically not only possible but ... urgent" (2014, p. 3). What Pappe considers the "very essence of the idea of Israel" parallels what I describe in Chapter 3 as identity. This term has profound peacemaking implications for both Israelis and Palestinians. Identities oscillate between ideals and actual experiences of violence and oppression. This struggle appears in many dialogues in Part II.

Pappe also suggests that the idea of Israel, for some, increasingly serves as a symbol of ethnic cleansing, occupation, and abuse of power. However, there remains a significant group for whom the idea of Israel symbolizes redemption and security. "Along the continuum between these two extremes lie innumerable gradations of strongly held opinion" (2014, p. 3). For peacemakers, moral and ethical dimensions of justice in this conflict must be considered essential capacities, deeply connected to personal and collective commitments to international law and a just peace.

Various forms of justice are central to peacemaking. Naim Ateek, founder of the Sabeel Center for Liberation Theology in Jerusalem, titled his first book *Justice and Only Justice* (1989). In our dialogue, he emphasized a close connection between justice and truth-telling (Part II, p. 133).

RH: Does the term "peace process" really hide more than it reveals?

NA: Yes. It's a kind of charade or game. People talk about the peace process, when there is no peace process.... You cannot build peace on

> a continuation of injustice, on domination, and on oppression.... We are building peace [on] foundational justice.

The theme of justice remains central in Ateek's later books (2008; 2017).

For other peace and justice leaders, truth-telling is also foundational for a just peace. For journalist Gideon Levy, the dominant Israeli "truth" is a most problematic half-truth.

RH: How do you see the interplay of telling the truth and ... building a just peace? What's the role of the truth-teller?

GL: It is not about the truth-telling, it's about the *whole* truth-telling.... There are many lies, but it's not about the lies, it's about the partial truth—the one-sided truth, being so concentrated on ourselves and not seeing the other at all. They don't exist. One of the roles of the Wall is to make it physical, [so] that you will not see Palestinians, ... hiding at least half of the truth.... I want you to know how brutal the occupation is, because it is there on your behalf. Every one of us is a checkpoint soldier. All of us carry this stain. Therefore, my journalistic role is to try to put a small light on the very, very dark backyard of Israel.... This will be my biggest contribution, if I can put some light there. (Part II, p. 248)

Many other peacemakers achieve situated knowledge by working for truth, justice, and in other ways to resist the occupation.

The dialogues in Part II provide contexts for each of 21 peacemakers, including liberal Zionists, anti-Zionists, Palestinians who still believe a two-state solution is necessary, and many others who believe it is no longer possible. Co-nominees for the Nobel Peace Prize in 2006 Ghassan Andoni and Jeff Halper have both expressed profound discouragement about the prospects for a just peace. Andoni says that his goal is to stop Israel from doing what it is trying to do (Part II, pp. 110–111). After the Israeli bombing of Gaza in 2014, Halper said, "No one will talk to me." However, by 2016, this began to change. Pappe hosted an important Israeli-Palestinian dialogue in England. This important turn will receive further attention in Chapter 6.

If and when government officials do commit themselves to develop a just peace, nongovernmental peacebuilders will have created a platform on which that just peace is built. Yousef Munayyer declares, "We are witnessing the writing of a very important and transitional chapter in the history of the Palestinian struggle that will be a major departure from recent history and will ultimately shape the future of the people in the land and how others relate to them" (2014, p. 2). Munayyer sees two related shifts. The first shift is from state or multistate actors—Israelis, the Palestinian Authority, the U.S., the Quartet, the UN—to nongovernmental leaders. As state actors recede, the role of civil society has grown, as shown by the leaders in this book. As Israeli leaders relentlessly build settlements on Palestinian land

and resist genuine peace efforts, the goals for what constitutes a just peace have also shifted—from land and partition to human rights.

In the quest for an Israeli-Palestinian peace, the stories of non-governmental peacemakers are compelling and deserve wider exposure. These stories provide strong evidence that both personal and structural change are possible, that peacemaking is possible, and that there are hundreds of peacemakers in Israel and Palestine resisting occupation, healing those who suffer, uttering prophetic insights, and developing strategies for achieving a just peace. These dialogues also reveal conflicts among peacemakers about how to analyze the conflict, and how to struggle effectively for a just peace. And yet, leadership for these challenging questions comes largely "from the middle." Here one finds the most vigorous dialogue about telling the truth, doing justice, pursuing reconciliation, and other peacemaking practices.

2.6 Multitrack Peacemaking

Since the 1990s, the broad field of peacemaking has recognized the role and importance of Track Two, mid-level peacemakers. According to the U.S. Institute of Peace, "There is a growing consensus among both official and unofficial actors that no single actor or activity is sufficient to build sustainable peace in situations of complex conflict, and that the achievement of that goal requires both top-down and bottom-up approaches" (n.d., p. 1). Most of the peacemakers in this book work from an interactive, "middle-out" approach. (See Fig. 1.1.) When traditional diplomacy is part of the problem, nongovernmental actors may be able to slow, stop, and even transform particular conflicts; peacemakers working from the middle can work from the middle up and from the middle down (Burgess & Burgess, 2010, p. 17). In the Israeli-Palestinian context, Track Two diplomacy has been widely used (Klein & Malki, 2006, p. 111). A multilayered approach is necessary, because this conflict has major international dimensions. "Palestinians can't shake off the occupation by themselves; so, the international civil society is a key partner" (Halper, Part II, p. 216). (See Fig. 1.1.)

Only a few peacebuilders, such as Hanan Ashrawi and Estephan Salameh, move among all three levels of peace and justice work, including Track Two diplomacy and international support. Salameh says that Palestine hasn't had a functioning parliament since the Hamas-Fatah split in 2006. So, "the role of civil society in Palestine is probably even more important than in other places" (Part II, p. 293). After Salameh finished a Ph.D. in the U.S., the Palestinian Authority (PA) put him in charge of international aid, working with 84 donor countries and agencies, and billions of dollars.

ES: I still work for the government, the UN, donor agencies, and local NGOS. I work across the spectrum.

RH: I argue that government leaders either can't or won't create a just peace, so NGOs, civil society, and Track Two diplomacy will have to lead this transformation … to a just peace, committed to … human rights and international law…. The vanguard will be leadership from the middle rather than from the top.

ES: I share this point of view. In Palestine, on the positive side, we have some of the most active civil-society organizations … in terms of numbers, in terms of activism (Part II, p. 293)

Salameh tries to bridge peacemaking arenas: "I work with civil society to bring them closer to the government, and the government closer to civil society" (Part II, p. 300).

Uri Avnery, a lifelong journalist and peace activist, served three terms in the Israeli parliament, the Knesset, cofounded an NGO, Gush Shalom, and engaged in grassroots peacemaking. Avnery's central goal was to change Israeli public opinion.

UA: Gush Shalom is unique. There are people who are very important in small movements … such as Courage to Refuse (Yesh Gvul), which encourages people to refuse military service in the Occupied Territories. Women in Black are extremely courageous.

RH: The Israeli Committee Against Home Demolitions …

UA: Of course. Each one doing excellent and important work…. Gush Shalom is trying to break new ground, [to] change Israeli public opinion (Part II, p. 152).

Gush Shalom is still working on this highly aspirational goal.

Hanan Ashrawi is a peacemaker for all seasons: a former member of the PLO Legislative Council, the highest level of PLO leadership; a member of Palestinian negotiating teams; a spokesperson on international media; director of an NGO, The Palestinian Initiative for the Promotion of Global Dialogue and Democracy (MIFTAH), and a grassroots peacemaker. She says,

> For decades we have been excluded and distorted. People of courage and conscience and justice have either been intimidated or silenced. We need to speak up. We need to regroup…. [We] have to have many different ways of addressing the issues … such as challenging [the U.S.] Congress (Part II, p. 129).

As noted earlier, Ashrawi says that we have to work on peacemaking and building civil society at the same time (Part II, p. 131). These three peacemakers demonstrate the need for in-depth dialogue among peacemakers and peacebuilders at all levels, including dialogue with international organizations.

2.7 What the Map Cuts Up

In Israel-Palestine, peacemakers are coming to terms with an emerging consensus that the old paradigm—of "land for peace" and a two-state solution—has died. The maps in Figure 2.1 pimpression of how successive Israeli governments have annexed, fragmented, separated, dismembered, walled off, and illegally settled the Occupied Palestinian Territories (OPT). Excellent research on this topic is available (Qumsiyeh, 2004; Pappe, 2006, 2016).

However, in a striking image, Michel de Certeau powerfully suggests that "what the map cuts up, the story cuts across" (1984, p. 12). Indeed, the compelling dialogues and narratives in Part II of this book have the capacity to recall, re-member, restore, and come to terms with what has been destroyed. A new paradigm is emerging, based on human rights and international law. This opens the way for new approaches, goals, and strategies. In the U.S., the intersectional strategies of Black Lives Matter and other social-justice movements are connecting their struggles for social justice with human-rights struggles in Israel-Palestine. Peace activists are engaged in dialogues about "uprisings" in the U.S. (Bahour, 2020a). I will extend this

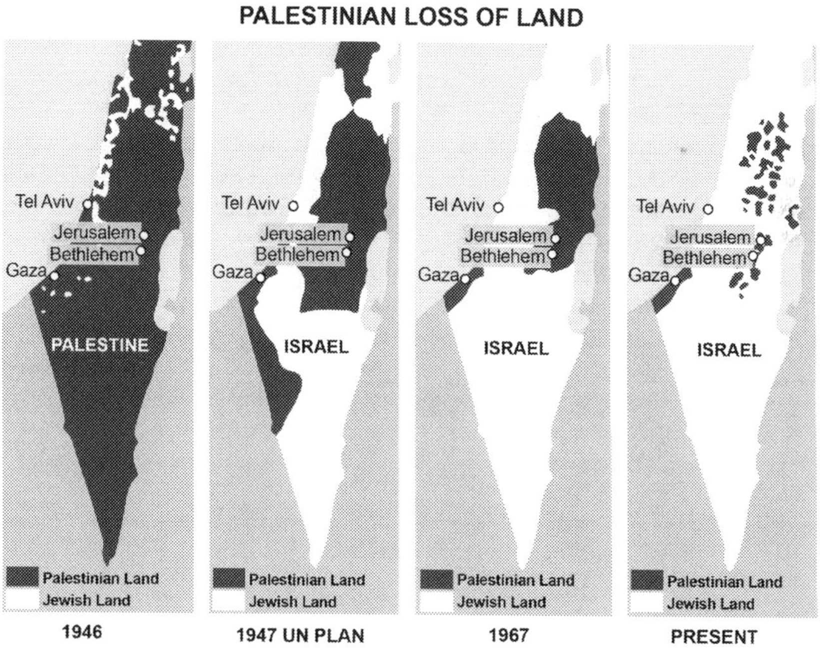

Figure 2.1 Loss of Palestinian Land.

Source: Mazin Qumsiyeh, (Pluto Press, 2004).

discussion of intersectionality in Chapter 6. To resist the occupation and make government elites accountable to international law will require strategic dialogue, aggressive nonviolence, and intersectional and international support. Government leaders in both Israel and Palestine continue to resist mid-level peacemaking, continue to annex more Palestinian land, and continue to build more illegal settlements. The task of transforming these challenges will be the focus of Chapter 3.

2.8 Conclusion

Coming to terms with the Israeli-Palestinian conflict encompasses multiple challenges: first, this is an existential challenge for both Palestinians and Israelis who perceiving this conflict as a matter of identity, even life and death; second, negotiating an agreement for things that can be more easily negotiated—land, housing, and policies; and third, literally coming to language, concepts, methods, and language for understanding and interpreting the conflict. Key terms include *positionality, situated knowledge, ethnography, critical ethnography, conflict, conflict transformation, and conflict resolution. Situated knowledge* is knowledge born of resistance to oppression. *Positionality* refers to a person's identity, values, and commitments. As theory and method, *ethnography* is a process of participant observation with a particular group of people in a particular time and place. *Critical ethnography* emphasizes the researcher's ethical responsibility to advocate for social justice for the group being studied. The researcher engages in transformational listening to create spaces for marginalized voices to be heard. Other key terms relate to *conflict,* which is generally defined as two or more incompatible goals or processes. In the context of this conflict, I have mostly used the process-oriented concept of *conflict transformation* rather than *conflict resolution.* To suggest that this conflict transformation process is still in the early stages of transformation, I have mostly used the term *peacemakers* rather than *peacebuilders.* In the next chapter, scholars and practitioners stress the major role of identities in conflict, and the crucial importance of mid-level peacemakers.

3 A Conflict of Identities

To transform the occupation, the role of identity is central. As suggested earlier, identities are often perceived as "a matter of life and death" (Pappe, 2014, p. 3), and I follow the premise that "issues of identity are at the root of most conflicts," protecting self and groups, "lodged in the narratives of how people see themselves, who they are, where they come from, and what they fear they will become or lose" (Lederach, 2003, p. 55). Israeli and Palestinian identities are constituted by ethnicity, personal and collective histories, ideologies, media images, fears and traumas, and national identities. Many writers have analyzed these competing identities (Khalidi, 1997, 2010; Hammack, 2011; Suleiman, 2011; Greenstein, 2014; Kahanoff, 2016).

3.1 Constructing Identities

I concur with Khalidi that identity is *constructed*, not primordial. In Part II, the dialogues show how both groups construct and sometimes transform their identities. These identities variously appear as tribal, both pre-conscious and highly articulated, deeply rooted and adaptable, exercised in policy and practice, and sometimes considered to be ascribed by God. Peacemakers often challenge the identities of others, because their own identities are not predetermined. As the dialogues in Part II will show, peacemakers have the capacity for radical, constructive change.

Modern historiography must interrogate and bridge both Israeli and Palestinian national narratives. Nationalism as a concept is seen as encompassing the lives of everyone in a given land. "In reality, it is a story of the few, not the many, of men, not women, of the wealthy, not the poor" (Pappe, 2004, p. 7). And identity is shaped by what is remembered, forgotten, denied, hidden, or erased. Pappe says, "Every identity is constructed by knowing not only who you are … but also, who you are not" (Part II, p. 269). For Pappe, the Israeli denial of Palestinian history and presence is deeply dishonest; it is coupled with a selective memory of what happened in 1947–49. The Israeli policy of *hafrada* officially separates Palestinians and Jewish Israelis. For Levy, the Israeli occupation is "the very dark backyard of Israel, … hidden from Israeli eyes" (Part II, p. 248). For Halper, the

DOI: 10.4324/9781003262817-4

Judaization of Palestine erases Palestinian history (Part II, p. 229). Since 1967, Israel has tried "by all means" to wipe out the Palestinian national, political, social, and cultural presence (Abuzayyad, 2017).

Elias Chacour (Part II, p. 195) expresses his identity in personal, collective, and religious terms:

> I was born in a village in the upper Galilee, ... an entirely Christian village.... I am proud to be a Palestinian Arab, [also] a Christian priest in the Melkite Catholic Church. I was not born a citizen of Israel; Israel was born in my country. I was born to speak Arabic. For a priority in my identity, I discovered that I was born in the image of God.

Most identities in Part II demonstrate a similar pattern of interconnections.

Palestinian national identity has evolved without a nation-state. During the Madrid Conference (1991), Rashid Khalidi discovered "how rapidly views of self and other, of history, and of time and space could shift in situations of extreme political stress, ... as watersheds in terms of identity" (2009, p. ix). For Mitri Raheb, nationalisms are constructed through the confluence of stories, histories, practices, and imagination. Both Palestinian and Israeli nationalisms are constructed to express what Raheb calls "mythistory" (in Wagner & Davis, 2014, p. xvii). According to Benedict Anderson, nation-states are "practices of sustained imagination," an "angle of vision" prior to the facts that shapes and positions the facts to serve an interest that requires obedience and resists criticism. For Walter Brueggemann, "nationalism" reflects "passion, eloquence, and courage along with some historical requirement" (in Wagner & Davis, 2014, p. xiv). The state of Israel and the quest for a Palestinian state reflect passion, idealism, and "practices of sustained imagination."

Nationalism presents challenges for peacemakers. When the Palestinian armed revolution emerged in 1967, Andoni questioned those who talked about Palestine as a "lost paradise."

GA: People are motivated by myths. Reality does not motivate anybody. But images do—heroic, ethical, sacrificing—those images actually motivate you to be part of it....

RH: Describe the myth that you said was dissolving for you.

GA: ... That a free Palestine is paradise [where] we can live in freedom, where we can show the world how good and effective Palestinians are. To achieve that, there was this image of the freedom fighter, the sacrificing, morally advanced person. (Part II, p. 106)

Khalidi writes that doubts about Palestinian national identity persist. Palestinian claims are considered "less genuine, deep-rooted, and valid than those of other peoples in the region" (2010, p. xxiv). The Palestinian national identity is challenged by the "matrix of control," an Israeli "settlement-occupation-industrial complex"; a Palestinian Authority (PA) with no real authority, serving as a subcontractor for Israel; villages functioning as "open-air prisons"; suffering geographical and political fragmentation; and opposition by the two great powers, the U.S. and the U.K. (2010, p. xxiii). For Palestinians, the central identity is the 1948 Nakba.

3.2 Demographics, Ethnicity, and Ethnocracy

Israelis are obsessed with demographics and ethnicity in their effort to re-main maintain a Jewish majority and a "Jewish democracy." In 1860, the population of 600,000 people in Palestine was 80% Arab, 10% Christian, 6% Jewish, and 4% other. By 1947, Jews made up 31% of the population (Rubenberg, 2003). Today, the Israeli population is 75% Jewish and 21% Palestinian. Within all of historic Palestine, Palestinians constitute half of the population; a million Palestinians are citizens of Israel, and over 700,000 Jews live in illegal settlements in the OPT. Avnery says:

UA: Jewish people don't want a state where there are 3, 4, 5 million Arabs.... Israelis are 99.9% unanimous: they don't want a binational state. They want a Jewish state.
RH: Would you include yourself?
UA: Including myself. Our national personality [must] be dominant.... We have 20% Arab citizens.... I am ready [for] another 5% if it solves the refugee problems. (Part II, p. 149)

Other Jewish peacemakers support a real democracy for all Israeli-Palestinian residents to overcome the discrimination against the 21% Palestinian minority in Israel. Palestinian citizens of Israel ('48 Palestinians) are sixth-class citizens, following Jewish ethnic groups (Kahanoff, 2016; Rouhana, 2017). Palestinians as "the unwanted" remain part of Zionist discourse (Pappe, 2006). But any Jew can move to Israel and become a citizen.

3.3 Zionism and Its Discontents

The ethics of Zionist exceptionalism and ethnic separation (*hafrada*) generate a rift among peacemakers. Avnery and Gila Svirsky are committed to a two-state solution in part to maintain a "Jewish state." Halper, Pappe, and Bronstein consider themselves to be "anti-Zionists," and they believe that the contradictions within liberal Zionism obstruct a genuine peace. Palestinian peacemakers unanimously reject Zionism as ideology, identity, and historical process. In its simplest form, Zionism is the historical quest for a "Jewish homeland." Two Zionist perspectives emerged in the late 1800s: Israel was a place in Palestine where Jews could escape persecution and develop a Hebrew culture; or it was an exclusive Jewish state developed through ethnic cleansing, secularization, and nationalism. Halper (Part II, p. 215) defines the two options as Western European-style democracy and Eastern European tribalism.

The Western model, like the American model, says the nation is the state. Everyone in the state can be a citizen. But Zionism adopted Eastern European tribalism and nationalism as an *ethnocracy*. When one ethnic group marginalizes everyone else, that leads to conflict.

From 1947 to 1949, Jews killed or transferred half of the Palestinian population and destroyed 450 Palestinian villages. Avnery participated in the expulsions. "I left the Irgun [at] 18 or 19, convinced that we must make peace with the Arabs ... against the colonial powers" (Part II, p. 146). Chacour, Ateek, and Salameh tell stories of being expelled. Pappe says that the Zionist motives for the ethnic cleansing of Palestinians were formal Zionist planning (Plan D, for *Dalet* [2005]). He calls this "a crime against humanity," the most "formative event" in the modern history of Palestine; and "a crime" that must be confronted politically and morally (2006).

In one of our dialogues, Pappe describes how Zionism is maintained and continues to function:

IP: Israel is still a very indoctrinating state. People still suckle, from the cradle to the grave, a very clear narrative, a Zionist metanarrative.

RH: Is this by design?

IP: Yes, it is by design. It is very systematic, ... very calculated. It is very difficult to deviate from it because it is based on deep fears of the Jewish people and their history.... [It's] a planned indoctrination.... If you want to challenge it from within, it is difficult, [or] from without, it is difficult. It is a very long process [to] deprogram people. (Part II, pp. 266–267)

Zionism, as an ideology, constantly resists peacemaking efforts. Ben-Gurion and most of the early Jewish leaders were secular, but "the Bible became both the justification and the map for the Zionist colonization of Palestine" (Pappe, 2017, p. 32). Based on a few biblical verses (e.g., Deuteronomy 14:2), Jewish and Christian Zionists claim that Jews are "chosen" by God, and they have special rights to the "promised land" of Israel. These arguments and counter-arguments are extensive (Wagner & Davis, 2014; Brueggemann, 2015). However, these promises are deeply connected to ethical requirements: "The Lord will establish you as a people holy unto himself ... if you ... walk in his ways.... But if you will not obey the voice of the Lord your God ... [and] do all his commandments ... all these curses shall come upon you (Deuteronomy 28: 9, 15). These warnings are explicit. A holistic interpretation of "chosenness" and the universal vision of the Hebrew prophets is necessary. Halper comments:

> The goal of Zionism and the Israeli elite is exclusive claim to the land.... As the victims, [they say,] "Palestinians brought it on themselves. *They* attacked us; *we're* the victims. This is all security, all defense." It's a very dangerous combination—tremendous *power* and aggressiveness, no responsibility and no accountability, all the freedom ... to do anything [they] want, *impunity* in relationship to the Palestinians. (Part II, p. 216)

Peacemakers find the arguments for a "promised land" and "chosenness" to be quite problematic. Some secular Jews believe that even if God does not exist, "God gave this land to us."

Jewish peacemaker identities exist along a continuum from liberal Zionism to anti-Zionism. Halper asserts that most peacemakers in the Israeli peace camp are Zionists in some form (Part II, p. 223). The dialogues in Part II include Svirsky's liberal Zionism, Avnery's "post-Zionism," and Halper's anti-Zionism. Svirsky accounts for Jewish suffering, fear, "land grabs," illegal settlements, and occupation. After the 1967 war, she hoped that "a land-for-peace" negotiation would happen. Avnery describes his transition from Zionism to "post-Zionism."

UA: Post-Zionist means that Zionism has fulfilled its mission. The moment the state of Israel came about ... it [became] a nation like other nations....
RH: So, the term [Zionism] was no longer useful.
UA: It was not useful at all. In our eyes, it was dangerous. (Part II, p. 147)

Liberal Zionists insist that a two-state solution to the conflict is the only solution, even if Israel has made this impossible. Avnery says, "We have two peoples in this country, and neither can be removed. So, the only solution is for the Palestinians to have a Palestinian state" (Part II, p. 155). Pappe declares, "However you define Zionism, it is a disincentive for reconciliation and peace" (Part II, p. 265).

3.4 Land, "Promised Land," and Illegal Settlements

The Israeli-Palestinian conflict is more about the land than religion. Since its founding, Israel has been obsessed with territory and territoriality, gained through military, administrative, and judicial means. Yosef Jabareen calls this "*obsessive territoriality*" and "a continuous, never completed, compulsive project" (in Rouhana, 1997, p. 238). Every piece of land is contested. Land, which the Zionists demanded, was not intended for persecuted Jews, but "to take as much of Palestine as possible with as few inhabitants as practical" (Pappe, 2017, p. 38). Karen Armstrong calls this land obsession a "holy war" (2001). To understand this geography of conflict, one must consult maps. The Occupied Palestinian Territories (OPT) comprise the West Bank, East Jerusalem, and Gaza—22% of historic Palestine. The West Bank is divided into "Bantustans" or "cantons" (see Fig. 2.1). Gaza is a "prison" with borders controlled by Israel and Egypt. Israel has divided the OPT into three administrative and military areas: Area A is under Palestinian control; Area B is under joint Palestinian-Israeli control; and Area C is completely under Israeli control. Israel also controls the air space above the land, and the resources under the land (Weizman, 2012). Halper calls the de-development of the OPT "holes in the grid" (Part II, p. 217).

In the early years, some religious Israelis rejected nationalism and Zionism as forces of secularization. Now, Ascherman says, Judaism, Zionism, land, and nationalism are closely linked.

AA: The dominant Judaism here says, God promised us in the Bible that this land is ours, but … the amount of land that we [control] will … [depend] on our moral behavior.
RH: In the Torah, promises are linked to doing the right thing, to doing justice.…
AA: … If we all got to the spiritual place of [saying] "the land doesn't belong to any of us" … we'd have less need … [to] control [it]. (Part II, p. 118)

Peacemakers are committed to sharing the land. El-Farra says that the land can be shared. Palestinian theologian Munther Isaac argues the "promised land" has lost theological significance; the "moral and ethical demands of God trump all claims of entitlement to the land" (2015, p. 177). Jewish and Palestinian peace activists speak of illegal Israeli settlements as a threat to the state of Israel. Gideon Levy says, "The settlers are living in total [separation] … [with] a different set of laws, a different way of behaving, and a different culture, creating such damage" (Part II, p. 247). Peacemakers must create a transformational concept of sharing the land.

3.5 Victimhood and War

Dialogues with Svirsky, Avnery, and Halper suggest that most Israelis are more preoccupied with security than with land. According to Nadera Shalhoub-Kevorkian, Ben-Gurion built a nation-state based on fear of surrounding Arab countries, Palestinians, and the feeling that "the whole world is against us." Israel's "security" was transformed into a religion, combining biblical claims of "promised land" with Jewish chosenness to frame Israeli violence against Palestinians as a "security necessity" (2015, p. 14). For Israelis, actual suffering and contemporary threats produce a national identity of fear and ethnic separation. Kuttab, a human-rights lawyer, says,

> I realized early on that the fight with Israelis was not a military fight; that I had to work with international law and international solidarity, and reject trying to defeat Israel, with its military might, technological superiority, weapons of mass destruction … and U.S. backing. It was important to find other ways to resist and end the occupation. (Part II, p. 233)

The concept of "victimhood" provides crucial insights for transforming this conflict. In the 1990s, Joseph Montville, a career diplomat and mediator, developed an understanding of how individuals and groups can hold simultaneous identities as both victims and victimizers. He applied this concept to Israel-Palestine and Northern Ireland. According to Montville, ethnic and religious conflicts are the most resistant to traditional diplomatic or political mediation (1993, p. 112). His workshops addressed three dimensions: an experience of violent trauma; a conviction that the aggression was totally unjustified; and victims' fears that "aggressors will strike again" (p. 113).

Peacemakers in both ethnic groups struggle with how to promote positive transformation rather than victimhood. Jewish suffering is well known. Palestinian suffering is less well known. Edward Said famously described Palestinians as "victims of victims" (in Halper, Part II, p. 220), but Palestinians resist victimhood as their core identity. Mitri Raheb declares:

MR: Israelis ... pretend they have a monopoly on suffering, which allows them to inflict so much suffering on Palestinians. We don't want to become like ... our oppressors. It is really important to provide ... something constructive.... Over 80% of the Palestinian people have some kind of trauma.... Right now in Bethlehem Israelis are building this Wall ... 35 miles around the city [and] 25 feet high. Each of our cities will be a prison.

RH: You ... are familiar with German [history] as well as the situation here.... How do you address a whole culture that has been traumatized, whether Israelis or Palestinians?

MR: People who have been persecuted often become persecutors themselves. [But] we are much more than victims.... We [must] become proactive actors. (Part II, p. 278)

Raheb has been quite proactive, as a longtime pastor and as president of a new university.

Ascherman and Pappe link Israeli victimhood and identity with a compensating quest as a mini-superpower. Ascherman confirms that Israelis deny human rights to Palestinians, while seeing themselves as victims. "There is an incredible symmetry in how we have all created seamless world views.... We fully see ourselves as the victims.... We cannot imagine that we can be both victims and victimizers" (Part II, p. 117). Pappe says that victimhood has a complex and contradictory relationship with Zionism. "You are the ... victimizer and you have a self-perception of yourself as a victim.... Israel embraces victimhood—'2000 years of suffering'—and thrives as a superpower. When Israel became a 'mini-empire,' the 'fifth largest [nuclear power] in the world,' Jews felt it compensated for their own history. Zionism makes Jews feel like they [are] powerful—the new Jew—compensating for years of being a victim" (Pappe, Part II, p. 268).

Since 1948, Palestinians have also been preoccupied with safety and security. But comparing suffering is a dubious activity. Halper says, "For Jews, nothing trump[s] the Holocaust.... If you try to play that game, you lose" (Part II, p. 220). There is a complicated way in which Israelis sustain the Israeli-Palestinian conflict by holding together their victim and victimizer roles. A military culture is deeply connected to the Israeli security state. It tends to choose aggression and war rather than dialogue and diplomacy to resolve conflicts. During the 2006 Israeli war with Lebanon, Gideon Levy offered this compelling insight (Part II, pp. 249, 250):

GL: Israel, usually *after* bloodshed, is ready to make compensation.... We could have had peace with Egypt before the [Yom Kippur] war and we refused. After 2,600 soldiers were killed ... Israel was able to make peace.... We needed the first *intifada* and the bloodshed to recognize the PLO.... A bigger bloodshed will bring a bigger outcome.

RH: What is the cultural dynamic that makes this so?

GL: Maybe there is a very deep need to have a war every few years. Maybe it's a physiological need, a national need.... It seems that [Israelis have] a real need for war.

For peacemakers, this is a haunting statement and a great challenge. Levy says that diplomatic leaders in Israel either can't or won't work out a just peace.

I asked Levy about Walter Wink's concept of "the myth of redemptive violence," the belief "that violence saves, that war brings peace, that might makes right" (1998, p. 42). Levy said,

> In Israel it's very true because it's a source of something that unites the people [and] makes the leadership very heroic.... It is like a ritual that comes back.... When it comes to negotiating, always it takes postponing and postponing and conditions and preconditions. When it comes to war, 15 minutes and there is a new war. (Part II, p. 250)

Avnery, Eitan Bronstein, and Yonatan Shapira also place militarism at the heart of Israeli culture and identity.

Jonathan Kuttab says Israel embraces a contradictory combination of idealism and uncritical Zionism.

> At the very heart of Zionism are ... positive, progressive, modern, even utopian ideas.... [and] the idea that the state should be [only] for the Jews, and that that goal must be achieved at almost any price, [serving] all Jews [but] not serving [all] its citizens, ... able to do anything [with] weapons of mass destruction, nuclear weapons, even genocide.... So, you can have your idealism, fascism, and racism at the same time. (Part II, p. 241)

Pappe also declares that Israeli exclusivity and supremacy are maintained "by all means and at all expense" (Part II, p. 269). Chapter 6 will address the security and safety needed by both groups.

3.6 Palestinian Identities and (Dis)orientations

While Israel differentiates among "non-Jews" according to religious, ethnic, and regional groups—Muslims, Christians, Druze, and Bedouins—each group has its own distinct identity. However, all Palestinians are discriminated against more or less equally (Peleg & Waxman, 2011).

3.6.1 Refugees

The most traumatic events affecting modern Palestinian identity are the catastrophes of 1948 and 1967. Estephan Salameh describes his family's disorientations and loss of identity.

> [Israel] captured 78% of the land, [and] 90% of the population ... became refugees. It was a complete loss of people, property, and identity.... What we were before is not what we are now.... That beautiful puzzle [of] 1,000 pieces—when somebody throws them around, there is no way you can put this puzzle together the way it was. For my dad ... it felt [like] a complete loss ... who he was, and who he had become. (Part II, p. 295)

This profound disorientation is common to the stories that appear in my play *The Longing* (2001), based on material I recorded during the 50th anniversary of Israel and the Nakba.

Ben-Gurion would not allow a single refugee to return. Avnery says, "We got orders to shoot any Arab who tried to come back to his village" (Part II, 149) When the 1948 war ended, the future of refugees and Israel's borders remained unresolved. The ceasefire lines of 1949—the Green Line—are still "fragile and contested" (Bunton, 2013, p. 65). Thousands of Palestinian refugees remain in Syria, Lebanon, and Jordan and thousands of internally displaced Palestinians remain in the West Bank and Gaza. For Avnery, the refugee issue is "by far the most difficult problem" of the whole conflict. Israel must clarify what really happened in 1948–49, assume responsibility and apologize for what it did, and recognize the moral principle that every refugee has the right to return. But Avnery rejects taking back 4 million Palestinian refugees. He supports only "a practical compromise" of 50,000 refugees a year for 10 years (Part II, p. 151).

3.6.2 Jerusalem

As "the city of peace," Jerusalem is the heart of both Israel and Palestine. For Khalidi, it is part history, story, and myth, and part geography, politics, holy war, and spiritual locus.

> Virtually all narratives about Palestine—religious, secular, Jewish, Christian, Muslim, Israeli, and Palestinian—revolve around the city of

> Jerusalem, which has long been the geographical, spiritual, political, and administrative center of Palestine. [It] has such great significance to so many people ... that contrasting narratives come most bitterly into conflict. (Khalidi, 1997, 2010, p. 13)

For thousands of years, religious groups and empires have fought for control of Jerusalem, waging the "holy wars" of the Christian Crusades, Islamic *jihad,* and Eretz Israel (Armstrong, 2001). In November 1947, to protect the legitimate rights and identities of all three major religious groups, the UN General Assembly passed UN Resolution 181, which called for "the partition of Palestine into Arab and Jewish states, with the city of Jerusalem as a *corpus separatum*" (separate entity) to be governed by an international coalition. But successive Israeli governments have increasingly made this a Jewish city, annexing East Jerusalem. In "Kairos Palestine 2009," leaders of Christian churches wrote: "Jerusalem is the heart of our reality. It is, at the same time, [a] symbol of peace and sign of conflict.... Jerusalem, city of reconciliation, has become a city of discrimination and exclusion, a source of struggle rather than peace" (p. 14).

Theologian Naim Ateek (1997) and other Christian leaders explore the ways in which Jerusalem may yet contribute to peacemaking in Israel. Ateek asserts that the New Testament "de-territorialises the Gospel ... universalizing God's reign" (p. 100). Conflict transformation in Jerusalem could be a catalyst for peacemaking in the whole country (Ateek, 2017, p. 71). But Israeli prime ministers have vowed that Jerusalem will never be divided. In 2018, the Trump Administration moved the U.S. Embassy from Tel Aviv to Jerusalem, calling Jerusalem the capital of Israel (but not of Palestine). Abuzayyad warns that Trump's decision lacks international vision; he concludes that "both Balfour and Trump gave away what they didn't own" (2018, p. 5).

3.6.3 Palestinian Citizens of Israel

At the end of the 1948 war, Palestinians constituted 20% of the state of Israel. Today, Palestinians still comprise about 21% of Israeli citizens—around 1 million people. They call themselves '48 Palestinians, or "Palestinian citizens of Israel." They have some loyalty to Israel, but a deeper loyalty to the Palestinian people. This places their national identities in a limbo of "forgotten Palestinians" (Avnery, Part II, p. 40); "unwelcome" in Zionist discourse (Pappe, 2011); subject to an ethnic Jewish state (Rouhana, 1997); "strangers in their homeland" (Cohen, 2009); and with "identities in conflict" with Jewish Israelis (Frisch, 2011; Kahanoff, 2016).

3.6.4 The PLO

Deborah Gerner (1994) writes that Palestinian national identity received a boost when Palestinians established the Palestine Liberation Organization

(PLO) in 1964. It served as an institutional expression of identity and self-determination. To set up the PLO as a nonstate national actor, Arab states followed the example of the Zionist movement 50 years earlier, with pre-state political, social, economic, humanitarian, and military institutions (Gerner, 1994, p. 85). Five political movements emerged. The secular Fatah Party became the largest group, with the Palestine National Council (PNC) as the highest Palestinian authority. Although illegal under Israeli law, the PLO worked through local institutions and served as the principal expression of Palestinian nationalism. Since 2006, pro-PLO groups have competed with the Islamic Resistance Movement (Hamas) for popular support.

3.6.5 The Six-Day War and Occupation

In 1967, Israel launched a pre-emptive war, capturing the Sinai from Egypt, the Golan Heights from Syria, and the Palestinian Territories (the West Bank, Gaza and East Jerusalem) from Jordan. Svirsky draws a sharp distinction between Israel's fighting the Egyptians "for survival" and grabbing as much Palestinian land as possible. The 1967 war forced many Palestinians into a second refugee experience, and another 20-year oppression. Ghassan Andoni describes how the 1967 war began to shape his early identity.

GA: That was my first ... shock of the real conflict between Israel and Palestinians ... my first scenes of bombardment, the [Israeli] army taking over, curfews imposed, and fear.
RH: So, very early on, critical questions began to form?
GA: Lots of them.... Everybody was involved ... knowing people who are part of the resistance.... Prison and the '67 war influenced me deeply.... Israelis arrested me to deprive me from taking the [big, senior] exam.
RH: You began to see a larger pattern of harassment and disruption?
GA: I was getting glimpses of "You can't have normal dreams of what you want in the future.... There is something much bigger.... It's invading all aspects of your life." (Part II, pp. 103–104)

After 1967, the land-for-peace option (UN Resolution 242) failed to materialize. Twenty years of brutal occupation followed, with low-intensity warfare, a decimation of Palestinian culture, and thousands more refugee dependent on the UN Relief and Works Agency (UNRWA).

3.6.6 The First Intifada: 1987–1993

For Ghassan Andoni, the first *intifada* (uprising) combined a civil-rights movement with a national independence struggle (in Carey, 2001, p. 209). It transformed whole communities. Andoni learned lessons about nonviolent resistance, prison, community organizing, academic preparation, and solidarity with Israelis and internationals.

GA: [I found] some answers to the many questions in my mind.... I saw real civilian-based, popular resistance [with] lots of creativity, lots of grassroots work, lots of new methods ... total civil disobedience as a way to force the occupation to lose control.

RH: Give examples of the civil disobedience.

GA: The first part was organizational.... We claimed independence [from Israel]. We started establishing the basis of our *sumud* or sustainability. (Part II, p. 107)

In response, the Israelis closed everything. In Beit Sahour, Andoni and other organizers opened 40 underground schools, taught people to raise vegetables instead of flowers, developed medical and judicial systems, practiced tax resistance, "the peak of civil disobedience," and completely replaced the occupation system (Andoni, Part II, p. 107). These events have been dramatized on film (Shomali & Cowan, 2014), and as a play (Hostetter, 2014). Estephan Salameh speaks of solidarity:

ES: The event itself was teaching us [through] people's stories [of] soldiers shooting everywhere, people thrown in jail.... But I still believed in peaceful resistance.... When classmates went to demonstrations and [didn't] come back, I had to deal with that trauma.

RH: You had friends who were killed?

ES: From another school. And friends got arrested, too.... They used to get arrested if [soldiers] saw them carrying books.... We call this the steadfast generation....

RH: So the concept of *sumud* was really palpable.

ES: It strengthened during the first *intifada* in every aspect. Carrying a book, that's a form of *sumud,* a kind of resistance. Going to school is a form of resilience.... The level of solidarity during the first intifada was unprecedented. I still believe that the peak of the Palestinian resistance is the first *intifada.* (Part II, pp. 297–298)

While the first *intifada* was spontaneous, some writers connect it to earlier forms of popular resistance to the Ottoman and British occupations (Andoni, 2001; Carey, 2001; Qumsiyeh, 2011).

The first *intifada* was generally nonviolent, but Israeli responses were brutal. Defense Minister Yitzhak Rabin ordered soldiers to "break the bones" of Palestinian protesters. B'Tselem reports that the Israeli government killed 1,070 Palestinians, including 257 children, arrested 175,000, and destroyed 2,000 Palestinian homes (Hammad, 2017, p. 1). The first *intifada* shook Israel's belief that Israel could indefinitely maintain the occupation (Khalidi, 2010). The *intifada* was likely the high point of Palestinian nationalism (Bunton, 2013).

3.6.7 A Failed "Peace Process"

The first *intifada* generated a "peace process," including the Oslo Accords (1993, 1995), facilitated by Norwegian and Israeli academics, PLO officials, and the U.S. government. Many Palestinians and Israelis cheered this process, believing that a two-state solution would emerge. More prescient analysts rejected the Accords. Alarmed, Edward Said (1993) wrote that the Accords were "an instrument of Palestinian surrender"; Israel conceded nothing and renounced all relevant UN resolutions except 242 and 338; Israel offered no reparations for 450 villages destroyed in 1948 and the expulsion of 750,000 Palestinians. The Accords called the OPT "disputed territories," rather than Palestinian territories, and demanded Israeli security but not Palestinian security. The Accords left in place "a victim and a victimizer" (Said, 2001, p. 3).

Peacemakers consider the Oslo Accords to be a masterful deception (Halper, Andoni, Pappe). Palestinian officials allowed Israelis to remove international law and human rights as the basis for the Accords, so the Accords strengthened the occupation. "Because of the fiction of a Palestinian Authority—supported by flags, honor guards, ministries ... the empty trappings of statehood—some are deluded into believing that Palestinians have all but achieved their national aims" (Khalidi, 2010, p. xxiii). Successive Israeli governments have created irreversible "facts on the ground," built illegal settlements in the West Bank, built a massive separation Wall, and placed hundreds of checkpoints in the OPT. Andoni mistrusted the whole "peace process." His friends accused him of not working for peace. But, he "spared no effort," establishing the Center for Rapprochement and other organizations (Part II, p. 107).

After the Accords, Israel pursued two goals: to control as much land as possible, with the fewest Palestinians possible on the land (Pappe). Israelis confined Palestinians to cantons (Fig. 2.1), annexed East Jerusalem, claimed large portions of the West Bank, legitimized illegal Jewish settlements, built bypass roads for Jewish settlers, restricted Palestinian movements, and seized most of the water resources for Israelis (Pacheco, 2001). Israel still controls the land it captured in 1967, and rejects provisions in the Fourth Geneva Convention to protect people under military occupation (1949). By the end of the 1990s, Israeli politicians believed that "Palestinians would have to relinquish most of their national, religious, and human rights because of Israel's ability to dictate terms" (Andoni, 2001, p. 211). Israel signals that Palestinians will "always remain subjugated" (Qumsiyeh, 2011, p. 168). For Chomsky, the Accords broke the world consensus that Israel has no claim to the OPT, and that the settlements are illegitimate. The Accords "wiped out virtually the entire record of Middle East diplomacy" (2016, pp. 9–10).

3.6.8 The Second Intifada

In October 2000, Israeli Prime Minister Ariel Sharon took 1,000 armed Israelis into the third-holiest site in Islam, the Al-Aqsa Mosque in the Old City. The second *intifada* (Al-Aqsa *intifada)* erupted. It was more violent and more costly than the first *intifada.* Israeli security forces killed 6,371 Palestinians, and Palestinians killed 1,083 Israelis. Rather than being a popular uprising, the second *intifada* was organized by Palestinian elites, and it involved much more violence. Israelis deepened attacks on resisters, the Fatah Party and Hamas fought each other, and the Israeli peace camp split up. The more progressive wing developed new initiatives such as the Coalition of Women for a Just Peace (Svirsky). Palestinian-Israeli dialogues ended.

3.6.9 Gaza, Hamas, and the Great March of Return

Two-thirds of the 2 million people living in Gaza are refugees from 1948 and 1967. In 1987, the Islamist resistance movement established Hamas in Gaza. The U.S. and other countries denounced Hamas as a terrorist organization. Hamas rejected the Oslo Accords, rivaled the Palestinian Authority (founded in 1993) and the secular Fatah Party, and positioned Gaza as a Muslim homeland and Israel as an illegitimate, occupying, colonial power. Israel withdrew illegal Jewish settlements from Gaza in 2005. But in 2006, Israel blockaded Gaza, limiting access to essential supplies and materials. It continues to control all of Gaza's borders by land, air, and sea. Two million people have been deprived of adequate water, electricity, medical supplies, access to the other OPT areas, and to the rest of the world. Human-rights organizations describe Gaza as "the world's largest open-air prison" (Pappe, 2016), suffering continuous de-development and humanitarian crises (Chomsky & Pappe, 2010; Roy, 2016; Finkelstein, 2018).

In 2018, the UN Office for the Coordination of Humanitarian Affairs (OCHA) identified 20 elements that constitute the humanitarian crisis in Gaza, among them that 98% of the water is contaminated, 50% of all children have been psychologically traumatized by war and blockades, and four out of 10 families struggle to acquire enough food. In our dialogue, Mona El-Farra, a medical doctor and development worker, says, Gaza is "unlivable": the number of deaths has increased, children are dying from a lack of medications, patients cannot get the right treatments, and borders are closed. El-Farra says, "We are trapped on this small piece of land" (Part II, p. 212) Shapira has tried to break the siege of Gaza by sailing there with supplies.

The humanitarian crisis in Gaza has been complicated by four military conflicts with Israel. Since 2007, Hamas has launched rockets into Israel and Israel has responded with disproportionate military attacks, killing thousands of people and destroying thousands of homes. The Israeli attacks on Gaza in 2014 and 2021 were brutal. About the 2014 war, Salameh says, "We have a whole generation with stress disorders, including 1,400 orphans, 10,000 injured, 2,100 killed, 100,000 houses damaged, and 12,000 houses destroyed completely" (Part II, p. 290). For Halper, this war was a "game changer" because Fatah collaborated with Israel rather than Gaza (Part II, p. 225-226).

Both Palestinian and Israeli identities are diverse and evolving. For Palestinians, Khalidi sees a story "of both failure and success…. In spite of all their sacrifices, the Palestinian people have not so far achieved… self-determination" (2010, pp. 208–209). According to Raheb, the Hamas leaders in Gaza are much more dialogical than what their adversaries perceive. Their multiple identities are a crucial starting point for dialogue. Raheb says that once you expose this, then Hamas appears to be very pragmatic (Raheb, Part II, pp. 281–282). In 2018, thousands of Gazans launched the nonviolent and remarkable Great March of Return, calling for an end to the Israeli blockade. In May 2021, Israel and Hamas engaged in another brutal war. Gaza remains under siege.

3.7 Conclusion

Most major conflicts are based in *identity* (Lederach), involving collective *positionalities* of ethnicity, ideology, fears, traumas, and national identities. Both ethnic groups sustain national identities in the "mythistory" of imagination (Raheb). *Zionism* emerged in Eastern Europe to relieve Jewish suffering, but it evolved into an ideology that many Jews believe made them divinely *chosen* and gave them a *promised land*. Israel supports this ideology with a policy of separation *(hafrada)* between ethnic groups. It annexes as much Palestinian land as possible, with as few Palestinians on that land as possible. This form of government is called an *ethnocracy*, rather than a democracy. Liberal Zionists support a two-state solution with a Palestinian state on 22% of historic Palestine. But most peacemakers in this study believe a two-state solution is no longer possible. Palestinian identities include the catastrophe (Nakba) of 1948, the war of 1967, the solidarity of the first *intifada*, a failed "peace process," a violent second *intifada*, the occupation, and four brutal wars between Israel and Gaza. To transform this conflict, the concept of *victimhood* (Montville) is crucial. It includes three elements; an experience of violence and trauma; a conviction that the trauma was completely unjustified; and fear that aggression will happen again. *Security* and *safety* are vital for both groups. Meanwhile, Palestinians cling to the practice of *sumud*—resistance, sustainability, steadfastness, and resilience. Chapter 4 examines the transformational identities of peacemakers.

4 Peacemaker Identities

In spite of the "fog of occupation" (Pappe) and the marginality of peacemakers in Israel-Palestine, their prophetic voices and strategic actions do emerge. Peacemakers share the conviction that government officials—of both groups—will not lead the way to a just peace, and that grassroots movements also need nongovernmental leaders to articulate and help implement a just peace. The peacemakers presented here are exemplary. A third have doctoral degrees. Chacour; Andoni; Halper; Boycott, Divestment, and Sanctions (BDS); and Combatants for Peace have been nominated for the Nobel Peace Prize. Eitan Bronstein and others struggle to name what they do.

RH: You have [written] that Zochrot's work is essential to create a ... platform [for] peace.

EB: Yeah, yeah. It's even more than peace, because usually when you talk [in Israel] about peace, it [is] a very bad word. The peace process here ... may even be good as a stage, but this doesn't mean that we'll have reconciliation between people.

RH: It may not have enough justice in it.

EB: Justice, I don't know.... Look, justice is a word that I wouldn't use, unfortunately, because ... it might even be dangerous.

RH: But there are many forms of justice.... Maybe restorative justice—

EB: [Or] transitional justice, ... not absolute justice.... In order to have reconciliation, we must acknowledge the Nakba and ... the parts we are responsible for. (Part II, pp. 190–191)

Though somewhat uncomfortable with the terminology of peace and justice, Bronstein links peacemaking with the goal of reconciliation.

Peace and justice workers are keenly aware that they work from the margins in both the Palestinian and Israeli cultures. For Halper and others, the image of "struggle" is central to their identities. They struggle to find dialogue partners within their own cultures as well as across ethnic fault lines. They struggle with the roles played by others (e.g., Part II, p. 226). I have generally followed Pappe's attitudes of inclusivity, considering both roles and goals. He firmly criticizes Peace Now's misguided "peacemaking,"

DOI: 10.4324/9781003262817-5

while celebrating a more dedicated core of peace and justice workers. "Those who are active against the occupation are crystal clear about what [the conflict] is all about.... We have now a much clearer group" (Part II, p. 267). Pappe includes a spectrum of peacemakers. "You have to be careful not to castigate people.... I don't define myself as [a Zionist], but I can work with people [who do] (Part II, p. 272). For Pappe, "tags" are not important.

4.1 Identity Formations

Most Palestinian peacemakers began wrestling with identity questions when they were young, and were caught in one of the cycles of violence—the Nakba (Ateek, Chacour), the 1967 war (Andoni, Kuttab, Abusrour), the first *intifada* (Raheb, Salameh), the second *intifada* (Awad), the Israel-Gaza wars (El-Farra), or refugee experiences (Ateek, Salameh, and Chacour). Palestinians began quests to understand Palestinian victimhood and Israeli oppression. As noted before, the 1967 war shaped Andoni's first understanding of the "real conflict" between Israelis and Palestinians (2006).

Jewish peacemakers exist along a continuum from "liberal Zionism" to anti-Zionism. Halper asserts that most peacemakers in the Israeli "peace camp" are Zionist in some form (Part II, p. 223). Halper and Avnery both affirm the renaissance of the Hebrew language and culture, but not the asymmetry of power, which is central to Israeli identity. This asymmetry is a huge challenge for all peacemakers in Israel-Palestine. Jewish peacemakers Bronstein, Halper, Pappe, and all of the Palestinian peacemakers identify themselves as anti-Zionists. They reject Zionist concepts of "chosenness," *hafrada* (separateness), exceptionalism, occupation, and two legal systems. This conflict has global implications. Halper says, "If the occupation wins, everyone loses, and apartheid wins" (Part II, p. 217). Pappe warns, "However you define Zionism, it has something in it that is a *disincentive* for reconciliation and peace" (Part II, p. 272).

Half of the Jewish peacemakers in Part II moved to Israel from other places—Canada, the U.S., Eastern Europe, or North Africa. All were born into families with stories of the Holocaust, founding the state of Israel, and war. For Pappe, these constitute a Zionist metanarrative.

IP: Israel is still a very indoctrinating state. People still suckle, from cradle to the grave, a very clear narrative, a Zionist metanarrative.
RH: Is this by design?
IP: Oh yes, it is by design. It is very systematic. It is very calculated. It is very difficult to deviate from it because it is based on the deep fears of the Jewish people and their history.... If you challenge it from within [or] from without, it is difficult. (Part II, pp. 266–267)

Pappe's identity changed when he left Israel for four years of graduate work in England. He learned to know Palestinian colleagues, researched the events of 1948, and examined Zionism both from within and from without. What he found in the archives about 1948, and what he heard from Palestinian and Arab friends were "eye-openers." These experiences "nurtured a decision to devote my life to asking for restitution and compensation, true reconciliation." He says, "This is not changing a position. This is almost changing your identity" (Part II, p. 265).

Shapira also tells a remarkable story of identity change. He grew up on Israeli air force bases in a traditional Jewish family. He became an air force pilot like his father. But he left the air force after a profound encounter at the School for Peace. "This Zionist poster boy ... found I [could] invest all this energy to do something ... I completely believed in, ... refuse [military service] ... [and] shake the system, the biggest shake I can ever think of" (Part II, p. 306). With his new identity, Shapira cofounded Combatants for Peace. His father called this "a betrayal, totally" (Part II, p. 306).

Concerning Jewish identity and the remarkable legacy of Jewish contributions to international law and human rights, Pappe makes a challenging comment:

> It depends on how you understand the precepts of Judaism. I claim in recent articles that Israel is *not* a Jewish state. I'm a Jew, and my heritage ... obliges me to put Jews ... in the U.S. civil-rights movement, against apartheid in South Africa, and where supporters of the Palestinians are today. If they don't do it, they are not Jewish. (Part II, p. 269)

Different long-term goals—a "Jewish state" and a "two-state solution"—create a rift among Jewish peacemakers. Halper, Pappe, and Bronstein are "anti-Zionists." They believe that contradictions within liberal Zionism are a major obstacle to a genuine peace.

4.2 Multiple Roles and Goals

Salameh says that since Palestine hasn't had a functioning parliament since the Hamas-Fatah split in 2006, "the role of the civil society in Palestine is probably even more important than in other places" (Part II, p. 293). Diamond and McDonald (1993) identify eight types of nongovernmental "diplomacy" or peacemaking. These examples appear in Part II:

- activism: Awad (p. 158); Halper (p. 214); Shapira (p. 302); Svirsky (p. 314); Bronstein (p. 182);
- nongovernmental professionals: Ashrawi (p. 125); Halper (p. 214);
- business: Bahour (p. 171);
- research, training, education: Chacour (p. 195); Pappe (p. 264); Raheb (p. 276); Awad (p. 158);

- religion: Chacour (p. 195); Raheb (p. 276); Ateek (p. 133); Ascherman (p. 113);
- funding: Bahour (p. 171); Salameh (p. 289);
- public opinion: Avnery (p. 145); Levy (p. 245).

From dialogical and conflict transformation perspectives, many additional peacemaking types appear in the dialogues presented in this book:

- dialogue facilitation: Pappe (p. 264);
- alternative tourism: Awad (p. 158); Halper (p. 214);
- the arts as "beautiful resistance": Abusrour (p. 91); Raheb (p. 276); Burnat (p. 192);
- boycott, divestment, and sanctions: Halper (p. 214); Pappe (p. 264);
- development work: El-Farra (p. 203); Salameh (p. 289);
- encounter groups: Shapira (p. 302); Bronstein (p. 182);
- human rights: Montell (p. 253); Ascherman (p. 113); Kuttab (p. 233);
- international law: Kuttab (p. 233);
- journalism: Avnery (p. 145); Awad (p. 158); Levy (p. 245);
- negotiations: Ashrawi (p. 125); Salameh (p. 289);
- nonviolence training: Awad (p. 158); Shapira (p. 302);
- restorative justice; Halper (p. 214); Pappe (p. 264);
- trauma healing: Salameh (p. 289); El-Farra (p. 203);
- strategic planning: Halper (p. 214); Andoni (p. 102).

Most of these peacemakers move between mid-level leadership and grassroots movements. As Diamond and MacDonald suggest, each of these approaches has its own philosophy, language, membership, and methods (1993, pp. 15–18).

Only a few peacemakers—Ashrawi, Salameh, and Avnery—have worked at all three levels of peace and justice work, as well as engaging with international peacemakers. Ashrawi is a peacemaker for all seasons: a former member of the PLO Legislative Council, the highest level of PLO leadership; a member of Palestinian negotiating teams; a spokesperson on international media; director of an NGO, The Palestinian Initiative for the Promotion of Global Dialogue & Democracy (MIFTAH); and a grassroots peacemaker. Ashrawi says that the world has given Palestinians impossible roles under occupation, to work on peacebuilding *or* nation building, but not both. "The best we can do right now is commit to peacemaking without falling into the trap of doing unto others what was done to us" (Part II, p. 127). She adds, "We need to speak up. We need to regroup.... [W]e have to have many different ways of addressing the issue, ... [such as] challenging [the U.S.] Congress" (Part II, p. 129).

Salameh connects social justice, community service, grassroots organizing, nonviolent resistance, coleading the Seraj library project, public policy work with government ministries, serving on the Sabeel board, consulting with

NGOs, and teaching at Birzeit University. Salameh describes himself as a teacher, diplomat, and politician with the ability to work in highly complex political environments. "My identity requires skills of diplomacy, politics, knowledge of policy, development, [and] community organizations as tools [for] change" (Part II, p. 300). After Salameh finished a Ph.D. in the U.S., the Palestinian Authority (PA) placed him in charge of international aid, to work with 84 donor countries and agencies, and billions of dollars.

ES: It was a really good experience.... I still do work for the government, the UN, donor agencies, and local NGOs. I work across the spectrum.

RH: I argue that government leaders either can't or won't create a just peace, [so] NGOs, civil society and Track Two diplomacy will have to lead this transformation, ... committed to ... human rights and international law.... The vanguard will be leadership from the middle rather than from the top.

ES: I share this point of view. In Palestine, on the positive side, we have some of the most active civil-society organizations ... in terms of number, in terms of activism. (Part II, p. 293)

Salameh tries to bridge peacemaking arenas: "I work with civil society to bring them closer to the government, and the government closer to civil society" (Part II, p. 300). Salameh translates his service roles as working for peace and justice.

Avnery, a lifelong journalist and peace activist, served three terms in the Israeli parliament, the Knesset, and cofounded Gush Shalom, a non-governmental organization.

UA: Gush Shalom is unique. There are people who are very important in small movements, ... Courage to Refuse (Yesh Gvul), which encourages people to refuse military service in the Occupied Territories; Women in Black are extremely courageous.

RH: The Israeli Committee Against Home Demolitions....

UA: Of course. Each one doing excellent and important work.... Gush Shalom is trying to break new ground, [to] change Israeli public opinion. (Part II, p. 151)

Gush Shalom is still working on this highly aspirational goal. However, I believe that changing Israeli public opinion will require a much more strategic approach. For example, Halper argues that the ideal peacemaker focuses on "political work with an endgame (intention), organization and strategy (effectiveness), leading to a genuinely just outcome" (2020b).

4.3 Human Rights: More than Naming and Shaming

Human-rights workers disagree about whether their work constitutes peacemaking or something more technical. Halper, who describes himself as both a human-rights worker and a peace activist, says that one of the advantages we have today is the concept of human rights, because they provide the basis of what a just society is. Human-rights workers document the physical, legal, and administrative violations of the occupation. Some human-rights workers accept a peacemaker identity, and some do not. El-Farra describes cycles of human-rights crises—bombings, demolitions, Israeli invasions, and other traumas that make Gaza "unlivable."

Some human-rights workers consider their task to be largely technical. Jessica Montell calls documenting human-rights violations a process of "naming and shaming."

> [H]uman rights is very narrow, almost technical. We are not involved in the big issues that are the root causes of those human-rights violations.... Our mandate is focused [on] international law, [and] basic human dignity ... the right to work, the right to housing, the right to be free of mistreatment and torture, the right to life. It is a ... legalistic approach [to] Jewish values and democratic values. (Part II, p. 254)

Montell distinguishes between the underlying causes of the conflict and "fire-brigade emergencies," what occupies the headlines: people killed, house demolitions. "We are not involved in political issues.... My job is to make sure that as long as there is a military occupation, it is conducted in as humane a way as possible" (Part II, p. 258). For example, if a Palestinian father is not allowed to take his daughter through a checkpoint for a medical emergency, and she dies, a human-rights worker may write press releases, or take journalists to meet the father, to put a human face on the event. Montell does connect her Jewish and democratic values with the Book of Genesis, B'Tselem (human dignity), and the Universal Declaration of Human Rights (2005). After leaving B'Tselem, Montell analyzed the gap between human-rights work and ending the occupation, "the number-one issue." She became more involved in political efforts to end the occupation, and concluded that human-rights work provides crucial support for peacemaking at every level; it is part of a "broader ecosystem," but limited in terms of political change. She says, "We should not attempt to fill the political vacuum that could be better filled by other actors" (Part II, p. 263).

Jonathan Kuttab, a human-rights lawyer, shares Montell's commitment to the importance of neutral, rigorous human-rights documentation, although he is deeply engaged in systemic, legal, political, religious, and cultural conflicts with Israelis. Kuttab identifies as a Christian, a pacifist, and a seeker of justice. Very early he realized that the conflict with Israelis was not a military fight; to end the occupation, he had to work with international law and international solidarity. He rejected trying to defeat Israel's military and technological superiority, and weapons of mass destruction (Part II, p. 234). He studied human-rights law, learned Hebrew, and joined the Israeli Bar Association to understand and expose Israeli legal systems.

> Israelis invest a huge amount of thought and creativity in maintaining a legal façade for what was a thoroughly oppressive, racist, colonial system ... intended for very good people to participate in very evil policies with a clear conscience. And for the Western world to support an extremely oppressive system without knowing it's so oppressive. (Part II, p. 234)

Like Gideon Levy, Kuttab uses strong images of darkness and light to express the challenges of peacemaking in this conflict. About trying to change Israeli law, Kuttab says, "You identify neutral and universal principles of human rights," not considering perpetrator or victim identities. All of these are illegal: torture, detention without trial, demolition of property, and building settlements in occupied territories. "The first thing I did in setting up a human-rights organization here was to train our field researchers in the need to be very, very accurate, very objective, very understated, not to use emotionally loaded terms," so no one could object (Part II, p. 236). But Israelis do claim exemptions from international law.

4.4 Perceptions of Truth and Justice

As Bronstein suggests, terms such as truth and justice may be problematic for peacemakers. The idea of justice, for example, is dangerous when victims press for absolute justice without keeping justice in creative tension with mercy and forgiveness. Within this conflict, truth-telling is a much-contested project. When I asked journalist Gideon Levy if Israelis know how Palestinians experience the occupation, he declared, "Israelis do not know. Israelis do not want to know" (Part II, p. 245). The publishers, the people, and the leaders are not interested in knowing. It's a "self-censorship of many years," and "those who want to know can very easily know because I am here and others are here" (Part II, p. 246). I pressed Levy on his identity as a journalist and committed truth-teller. Like Kuttab, Levy uses images of light and darkness.

RH: How do you see the interplay of telling the truth and its connection to justice, to the health of society, and [to] building a just peace? What's the role of the truth-teller?

GL: It's about the *whole* truth-telling. The main problem of Israel is about the lies, the partial truth, ... being so concentrated on ourselves, and not seeing the other at all. They don't exist. The Wall makes it physical, [so] you will not see Palestinians. It's about hiding at least half of the truth.... [You should] know how brutal the occupation is, because it is there on your behalf. Every one of us is a checkpoint soldier.... My journalistic role is to put a small light on the very, very dark backyard of Israel. it's very hidden from Israeli eyes. This will be my biggest contribution, if I could put light there.

RH: Why do you refer to it as a "backyard?" Because it's ... out of sight, out of mind?

GL: You've heard that Israel is the only democracy in the Middle East. It is Western and liberal. For Jews, it is by far very liberal—freedom of speech, freedom of movement, a free press—in the front yard. Then in the backyard, there is the occupation. See if you can be half-pregnant, then see if you can be half-democratic.

RH: That is the conundrum. The difficulty of [having] a "Jewish democracy."

GL: Right. Israel is a real democracy for Jews, no doubt, but this is not in [line] with our demographics.... If it is democracy, it is ... for everyone. (Part II, p. 248)

The metaphors may be mixed, but the meanings are clear: profound contradictions in Israeli culture suppress the truth. Without holistic truth-telling in Israel, a just peace will be impossible.

In his development of Palestinian liberation theology, Ateek focused on "justice and only justice" (1989). Some 15 years later, his organization, Sabeel, issued "Principles for a Just Peace in Israel-Palestine" (2004). After affirming that God loves all people equally, Ateek wrote that "God demands that justice be done" (p. 3). The principles conclude with the same emphasis: "Justice alone guarantees a peace that will lead to reconciliation ... security and prosperity for all the people of our land" (p. 16).

4.5 Nonviolence, Popular Resistance, and *Sumud*

Peacemakers recognize that oppressed people do have the right, under international law, to resist oppression through armed struggle (Awad, Halper). However, they agree that armed struggle for Palestinians has failed in the past and would fail in the future. (Part II, p. 00). Israel's overwhelming military, economic, and political power constantly resists a just peace. Kuttab says, "Israel can deal very well with any military threat. They can outgun, outshoot, outkill, outviolence Palestinians ... any day. But how do they deal with people who won't carry guns ... but insist on their rights, their freedoms, ... their dignity, and their equality with Jews?" (Part II, p. 237). Abu-Nimer writes that "Islamic values shun aggression, violent confrontation, and bigotry, and favor … peace-building and nonviolence for resolving conflicts" (2003, p. 63). Nonviolence in Israel-Palestine is well documented (Kaufman et al., 2006; Kaufman-Lucasta, 2010; Pearlman, 2011; Qumsiyeh, 2011).

The Palestinian sense of nonviolence is complicated by questions of how to translate peacemaking terms into Arabic, and how to transform what Kuttab calls the "poetry of violence":

JK: There is a lot of support for nonviolence. The problem is that [we] have perfected the *language of violence,* and have a hard time giving up the *poetry of violence*—

RH: The heroic struggle—

JK: The heroics, the bombastic language of violence, in favor of nonviolence. [So,] "peace" has been given a bad name. "Nonviolence" in Arabic [*la'ounf*] sounds so passive rather than being an active method of fighting the occupation. [Advocates] for nonviolence were viewed as being passive, [refusing] to fight the occupation.

RH: So, other terms are necessary.

JK: Exactly. Everyone has used the word peace so much, it's gotten a bad rap. The so-called "peace process" was a cover for legitimizing and continuing the occupation with Palestinian cooperation…. We really need a different word.

RH: [For Israelis, nonviolence] is more threatening than violence.

JK: Far more threatening. (Part II, p. 237)

Kuttab describes nonviolent resistance as having "tremendous potential."

Liberation theologian Naim Ateek hopes that the PLO will officially abandon an armed struggle and adopt a nonviolent struggle. "A massive campaign would follow to train the Palestinian community in the techniques and tactics of nonviolent resistance" (2008, p. 179). For Ateek, this would mobilize the entire nation, restore the dignity of Palestinians, and involve the whole community, as the first *intifada* did. "Palestine needs a new, nonviolent *intifada* that is willing to accept suffering rather than inflict it on others" (2008, p. 179). The stories of nonviolence and popular resistance during the first *intifada* are compelling, including the tax revolt in Beit Sahour (Andoni, 2006; Qumsiyeh, 2011; Hostetter, 2014). When Mubarak Awad founded the Palestine Center for the Study of Nonviolence in the 1980s, Sami, his nephew, became involved, too. Mubarak's nonviolence threatened the Israeli army, and it also threatened Palestinian leaders who believed that nonviolence was a rejection of their armed resistance. When Israel deported Mubarak, Sami cofounded Holy Land Trust in Bethlehem to continue Mubarak's work.

During the first *intifada,* Sami Awad saw "David and Goliath reverse roles," and he saw that armed resistance "was not achieving the results that we wanted" (Part II, p. 165). So, Holy Land Trust developed a four-day training in nonviolence—conflict analysis; different types and levels of violence, communal, psychological, structural, psychological, social, and cultural violence. Awad promotes both principled and pragmatic approaches to nonviolence. The pragmatic approach deals with tactics and strategies of resistance; the principled approach is a communal and a faith-based approach (Part II, p. 161). Awad convinces as many people as possible to engage in pragmatic nonviolence, and that brings them closer to engagement with the practice and philosophy of internal, communal nonviolence.

When the second *intifada* erupted in 2000, the role of Awad's organization for nonviolence became even stronger. Even former combatants explored nonviolence as a powerful symbol of Islam and *jihad.* Holy Land Trust has trained hundreds of trainers in nonviolent resistance—some 800 individuals all across the West Bank, representing different political factions and organizations. Hamas has monitored this training and given Awad "positive remarks" (Part II, p. 166). Awad calls for both short-term and long-term approaches to nonviolent resistance. Many Palestinians are not fully engaged at either level. So, Awad says, "We are working … to build a continuous nonviolent strategy" (Part II, p. 161). Awad says the majority of Palestinian people "are in the middle," not engaged in resistance, but refusing to surrender. Awad sees nonviolence as the only viable way for Palestinians to approach internationals, the U.S., and the Israeli public.

Palestinian peacemakers often invoke the concept and practice of *sumud* in relationship to nonviolence. It "relates to a shared sense of identity, the maintenance of inner strength in the face of all odds—wholeness in the face of fragmentation, life in the face of death [and] steadfastness" (van Teeffelen, 2011, p. 9). *Sumud* is connected to family, community, and national values of struggle, solidarity, resilience, and resistance. For Ateek, *sumud* describes "holding on, no matter what"; it is central to Palestinian identity, "in both the Christian and the Islamic view" (Part II, p. 135).

4.6 South Africa and BDS

South Africa is the most frequently mentioned paradigm for transforming the conflict in Israel-Palestine. In our dialogues, Halper makes a dozen references to South Africa as a model of an anti-apartheid struggle. He says Israel will not voluntarily change its patterns of oppression. Consequently, "the international civil society has to play a key role.… Church groups, Jewish groups, NGOs, trade unions, universities, political groups—everybody's got to play a role, just like we all did with the anti-apartheid struggle in South Africa" (Part II, p. 216). For Halper, the anti-apartheid struggle must be inclusive; "Everybody who's here is a part of this" (Part II, p. 225).

Pappe declares that since the diplomatic efforts and the armed struggle have failed, "A just peace is the only nonviolent alternative" (Part II, p. 272). Therefore, Pappe supports the Boycott, Divestment, and Sanctions (BDS) campaign against Israel, because it is important and effective.

Halper also supports BDS as a "very strong campaign" against Israeli consumer goods, settlement products, and arms, because "companies profit from the occupation" (Part II, p. 225), and they work closely with the Israeli army. Halper and the Israeli Committee Against Home Demolitions resist the huge, U.S.-made Caterpillar bulldozers used to demolish Palestinian houses. In support of the BDS campaign, Halper cites the Fourth Geneva Convention, which "prohibits an occupying power from using the resources of an occupied territory" (Part II, p. 225).

Omar Barghouti, cofounder of the BDS movement, participated in the anti-apartheid movement when he was a student in New York. In his manifesto, Barghouti devotes several chapters to comparing the South African apartheid to the Israeli occupation. He writes that international law considers apartheid a crime against humanity. Therefore, Israel should receive sanctions similar to those imposed on apartheid South Africa. Barghouti concludes, "Israel's regime of oppression is … worse than apartheid" (2011, pp. 63–64). Barghouti articulates the three dimensions of BDS—an academic and cultural boycott of Israeli organizations, divestment, and sanctions—to achieve three goals: to end the occupation, to grant full rights to the Palestinian citizens of Israel, and to promote the rights of Palestinian refugees, as called for in UN Resolution 194 (1948). These goals suggest a platform "for *any* just solution to the Palestinian-Israeli conflict" (2011, p. 17). BDS challenges Israel's colonial rule in "a morally consistent, effective, and … intelligent manner" (2011, pp. 16–17). BDS applies not to individuals, but to institutions, because institutions are unwilling to oppose the occupation. Divestment and sanctions are primarily international, economic strategies for pressuring institutions to pressure Israel to end the occupation. BDS organizers have secured support from religious institutions such as the Presbyterian Church, the World Council of Churches, trade unions, educational institutions such as TIAA-CREF, and corporations to withdraw their investments from Israeli assets. The "sanctions" campaign is difficult to implement because it requires the cooperation of governments. Important differences between the South African conflict and the Israeli-Palestinian conflict include the lack of effective Palestinian leaders and the right of return for Palestinian refugees (2011, pp. 77–82).

4.7 Religion and Peacemaking

Peace and justice workers from Jewish, Muslim, and Christian traditions have frequently tried to use those traditions for conflict transformation, resisting the occupation, developing liberation and contextual theology, developing educational programs, and affirming that they are all "children of God." Since the failure of the Oslo process, and the fury of the second *intifada*, faith-based organizations have published requirements for a just peace. The Sabeel Ecumenical Center for Liberation Theology released "Principles for a Just Peace in Palestine-Israel" (2004), affirming God's care for all humanity and identifying the challenges of the occupation. Other Christian leaders published "Kairos Palestine" (2009, 2021), beginning with words of crisis and lament. "[We] cry out from within the suffering in our country, under the Israeli occupation, with a cry of hope in the absence of all hope, a cry full of prayer and faith in ... God's providence.... [W]e have reached a dead end in the tragedy of the Palestinian people" (p. 13). The decision-makers "manage the crisis" rather than resolving it (p. 13). The document affirms God's presence, gives biblical perspectives, questions the church's mission, and appeals for solidarity.

In one of our dialogues, I asked Rabbi Arik Ascherman to give me a theological interpretation for why the Israeli-Palestinian conflict grinds on year after year.

AA: As a rabbi, I would first say it is a spiritual problem....
RH: How do you link spiritual resources to a political movement?
AA: That's a very good question.... We religious Israelis may be best poised to empower Palestinian peacemakers, and Palestinians have to empower us ... so whenever [transformation] comes, we'll be ready to embrace it. (Part II, p. 118)

It is intriguing to think that religious leaders of one community may be "poised to empower" peacemakers in another community.

Mitri Raheb, the president of Dar al-Kalima University College of Arts and Culture in Bethlehem, uses the term "contextual theology" to describe his work. He focuses on building infrastructure to create something constructive "in a context where everything around us is ... very destructive," and "to transform the lives of those who feel broken into something that is whole" (Part II, p. 278). Raheb calls his approach "building the infrastructure of hope." At Sabeel, Ateek's Palestinian liberation theology (1989) links Christian faith with seeking justice, a path that moves through justice to something more holistic, including reconciliation (2008) and liberation (2017). For Ateek, Sabeel means "a journey of peace, justice, and reconciliation in the footsteps of Christ" (Part II, p. 133). Ateek's ecumenical approach helps people "live their faith under occupation" (Part II, p. 136). Sabeel urges people to move from education to advocacy, developing relationships with Israeli organizations "that dare to speak out against occupation" (Part II, p. 139).

Pappe provides an example of Jeremiah's prophetic mandate to tear down injustice and to rebuild with justice. He confronts the moral quandaries of Zionism. His goal is to convince Jews, not just Palestinians, that Zionism works against their interests. So, he tries to enable them to get over their fears in order to accept alternative ways of thinking.

> They say, "But what you suggest to us—a state where Jews and Arabs would be equal—is the end of Judaism. So, we cannot accept it. We

> would rather occupy and oppress.... Sure, we will be immoral, but we will be alive." Of course, they are utterly wrong, but it is not easy to show them the way. (Part II, p. 269)

Pappe's religious references are compelling. He says he focuses on what Christianity refers to as "original sin, ... untangling the manipulation of the story of 1948—through the visible remnants of 1948, and the oral histories of soldiers who confess.... It is a very Christian thing—confession, and a theology of liberation" (Part II, p. 270).

4.8 Education and Peacemaking

Education is a major part of the identity for peacemakers in this study. A third of them have doctoral degrees or other advanced training: Abusrour in biological and medical engineering; Andoni in physics; Ashrawi in literature; Ateek, Chacour, and Raheb in theology; El-Farra in medicine; Halper in anthropology; and Salameh in planning and public policy. For the peace and justice workers, it is crucial to educate Palestinian communities. When the Israeli army closed schools during the first *intifada*, villages held classes in private homes.

Archbishop Elias Chacour, founder of the Mar Elias schools and college in Ibilin, has been a longtime advocate for peacebuilding through education. He often says that peacemaking begins on the tops of school desks. Chacour's vision for education emerged from his experience of trauma in 1948, his identity as a Palestinian Christian priest living in Israel, and his awareness of the huge educational and social needs of his village. He says, "I was invited by the experience of deprivation, of belonging to a community that was stripped, literally stripped, of all its human rights" (Part II, p. 196). When Israeli officials refused to give him permits to build school buildings, he built them anyway. Officials hauled him into court 35 times, but Chacour's commitment to ethnic diversity, inclusion, and reconciliation has produced a remarkable educational campus. Chacour's main goal is to prove to Israelis and Palestinians that the only way to solve the conflict is to accept diversity and to make that diversity itself the community goal. Chacour says, "We are to get up, to move, to go ahead, to get our hands dirty, to implement and pursue justice, from which peace and security will come" (Part II, p. 200).

4.9 The Arts as "Beautiful Resistance"

Peacemaking through the arts is also a long-term strategy. Abdelfatah Abusrour grew up in the Aida Refugee Camp in Bethlehem, and he became involved in theatre and in activism about land issues. Later, while earning a Ph.D. in biological and medical engineering in France, Abusrour continued his theatre work. When he returned to the refugee camp, theatre won out. He founded the Al-Rowwad Cultural Center, and created the concept of "beautiful resistance through theatre." For Abusrour, theatre is "a most amazing, powerful, civilized and unarmed way ... to express yourself, to tell ... your version of your story [and] to build peace within" (Part II, p. 93). He has received numerous awards as a "social entrepreneur."

In 2006, Raheb founded Dar al-Kalima University College of Arts and Culture in Bethlehem, with a focus on the arts and Palestinian sustainability. He emphasizes that culture is vitally important for people who live under occupation. People were thinking that the Israeli-Palestinian conflict is like a hundred-meter run, requiring full power, but Raheb says the conflict is more like a marathon of 30 miles. "You have to learn different techniques; otherwise, you will kill yourself." Culture teaches people "how to breathe, how to survive, in order to reach the goal and not die" (Part II, p. 283). Raheb's students learn how to survive through painting, music, theatre, and filmmaking.

Another example of "beautiful resistance" through the arts appears in the Oscar-nominated film *5 Broken Cameras.* Director Emad Burnat documents the daily humiliations of the occupation and the nonviolent resistance of his Muslim village. He describes his multiple challenges.

EB: I was nominated [for an] Academy Award, but [U.S.] officials ... thought I was lying. So, I called Michael Moore.... He tweeted this to 1.5 million people....

RH: How was [the film] received?

EB: It was received well at the UN ... and everywhere around the world....

RH: Is there a difficult side to the success?

EB: Sometimes it's difficult, especially here in Palestine. We live in the same situation [shown in the film]. The Palestinian community [is] very scattered around the world. It was very difficult for them to see the many sides of [Palestinian] lives.... My camera is my weapon. It's a very strong weapon, and it's the truth—my experience, my point of view.

RH: Your voice-over style was very effective.

EB: The point is to tell my story to the world.... You have to talk to the people in their language. I think our language ... is the language of humanity. (Part II, p. 194)

Burnat's film is simultaneously a father-son story, a documentary about nonviolent resistance in a Muslim village, and an example of the crucial role of the arts under oppression.

4.10 The Price of Peacemaking

Peacemakers describe the cost of their resistance and peacemaking as being occupied (Awad), marginalized (Levy), threatened (Chacour), jailed (Burnat,

Halper), unemployed (Shapira), and tortured (Andoni). After Pappe began to support the BDS campaign, he received frequent death threats, and moved his family to England. After several attempts to sail into Gaza to break the Israeli siege, Shapira is unable to find employment in Israel.

As regards paying a high price for resistance, after church services in the Old City of Jerusalem, Mordechai Vanunu told me his compelling story of confirming and protesting the existence of Israel's nuclear-weapons program. Vanunu's family moved from Morocco to Israel. Vanunu served in the Israeli army for three years, studied physics, and went to work in the Israeli nuclear program at the Shimon Peres Negev Nuclear Research Center, near Dimona. As a technician, he produced material for atomic and hydrogen bombs. He discovered that Israel was producing "a lot of bombs"—10 atomic bombs every year, or about 200 bombs total when he left in 1985. To reveal the Israeli bomb-making program to the world, and to work against the occupation, he "began a new life" by taking 200 pictures inside the Dimona nuclear plant, going to Australia to become a Christian, and publishing his pictures in a London newspaper. Later, in Rome, British, French, and Israeli agents kidnapped him and took him back to Israel. He spent 18 years in prison, most of the time in solitary confinement. Though he has served his full prison term, Vanunu is not allowed to leave Israel, but he wants the world to hear "*my* story, *my* experience in prison," and to know that he has paid a "huge, huge price" for peace.

4.11 Conclusion

Because the Israeli-Palestinian conflict remains in the early stage of conflict transformation rather than a more advanced stage, this chapter mostly refers to peacemakers rather than to peacebuilders. Peacemaker identities encompass some combination of the peacemaker's positionality; experiences; sense of "calling" or vocation; commitments to truth, justice, and reconciliation; a keen ability to listen; empathy; and, for many people, professional associations, colleagues, and dialogue partners. Building on the work of Montville, Diamond, and McDonald, this chapter identifies more than 20 "tracks" or roles for nongovernmental peacemaking. Some peacemakers struggle to find new, nontraditional terms, such as dialogue facilitator, for their peacemaking identities. Peacemakers committed to a just peace must contend with Zionism as an exclusive ideology that privileges one ethnic group over another. Consequently, peacemakers are change agents, with large capacities to employ nonviolent resistance and transformation (*sumud*); for finding historical change models (South Africa); and for creating new ways to generate peace through religious practices, educational institutions, through the arts as "beautiful resistance," and through in-depth and strategic dialogue.

5 Dialogues for a Just Peace

This chapter examines the forms, goals, implications, and practices of dialogue for a just and sustainable peace in Israel-Palestine. In everyday language, the term dialogue is often used as another word for conversation, debate, discussion, or negotiation. These communication processes are necessary for developing thought, exercising power, building relationships, and transforming conflict. In-depth dialogue is the primary mode of communication for peacemaking. Multiple definitions describe dialogue as both content and process. In my dramatic writing classes, I insist that dialogue is different from informal conversation. In plays, films, and narrative fiction, dialogue is purposeful and strategic—meant to reveal character, to express ideas, and to achieve goals. Schirch and Campt (2007) also insist that dialogue is different from conversation, though they acknowledge that dialogical communication is fluid and often moves in and out of various modes; dialogue can have the informal quality of conversation, the focused approach of training, or "the heated passion [or] anger of a debate" (2007, p. 8). For communication scholar Julia Woods (2004), this suggests theories that view contemporary dialogue as contingent, nonlinear, structured around tension, subject to surprise, emergent, unpredictable, dependent on process as much as content, fragmented, experimental, and not necessarily committed to resolving differences.

Despite these ambiguities, in-depth dialogue is the primary mode of communication for peacemaking. In the Israeli-Palestinian conflict, the term dialogue often merges with other words for talking and other exchanges. In this context, the most relevant theories and definitions of dialogue pertain to transformative goals, and the quest for a just peace. Lederach (2003) writes,

> We need to engage in change processes at all levels of relationships: interpersonal, inter-group, and social-structural.... A fundamental way to promote constructive change on all these levels is dialogue. Dialogue is essential to justice and peace on both an interpersonal and a structural level. It is not the only mechanism, but it is an essential one. (2003, p. 21)

DOI: 10.4324/9781003262817-6

For Lederach, a transformational view approaches dialogue as "necessary for both creating and addressing social and public spheres where human institutions, structures, and patterns of relationships are constructed" (2003, p. 22). He connects dialogue and social change through intentionality, as "ways forward toward solutions" (2003, p. 22).

Mohan Dutta, another communication scholar, also emphasizes transformational goals, focusing on the political changes that emerge when subaltern or marginalized voices are brought into serious dialogue. For Dutta, the goal of dialogue is "to change the structures in order to address the inequities and injustices perpetuated by them.... The politics of a dialogic approach to social change lie in the articulation of issues from subaltern standpoints" (2011, p. 169). Peter Kellett also holds a transformational view: dialogue is, by definition, a "moving through" to a new understanding through talk (2020, p. 49). Kellett's concept of "dialogic negotiation" is useful for approaching the failed Israeli-Palestinian negotiations.

This conflict encompasses multiple dialogical forms and issues: informal discussion (Shapira), training (Awad), dialogue between peacemakers and their own communities (Andoni, Awad, Halper), facilitated dialogue and encounter groups (Bronstein, Shapira), dialogues between Israeli and Palestinian peacemakers (Andoni), dialogue between peacemakers and government officials (Halper), debate and argument (Pappe, Avnery), negotiations (Ashrawi, Salameh), interreligious dialogue (Ascherman, Ateek, Raheb), lament (El-Farra, Halper), and strategic dialogue (Halper).

5.1 Voice and Transformational Listening

Dialogue is often contingent on experiences of discovery as one speaks and listens. During the recording of more than 50 dialogues, I have experienced what Salameh calls "meaningful dialogue" (2018) and what Ashrawi calls dialogue that is truthful (2005). I have brought my existential questions into dialogue with an exemplary group of peace and justice workers. In Dutta's "culture-centered approach" (2011) to dialogue, "voice" is a key theoretical concept. It offers an opening for the voices that have been excluded from the dominant discourse. Since most of the peacemakers in this study are part of marginalized groups, the dialogical approach in this study makes these voices more accessible to more people. These dialogues open spaces where others' voices can emerge, spaces in which peacemakers can speak their truth, their situated knowledge, sometimes for the first time. For example, after graduate work in the U.S., Salameh worked on international financial agreements for the Palestinian Authority. He commented, "This is the first time I get to talk about [my work].... Thank you for that" (Part II, p. 299).

Dialogue has the potential to create profound transformations, moving beyond understanding and empathy to engagement. As I described earlier, Shapira provides a compelling example of change, from being a Zionist "poster boy," to becoming the cofounder of Combatants for Peace, and "shaking the system" (Part II, p. 306). For me, dialogue with peacemakers who work in the crucible of injustice has been a profound experience. I have experienced moments of profound agitation. Theologian Paul Tillich called this existential experience the "shaking of the foundations" (1948). In dialogues with Palestinian and Israeli peacemakers, I have experienced moments of profound existential shaking. Levy declares that we are all responsible for this conflict; "every one of us is a checkpoint soldier" (Part II, p. 248). So, I am included.

In dialogue with Halper, I have had to reconsider my understanding of forgiveness, reconciliation, and real-world politics. Referring to South Africa, Halper declares, "The oppressor ... before it gives up control, has to be convinced that you're not going to get revenge. You're not going to do to us what we deserve" (Part II, p. 227). This is a profound and haunting insight.

5.2 Dimensions of Dialogue

The dialogues in Part Two promote constructive change at all levels of the conflict—interpersonal, community, structural, national, and international conflict—in the form of listening, speaking, encounter programs, dialogues among peacemakers, debates, and efforts to link dialogue among grassroots movements, mid-level activists, and governmental officials (Lederach, 2005, p. 79). All of these levels have the goal of discovery, understanding, building relationships, and strategic work for social justice. Ramsbotham offers useful terms for promoting strategic dialogue: *agonistic dialogue*, the dialogue of struggle; dialogue for mutual understanding; and *strategic engagement of discourses* (2010, p. 254). These dialogues address both radical intraparty and interparty disagreements, and disagreements among and within third parties (p. 254).

5.2.1 Listening for Understanding

We commonly associate dialogue with speaking, but informed listening is also a key component. For Schirch and Campt, dialogue is a unique communication process because it focuses participants' attention on "listening for understanding" (2007, p. 7). Simply understood, dialogue is a process of exchange, of communication through speaking and listening. Salameh says, "You have to work with everybody, listen to everybody ... find a middle ground for everybody; try, under pressure, to find a common way forward" (Part II, pp. 300–301).

5.2.2 Building Relationships

There is a broad consensus that dialogues are central for beginning, building, and maintaining relationships. Montville writes, "Dialogue, the engine of relationships, promotes mutual confirmation and thereby serves a fundamental need of parties to a conflict to be recognized as individuals with values and unique (and valued) identities" (1993, p. 115). According to Schirch and Campt, dialogue is a communication process that attempts to build relationships, enhance experiences, and wrestle with common concerns (2007, p. 6).

5.2.3 Dialogues between Peacemakers

Dialogue between Israeli and Palestinian peacemakers is a kind of roller coaster, driven by ideologies and the presence or absence of violence. During the first *intifada,* Andoni became a resistance leader in Beit Sahour, while teaching at Birzeit University. "For the first time, I saw real, civilian-based, popular resistance.... You could see lots of creativity, lots of grassroots work, lots of new methods" (Part II, p. 107). Andoni developed the Palestine Centre for Rapprochement between People (PCR), building relationships with international and Israeli peace activists. This all fell apart after the Oslo process. The policy of "separation," which Palestinians thought would yield a two-state solution, turned into the Israeli policy of *hafrada*, an official separation between ethnic groups.

In 2000, after the second *intifada* began, Andoni cofounded a movement dedicated to nonviolent direct action, the International Solidarity Movement (ISM). But he discovered that most of ISM's functionality depended on internationals, so, he chose "to act more with my people, not as isolated communities, but with the national [Palestinian] bodies" (Part II, p. 109). Andoni gave to others the leadership of his activist organizations. He shifted from working with a select group of Palestinians and internationals to "stepping into the dynamic of the community" (Part II, p. 110). He calls this a dialogical approach. "It's not really a plan. It's an experiment" (Part II, p. 110). This strengthened dialogue among Palestinians, but it weakened dialogue with Israelis. In 2014, Halper pondered the challenges of Israeli-Palestinian dialogue in general, and Andoni's initiatives in particular.

RH: Dialogue is such a fraught topic between Palestinians and Jews. [Is] genuine dialogue possible? You are suggesting that genuine dialogue is rare....

JH: Ghassan got completely burned out with dialogue.

RH: He withdrew from the [International Solidarity Movement], right?

JH: Yeah. He was very involved with all the dialogues during the Oslo process. When the second *intifada* hit, all the [Israelis] he had talked to ... for all those years—WHOOM!—they completely cut him off, within minutes. (Part II, p. 226)

After the brutal Israeli-Gaza war in 2014, Halper lamented that he had no Palestinian or Israeli dialogue partner, because of the war and because of the alienating discourse about Zionism and "settler colonialism." Ironically, Halper says, "enemies" are able to talk with each other.

JH: We're all stuck. The political process is gone, the two-state solution is over, the PA is on its last legs.... Palestinian partners are not talking to us at all.

They have completely cut off all ties. Even with us, who are anti-Zionist.... An obsession with Zionism and "settler colonialism" [is] not going to lead you to liberation.... This discourse is so... disconnected from political realities that we're not able to strategize. The Israeli Right and the Palestinian Right know where they want to go, and the Left doesn't. The Israeli military and Palestinian military talk to each other, the security people talk to each other, the business people talk to each, the criminals talk to each other, but the intellectuals don't talk to each other. In terms of strategy, nothing is going on, zero.

RH: There's no entity that can convene or create a common ground?

JH: Palestinians have to lead this movement.... It can't be done by the Israeli Left. If [Palestinians are] not going to do it, then we're really stuck. (Part II, p. 226)

Halper's insistence that Palestinians must lead the peacemaking dialogue began to change in 2016.

5.2.4 Dialogue with Government Officials and Grassroots Movements

Most peacemakers, working from the middle, do not have adequate access to government officials. Exceptions include Ashrawi and Salameh, who have access to PLO and PA officials, and Uri Avnery, a member of the Israeli Knesset for 10 years. Ascherman's human-rights work is connected to both grassroots movements and "the halls of power." The prevailing attitude is that government officials *manage* conflict to gain and maintain power rather than to work for justice. Halper will work with governments to end the occupation, but they "will not do the right thing, period.... We look to governments to lead, but they are not going to do it unless they're pressured into it" (Part II, p. 224).

Halper declares that he has ideas of what to do with all this, "but I'm not a Palestinian and I don't have access to the Palestinian leadership. If they would say, 'Jeff, have a cup of coffee with us on Wednesday and let's talk,' that would be nice, but it is not going to happen." (Part II, p. 220). So, instead of advocating for particular strategies, Halper makes "suggestions." His frustration becomes a theme:

RH: The other day … Sami [Awad] admitted that he [is] still groping for guidance.…

JH: We, as an organization, have earned the right to put in our two cents. And we are doing it constructively … [as] part of the dialogue and part of the partnership.… We can't lead their struggle of national liberation. They have to do it. Otherwise, we're in an impossible situation of representing Palestinians. (Part II, p. 222)

Two years later, the same topic emerged, as Halper simultaneously described what he does as dialogue, discussion, and debate.

RH: You're part of the dialogue.

JH: I'm part of the dialogue. What I try to do is to throw out options like the "two-stage" solution and say, … let's have a *discussion* about it. I can help sharpen the *debate*.… (Part II, p. 223)

In this moment, these terms all converge: dialogue, options, discussion, and debate.

Ramsbotham et al. write that it is "now generally established that a sustainable peace process must be embedded in the grassroots or communal levels of Lederach's conflict pyramid, though what constitutes authentic grassroots or local community is frequently difficult to discern" (2011, p. 244). However, I believe that some mid-level peacemakers have the capacity to provide conceptual leadership and vision to people at both grassroots and government levels.

5.2.5 Dialogue and Debate

Dialogue as "debate" appears as intense discussion, a public exchange between experts, and a wider cultural encounter between Israeli and Palestinian communities. Ramsbotham calls this "agonistic dialogue, the dialogue of struggle," and "the dialogue between enemies in intense and intractable conflict, … radical disagreement[s] in which conflict parties directly engage each other's utterances" (2010, p. 254). Avnery describes his debate with Pappe:

RH: You've had extended debates with Ilan Pappe and others about [nationalism]?

UA: Yes, we had a public debate. His ideas run counter to the current of history. Nationalism is a basic force in our world. Maybe in a thousand years it will be overcome. But in the last hundred years, anyone who ran counter to nationalism has lost. (Part II, p. 155)

Avnery's nationalism is connected to his determination to maintain a Jewish state.

In one of my dialogues with Awad, he uses the terms discussion and debate interchangeably to describe intense exchanges between Palestinian factions about nonviolent and violent resistance.

RH: Your internal conflict is nearly as large as the external conflict [with Israelis]?

SA: It is a very difficult debate within the Palestinian community. We will not be able to address the bigger conflicts of the occupation if we fail to address … internal issues.

RH: Is that dialogue beginning to happen now, since the elections, or is it still too soon?

SA: There have been many discussions between political factions. (Part II, p. 164)

Debate is a form of both internal and external cultural dialogue. For Ramsbotham, intraparty dialogue can be a harbinger of peacemaking at interparty and higher levels of conflict (2011).

5.2.6 *Fatah and Hamas*

In 2006, when negotiations broke down between the two largest Palestinian political parties, Palestinians in the OPT experienced further political, geographical, and strategic fragmentation (Barron, 2019, p. 1). Israel blockaded all of Gaza's borders and the passage of materials and humanitarian supplies. Dialogical efforts to create a unity government failed, and the Israeli siege of Gaza continues. But according to Raheb (2006), there is space for both intraparty and interparty dialogue. As he noted earlier, "Hamas doesn't have one narrative, but several narratives.… There are lots of possibilities for a dialogue because within Hamas there is a big dialogue. And the question at the end is, who will win in the dialogue"? (Part II, p. 282). So, the Israeli approach to conflict with Hamas follows Levy's model of "first war, then negotiation."

5.2.7 *Argument and Advocacy*

Halper says that he "argues all the time" with Arik Ascherman about the limits of activism and the virtues of mid-level advocacy. This constitutes an ongoing dialogue:

> I [argue] with [him] all the time. [He runs] around doing things. I said, "Let the 18-year-old kids plant olive trees.… You should be writing articles on how the uprooting of olive trees is against Jewish law. You're a rabbi. You should be doing the advocacy…." But it's easier to be an activist. You do an action, but nothing is really delivered. (Part II, p. 223)

In other dialogues, Halper insists that both activism and strategic efforts are necessary.

5.2.8 Interreligious Dialogue

Since this land, often called the Holy Land, is home to three world religions, "interreligious dialogue" frequently emerges. Most Palestinians are Muslims; only 1% are Christians. Roughly half of Israeli Jews are secular, and half are religious. When David Ben-Gurion, the secular first prime minister of Israel, declared that the Bible would be the "guidebook" for the state of Israel, it was a political strategy, not a faith statement. David Smock writes that "interfaith dialogue," defined simply as "persons of different faiths meeting to have a conversation" (2002, p. 6), can be an effective tool to advance peacebuilding. But "anyone in a situation of serious conflict recognizes how difficult it is to organize and conduct meaningful interfaith dialogue" (2002, pp. 8–9). Smock identifies multiple peacemaking roles for religion: leaders advocating for peace, organizations mediating among combatants, training for conflict resolution, providing resources for peacemaking, and doing reconciling acts—efforts "beyond talk" (2002, pp. 7–8). Abu-Nimer insists that dialogue is not a substitute for social action. "Protest and resistance to oppression are still needed for social and political change to occur" (2002, pp. 15–16).

Naim Ateek has developed ecumenical, dialogical approaches to liberation theology. After doing graduate work in the U.S., Ateek joined the leadership team at St. George's Cathedral in Jerusalem. He published *Justice and Only Justice* (1989), and cofounded and directed the Sabeel Ecumenical Liberation Theology Center. During the first *intifada,* he began to articulate a "grassroots theology of liberation … a prophetic voice … [to] resist the occupation" (Part II, p. 138). Sabeel focuses on ecumenical dialogue and peace education, interfaith dialogue with Muslims, intercultural dialogue with Jewish peace activists, and leadership roles for women and young adults—all to help people live their faith under occupation and through nonviolence.

NA: Some [people] are shocked when they hear what's really happening [here]. Some resist. They don't want to hear the truth.
RH: For theological or ideological reasons?
NA: They've been taught to interpret the Bible in a pro-Israel way, rather than a pro-justice way.… We encourage people to move from education to advocacy. (Part II, p. 139)

Ateek's Sabeel organizations are located in the OPT, Israel, and around the world.

Mitri Raheb affirms the benefits of dialogue, and focuses on "intra-faith dialogue" rather than interfaith dialogue. Raheb employs "contextual theology" and cultural analysis to address future leaders, the role of women, and the role of law and social justice. As the pastor of Christmas Lutheran

Church in Bethlehem, Raheb created "a holistic ministry for the spirit, for the body, and for the soul," empowering people to resist the role of victim and to become actors rather than spectators (2006, p. 2). Raheb builds infrastructure for every project, creating something constructive and visible in a context where everything is "very destructive." In an elegant phrase, Raheb calls this building process the "infrastructure of hope." Raheb also works with Christian and Muslim academics to combat religious fundamentalisms, because they "close off dialogue" (Part II, p. 286)

5.2.9 Encounter Programs

People often criticize People to People (P2P) programs, for having only a short-term impact. According to Schirch and Campt, effective dialogue between people of diverse backgrounds usually requires the guidance of facilitators, since "facilitators help create a safe space by setting ground rules or guidelines to keep dialogue participants focused on listening to and working with each other" (2007, p. 8). In a study of "dialogues for peace" in six Arab-Jewish encounter groups in Israel, Abu-Nimer questions whether these programs are designed to change "political structures of dominance and control of one group over the others" (1999, p. xviii).

At Neve Shalom/Wahat al-Salam, facilitator Rabah Halabi organizes encounters between "Palestinian and Jewish identities" in the School for Peace. Three-day encounters involve equal numbers of Jewish and Palestinian citizens of Israel (not Palestinians from the OPT). Facilitators help participants understand more about the conflict, more about themselves, and what roles they play in the conflict. As facilitator, Halabi focuses on identities, and why Jewish people feel endangered when Palestinians become more empowered (2004). Halabi concludes that the prevailing political and economic systems in Israel overwhelm such efforts. Palestinian citizens of Israel affirm their connections to Palestinians in the OPT and desire some national identity within Israel. Bronstein and Shapira describe how their participation in School for Peace encounter groups changed their lives. Bronstein, jailed three times for quitting the Israeli Army, facilitated many dialogues, and concluded that, as a Jewish Israeli, he was part of the occupation (Part II, p. 185). As noted earlier, Shapira participated in an encounter group at the School for Peace, but found himself unable to say that he was "an air force pilot who wants peace" (Part II, p. 305). Later he cofounded Combatants for Peace, and became a School for Peace facilitator.

5.2.10 Parents' Circle-Families Forum

Although P2P programs are generally relationship-oriented and "not political," the remarkable Parents' Circle-Families Forum (PC-FF) is a compelling, transformative program for those who have paid "the ultimate price," the death of a family member because of the ongoing conflict. PC-FF appeals to both ethnic groups to stop the killing, end the occupation, and pursue peace and reconciliation through dialogue.

5.2.11 Living Together as Dialogue

Experiments involving Jewish Israelis' and Palestinian citizens of Israel's living together can be understood as *existential dialogues.* In the community of Neve Shalom/Wahat Al-Salam (Oasis of Peace), equal numbers of Israeli Jews and Israeli Palestinians live together to show that coexistence and peace are possible. Pappe's peacemaking initiatives with "small enclaves" also include experiments with dialogical relationships:

> We are trying to nourish, in Palestine and Israel, joint kindergartens, joint school systems, joint academic dialogues, joint [groups of] artists … not in terms of the old Oslo concept of dialogue between two segregated partners, but based on a de-Zionized understanding of the situation, but also a denationalized one, as far as the Palestinians are concerned. [We] want to create small enclaves that allow people who feel the burden of living within this dismal situation to [do that]. You cannot do it in the occupied territories. (Part II, pp. 268–269)

The experiments of Jewish and Palestinian families coexisting at Neve Shalom/Wahat Al-Salam and in Pappe's "small enclaves" require existential dialogues at all levels.

5.3 Dialogue and Negotiation

In the Israeli-Palestinian discourse, "negotiation" is one of the most common dialogical terms. During the Oslo process, Palestinian leaders were not allowed to negotiate from a platform of international law and human rights (Halper, Part II, p. 216). That is, the Oslo negotiations were not genuinely dialogical. To explain the discourse of negotiation and dialogue, Kellett's concept of "dialogic negotiation" is apt (2007). It begins with an understanding of the meaning of the conflict, and how parties might negotiate the things that are important to them. For Kellett, dialogue integrates oppositional perspectives as a way to achieve win-win solutions: dialogue "moves participants beyond argumentation and competitive negotiating," it is "based on systemic analysis and leads to plausible scenario building," it "integrates the surface and deeper issues in conflict management practices," and it "develops a conflict discourse that explores shared and different meanings." For Kellett, dialogic negotiation embraces narrative, rather than dialogue, as the structural form of communication for promoting emergent meanings. It "broadens options for pre-conflict and post-conflict management" (2007, pp. 49–53). Ramsbotham's concept of "agonistic dialogue" is also an important concept for finding ways through intractable conflicts (2017).

5.3.1 "No One to Talk to"?

Some of the most common charges in this conflict are that "there is no one to talk to," "no partner for peace," and "no one to negotiate with." This charge is hurled back and forth between Israeli and Palestinian officials as both a lament and an accusation. Ashrawi, a PLO spokesperson and dialogue practitioner extraordinaire, characterizes authentic dialogue as conducted with trusted partners, truthful, and motivated by concerns for justice, in contrast to inauthentic dialogue, conducted with no peace partner, unilateral communication, and power politics.

RH: [Prime Minister] Ariel Sharon said he did not have any [Palestinians] to talk to.

HA: Which, of course, was fiction. Sharon claimed that he had no peace partner, but he was not interested in peace.... There is no peace partner in Israel. The peace camp is in disarray, and has been really undermined and excluded.... [We have] power politics; the strong dictating to the weak, the perpetuation of the occupation.... Any type of dialogue ... even intellectual attempts at creating a new discourse for peace are undermined.... The dominant logic is one of violence and negation ... to prevent like-minded Palestinians and Israelis from meeting and exposing a ... fraudulent [government] agenda.

RH: At this point, there is no official negotiation process at all.

HA: The issue has never been bilateral and cannot be bilateral. We need third-party internationals [to intervene]....

RH: [If] the only one who can [intervene] doesn't want to, how do [you] create that space?

HA: It is very hard to create that space where you can re-energize and relegitimize negotiations ... with substance [and] with a clear view of the outcome. (Part II, p. 127)

Ashrawi's compelling remarks identify the ways in which Israeli officials reject dialogical negotiations, combine asymmetrical power with refusals to meet, insist on preconditions and "unilateral dialogue," and reject an international third party as a facilitator.

5.3.2 First War, then Negotiations

Where there are major conflicts and no dialogue, the people perish. Levy warns that the absence of negotiations and in-depth dialogue may have dire consequences for Israelis, Palestinians, and the Middle East region. Levy says that among Israeli government officials, "Never will you find any kind of ... initiative [or giving up] anything before bloodshed.... When it comes to negotiating, [Israel keeps] postponing and postponing, and [making] conditions and preconditions. [But] when it comes to war, 15 minutes, and there is a new war" (Part II, p. 250).

5.3.3 Endless Negotiations

If the prevailing cultural dynamics favor war over peace, and deceptive negotiations rather than authentic, dialogical negotiations, what happens if one or both parties insist on negotiation? In that case, Levy suggests, false negotiations may be dangerous, as in the Oslo process. Israeli and Palestinian leaders participate in endless negotiations over minor issues to maintain the status quo, and to avoid real peacemaking. Salameh says, "If you want to continue negotiations, that's fine, but don't make it the only way of resisting the occupation. You've got to have other ways, nonviolent ways" (Part II, p. 291). Both the PA and the Israeli government insist on using one dialogical approach, negotiation, in order to maintain the status quo and to hold on to power. During the Oslo process, Israelis engaged in endless dialogues to distract attention from illegal settlement-building, which was done to make a two-state solution impossible.

5.4 An Exchange on Dialogue

During the first *intifada*, Jonathan Kuttab, a Palestinian human-rights lawyer, and Edy Kaufman, an Israeli academic, published "An Exchange on Dialogue" (1988). Kuttab identifies six "pitfalls" that create a "false dialogue" (pp. 85–107). Peacemakers cannot assume "a false symmetry" between the oppressor and the oppressed; they cannot ignore basic conflict issues, such as land, water, and national rights; Palestinians cannot accept the existence of a Jewish state as a precondition for dialogue; in the name of moderation, people in dialogue cannot compromise genuine principles, and they cannot abandon positions generally held within their own community; and everyone must resist the tendency to make dialogue a substitute for actions to empower the oppressed. For Kuttab, "authentic dialogue" must seek the truth, pursue dialogue with real enemies, avoid trying to solve the whole problem at once, "keep your whole society in mind when you dialogue with members of another society," and hold a perspective which encompasses other perspectives. Dialogue must be a first step toward action, developing the power of the oppressed (pp. 85–107).

In response to Kuttab, Kaufman (1988) believes that dialogue is "intrinsically positive," a necessary but not sufficient condition for peaceful resolution of… disputes in the region"; Israelis must realize "that the practical realities of dialogue are not the same on both sides"; there must be a mutual understanding that real issues will be addressed, or the whole dialogue will fail; and dialogue must be sustained over time, concentrating on process as well as outcomes. Starting dialogues with present circumstances may be as useful as digging into the past; while dialogue may lead participants into concrete efforts for social change, it may also lead participants to give up in frustration. Security is a dominant concern for most Israelis, and "military strength is not perceived as a sufficient guarantee against acts of terror"; dialogue with the enemy is not a weakness, but "another means of struggling to accomplish national goals." Further, one should talk with enemies as well as fellow travelers; one should be cautious about developing a class of "professional dialoguers" who talk with the other side, but forget about their own people (pp. 85–107). To conceptualize a platform in Chapter 6, one must remember that safety and security are vital for Palestinians, too.

5.5 Narratives as Dialogue

In this study I foreground dialogue as theory, method, and practice. However, embedded narratives constitute the core of many dialogues. People use narratives "to do things—to connect with other people, to deal with social structures ... to make sense of what is going on around them ... and sometimes to change [things]" (Daiute, 2014, p. 3). As noted earlier, "identity is lodged in the narratives of how people see themselves, who they are, where they come from, and what they fear they will become or lose" (Lederach, 2003, p. 55). In this study, there is movement back and forth between dialogue and narrative. Avnery, Bronstein, and Pappe have worked for many years to construct authentic narratives about "what really happened" in the 1948 war. They struggle with contested, historical narratives, collective memory, metanarratives, and "myths"—narratives that express or carry the deepest values for a particular person or group. Rotberg writes, "Narratives are motivational tools. Without the legitimacy conferred by collective memory, mobilizing followers would be impossible. Both Palestinians and Israelis are urged by ... collective memories to act in the group interest" (2006, p. 4).

As noted earlier, in Michel de Certeau's compelling image, "what the map cuts up, the story cuts across" 1984, p. 129. Since 1948, Israelis have literally cut up and fragmented the map of Palestine, dividing the West Bank into military and administrative zones A, B, and C, pressing Palestinian population centers into "Bantustans," isolating Gaza and controlling Palestinian resources underground, in the sea, and in the air (Weizman, 2007). But the stories about these events are more powerful than the maps. In this context, the Israeli fragmentation and erasure of Palestinian culture and the distortions of the occupation and Israeli collective memory are most powerfully healed, corrected, or transcended not by maps, but by authentic narratives.

Holocaust narratives hold a unique and problematic place in the warehouse of Israeli and Palestinian victimhood and suffering. Pappe says that Israelis are deeply ambivalent about Holocaust narratives. The Holocaust plays a role, [but] "I have a very different theory about it.... When Israel became a mini-empire, suddenly Jews felt it compensated for their own history, ... compensating for years of being a victim" (Part II, p. 268).

5.6 Dialogue as Difficult Work

Kuttab reminds us that there are major challenges for generating the quality of dialogue needed to transform this conflict: "In every oppressive situation, the status quo is in favor of the oppressor, and it cannot be assumed as the proper or legitimate starting point" (1988, pp. 105–106). Kuttab concludes, "In my experience, dialoguing is such a difficult and exhausting business, so demanding intellectually and emotionally, and so fraught with pitfalls, that few would ... seek out its rigors" (p. 107). Chapter 6 will identify principles, processes, and other rigors for a just peace.

5.7 Conclusion

In this chapter, the concept and practice of dialogue are understood as *a form of human communication with intentionality and purpose.* Dialogue is an essential component of conflict transformation at all levels—at the interpersonal, institutional, and structural levels. In Dutta's culture-centered approach to dialogue, the ethnographic researcher serves as an "informed listener" with marginalized people, enabling them to "give voice" to their situation, what Ashrawi calls "in-depth" dialogue for peace and justice. Dialogue is necessary for developing understanding, building relationships between grassroots and mid-level peacemakers. These peacemakers often find it difficult to develop meaningful dialogues with government officials, even though peacemakers are an important part of the cultural and political dialogue. For genuine social change and conflict transformation, peacemaker dialogues must lead "beyond talk," and must overcome the challenges discussed in "An exchange on dialogue" (Kuttab & Kaufman, 1988). To move beyond understanding and advocacy to effective conflict transformation, peacemakers must engage in strategic dialogue. Only through "dialogue as hard work" at all levels—interpersonal, communal, and systemic levels—can change occur. As Chapter 6 will suggest, strategic dialogue is necessary for creating a platform for a just peace.

6 A Platform for a Just Peace

From the Nakba of 1948 until the present, Palestinians have experienced exile, violence, ethnic cleansing, cultural erasure, and persistent de-development. As the infrastructure in the OPT broke down, peacemakers engaged in "surreal discussions" about one- and two-state solutions for the Israeli-Palestinian conflict. Khalidi declares that we must not debate "how many states can dance on the head of a pin," but rather discover the means of rapidly reversing the current situation and "extricating the Palestinian people from their present state" (2010, p. xxxix). In parallel terms, it is not important to ask how many peacemakers can dance on the head of a pin, but to ask strategically how peacemakers can develop and implement a just, sustainable peace.

For Lederach, the central challenge for transforming a major conflict is how to respond to immediate needs while simultaneously developing long-term capacities for building and sustaining a platform for positive change. "We can do this by thinking about platforms as 'process-structures'" (2003, p. 4), combining adaptability with a sustained purpose (or structure). Since this conflict changes both "by the day" and over time, adaptability is crucial. Salameh says, "I was a longtime believer [in] the two-state solution. I changed … because I realized, as many people did, that the two-state solution is dead" (Part II, p. 291). The capacity of peacemakers to make creative and strategic changes at every level is a central concern of this book. Platforms "emerge from an adaptive base at the epicenter of conflict," understanding the levels of the conflict ("the big picture"), processes for addressing immediate conflicts, and a vision for a "strategic, long-term, constructive change in systems and relationships" (Lederach, 2003, pp. 45–46). This conflict presents many immediate problems: travel restrictions, war, house demolitions, checkpoints, water, long-term conflicts with Zionism, occupation, victimhood, racism, settler colonialism, nationalism, and religion. Complex, protracted conflicts must use simultaneous processes and approaches (see Awad, Ashrawi, Halper, and El-Farra).

6.1 Conflict Analyses: "If" and "Poof"

In 2003, Halper signaled that a two-state solution for ending the occupation had vanished because of Israeli policies and "facts on the ground." For

DOI: 10.4324/9781003262817-7

Halper, the Israeli project of the last 40 years had reached a climax and a point of no return. Facts on the ground had been internalized by Palestinian leaders as well as Israeli leaders. Years of discussion about one-state and two-state solutions had been attempts to achieve a peace and avoid apartheid. Halper changed his global strategy to say, "This is apartheid; now, how do we get out of it?" (Part II, p. 221).

Avnery, a strong advocate for a two-state solution, rejects the apartheid analogy.

UA: There will be no peace for Israel … if we do not change our perceptions.… We must understand the hopes … and fears of the other side.… Contrary to appearances, we have won a major part of the necessary victory, … the world consensus.

RH: But things are so much worse than two years ago.…

UA: By far; life in the Occupied Territories is becoming worse and worse.… New settlements are going up all the time.… [But] it's now accepted in Israel by the vast majority that there will be no solution without a Palestinian state.…

RH: [But] Israeli governments have made a Palestinian state impossible.

UA: It makes it difficult, but far from impossible.

RH: *If* there's a political will.

UA: *If* there's a political will, everything can be adjusted to this. As Theodor Hertzl once said, "If you want it, it won't be a fable." (Part II, pp. 153–155)

This is a very aspirational *if*. After the 1948 war, Avnery tried to change Israeli public opinion by writing books and articles. But his commitment to a Jewish state limited his vision (Part II, p. 155).

Recent U.S. presidents of both parties have also made flawed analyses of this conflict. During President Barack Obama's second term, Secretary of State John Kerry made a good-faith effort to revive a diplomatic peace process. But in a defining moment, Halper says, Kerry cleared away the "fog of the two-state solution." Testifying before a U.S. Senate committee, Kerry reported that while he negotiated an agenda with Israel, Israel announced it would build thousands more illegal housing units in the West Bank. Kerry said his peacemaking efforts went "*POOF!*" For Halper, "*POOF*" cleared the air and moved peacemakers past the fiction of a two-state solution; it was "the most accurate assessment of where we are." (Part II, pp. 230–231). President Donald Trump also ignored diplomacy by moving the U.S. embassy from Tel Aviv to Jerusalem, cutting humanitarian aid to Palestinians, promoting a bogus "Deal of the Century," and supporting Israel's plan to annex more of the West Bank. At this writing, President Joe Biden has not announced a just vision.

6.2 Principles for a Just Peace

Principles are general statements of values and perspectives, and they serve as the bases for peacemaking platforms. For example, Edward Said called for "the idea and practice of *citizenship*, not of ethnic or racial community, as the main vehicle of coexistence" (1999). I have already examined some of the essential principles for a platform for peace: commitments to dialogue, upholding human rights, and international law.

6.3 A Minimum Basis for Peace

Mid-level peacemakers have provided ample guidance for pursuing peace. Between 2004 and the 2014 war in Gaza, most peacemakers supported the "end game" of a two-state solution. In 2004, the Sabeel Liberation Theology Center issued "Principles for a Just Peace," declaring that a two-state solution provided "the minimum basis" for resolving the conflict, a combination of principles and processes requiring Israel to acknowledge its injustices against the Palestinian people; end the occupation; pay reparations; pursue reconciliation through "repentance, forgiveness, and redress"; establish a Truth and Reconciliation Commission; fulfill the right of return for Palestinian refugees; make all Israeli settlements built on Palestinian land since 1967 a part of Palestine; require all Arab states to accept a Palestinian state within the 1967 borders; and promote peace programs (2004, pp. 6–8). Five years later, Christian leaders also published "Kairos Palestine" (2009), recognizing the failure of both armed resistance and negotiations, and urging nonviolent resistance to end the occupation. ("Kairos Palestine" was updated in 2021.)

6.4 Limbo, Collapse, or Something Worse

Since 2006, the major Palestinian factions exist in limbo. Fatah and Hamas have struggled for control of the OPT. Fatah collaborates with the Israeli government, providing police security in the West Bank, and Hamas struggles to survive Israel's air attacks. From 2007 to 2021, Israel and Hamas have fought four wars. The 2014 and 2021 wars were game-changers. Halper says,

> We're in [a] collapse we weren't in five years ago, the collapse of everything—the two-state solution, the political actors that exist today, the occupation. We're headed towards a whole new situation ... maybe a whole new occupation.... The two-state solution is gone, but many Palestinians haven't moved to a one-state solution. (Part II, pp. 226–227)

Raheb says Palestinians are in limbo—"it's too late for a two-state solution and too early for a one-state solution.... that's the danger" (Part II, p. 287); Palestinians are under an oppression copied from East Germany, South Africa, and U.S. reservations, but the occupation is not sustainable. "When the egg break[s], we will see what ... solution comes out" (Part II, p. 288). Bahour fears "something worse" than the *intifadas*. El-Farra warns that Gaza will explode.

Gaza did explode for 11 days in May 2021, the fourth major conflict between Israel and Hamas since 2007. Israel killed some 250 people in Gaza, injured 2,000 others, and displaced or left homeless more than 70,000 Gazans.

Hamas launched more than 4,000 rockets into Israel, killing 13 Israelis. Commentators perceived this war as qualitatively different from the three earlier wars between Gaza and Israel. Israel "must face a changed reality" (Avishai, 2021, p. 1) of how it is perceived in the world. *The New York Times* printed all the pictures of 65 children who were killed; all but two were Palestinian (May 28, 2021, p. 1). The UNRWA staff in Gaza reported that this war was "worse in intensity and terror" than the war in 2014 (UN Report, May 21, 2021). Journalists observed that the roots of the Israel-Palestinian conflict persist—apartheid, occupation, and collective punishment. New dynamics include Jerusalem as the epicenter of Palestinian resistance, a unified Palestinian resistance in all of the OPT, intersectional solidarity with other resistance movements, young people's resisting in spite of fear and collective punishment, a movement not tied to a "two-state" solution, and more international journalists' listening to Palestinian voices (Mattar & Caplan, 2018). Michelle Bachelet, UN High Commissioner for Human Rights, declared that Hamas violated international law by launching thousands of rockets into Israel, and that Israel's air strikes on Gaza may constitute "war crimes" (in Keaten, 2021).

6.5 International Law and Human Rights Redux

As noted in Chapter 4, a human-rights paradigm is replacing the land-for-peace paradigm. State actors have receded, the role of civil society has grown, and strategies for a just peace have shifted to human-rights strategies. "Civil-society actors are far more inclined to focus on people and their rights rather than borders and the brokering of political power between factions or states" (Munayyer, 2014, p. 3). This shift is forcing a global discussion of why Palestinian rights are being denied. Peacemakers insist on following international law, UN resolutions, and the Fourth Geneva Convention. In the Universal Declaration of Human Rights, Article 2, everyone is entitled to all rights and freedoms without distinctions of any kind—race, color, sex, language, religion, politics, national or social origin, property, birth, or other status (p. 25).

For Kuttab, a human-rights lawyer, "There's no system in the world that rivals the Israeli system in the manipulative use of law, because Israel doesn't have a constitution to appeal to.... Clever scholars [use] the law to defeat the spirit of the law" (Part II, p. 234). The Fourth Geneva Convention protects civilians in war zones and occupied territories, but Israel claims that there is no occupation, that the occupied territories are "disputed territories," so, Palestinians have no protected status. Israel argues it is exempt from the Fourth Geneva Convention. Halper contends that Israel has created a whole new category of conflict, a stage "short of war," although there is no such concept in international law. Israel wants to use all of its military equipment, but in war, enemies have rights. Palestinians are neither citizens, protected persons, nor enemy combatants. Palestinians are living in a Kafkaesque bubble, completely at the mercy of Israel" (Part II, p. 219). Israel wants all the rights of war but none of the obligations.

6.6 Prophetic Mourning and Warning

Developing a platform for a just peace includes both secular and religious forms of prophetic discourse—mourning, warning, and radical imagination. Prophets are much more than sour human beings who call out the misdeeds of others. Walter Brueggemann (1978) writes that prophets "engage in imagination before implementation" (1978, p. 45). Jeremiah is his model for prophetic imagination (p. 51). Prophets announce the end of the royal fantasy, identify massive deceptions, bring fears and terrors into public consciousness, and "speak neither in rage nor in cheap grace, but with the candor born of anguish and passion" (pp. 49–50). For Brueggemann, the central task of prophetic leaders is "to nurture, nourish, and evoke a consciousness and perception alternative to the consciousness and perception of the dominant culture" (p. 13). The "proper idiom" for prophets is to cut through royal numbness, denial, and oppression, and to substitute the language of grief and mourning. Prophets use the language of lament "to [bring] to reality what the king must see and will not, … that crying in pathos is the ultimate form of criticism, for it announces the sure end of the whole royal arrangement" (1978, p. 51).

For both secular and religious peacemakers, collective mourning is enormously challenging; it includes prophetic imagination, lament, grief, trauma, *sumud*, and warning. Palestinians grieve the end of a two-state solution, and a long national liberation struggle (Halper, Part II, p. 226). Pappe mourns the loss of prophetic imagination during the all-consuming occupation and the triumphalism of "the new Jew" (Part II, p. 268). Levy mourns being ignored.

RH: In *Ha'aretz*, you used very strong language, such as "vengeance," … [in] the tone of the Hebrew prophets. Tell me how you see your role as a writer and as an analyst.

GL: I was very flattered to get the other day an e-mail from Noam Chomsky, whom I've never met, who compared me to the prophets. He used this term. It's not for me to judge my role. It's too early to judge. Many times I feel that I am writing for the archives….

RH: Writing for the future?

GL: I think so, because I don't see a real influence right now. (Part II, pp. 247–248)

In "Kairos Palestine" (2009), the "prophetic mission" of Christian leaders focuses on truth-telling (p. 18). "We will not understand the meaning of prophetic imagination unless we see the connection between the religion of static triumphalism and the politics of oppression and exploitation" (p. 17). Mourning must be practiced with the consciousness of illegal settlements, terrorism, the Holocaust, the Nakba, occupation, and the right of return. Ateek's theology of liberation speaks "prophetically and contextually" to this suffering and injustice (2017, p. 7).

Within a strategic framework, mid-level peacemakers must assess the efficacy of their work. After the Israeli-Hamas war of 2014, Halper mourned the failures of peacemakers:

> People are trying to pass the ball [to us] and we're not there.... We are not talking to each other. We're ... isolated from political agency. [Intellectuals] can create the alternatives that the higher political people pick up on.... There's a whole gap between the agency of the people, and the agency of the political leadership, without that connecting link in the middle. That's where we have failed. (Part II, p. 228)

Sami Awad yearns for new communities in which political, religious, and prophetic capacities converge "to launch a new peace process" with a vision of justice, equality, and human rights for all, creating a new model for resolving global conflicts. "You give up on what you were promised ... the two-state solution and our own leaders"; this "cleanses the land for new hope to be planted, hope in the growing hopelessness" (Part II, pp. 168–169). I believe that when Israelis mourn the Nakba, and Palestinians mourn the Holocaust, profound transformations will emerge.

6.7 Security and Safety

In this conflict, the principles of security and safety are primary concerns. Referring to Mariame Kaba, Sandra Tamari suggests that safety and security are different concepts; *security* is associated with surveillance, force, and violence; *safety* is a psychological dynamic based on relationships and trust (Tamari, 2021). Svirsky says, "Israelis desperately need a sense of safety, and they will never have it if they are part of a bigger state" (Part II, p. 317). However, most peacemakers in this study believe that safety and real security derive from coexistence and racial integration (Halper, Part II, p. 218). Chacour, founder of Mar Elias schools, says cultural diversity is the only way to solve the conflict: diversity means sharing, justice, peace, and security (Part II, pp. 198–199).

Israel has created a militarized culture of "might makes right" (Ashrawi, Part II, p. 128). Nadera Shalhoub-Kevorkian (2015) analyzes how Israel generates fear among Palestinians through a "security theology" of violence, surveillance, and a "settler-colonial logic of elimination and erasure" (p. 1). Both ethnic groups have enormous needs for safety. But Halper's caveat is confounding: "The oppressor ... before it gives up control, has to be convinced that you're not going to get revenge.... You're not going to do to us what we deserve.... For oppressed people, that's very hard to do" (Part II, p. 227). The ANC did that in South Africa. Palestinians may also have to do that.

6.8 Strategic Dialogues

The purpose of strategic dialogues is to achieve specific goals. Peacemakers attempt to answer questions of *why* and *how* they are engaged in conflict transformation—the principles and processes concerning goals, systemic change, simultaneous actions, and effectiveness. Strategic peacemaking must be comprehensive, a *system* of interconnected people, roles, activities, design, and infrastructure, sustainable and integrative (Lederach & Appleby, 2010, pp. 39–41). Peter Kellett (2007) calls for similar strategies: analyze the meaning of the conflict; develop a working model of how to negotiate what is important; focus on shared questions about the conflict; integrate "diverse and oppositional perspectives as a way to achieve win-win solutions"; move beyond arguments; base dialogue on systemic analysis, build scenarios; integrate surface and deeper issues; and develop new meanings (pp. 46–53).

While dialogue is an in-depth, purposeful exchange, *strategic dialogue* is even more goal-oriented. Conceptually and procedurally, strategic dialogue must respond to the complexity of peacemaking and peacebuilding in Israel-Palestine. According to Lederach (2005),

> Peacebuilding is an enormously complex endeavor in unbelievably complex, dynamic and ... destructive settings of violence ... [with] multiple actors, pursuing a multiplicity of actions and initiatives, at numerous levels of social relationships in an interdependent setting at the same time.... This is *the* great challenge of peacebuilding. (p. 33)

An example appears in this scenario regarding an effort to create a draft constitution for Israel-Palestine to show people what the new system would be, how it would work, how to transform power relationships, how to decolonize the country, and how to establish an egalitarian society.

JH: If we can show *that*, then we can try to address [Israeli and Palestinian] fears....

RH: Along with a constitution, which is a conceptual framework, create another document [for] implementation. Who would administer or oversee this [process]? Are there third parties that could put some muscle behind it? ... You need trust-building [steps]....

JH: We have to find a strategy that allays Israeli fears but that doesn't assume that they're going to be active partners.... But it's true what you're saying.... implementation is key to it. If you ... address [Israeli] fears, you have a shot at [transformation]. (Part II, p. 231)

Ending and transforming the occupation will be possible only with a robust vision for a just peace, strategic implementation, simultaneous peacemaking processes at all levels, and mourning personal and collective losses, with all groups accountable through international law. According to Ramsbotham, the very complexity of some conflicts presents peacemaking opportunities: "During times of maximum attrition, the radical disagreements that constitute the core of linguistic intractability are best seen as an opportunity rather than a terminus" (2017, p. 6); that is, more disagreement, not less, may be needed to clarify strategic issues. For Ramsbotham, collective strategic thinking is more viable than individual strategic thinking. It asks, Where are we? Where do we want to go? And how do we get there? Collective strategic thinking begins with "identity groups" (2017, p. 51); it examines questions of strategic unity, context, power, possible futures, goals, paths, means, alternatives, opponents, allies, and communication (2017, pp. 132–134).

It is crucial to consider and celebrate the recent surge in intersectional dialogues and strategies, addressing the dynamics of power, racism, human rights, poverty, gender, militarism, colonialism, health, and climate justice. Over the past 15 years, Pappe (2021) has observed a significant increase in intersectional, postcolonial studies in academic circles and a positive change in how Palestinian studies are taught: "There is a new identification and solidarity between [Palestine] and oppressed groups around the world" (Part II, p. 274). For example, Jewish Voice for Peace (JVP) supports the Black Lives Matter (BLM) movement, and sharply criticizes Jewish organizations that facilitate the "worst practices" among the U.S. police, the FBI, immigration officials, and the Israeli military, who tests its weapons on occupied Palestinians (Fox, 2021).

For Palestinians, many years of occupation and the pandemic of 2020–2022 have produced a "double lockdown" of the virus and the occupation. As the world seeks effective global responses to the current pandemic, Mitri Raheb and Palestinian negotiator Saeb Erakat hope for "an effective international coalition to bring an end to the occupation" (2020, p. 7). They hope for a turning point in which the world values the role of international law and a rule-based world order.

6.9 Strategic Nonviolence

With Pappe, I believe that both the armed struggle and the diplomatic efforts to end the Israeli occupation are "failed projects," and that "a just peace is the only nonviolent alternative" (Part II, p. 272). I also believe that the transition from an Israeli apartheid regime to a just peace will require aggressive and offensive forms of nonviolence. This follows Judith Butler's argument for "the force of nonviolence" that "nonviolent forms of resistance can and must be aggressively pursued" (2020, p. 21). For peacemakers, nonviolence is an ongoing, intersectional struggle. Butler writes, "When the critique of continuing colonial violence is deemed violent (Palestine), when struggles for equality and freedom are construed as violent threats to state security (Black Lives Matter) … we are operating in the midst of politically consequential forms of phantasmagoria" (2020, p. 24). Nonviolence is "a physical assertion of the claims of life" through speech, actions, networks, and assemblies—"recasting the living as worthy of value, as … grievable precisely under conditions in which they are either erased from view or cast into irreversible forms of precarity" (2020, pp. 24–25).

Several peacemakers connect Palestinian oppression with security issues in the U.S., the BLM movement, and U.S. military interventions. Bahour, a Palestinian-American businessman and commentator, writes, "The oppressed around the world are watching … our struggles for freedom [in] America's narrow military-industrial-congressional complex" (2020, p. 7). Following Naomi Klein's concept of "warehousing"—how capitalism makes half of the world's population superfluous—Halper says, "Palestinians are the first people to be declared by the international community as surplus humanity"

(Part II, p. 224). This has profound implications for transforming Palestinian "grievability" (Butler) into aggressive nonviolence, decolonizing Israel (Halper, 2021), and pursuing reconciliation (Ateek, 2008). Transforming the current occupation-apartheid-warehousing complex into peacemaking will require processes of creative and strategic nonviolence as practiced by Andoni, Salameh, and many others during the first *intifada.* Andoni says, "We were ready to take huge risks, to invest all of our effort, energy, and people. We needed to make it sustainable because it is impossible that you can arrive at a just peace during a short period of time" (Part II, p. 108). Wendy Pearlman (2011) argues that to avoid fragmentation and violence, movements need both strong institutions and strong leadership.

6.10 Transformations and Restorations

As peacemakers exercise "the force of nonviolence," they must also exercise capacities for empathy, understanding, trauma healing, and other restorative practices. As I argue in Chapter 5, the capacity for building inclusive relationships is at the heart of strategic practice. For El-Farra, land can be shared. For Halper, rebuilding demolished houses says to Palestinians, "You belong here." For Burnat, showing *5 Broken Cameras* reveals the suffering and nonviolent humanity of his Muslim village. Pappe facilitates writing a "bridging narrative" and imagines coexistence. Raheb and Abusrour develop resistance and healing through the arts. Positive transformations also occur through theatre, fun, laughter, and dialogue as shared work (Lederach, 2003, p. 59).

Gaza's mostly nonviolent Great March of Return (2019) demonstrates the possibility and power of nonviolent transformations. As noted earlier, Ramsbotham et al. (2011, pp. 175–176) identify "generic transformers" in protracted conflicts. All five appear in the Israeli-Palestinian conflict:

- **Context transformation.** The fragmentation of the OPT is a negative, ongoing transformation of Palestinian geography. One of the most significant context changes will occur when thousands of Palestinians leave refugee camps and access the right of return.
- **Structural transformation.** The structures that sustain this conflict must undergo radical transformations, including writing a constitution and creating institutions that conform to international law, the Fourth Geneva Convention, and the Declaration of Human Rights.
- **Actor transformation**. There is an enormous need for more visionary and prophetic leaders in both Israeli and Palestinian communities, and at all levels—government leaders, nongovernmental leaders, and grassroots movements.
- **Issue transformation.** Issue transformations are profoundly needed—cultural shifts to equity and inclusivity, and away from Zionism, nationalism, and other forms of exclusivity.
- **Personal and group transformations.** At every level, profound transformations must occur, through in-depth dialogue, encounter groups,

religious programs, letting go of "victimhood," and developing capacities for personal and collective mourning.

6.10.1 Trauma Healing

While the term "trauma" occurs only a few times in Part II, traumatic experiences are related in almost all of the dialogues—personal, historical, and collective trauma, living with traumatized people, refugee experiences, racism, anti-Semitism, Holocaust and Nakba experiences, politicide, memoricide, war, terrorism, checkpoints, bombings, the Wall, house demolitions, arrests, detention of children, separation of families, torture, even trauma through peacemaking. Raheb cites a U.S. study in which more than 80% of the people living in the OPT are traumatized (Part II, p. 277). The horrific bombing of Gaza in 2014 caused persistent trauma to Palestinian children. Salameh says, "We have a whole generation [with] stress disorders" (Part II, p. 290). Trauma healing must be applied both to groups and individuals. Carolyn Yoder says, "At its core, addressing trauma is bio-psycho-social-spiritual work of the deepest sort, calling forth nothing less than our noblest ideals, and the faith, hope, love, and resilience of the human spirit" (Yoder, 2020, p. 3).

Healing generally suggests physical and psychological processes, while liberation often suggests political processes. As noted earlier, Montville promoted "the healing function in political conflict resolution" in the 1990s. In this study, dialogue partners use healing, liberation, forgiveness, and reconciliation in multiple, overlapping ways. There are numerous definitions of these terms, rather than "consensus definitions" (Waldron & Kelley, 2008). Trauma healing appears in dialogues with El-Farra (2007, 2018), Raheb (2006, 2018), and Abusrour (2014).

6.10.2 Restorative Justice

The principles and practices of restorative justice offer a creative approach for addressing the challenges of accountability, the rule of law, justice, amnesty, and restitution. Since the 1970s, numerous restorative justice practices have emerged. Howard Zehr (2002), one of the founders of this movement, writes, "Restorative justice is a process to involve … those who have a stake in specific offenses and to collectively identify and address harms, needs, and obligations, in order to heal and put things as right as possible" (p. 37). For Zehr, these are the guiding questions: Who has been hurt? What are their needs? Whose obligations are these? Who has a stake in the situation, and how should they put things right? (p. 38). He writes,

> Show equal concern and commitment to victims and offenders, involving both in the process of justice. Work toward the restoration of victims, empowering them and responding to their needs as they see them. Support offenders, while encouraging them to understand, accept, and carry out their obligations. (2002, pp. 40–41)

Stakeholders in the Israeli-Palestinian conflict—grassroots groups, peacemakers, government officials, and restorative justice practitioners—must decide the appropriate mix of restorative justice and retributive justice. Restitution is vitally important to victims in compensating actual losses, but also for "the symbolic recognition [that] restitution implies" (Zehr, 2002, p. 15).

"The victim deserves something and the offender owes something.... Restorative justice has the potential to affirm both victim and offender and to help them transform their lives" (p. 59). Zehr also says that restorative approaches are being adapted to larger community issues and processes, how to do justice after large-scale societal conflicts, and how to think concretely about justice within "the theory and practice of conflict transformation and peacebuilding" (pp. 42–43). For Zehr, restorative justice is more about concrete restoration rather than forgiveness and reconciliation (p. 8).

6.10.3 Forgiveness and Reconciliation

In these dialogues, references to reconciliation and forgiveness are rare. These processes are among the most difficult to contemplate and to practice. Waldron and Kelley (2008) place forgiveness and mercy at one end of a continuum and justice at the other end. Near the middle, they situate forgiveness and trauma healing. They define forgiveness in terms of relationships: a wrong is identified, and the relationship is renegotiated (p. 19). Shapira provides a compelling model of forgiveness and mutual liberation at all levels: acknowledge wrongdoing, take responsibility, and engage in restoration; then translate one's conflicts and solutions for oneself, one's society, and one's social or political context, and work with the people one oppressed to stop and transform the oppression (Part II, p. 319).

6.10.4 Liberation

Both Israelis and Palestinians have a liberation discourse. Israelis refer to the 1947–1949 war of liberation, and Palestinians traditionally refer to their national liberation struggle. I argue that a platform for a just peace must pursue more radical liberation processes for everyone in Israel-Palestine—both political and spiritual liberations. Liberation theologian Ateek articulates this vision. While he resists "the evil of illegal occupation," he also affirms the importance of mutual liberation. "We must work for the liberation of the oppressors as well as the liberation of the oppressed.... Nonviolence respect[s] ... the humanity of the antagonist" (2017, pp. 4–5).

6.11 Processes, Structures, and Scenarios

The struggle to end the occupation is part of a global conflict, and part of a global resistance. Halper says:

JH: Human rights and international law give me a handle. I have friends, I have allies.

RH: So, it's meaningful to talk about the ongoing work [for] peace and justice?

JH: That's right, you have a vision of where you're going. You make corrections in that as you go along and as new concepts emerge, and things change, and you re-evaluate.... (Part II, p. 222)

I concur with Halper that activism must be linked with strategy. He says, "Our job is not to protest. Our job is to end the occupation ... to bring about a just peace" (part II, p. 223).

Peacemakers and peacebuilders use many terms to name their work: struggles, stages, approaches, elements, principles, and solutions. "Solution" is the most common term, but perhaps the most problematic. In 2016, Halper proclaimed that the two-state solution had died. "There is one, Israel-controlled country, with borders, government, army, currency. Now, how do we transform it? We are not ready yet for a solution.... We can't just jump to that, even though this is urgent" (Part II, p. 229). Many peacemakers refer to their work as a struggle, engaging in what Ramsbotham calls *agonistic dialogue* (2017, p. 47). Levy and Ascherman do not care how many states emerge, as long as "the process is fair." Meanwhile, struggles, strategies, scenarios, and solutions proliferate. See journalist Judy Maltz's (2019, pp. 1, 21) seven "solutions."

Halper's terms have evolved from a binational, two-state solution (2003) to two stages (2006) to strategic dialogues (2008) to elements, processes, and approaches (2010). He proposes to:

- include both Israelis and Palestinians in two national groups, like the South African model.
- accept the right of return for refugees and acknowledge their long-term suffering.
- base this state on international law and human rights to guarantee that it will be just.
- develop regional approaches to refugees, water, and economic development.
- provide security for all communities. (Part II, p. 225)

By 2016, Halper and at least half of the peacemakers in this study dropped the demand for a Palestinian state and advocated for some form of a One Democratic State (ODS). Halper says,

JH: I am looking at the Palestinian-Israeli version of the [ANC's] Freedom Charter in South Africa. It's a vision document.... You could move Israelis towards a one-state solution, if they could see that the Palestinian concept is inclusive. I would love to get together a group [of] 10 Israelis and 10 Palestinians—from ... the West Bank, East Jerusalem, Gaza, inside Israel, [the refugee] camps, and the diaspora.... Once you accept the principles of a Freedom Charter, there are alternatives.... People say, "Let's think of a joint future," [and] "Let's move on to a real detailed plan," ... a platform.

RH: A platform, yes.

JH: The *process* develop[s] the Freedom Charter. The platform *is* the Freedom Charter. (Part II, pp. 229–230)

In 2018, at the University of Exeter in the U.K., Pappe hosted such a dialogue with a diverse group of Palestinians and Israelis. This group, including Halper, launched the One Democratic State Campaign (ODSC), based on a multicultural democracy, the right of return, "the dismantling of all structures of domination; and construction of a new, shared, civil society" (Halper, 2019a). Yousef Aljamal et al. welcomed the ODSC as an "inclusive umbrella group," although he could not predict which groups and individuals "perceive enough common ground to work together" (2019, p. 1).

For example, facilitators must give careful attention to identities—"how identity is linked to power and to the systems and structures which organize and govern their relationships" (Lederach, 2003, pp. 58–60), and how to transform Israeli and Palestinian fundamentalisms that combine religion and nationalism and cut off dialogue (Raheb, Part II, p. 280).

6.12 A Platform for a Just Peace

I endorse Pappe's declaration that both negotiation and armed struggle are "failed projects," and the only alternative is strategic nonviolence, including these elements: a prophetic, comprehensive platform, international law, human rights, mourning, diverse and transformational identities, intersectional solidarity, bridging narratives, truth, justice, and accountability:

- **Nonviolent resistance.** Peacemakers must employ aggressive, nonviolent resistance until officials accept international law, human rights, and a genuine peace process.
- **The end of occupation.** Israel must meet immediate needs of water, food, and medical care; at the same time, it must dismantle the occupation as quickly as possible.
- **Security.** Security must be provided for all. UN peacekeepers should be deployed as needed; peacemakers and peacebuilders must facilitate trust-building programs.
- **Strategic dialogue and a constitution.** Representatives of all ethnic groups, parties, and factions must draft a constitution, design new institutions, and appoint temporary leaders.
- **The right of return and restorative justice.** As required by UN Resolution 194, the right of return for refugees and the principles of restorative justice must be implemented.
- **A secular, multicultural state.** All residents must be given equal rights and resources for transforming Zionism and Palestinian nationalism into a multi-ethnic, secular state.

- **Accountability and reconciliation.** An interim government should appoint a commission to hold individuals accountable for ethnic cleansing, torture, and other crimes against humanity, and appoint a commission to develop truth-telling, mercy, and reconciliation.
- **Regional approaches.** Regional approaches should address security, water, climate change, borders, nuclear weapons, and other regional issues.

All of these elements require struggle and thoroughly dialogical processes. Peacemakers and peacebuilders, working "from the middle," must provide strong and creative leadership, similar to the emergent leadership during the first *intifada* (Andoni, Salameh), combined with high levels of grassroots participation and buy-in from government leaders.

6.12.1 The "Infrastructure of Hope"

Raheb's elegant phrase sings out the possibility of transforming Israel-Palestine into a new country, emergent through prophetic vision, mourning, strategic dialogue, and implementation for all of its residents. This will require the combined passion of grassroots movements, nongovernmental leaders, and government leaders. This country can be reborn with a constitution, equal rights, the right of return, restorative justice, rebuilding "the old waste places, [and] raising up the foundations of many generations" (Isaiah 58:12).

6.13 Conclusion

The concept of constructing a flexible platform for a just peace emerges from a "process-structure" (Lederach). This concept combines a clear and sustained purpose and the adaptability of complex processes. This paradox confronts many challenges; the failures of Israeli and Palestinian government officials; collective victimhood; the violence of settlers; the ideologies of Zionism, nationalism, and exclusivity; and the Jewish Nation-State Basic Law (2018), which justifies Jewish domination of Palestinians. The resistance, aggressive nonviolence, and vision of mid-level peacemakers provide hope for a just and sustainable transformation: a commitment to human rights and international law, capacities for prophetic pathos and mourning, and an understanding that security and safety for all will only emerge when systemic racism is curtailed and replaced by trauma healing and other restorative and transformational processes. At this writing, there is a broad sense among activists, scholars, journalists, and intersectional allies that strategic dialogue, process-structures, scenarios, and platforms can lead to peace in a new country. As in the struggle against apartheid and for justice in South Africa, many people are needed to join this struggle for a just peace. In Part II, 21 peace and justice activists extend their compelling narratives, analyses of the conflict, and their visions for a just peace.

Part II

Dialogues with Peacemakers

7 The Arts as Beautiful Resistance

Abdelfattah Abusrour

Abdelfattah Abusrour was born and raised in Aida refugee camp in Bethlehem. Eventually he left Palestine and went to France to earn a Ph.D. in biological and medical engineering. When he returned to Aida camp, Abusrour created the Alrowwad Cultural Center. Some 66% of the 6,000 people in the camp are under the age of 24. Abusrour teaches young people to develop theatre as "beautiful resistance." He has received the Ashoka Social Entrepreneurial Fellowship (2006) and many other awards.

Aida Camp, Bethlehem, September 2014

RH: As both a writer and a teacher, I'm looking for people who have figured out how to do cultural resistance using the arts.... You were in France, studying medicine?

AA: I was in biological and medical engineering. I was born in Aida Camp. My father and mother come from villages 17 to 20 kilometers to the southwest of Jerusalem. There were 534 other [Palestinian] villages that were completely destroyed and annexed [in 1948] and now are part of what is known as Israel. My parents became refugees. They stayed in the hills for two months, and finally ... they rented a room in Beit Sahour. The UN created UNRWA [The United Nations Refugee and Works Agency], which registered refugees and allocated tents.... In 1950, Aida refugee camp was established, and one of my uncles registered the Abusrour family. So my parents moved here. My family was about 70% of the population here. Now it's about 30 to 35% of the camp. When I was a child, I had a love for writing, for theatre, and painting. I took lessons in East Jerusalem for painting. As I grew up, I became part of the Aida youth club, a board member, and a part of the popular committees. We improvised, and demonstrated about land issues.

RH: Was this in the 1960s?

AA: It was the mid-1970s and mid-1980s. I was born in 1963 and came on the board in 1978 or '79. I finished my high school in 1981 and finished my bachelor's degree at Bethlehem University in 1984. I started learning French and got a scholarship to continue my studies

DOI: 10.4324/9781003262817-9

in France. To leave, you needed a permit from the Israeli military administration. Today it's not really necessary. Even if you wanted to have a phone in the house, you needed a permit from them.

RH: The Israelis had an obsession with control.

AA: Yeah, like today! Nothing comes in or comes out without permission. They decide who can fall in love and who marries who. After six rejections by the Israelis, I got the permit. I arrived in France with an Israeli document, but not a passport. Israelis did not recognize Palestinians. The French police gave me the nationality of a Jordanian refugee under Israeli mandate. I am a Palestinian refugee under the Israeli occupation. So that created a long debate with French police. When I came back, they gave me a residency card that said "Nationality to be determined." So that was the starting point of my thinking, How can we control the image of Palestine because we have the right to resist occupation? Some people chose armed struggle, while 99% of Palestinian people never carried a gun in their life. There are a lot of creative and unarmed ways [to resist]. And so the idea of what I call "beautiful resistance" was necessary.

RH: The phrase is very elegant!

AA: When I started talking about that in 1998, some people started saying, What do you mean? Other resistance is ugly? [I said,] the act of resisting the occupation—resisting a dictatorship, or any sort of injustice—is beautiful.... I wanted to use this terminology to get beauty out of all the deeds we are doing as human beings—the act of living is beautiful—while refusing oppression.

RH: I was at the Mahmoud Darwish Museum yesterday, which is a good example of what you're talking about. The building, the poetry, the life, the beauty.

AA: The beauty of his language and expression, yes. I stayed for nine years in France. Even while working for my master's and Ph.D. in biological and medical engineering, which I loved as well, I was doing painting and theatre as an actor and writer. I amused myself in working on my paintings, and deepened my theatre work. In 1988, we created our own theatre at my university in the north of Paris. I almost quit the Ph.D. for the theatre. But I finished my Ph.D. For my parents, it was important, and for me as well, because I was the first Ph.D. in the family and in Aida Camp.

RH: Everyone was applauding you?

AA: Yes. I finished my Ph.D. in October 1993. When I returned to Palestine, I worked with my bioengineering diploma for a living, and then in my spare time did painting and theatre.... In 1994 I came back, expecting Palestine to be waiting for me. I didn't get married to a beautiful girl to get French nationality, because I was still idealistic. [I said,] We are going to come back to serve our country. Part of the plan of the Israelis is to push us to leave. If I decided to stay in Paris, no one could blame it on the Israelis.... I didn't want to run away in case this [occupation] got worse. It got worse. I started ... teaching at Bethlehem University and doing microbiology for a Beit Jala company.

But afternoons and weekends, I volunteered at theatres and schools. In 1998 I founded the concept of "beautiful resistance through theatre," the most amazing, powerful, civilized, and unarmed ways to express yourself, to tell your story, your version of your story, without hypocrisy or compromise or trying to please anybody. This is a way to build a peace within, before talking about peace with anybody else. If you are not truthful with yourself, you cannot be truthful with anybody else. And if you are not at peace with yourself, how can you make peace with anybody else? As Palestinians, weapons should not be the answer for any conflict resolution.

RH: Was that a widespread commitment? Did you come to that through your teachers?

AA: Not really; they came later. In fact, it was part of the religion as a Muslim....

RH: Most people in the west don't know that.

AA: No. When you look at how many have been killed in Muslim wars compared to other wars.

RH: And most people don't know that the first *intifada* [1987–91] was mostly nonviolent.

AA: In fact, that was probably the twelfth *intifada*, because when you look at the first demonstration against the first dynasty, it was in 1881. And the big, big intifada in 1936.

RH: I'm familiar with that, yes.

AA: You probably have read the book of Dr. Qumsiyeh about "popular resistance" in Palestine?

RH: Yes. I'm going to hear him speak in Ramallah later today.

AA: [Chuckles.] Excellent. He was on our board until last June. We became very, very good friends. And we worked together on many things. We are both biologists as well.... My parents also have been great teachers because, it was the biggest idea and heritage that they left us. It wasn't money. It was that even with a just cause, if you practice violence, you lose part of your humanity. My father could not tolerate us or anybody speaking badly about anybody else

RH: Even if it was an Israeli soldier?

AA: Whoever. The Israelis wanted my father to be the chief of the camp, to be the correspondent when they wanted to arrest somebody. So, they negotiated with him because he was among the eldest of the Abusrour families and he was expected to be the *muktar*. In exchange, the Israelis would facilitate the return of my second brother, who was exiled in 1972. My father refused, even if my second brother never returns; and, unfortunately, until today he never returned.

RH: Where did he go?

AA: He was imprisoned for six months in a Hebron prison. He was transferred to Jordan and stayed there, and never allowed to come back, even for the funerals of my parents.... My mother was a midwife and a wonderful woman. Part of my theatre came from there. If she was in another country, she would have been a great actress. So, this is the teaching part of my Islamic faith, part of the family life that I was in, and part of the culture. People negotiated things in families. The elder resolved the issues. Even today a lot of things are resolved this way.

RH: The community was more important than the individual.

AA: Yes, and there was a social code for people about what is shameful.... Faith has given me a lot of peace. I was never keen on weapons and I never used a weapon and my father, either. He never was involved in any way in an armed struggle. The one who was exiled was accused of being part of the Popular Front. Someone confessed against him; he never confessed anything.

RH: And he is still in prison?

AA: Yes. You know that Jordan is our only passageway when we travel outside. And, of course, patience is a big part of my parents' example. My parents lost 10 children out of 14. Four girls and six boys died; now, we are only four boys living. And so, losing 10 children and still having this faith and patience and belief is extraordinary. At the same time, I could see that my father was imprisoned by this fear of what comes next.

RH: He was fearful?

AA: He was fearful for us, when we went out. He was always at the door saying, "Don't be late. Where are you going?"

AA: And also, he said, "Do you think that's the end of it? 1948 and 1967 are not very good." He was never in any political party. All my living brothers were not engaged in any political party.

RH: Faith was much more central than politics?

AA: Faith, and we had politics in a sense, but not under the umbrella of any political party. I never saw that any party meant priority to people and the country. They are more focused on small things that concern the parties. I don't see any political party that gives priorities to the people.

RH: I have had many conversations with people about the Palestinian Authority....

AA: It is really pitiful, especially after 2006, with the segregation between Hamas and the Palestinian Authority [and with] shooting each other. It is horrible, and does not serve us in any way. [They] talk about unity when it's in their interest. That is why I work with everybody, but not under the umbrella of anybody. And I refuse to be part of any party.

RH: That gives you a lot of freedom.

AA: The ability to be critical as well. And also, it means that you do not have money from anybody, but at least you are truthful to yourself.

RH: Tell me about your artistic strategies and your theatre sources. Were you deeply influenced by the French and by the generation of 1967–68?

AA: In Palestine, it was really new. Even when we talked about civil disobedience, it was mainly on political action and demonstrations and confrontations with the Israelis on refusing to pay taxes, throwing stones, or burning tires. After 1967, there was an active movement of artwork and songs and poetry, and to a lesser extent theatre. There were a lot of times when we were doing plays or professional actors were doing plays in the 1970s. Actors were arrested and imprisoned or made to [promise] not to perform again ever. I was very much influenced by French theatre, more modern ones than the classical theatre, [but] I was even training within the classical theatre.

RH: Shakespeare? Moliere?

AA: To a lesser extent Moliere. The people I worked with liked Racine, Shakespeare's *Twelfth Night*, and *Romeo and Juliet*. I performed *Andromache*, with Racine again.

RH: So how did you move from classical theatre to the theatre of resistance?

AA: We started our own theatre group in Paris in 1988. We created our own plays. I was the only Palestinian, and Arab even, with mostly French actors. Some were Jewish or Christian. All of us were very young. [We wore] things that represented us and our communities. For me the issue was being Palestinian, and talking about my country, but in a way that everybody agreed. We were five co-writers for the play and 12 or 13 actors. We wrote pieces and connected them together. One of the things that I wrote was about an immigrant Palestinian who says that he forgot everything about his country and he started saying exactly what he forgot.

RH: That sounds like Darwish's poetry.

AA: In 1989 or 1990, this shocked a lot of Jewish audiences. But the director said, "This is what we have. If they like it, then great; if they don't, then that's their problem." Of course, Ionesco was a great influence. So we were starting to become more and more engaged on a political level with the power of theatre to make a change. We started on the level of the individual, building peace within before talking about building it with anybody else. That was an important way for me to start building peace because it does not come from [demanding], "You should make peace. You should be together." [In] some organizations.... Palestinian children and Israeli children have a good time and then return everybody to his corner and nothing has changed.

RH: And then the Israeli children go into the army.

AA: The [theatre] concept was new at that time. Up until today it creates an impact and people believe that they can go and change the world. Or, they are going to go and shoot everybody else or explode themselves or burn themselves to stay alive because in a refugee camp like Aida, where there are about 6,000 people, 66% are under 24 years old. [There are] no playgrounds or green spaces and [they are] surrounded by the Israeli army.

RH: 66% of 6,000 people?

AA: 6,000. They originate from 41 different villages. Three days ago, the Israeli army comes and tear gasses us. They came into the center of the camp at four in the morning. They broke in our main door. They broke in the door to the roof.

RH: Four o'clock in the morning? Why?

AA: They came to arrest the son of our neighbor, his third son to be arrested in the last three months. He was injured while trying to save another young man who was injured in one of the confrontations. He was not really involved in anything except that he was trying to pull someone who was shot to safety. Here it is enough if somebody says, "You did something." Or, "We suspect that you did something." So, you are guilty even if you are innocent.

RH: Because everything is stacked against a young person like that?

AA: [In Aida Camp,] we started with theatre, but not everyone wants to do theatre, so we have dance, photography, video to hold the camera, not always in front of it, activities with kindergarten, with schools, with parents. We do a lot of stuff with mothers and with women because I believe it is the women who change the world more than the men.

RH: Yes, interesting.

AA: In order to make a long-term change, the community should be involved, mothers and other women should be involved. Also, our touring groups are a mobile, beautiful resistance—the theatre training, dance training, music, or photography. We go to libraries and all over the West Bank, ending with a program where we manufacture games. We also try to renovate educational levels so that education could be fun, not just memorization. We teach them to ask questions.

RH: So, you are able to travel all over the West Bank?

AA: Yeah, and to tour internationally, since the year 2000, with our theatre group. It was the first professionally trained children's theatre troupe in Palestine at that time. Touring internationally was important because it was a way to show them normal life in different countries.

RH: That's absolutely crucial.

AA: Also to connect with others. To look at each other as equal human beings, potential partners, not as potential enemies. To see that we share a lot of things which bring us closer to each other and also see that we have our differences. For me, the differences are beautiful—what a beautiful gift that you could have to enrich us and not marginalize us and make us afraid of each other. So, my main worry was how to save lives and inspire hope in such times of death and despair; how to give our children and young people the ability to express themselves, and change the world without needing to carry a weapon and shoot everybody else.

RH: Do you work with games or other storytelling forms to draw stories out of the young people?

AA: In the beginning, mostly my interest was to get their stories. Some stories took three to four years to come out.

RH: Because they were so buried?

AA: Yes, because as Palestinians, our personal narratives are buried beneath the collective narrative. So, your personal narrative seems meaningless compared to big narratives. So, when you ask children, "What is your dream?" and they say, "Liberation of Palestine," so the little me doesn't exist a lot of the time. Palestinians mostly have a collective voice. We say, "We do this," not, "I do this."

RH: I have a friend in Chicago; when I asked about his personal experiences in Palestine, he would talk about his village.

AA: Of course; self-consciousness is shaped, for us, in our collective narrative. It took me a long time [to change]. Realizing "I" came about in 2005–2006 for me, when I came into Ashoka. Ashoka is in the U.S., actually. They find people who they call "social entrepreneurs" who have a creative idea that has an impact on the community that can be replicated elsewhere. You would be nominated for this organization by someone and it is your idea, it is an original idea, and you are trustworthy, you are morally "clean," not corrupted, you are not in the government. It was started in India by an American named Bill Drayton, a Harvard graduate, who moved Ashoka to the U.S. in 1990. They have a long process of assuring that you are actually a social entrepreneur and that you are the originator of this idea. "What did you do?" "We?" "If you are you, then I is not a 'we.'" In the beginning, it wasn't easy.

RH: So, do you work mostly from community stories and experiences or do you combine contemporary work with adaptations of older work?

AA: There are different levels. When we work with children, it is based on encouraging them to speak, because their stories need to get out; and building peace within means that they think of life's worth. As parents or as human beings, we will want to see our children grow up and go on to celebrate their lives and their successes. So, it was important to get things out, whether through activities, storytelling, games, or even the supportive education program for children who have difficulties in learning. Part of the difficulties were health issues; they did not see well or they did not hear well. Their parents don't know how to read or write. Our children are in the streets at 2:30 in the morning. The parents are working day and night and so nobody is taking care of the children. So, we have worked in plays that we created like *Handala*. Are you familiar with *Handala*?

RH: Yes.

AA: I adapted the cartoons of *Naji Al-Ali* into a theatre play. And these are also parts of this beautiful resistance work, drawings, and cartoons. And the symbol of Handala should not be hijacked by political groups like the Popular Front. Naji was also not part of a political party. He criticized anybody who deviated from Palestine, whether it is Palestinian or Arab or American or whoever. We also worked together with some other theatre groups, American or French. In 2011, we did a collaboration with a French group on *Facts*, the play. *Facts* was a play performed in 2011–2012 about an American archeologist who was killed in Jerusalem in the early '90s. He established the archeological department at Birzeit University, and his death remains a mystery. The author Arthur Milner, who is Jewish-Canadian, made this story and made it happen in Hebron and made the suspect of the killing a settler from the illegal colony of Karyat Arba in Hebron. The investigation is carried out by an Israeli and a Palestinian officer, which is, of course, a complete fiction.

RH: But it is a good device for getting out of the whole situation.

AA: So, his main focus was to show the two sides of Jews. The religious fanatic and …

RH: Those who want the truth.

AA: Not even the truth; the other who tried to portray themselves as the non-fanatic and still supports the occupation. This is a struggle between them. The settler said to him, "You are not even a Jew." And then he said to him, "What do you mean I am not a Jew? I am circumcised…." This Zionist settler also looked at the Palestinian and said, "This is our land. God gave us this land." At the end, the Israeli worked to falsify evidence to frame the settler because he hates settlers. The Palestinian refuses to play the game and said Well, it was not people like him who occupied us; it was people like you Zionists, when they came to make the desert bloom. We're not even talking about religion….

RH: Zionism is still deeply rooted in the whole culture.

AA: This is part of the problem, but not the whole issue. In 2013, the play *Intimate Brothers* was made by a French writer and director. It was a documentary film, so she had interviews or read interviews with different Palestinians and Israelis and put them on stage. Israeli characters are very easy to identify; her Palestinian characters are very vague. The only character in between is Juliano Mer-Khamis. She had, among the clear Israeli characters, Ms. Holocaust. I don't know if you are familiar with this competition of beauty queens—Ms. Holocaust, in 1998.

RH: Was that a satire?

AA: It really happened. In 1998, in Haifa, they made a competition to name a Miss Holocaust.

RH: That's bizarre.

AA: It is bizarre. This Miss Holocaust made a speech, and in her speech she said, "We [Jews] have suffered, so leave us this Israel. You [Palestinians] have a lot of countries to go to." One of the founders of Breaking the Silence in Israel is an organization that enabled us to talk about what was happening. So, the Israeli characters are well defined somehow and when you hear the Israeli who created Breaking the Silence, he seems more Palestinian than a Palestinian. But the other Palestinian characters are not equal artistically or even humanly.

RH: Where are the actors drawn from—all over, or are most from within Aida Camp?

AA: Not from the camp, but from all around, because we work in different areas. Actors come from all over—Bethlehem mostly, but some from Hebron and some from East Jerusalem.

RH: So, your work occurs at many different levels. You are deeply involved in day-to-day education and theatre games and then professional theatre.

AA: We start with five- and six-year-olds. We do work in kindergartens and sometimes the schools come here. In one year there are 6,000 to 8,000 children who come here for different activities. With mobile Beautiful Resistance, we also reach 40,000 to 50,000 people all over the West Bank.

RH: When was the last time that you were in the United States?

AA: My last time was in March and April, when I directed *The Diary of Anne Frank* for Burning Coal Theater in North Carolina, in Raleigh.

RH: Yes, I read about that. Have you ever come to Chicago?

AA: I did. I came for the first time to Chicago in November 2013.

RH: I teach a course once a year called Performance and Social Change. So, the next time you come, I want to be sure to be a part of the conversation.

AA: That would be great. I was invited to speak to students in two schools and one university.

RH: Chicago is a great theatre town. We have over 200 producing theatres in Chicago. Many of them are storefront theatres, very small, but a lot of creative work is being done.

AA: We did not tour in Chicago. Hopefully next time. We toured 2005 and 2009 on the east coast.

RH: So, what is the vision? Has anything changed since the recent war in Gaza? Has your perspective changed? Is your perspective one of tragedy, comedy, tragi-comedy?

AA: Comedy is the biggest challenge for responding to this oppression; and at the same time, honor those who died justly and … for the realization of their cause. Theatre remains one of the most amazing, powerful tools that we could use to tell stories and make people connect on a human level. The arts have such power to make people as naked human beings in their consciousness and make them look at things with their hearts … and to change. It works both ways—for the audience and for the persons themselves.

I believe, also, that injustice cannot dominate the world and that great civilizations come and go, and great dictatorships come and go, great occupations come and go, and people stay. This is a constant. We fought against the Ottomans, even as Muslims, because it was an injustice. We fought against British Christians because it was an injustice. We fight against this Zionist occupation because it is an injustice. These are not fights against Muslims or Christians or Jews. Regardless of who is doing what, oppression is oppression, and it doesn't matter who is part of what religion or ethnicity. We have resisted the persecution of our identity and culture for hundreds and thousands of years. Now we resist the Israeli state. Even as a Muslim, I cannot say Palestine is only for Muslims, or Christians, or Jews. It doesn't work.

RH: Diversity is very important for all of us.

AA: In every place where you go. You cannot go to Bethlehem and say, "This is Muslim only." Or go to Jerusalem and say, "This is only Muslim." Everybody has a part. So, nobody has the monopoly to say, "This is mine and everybody else go to hell."

RH: I have read a few essays about biological diversity, and the more biological diversity you have, the better the ecosystem. So, culture has some parallels with that.

AA: It does, it does. Specifically here. People through history look at the U.S. and ask, What is a typical American? You came from everywhere. You are a young nation, 200 years. So, when people say, "We Americans," their grandfather probably was Italian or Greek or Polish.

RH: My grandfather was German American.

AA: Or German or Palestinian or Brazilian or whatever.

RH: That is what my book is about—that people have the capacity to change. If you are born Jewish or Palestinian, that doesn't determine your future.

AA: I am the same. When I was 14 or 15, I started reading the Bible—the Old Testament, the New Testament—as well as Buddha, and Confucius. I read a lot of things because I wanted to. I was seeking for why being a Muslim means that you are imprisoned in a system. Even when you look at Islam. All of the Qur'an is based on questions: "Don't you see?" "Don't you understand?" "Don't you think about it?" "Don't you question it?"—always questioning. God does not like people to just adore him in all ignorance and say, "Because He said so." No, He wants you to have full consciousness in adoring Him, with full understanding of why you do that. But not like ISIS, what they are doing, and saying it is in the name of Islam; or the Crusaders, claiming the name of Christianity, while their actions have no basis in religion.

RH: It is a corruption or a distortion.

AA: It is a distortion of the whole thing, like what Zionism is doing in the name of Judaism, with all the pain, sympathy and empathy going to the Jews. But we were not the cause of their suffering, so why should we pay for the crimes of the Nazis or the Holocaust? We cannot. And even though Jesus was born here, we cannot continue to turn our cheeks to flak from everyone and say we are fine with it; we are not. We are not superheroes and we do not want to carry the burden of humiliating the Jews.

At the same time, we also have a heritage to leave behind us. We are fortunate to get this possibility as actors, as artists, as educators. To leave a better heritage for our children than what we have inherited. I guess my worst nightmare is that one of my children or your children would come and look me in the face and say, "What did you do to make a change? What heritage are you leaving us?" Shall we feel shameful and say, "I thought Obama would do it. Or Queen Elizabeth or the pope or even God"? Even God will not help those who will not help themselves.

RH: We have a responsibility to use whatever gifts we have been given for liberation.

AA: That is why I made the choice for quitting my job in biology in 2005, and thinking that I can do better for the world through theatre and art and education.

RH: Are any of your scripts online or available in English?

AA: There are some; *Handala* has an English version. *We are the Children of the Camp* was the first big production that we did and toured with in many countries. In 2005 I cowrote a play with Naomi Wallace and Lisa Stressinger, *Twenty-One Positions*, which was commissioned by the Guthrie Theatre. Some people said it was not "balanced"; so, it was performed at Lincoln Center in New York [Broadway Play Publishing, 2015]. This is a story about two Palestinian young people who are born in the U.S. and decide to come here to discover the occupation. It has Israeli characters and Palestinian characters, even the architect of the Wall [Dany Tirza].

RH: There really are an endless number of stories. Endless.

AA: We are preparing for two other plays for the professional group: *Tales of the City by the Sea* is about the siege in Gaza, when boats were bringing solidarity groups; the other play is a friendship story, *The Silence of the Sea,* about fighting the Nazis in France in the 1940s.

RH: Thank you so much for the dialogue.

AA: It was my pleasure.

8 The Lessons of Engagement

Ghassan Andoni

Ghassan Andoni is a physics professor, a brilliant community organizer, and a peace activist. In response to the first intifada (1987–1991) and the second intifada (2000–20005), Andoni cofounded the International Solidarity Movement (ISM) and the Center for Rapprochement in Beit Sahour. Andoni is widely known for his leadership of the tax revolt and community organizing during the first intifada. In 2006, the American Friends Service Committee nominated Ghassan Andoni and Jeff Halper to share the Nobel Peace Prize.

Birzeit University, 2006

GA: My name is Ghasson Andoni. I am the director of public relations at Birzeit University, cofounder of the Palestinian Centre for Rapprochement (PCR), cofounder of the International Solidarity Movement (ISM) and the Alternative Tourism Group (ATG).

RH: I'm fascinated with how people come to do what they do. I know that you are a master storyteller; so, tell me where you were born, family experiences, and major turning points.

GA: I was born in the little town of Beit Sahour in 1956 to a Christian family and raised until the age of six in that town. And then we moved to Amman, Jordan, due to my father's work.

RH: That would have been the early 1960s?

GA: Yes, 1962. As I moved to Jordan, I moved also from being in private Christian schools into public schools. So, I got the opportunity—I think I was the only Christian in the school—to be raised among Muslims, among refugees, among real kids in a diverse community. In fourth grade I started being very fascinated with Islam and the Koran. By the age of 12 I memorized [major parts of] the Koran.

When I was a teenager, after 1967, the environment in Jordan changed very much. The modern Palestinian armed revolution started to be more obvious, especially in the Al Hussein refugee camp which I lived close to. Even if I was a middle-class kid, I lived with people in poverty. You would [see] a family crowded in one room without any other facilities. That poverty was hard to understand. I was fascinated by those who showed up there, sometimes holding guns,

DOI: 10.4324/9781003262817-10

and always talking about Palestine and a "lost paradise." I was of an age to understand but not fully apprehend the situation. From that time I have been closely looking at what's happening in my own country rather than in Jordan. Why is this happening? For what? In 1967, when the war happened, I was the only member of my family visiting my grandmother in Beit Sahour. I got caught by the war. That was my first idea, my first shock of the real conflict between Israel and the Palestinians. Those were my first scenes of bombardment, of the army taking over, curfews imposed, and fear....

RH: So very early on, critical questions began to form?

GA: Lots of them. You cannot but get involved somehow because everybody was involved, visiting, looking, knowing people who are part of the resistance, admiring some people and regretting others. You are raised in this environment where things are going on around you and you cannot but notice them and interact with them. But still a young 13- or 14-year-old kid was more confused than actually understanding what's happening.

In 1970, Black September happened and I was living in Amman, Jordan, and I lived for the first time in Syria's war environment. Our home was destroyed from bombardments by the Jordanian Army. Because we were living close to the refugee camp, we were more targeted than other places in Jordan. My father's car was smashed and destroyed. As a family, we almost lost everything that my father worked hard for his entire life. Then, after the Jordanian army managed to take control over Amman, the Jordanian army arrested everybody from the age of 13 to 18. So I was the first time arrested together with my father for 14 days in a desert detention camp.

RH: King Hussein arrested everybody?

GA: Yes. That was hard and confusing....

RH: Were you accused of something specific?

GA: No. I don't think they had time to check everybody. So I think it was more of a punishment for hosting troublemakers among us....

RH: Collective punishment.

GA: Yeah, if you collect everybody from 13 to 18, then by no means are you selective. Of course they were looking at your shoulder to see if it has any mark of holding a gun. They were looking for signs of involvement and treating more severely young adults than others. The conditions were harsh and you have to fight to get water to drink or food to eat. The level of humiliation was high. There are things that you can never forget about such experiences. It was impossible for us as a family to continue living in Amman, so we came back to Beit Sahour.

RH: You had been in Amman for—

GA: Eight years.... Those two major incidents in my life—prison and the '67 war—influenced me deeply.... We moved back in 1970, and I continued my schooling in Bethlehem. During my senior year when we take the big exam called the *tawjihi,* the Israelis arrested me on September third at midnight. So my first time in prison was in 1972.

RH: First time in an Israeli prison?

GA: Yeah, in an Israeli prison. Of course, we were active as students in terms of discussing what's happening; and sometimes I'd go to demonstrations to show that there is something wrong happening here and to confirm that we are Palestinians. I spent four months in jail. I think that the main purpose of arresting me among other students was to punish us and deprive us from taking the *tawjihi* exam.

RH: You began to see a larger pattern of harassment and disruption?

GA: I was getting glimpses of "You can't have normal dreams of what you want in the future, how much money you will gain, and when are you going to get married." I started seeing there is something much bigger that needs to be dealt with. And it can harshly disrupt your life and block your dreams. So from that time on I became more serious about [saying], "You cannot be a third party to this conflict. It's in you. It's invading all aspects of your life."

RH: So you moved abruptly from high school to prison?

GA: Yeah. I was released from prison just one month before the final exam, the *tawjihi,* and that was [my] first challenge. I said, I'm going to sit through that exam and I am not going to allow them to disrupt my life. So I did. I gained a very high grade that surprised many. At that time there were no universities in the Occupied Territories.

RH: Birzeit was not open at that point?

GA: No. Birzeit was a college, not a university, and they were not offering [what I needed]. So I decided to go to Baghdad to get my first university degree in physics. I really fell in love with Iraq. It was probably the Golden Age of Iraq, with wonderful people, warm, very hospitable, having a high level of dignity. I really explored Iraqi society. I developed deep relations with Kurds, Shiites, Sunnis, all of them. Up to the end of my studies, things were okay. Things started changing in Iraq when Saddam Hussein took power.

RH: Were you there when he came to power?

GA: Yes. In the last year I was in Baghdad, he became the power in Iraq. It was evident that the vice president, not the president, was the one who had everything in his hand. You could see rising levels of enmity and brutality. I hated this change. During my study in Baghdad, another dramatic thing happened in my life, the civil war in Lebanon in 1975. I realized that it's not possible for me to *not* be part of this, especially with the massacres of Palestinian refugees. So I volunteered to go to Lebanon and be with my people and try to help as much as I can. I left my studies in 1976 and spent three months in Lebanon. It was a very dangerous trip. I was lucky to escape being killed during the trip. Many of my friends were killed.

RH: Were you in Sabra and Shatila [refugee camps] or elsewhere?

GA: When the massacre happened in the Tel al-Zaatar refugee camp (near Beirut), I was in Shatila camp. I was one of the people who received the survivors. All of them were women, children, or very elderly people. Nobody else managed to arrive. And that's a very tough scar inside me. That period was a very hard period in terms of what I experienced. It left so many questions unanswered in my mind. At that time, I realized that much of what was happening was meaningless, and I started very much questioning, Are we controlling the gun, or is the gun controlling us? And I talked to so many leaders and I said, what is it that we are doing here? If things are so out of hand, everybody who's not solid in his norms and ethics will sometimes get seduced to do things that destroy the whole picture around the ones who fight for freedom.

RH: You get a disconnect between ends and means?

GA: You know, people are not motivated by reality. People are motivated by myths. Reality does not motivate anybody. But images do—heroic, ethical, sacrificing—those images actually motivate you to join and be part of it.

RH: People are working inside a myth that is not deeply connected to reality.

GA: Yes. [If] there is a severe contradiction between myth and reality, then you feel as if you are stuck somewhere that is meaningless and you don't feel belonging there. It has nothing to do with fear or safety. But it has to do with [feeling] this is not what it should be.

RH: After your experience in Lebanon, what was your next major turning point?

GA: I started questioning whether the basics of the modern Palestinian revolution were correct. I realized that there must be something else where I belonged.

RH: You had to stay engaged, but the question was how?

GA: Yes, I felt that there was a problem in the engagement process. So I went back to Baghdad, continued my studies, graduated, and decided to come back and live in occupied Palestine at the end of 1977. The Israelis arrested me ten days after I arrived. They interrogated me for three months and then released me because they couldn't prove any of the charges against me. It was a very tough period.

RH: Did that include physical torture?

GA: I experienced severe physical torture in 1972. In 1977 I experienced torture of a different sort—not severe but very painful and prolonged—being locked into a small cabinet for long periods of time, forced to stand with a sack on my face for days and days, little beatings but not severe ones. This was mostly focused around psychological torture and inflicting a level of pain that, if prolonged, could crack you. I went out of interrogation without marks on my body, as happened in 1972, but with so much damage inside. Eight or nine months later, I was arrested again and went through the same course. That time they managed to prove that I was in Lebanon. So, I was sentenced to two years in prison, and I lived in prison for a long time. It's another world. It's extremely important to live that experience. It gets you to understand more about yourself, your society, the potential that exists. And it's not your impression about prisons in the States. Here it's more of a tough life but organized and educational.

RH: It's a profound social experience.

GA: Yeah. It's like living in a military camp where discipline, education, and training are important. You have a mini-state that organizes your life but then you have a big oppressor that always steps in and tries to mess that up and create chaos and inflict fear and pain. So it's this combination that you have to find your way through, live the challenge, also live the harmony, and contribute to processes that are taking place.

RH: So now you're in your mid-20s....

GA: I managed to get a scholarship and went to the UK to do my master's degree and then came back and started working at Birzeit University.

RH: You began teaching?

GA: Yes. At that time, I was much more confused than any other time in my life because I already lost part of this myth, and I couldn't find the way to connect again. So I focused more on my work, my study, and my future, which was obviously difficult because I struggled with every step of my life. After a year at Birzeit, I contracted at Amsterdam University to go and do my Ph.D. Suddenly I realized that I'm not allowed to travel.

RH: Describe the myth that you said was dissolving for you.

GA: My myth was around this (idea) that a free Palestine is paradise. And we need to regain paradise, where we can live in freedom, where we can have an opportunity to compete with others, and show the world how good and effective Palestinians are. To achieve that there was this image of the freedom fighter, the sacrificing, morally advanced person. And the revolution will organize people. The whole picture of the means and ends.

RH: The pure liberation.

GA: That wasn't me only. That was our generation. This is what motivated us. Because I had problems with this, because I couldn't find a solution, I started looking to invest in me. My priorities shifted and I wanted to focus on continuing my studies. But I was blacklisted from 1984 until 1993 and I was totally banned from traveling.

Then all of us were surprised by the first *intifada* [in 1987]. There I managed to find some answers to the many questions in my mind. I kept the work at Birzeit, but whatever time I had I focused on this new phenomenon and how to develop that as an effective tool of fighting the occupation. For the first time, I saw real civilian-based, popular resistance emerging without anybody designing it.

RH: A grassroots movement.

GA: Yes, it was a grassroots movement.

RH: It began in Gaza and moved up into the West Bank?

GA: An incident happened at the border of Gaza, and then clashes started in Gaza. In two or three weeks everything went into flames. You could see lots of creativity, lots of grassroots work, lots of new methods. I got really interested. In Beit Sahour we started moving to total civil disobedience as a way to force the occupation to lose control, or at least help crack up the system that imposes this military occupation on us. There are plenty of stories. Probably you have heard most of them.

RH: Give examples of the civil disobedience.

GA: It had two parts. The first part was organizational. We managed to divide the town into 35 neighborhoods and [organized] four main central committees to run the town. I was a member of the central committee that was in charge of the town, and we claimed independence [from Israel]. We started establishing the basis of our *sumud* or sustainability....

Because Israel closed the schools for years and years, we opened schools. We operated an educational system with 40 underground schools. Because Beit Sahour is not a farming place, we started victory gardens, teaching people how to sustain themselves, how to plant [vegetables] instead of flowers, and how to raise rabbits and chickens. We also started running our own medical system. We started first aid, organized teams of doctors, and then found money to build Beit Sahour Medical Center, which is one of the most advanced. From the agriculture work, we established the Applied Research Institute, which is one of the major applied research institutes in the region. We started a Rapprochement Center, and started working out our system of communication with Israelis and international media.

RH: The Rapprochement Center began during the first *intifada*?

GA: Yes, and we also started running our own judicial system. We started having courts and saying, Whoever makes mistakes will be fined. We started replacing entirely the system of occupation in that little town. And that was combined always with protests, marches....

RH: Tax resistance?

GA: Yeah. We started tax resistance because we believed that this was the peak of total civil disobedience. We also threw away our military identity cards. So we started with all of those steps.... The Israelis accused me of being the mastermind of this tax revolt, that our end is to establish an independent state, and said they are going to crack this. What they said was somehow true, but I think it was much more collective than one person or two persons, because none of us could do it without this level of community work.

RH: But you were a crucial part of the leadership.

GA: Yeah, I was a part of the leadership, [but] because of that, I turned into being useless because I have been most of the time arrested or under day arrest. I was so proctored that by the summer of 1988 I was almost useless. I took the file of international Israeli relations and I was still organizing and talking, but in terms of actual resistance in the community, when everything happened there, I was in jail.

RH: What was the focus of the Rapprochement Center?

GA: The focus for the Rapprochement Center was the outreach of the town, building relations with internationals and opening channels of communication with Israeli leaders, trying to examine whether it's viable to have allies from the enemy side. Can you have Israelis who you can identify with?

RH: With whatever Israeli peace movement there was?

GA: Whoever was willing to cross the border and to separate between Israel and the occupation and then be willing to say, I will do that little bit against the occupation. At that time we were functioning from this standpoint of hope, that we can solve this problem; we can have two states. This could achieve something very inspiring. We believed that it is possible. So much of what we did, we did without thinking of survival afterwards. We were ready to take huge risks, to invest all of our effort, energy, and people into that matter. And we needed to make it sustainable because it is impossible that you can arrive at a just peace during a short period of time. I am talking about years, not months or weeks. That's why everybody was in the battlefield.

RH: I understand.

GA: I believe there were so many achievements, but there was a total political and diplomatic failure afterwards. The concept of separation, that in our point of view was a two-state solution, paved the way politically and diplomatically into a separation that's more demographic, discriminatory, apartheid-like. That's what happened afterwards. I was extremely disappointed.

RH: I assume that you had optimism when the Oslo process began?

GA: No, I personally took a very strong stand against Oslo from the beginning.

RH: Really, you were able to see—

GA: Yes. So many friends accused me of being radical, not actually working for peace, disguised as a peacemaker.... because I couldn't fake [support for] Oslo. Nevertheless, during the Oslo period I spared no effort in trying to develop Palestinian society, including establishing the Alternative Tourism Group, the Applied Research Institute, and in developing Rapprochement as an organization with a vision and projects....

RH: So you stayed very grounded?

GA: I stayed very engaged. I was so disappointed, but I stayed very engaged.... When the recent crisis erupted—

RH: The second *intifada*?

GA: The second *intifida*. I started seriously looking at methods of engagement in such a violent conflict. I started working with the idea of establishing a group that is more offensive in its nonviolent resistance. From there came the idea of nonviolent direct actions and the establishment of the ISM [International Solidarity Movement] and all the work that probably you know about.

RH: For you, had nonviolent resistance been part of an existential philosophy or more of a strategy?

GA: For me, it was my only comfort. I wanted to engage in the conflict but I found it hard to engage in the norms that existed. I started looking at the concept of civil resistance. Since Lebanon, I swear to myself that I will never hold a gun in my life. I will never use violence against anybody. My commitment is to engage in a civilian-based grassroots movement rather than in a selected or elite [group].

RH: So you can provide leadership and analysis while staying very close to the grassroots?

GA: When I engage, I am usually in the front lines. But I realized that it's hard for me to be in the front lines because I felt that we lost the direction and there is no strategic long-term benefit of this right now. So I started seeing that it was great to have ISM, but this is not a tool possible to lead Palestinians. Regardless of the name and saying that this is Palestinian land, in reality, most of ISM's functionality depended on internationals. So my choice was to act more with my people, not as isolated communities, but with the national bodies—like university students, like people affiliated with national bodies, like Fatah. And this is what I'm trying to spend energy on these days, rather than spending my energy with internationals.

RH: I understand.

GA: I want to focus efforts in another direction. I can't really be on the leading [edge] of ISM, and therefore I shouldn't give myself the privilege of being the leader or planner. I should provide support and guidance, but people under struggle should run the struggle from A to Z.

RH: So ISM began in 2000?

GA: December 2000.

RH: It continues, but other people are running with that?

GA: Yes. I also gave the Alternative Tourism Group to young people fully, and I'm on the board only. And I gave Rapprochement to other people and said, I'm not the executive anymore; this is your work.

RH: So how would you define your personal focus at the moment?

GA: At the moment I am trying my best to work very closely with the student body [at Birzeit University]. I managed to make some breakthroughs here. The whole idea is to open different alternatives and get them to do useful things that make them realize that there is so much [more] in organized grassroots work than you think. The whole struggle is not based on heroic actions; it's not based on the glorious fighter. You cannot just contract people to fight for you. You have to join, join fully or provide [at least] part of your time. When you add all of those parts together, it becomes big. I am trying to get them involved in projects that have a national meaning, that seek freedom, that have a potential to make their lives and respect for themselves better. It's a long process, but I believe it's an extremely needed process.

RH: It's a process that will help to sustain the movement for the long haul?

GA: Hopefully. I am not really looking at that at this moment. I have shifted from working with a selected group of Palestinians and internationals to stepping into the dynamic of the community. And those are totally different.

RH: The dynamic of community?

GA: Yes, the community has its own dynamic. What you need to do is to step into that. As you step there you have to become part of this dynamic, and then you might be able to influence this, you might not be able to influence it. You might be influenced by it. In a way that's an open option

RH: It's a very dialogical process.

GA: Yes, it's not really a plan. It's an experiment.

RH: Yes, it's a process.

GA: And that's why I cannot really talk about a strategy of mine right now. I have started a process and I'd like to see how this process, develops.

RH: How do you understand the situation at the moment for the larger Palestinian community in relationship to Israel, to "facts on the ground," the Wall, closures, checkpoints, the legal system, all of it?

GA: For Palestinians, with all of what you described right now, the idea of a two-state solution has been damaged fully, and I doubt it can be revived. Palestinians are convinced that Israel has destroyed this, and therefore why continue running after a ghost?

RH: They have killed it.

GA: Yes, they have killed it. Most Palestinians are convinced that right now we are not fighting for a two-state solution, but we are fighting to not allow them to implement what they want to implement. And therefore, there is no target you want to arrive at.

RH: You have the process of resistance.

GA: That's it. This is a process of resistance, not a [specific] target.

RH: I have talked extensively to Jeff Halper, who is frustrated, and says he keeps waiting for Palestinians to provide a vision [for the peace movement]. Is it unfair for him to ask for something specific under these difficult circumstances?

RA: It's not possible right now. It's not possible. For Palestinians, what is happening right now is resistance to [Israeli plans], but there is nothing beyond that. You cannot start a process of resistance and define an outcome, because it's not clear. The only outcome that could unify a majority of Palestinians was the concept of two states. That was possible. At least 70 to 80% of Palestinians were convinced that this is the suitable solution to the problem, taking into consideration other Palestinian rights in Jerusalem or for refugees. But that target (of two states) is not on the table anymore. This is dead, and there is [only] something that they want to stop.

RH: At some point some new image or metaphor may emerge.

GA: Yes, that's true. You can never tell what will come out of that [process]. This is exactly why the conflict needs to cross borders. Because here there is no prospect for a solution; there is an endless fight. Crossing borders is what we saw in Lebanon [in 2006]. The conflict crossed borders. And it could cross more borders until it creates the metaphor needed.

RH: It can be a violent conflict, or it could also become a nonviolent process.

GA: Hopefully.

RH: It might have more possibility for resolution?

GA: It depends from which angle you look at it. Most people right now are looking at the military-strategic aspect of the conflict....

RH: What is the particular role for the nonviolence movement, for education, your work with the university, for other NGOs?

GA: Look, it's not a dominant role, it's an important role. Right now, you want to identify what side you belong to. To me this is clear. I'm on the Palestinian side. Identify the field you want to work in, the field where people are resisting collective punishment. You keep doing useful things, rather than looking for strategies. And give an eye to what potential this conflict is creating. I don't think you can go beyond this.

RH: You stay alert to possibilities.

GA: Yes, you stay alert to possibilities, you keep doing good things, and you consider yourself as complementary to whatever grassroots resistance that exists in Palestine.

RH: When did the American Friends Service Committee nominate you for a Nobel Peace Prize?

GA: This year [2006].

RH: How did that make you feel?

GA: I felt grateful. I wasn't consulted. I'm proud that they thought of me as eligible for nomination. It feels out of place to be talking about peace in such an environment in the Middle East. I never hunted for appreciation. I was trying to promote my cause, my people.

RH: A final question. Is hope a useful concept? Are there processes that give you hope?

GA: Right now I don't see them, honestly. It's always good to be hopeful but never allow the work to create illusions for you. If you are not hopeful, you don't engage.

RH: So hope is in the commitment, and you just continue?

GA: Yes; if you believe in the good in humans, good will happen sometime, somewhere. You have to be ready for that. You can see with your engagement that you are making hope real. If you are out of the scene, others will do whatever they believe is right and you won't be there. So it's important to be engaged. That's the most precious lesson I learned in my entire life.

RH: *Shukran.*

GA: *Shukran.*

9 Jewish Tradition and Human Rights

Arik Ascherman

For 21 years, Arik Ascherman worked with Rabbis for Human Rights, serving as executive director from 1998 to 2016. In December 2017, Rabbi Ascherman created a new organization, Torat Tzedek-Torah of Justice, to pursue his vision of justice and human rights. He has been arrested many times while trying to prevent a house demolition or other injustice. For Rabbi Ascherman, human-rights work must involve one's body as well as dialogue.

Jerusalem, May 2003

RH: People with the same background often go in very different directions. Where did you start in terms of family experiences, and what were the turning points to arrive here?

AA: I was interested in becoming a rabbi since about age seven. I said, I'm special, and only Jews can be rabbis, so that is special.

RH: Where was this?

AA: This was in Erie, Pennsylvania.... I was going to become an Orthodox rabbi and live on a kibbutz here in Israel.... By the time of my bar mitzvah ... what was increasingly significant to me was the ethical and moral aspects of the Jewish tradition, and issues of social justice.

RH: Can you give us a couple of the major changes?

AA: I got a political education at Harvard University. Those were the years of the anti-apartheid movement. I spent more time in protests and with the Jewish community than I did in class.

RH: So there was already a strong ethical foundation based on your Jewish upbringing.

AA: The lessons that I had from my parents, rabbis, and teachers was that a basic part of being a Jew was to be concerned with universal human rights and social justice. One of my greatest shocks coming to Israel was finding out that not all Israelis thought ... the way that I did as I grew up. A North American Jewish survey showed that of all the different measures of Jewish identity, more Jews identified with [the] connection between Judaism and social justice.

RH: What were the lessons that you learned in your work against apartheid in South Africa?

DOI: 10.4324/9781003262817-11

AA: ... How much pain and injustice there is in the world. The other important lesson that I learned ... was that you can be very intelligent but still do very wrong things.

RH: When did you begin coming here?

AA: Right after high school I spent a few days here with my family, and I fell in love with this country.... In college I had debates on Zionism with one of my roommates. I read through *The Zionist Idea*, by Arthur Hertzberg. I began to feel that if these people with so many views all considered themselves Zionists, with a common denominator [of] the national liberation movement of the Jewish people, then I too was a Zionist.... I was going to go straight into rabbinical school. But I didn't get accepted to rabbinical school; they told me I needed more experience in the real world. When I spoke about an internship for peace, they said that is exactly the kind of thing you should be doing.... Although I was very angry.... I can't imagine where I would be today ... if I hadn't spent those two years dedicated to peace. I decided to live in Israel and contribute to what Christians call co-creationism: we are God's partners in the ongoing work of creation and repairing the world. That is the Midrash, the narrative, which brings my worlds together more than anything else.... In '83 I started rabbinic school, where I met my wife. Today, we are Israel's only rabbinic couple.... After we were both ordained in '89, we spent five years in California, [where] I went to do a doctorate at Stanford. When I came back in '94, I worked for a congregation with Orthodox, Conservative, and Reconstruction members. I also wanted to find work for that other part of my soul, dealing with issues of social justice....

RH: Outline for me the philosophy of Rabbis for Human Rights.

AA: [It] was founded during the first *intifada*. We focused on the occupied territories, and worked closely with B'Tselem. It was unusual for rabbis to be involved.

RH: So your base was human rights, linked to the concept of Jewish ethical responsibility.

AA: Correct. We were then the only rabbinic organization which brings together rabbis from different movements within Judaism—orthodox, reform, conservative, reconstructionist, and renewal rabbis. What brought us together was this sense that our tradition had something to say about human rights, a humanistic reading of the tradition that was not being heard.

RH: So, there were several approaches based on this foundation.

AA: At the time, we were media-oriented. Our main role was our presence.... Since I've been involved, we do a lot more in-depth work—95% in the occupied territories.

RH: I know you work with the Israeli Committee Against Home Demolitions....

AA: We have been very involved with ICAHD. In summer 1998, Israel demolished [Palestinian houses] at a pace of one or two per day. The Civil Administration said there were hundreds [of houses] on the chopping block. One day, we got word that five homes would be demolished, including the Shawarmah family home, which has become the symbol around the world of the struggle against demolitions. We had a Knesset member and a bus full of activists who were seeing this for the first time. It didn't do any good. To go back to Jerusalem, where life goes on for everybody else like nothing has happened—but everything has happened—was the worst day of my life. The best day of my life was an act of civil disobedience; we came back and rebuilt that home. That home has now been rebuilt and demolished and rebuilt and demolished several times. For a family [to see] its home demolished is a personal tragedy. Publicity around the demolition and rebuilding was a turning point. People realized that this was a "Catch-22": [Palestinians] can't get a building permit; then they are punished for building without a permit.

In 2000, after the [second] *intifada* began, the Palestinians that we have been working with said this is not the time to come [to the West Bank]. Your job is to demonstrate in Tel Aviv. There is a disappointment and anger with the Israeli Left, that they weren't effective. Palestinians now had to take this into their own hands. In principle we are very opposed to violence, and we think this whole *intifada* was morally wrong. But I organized the first major Israeli/Palestinian joint activity, a joint harvest. One of the most basic Jewish teachings is that people can change.

RH: I agree with you. It is one hope that I hang onto, that individuals can change....

AA: [I saw] Israeli soldiers digging trenches all around Ramallah. This was not about security. So, I pushed other organizations into bolder activities. We dismantled a roadblock.

RH: Literally by hand, with shovels?

AA: We ignored the police. They confiscated our tools, so we worked with our hands. They arrested people and said we will give them back if—We [didn't negotiate]. We removed the roadblocks and got the people and tools back. It didn't stay open, but it was a significant activity. After we left, Palestinians would often get injured, though they knew what they were getting into.

RH: So, you were having second thoughts about that type of work?

AA: We abandoned it too quickly. Personally, I would go back to some of those activities. There was an upsurge in the number of Israelis being murdered. So, people saw things differently.

RH: When I talked to Jeff yesterday, he lamented the collapse of the broad middle ground in which people could talk with each other, but suicide bombings have caused people to withdraw.

AA: True, although we haven't done enough of the difficult work of speaking to people that we don't agree with. There is nothing as important as going and speaking with people one on one or in small groups. When you do that, you can get through to a lot of people.

RH: Education and teaching in the rabbinic sense are clearly a part of your central approach.

AA: Absolutely. In late January 2002, a poll was published showing that 59% of Israelis believed that we were acting immorally in the [Palestinian] territories.... I realized that the issue was much more complicated than just making people aware. Polls show a slim majority of both Israelis and Palestinians want to negotiate a compromise settlement, and an even larger majority on both sides who think that there is nobody on the other side to talk to.

RH: The majority on both sides say, We don't have anybody to talk to?

AA: Yeah, people say, There is no one to talk to.... A lot people feel there is no military solution, there will be a compromise, and [Israelis] will have to leave the territories. But for now, use full military force to uproot the infrastructure of terror. We know it is wrong, but if it gives us a day or a month of respite from suicide bombings, nuke 'em. It is wrong, but do it anyway.

RH: I understand that moral dilemma.

AA: I was one of the only Israelis who went to the Jenin refugee camp right after the army left in April 2002. I went undercover.... I was blown away by the enormity of the destruction.... But after 13 soldiers were killed, a decision was made to rain down fire. What were their alternatives?... In July I got a call at 11:30 at night. A baby was born at home. This baby is going to die if we don't get her to a hospital in a few hours. I got a call on another three-month-old girl who had been trying to go to a hospital for a couple of days with a life-threatening condition. She didn't get a permit, and died that night.... Israeli policy led to the death of one little girl and endangered another. Why are the roadblocks there? We are like two roosters put in the ring to fight. We stick to the micro-level. We are a human-rights organization, not a political organization. But even within a narrow focus; we are still needed to talk about the occupation.

RH: This root cause has caused violence in and of itself.

AA: Right. The occupation is a situation which creates human-rights violations.

RH: The foundation for that understanding is in the Geneva Conventions and international law.

AA: These two events in the last year and a half drove it home for me in a very personal way.

RH: From your perspective as a rabbi and a student of history.... how does one approach this matrix that combines denial, partial justification, historic victims, [and] perpetual victims?

AA: I don't see the situation between Israelis and Palestinians as symmetrical. We are the dominant military and economic power. [But] there is an incredible symmetry in how we have all created these seamless world views which are very impenetrable and closed. We all so fully see ourselves as the victims that we cannot imagine that maybe at the same time we can be both victims and victimizers.... There is a hair's difference between being a victim and a victimizer, especially when your cause is just. It is very simple to go from one to the other or be both at the same time.... We have begun working more intensively with Christian and Muslim religious leaders. We've created an interfaith declaration in which we say that human rights are God's will for humanity.... When we go out to rebuild a demolished home, the parents insist that the kids meet us. We want them to know that not all Israelis who come have guns.

RH: It is relevant that people-to-people contact occurs whenever possible?

AA: People-to-people, not just in the sense of dialogue, [but] contact where we demonstrate with our bodies our commitment to human rights and justice for Palestinians. We need Palestinians who will do the same thing to convince Israelis.

RH: It sounds like what you are calling for is a ... nonviolent resistance movement.

AA: It all comes down to how do you restore hope? When people have hope that things can be different, all kinds of things are possible.

* * * * * * * * *

Jerusalem, 2014

RH: I want to talk with you again because you are a rabbi and you are committed to human rights. What keeps the conflict going—political, economic, and/or spiritual problems?

AA: I think it's all of the above, but as a rabbi I would first say it is a spiritual problem. I write about spiritual blindness and spiritual myopia. There are many factors, starting with what we learn from psychologists—that people who have been beaten as children are more likely to beat others. Israelis and Jews have a long history of being beaten, and Palestinians certainly have been beaten as well. One of the things that happens when you've been beaten is you believe that it gives you privileges, that is, exceptionalism. [Some say,] because of all the things we have suffered—2,000 years of suffering—no one can tell us what to do....

During the recent 2014 war, we had every right to defend ourselves, but even self-defense has limits; there are red lines in Judaism, and in international law. The fact that we [Israelis] have much greater power also gives us a much greater responsibility. You see incredible spiritual myopia on both sides. The dominant Judaism here is *not* what I believe—"It's all ours by right from God." The dominant Judaism here says, God promised us in the Bible that this land is ours, which is true, but … if you really look at those promises, they make it very clear that at any point in history, the amount of land that we control will expand or contract depending on our moral behavior. [We] need to think outside the box…. If we all got to the spiritual place of [saying] the land doesn't belong to any of us, we'd have less need to exercise temporal control.

Another challenge is, we have a very narrow understanding of democracy. In the U.S. you have a Constitution and a Bill of Rights. More and more Israelis see democracy as being simple majority rule. We've lost this idea that democracy is also about what the majority cannot do—to respect the rights of minorities. So we need to have that as part of our spiritual base.

RH: [Israelis say,] Because we have survived, we are entitled?

AA: We will do X, Y, and Z because that's what we need to do to survive, and we're entitled.

RH: To what extent are generations of suffering still powerful, and to what extent are they manipulated politically?

AA: Well, they could be manipulated because they're incredibly powerful.

RH: You have passion and concern but you also carry hope.

AA: My basic hope comes with the fact that the situation looks pretty bad right now. In all likelihood, we are on the brink of another round of five to ten years of conflict before we get so weary of killing each other that we say, Let's try something else…. I hope I'm wrong.

RH: … How do you link spiritual resources to a political movement?

AA: That's a very good question. That's a tough question. There may be shortcuts, but I don't know them. [Some] people become leaders, create movements, and almost overnight change things…. We religious Israelis may be best poised to empower Palestinian peacemakers, and Palestinians have to empower us…. You don't just say, "There's nothing I can do" because then nothing will happen…. I will keep doing everything that I can, everything possible, so whenever [transformation] comes, we'll be ready to embrace it.

* * * * * * * *

Jerusalem, June 2018

AA: In September 2017, I left Rabbis for Human Rights and formed an organization doing legal work in the Occupied Territories. Torat Tzedek-Torah of Justice is a vehicle for me to continue my life's work from the point of view of international human rights and the Jewish tradition.

RH: Talk to me about your perspective of more than 20 years of doing human-rights work, about the short term versus the longer term.

There are so many human-rights needs here—the West Bank, Gaza. Do you primarily work on short-term crises or some combination?

AA: Human-rights work always has one foot in the grassroots and the other in the corridors of power. Short-term work gives you the ability to make major changes of policy in the long term.

RH: In the peacemaking and peacebuilding literature, there are theories about different layers, related to what you just said—a grassroots level, the political elite, and intellectuals and NGO people in the middle.... The grassroots level has the most people and the corridors of power the least people. The middle group has access to the corridors of power, and to the grassroots.

AA: First of all, I do human-rights work, which is related to but different than peace work.... My job is *not* to bring about an ultimate peace treaty or final status solution to the conflict, although we do contribute to that. I probably [said] four years ago that [people give up] when a majority of Israelis and Palestinians want a compromise, a negotiated, nonviolent solution, but an even larger percentage of both sides say, "We want peace, but there's no one to talk to." In the last few years so many Israelis and Palestinians have given up and don't believe that peace is possible, and therefore vote against their own positions. They support parties and groups that are inconsistent with what they say they believe. The ironic thing is that my work can break down stereotypes held by Palestinians about Israelis, particularly religious Israelis, thereby empowering Palestinian peacemakers from the Palestinian street to make peace with them possible, allowing people to empower me in the same way. That is certainly a contribution to the possibility of peace. [And] if we return land to Palestinians or prevent it from being taken over, that changes the facts on the ground, which is important to any potential peace process.

My role, from a religious perspective, is influencing the moral outlook of our society, building a society which honors God's image in every human being, which honors the values ensconced in our Declaration of Independence. The prophetic values are clear. We have a goal of changing society as an ultimate big-picture goal, even more than an ultimate goal of achieving peace.

RH: How do you work at that? I know you write.

AA: We try, in every way possible, to frame the human-rights discussions on large issues and small issues ... in a Jewish ethical framework.

RH: So you see yourself working both near term, short term, and longer term simultaneously.

AA: Yes. A lot of what we do is very focused on helping a particular farmer, a particular village, but it's always with the eye of changing the big picture.

RH: Give me an example.

AA: I've been writing a lot and working with Bedouin villages inside Israel, in the Negev Desert.

RH: I went down there three days ago.

AA: OK. So you're familiar with that situation. [I write] Op-Eds on Friday. In both projects, we're trying to achieve specific policy goals. We talk about all the to-do items in terms of the values of our Declaration of Independence. Frequently Independence Day falls on the week that we read Leviticus 19 with all its ethical codes. I'm working with elected officials to find a solution so it all comes together. [In] one of our major accomplishments, we acted as human shields to help Palestinian farmers get to their olive trees. They were being attacked by settlers and soldiers.

RH: This was on the West Bank?

AA: Right. In 2006, we started with the micro [approach] of day-in and day-out accompanying in the villages [and] farmers taking all that experience to the high court, winning a major victory. We [resist] all the ways that the army is trying to turn the clock back to the situation before 2006. We go from village to village to document what people would ideally do on their land versus what they're actually able to do, and why. Maybe we can go back to the powers that be to make the macro change. We find so many immediate needs. Some we pass on; some we take care of.

RH: Immediate needs, like really elemental things—

AA: Like right now, even changing the overall policy of Palestinian access to the land is still not a full picture. But that is the role of a human-rights organization, working at that level.

RH: Talk to me about land. Jeff Halper says [the conflict] is not really about land; it's about security. But almost everybody else that I talk to says land is central to the conflict.

AA: It is central. What Jeff is saying is that your average Israeli is concerned about security.

RH: At the personal and family level.

AA: Right. Your average Israeli is not ideologically committed to holding on to all the land. Although they may believe that in an ideal world they would have it. In some of the old footage, Ben-Gurion says, "It's all ours, but I would give up all of the Occupied Territories for real peace."

RH: Was he being sincere, or was he disingenuous?

AA: He was being sincere. He was always a pragmatist. I think he absolutely meant that. After he was no longer in power, he said we should give it all back for peace. Ben-Gurion, from 1929 to 1936, was in favor of a binational state. Then, after the uprising [in the 1930s], he decided that that wasn't workable.... He was much more pragmatic than the Arab world in 1947. He said that the two-state solution [proposed] by the UN is not fair; this is our land. But he was statesman enough to say that the greater good is served by our accepting this partition plan.

RH: Interesting.... The question was about land and the extent to which it's central or not.

AA: Remember that we are being led by the nose in this country by people who are very ideologically committed, in most cases from a religious point of view, to the entire biblical land of Israel and God's promise. They present that to the larger Israeli public as "We need this land for security reasons," although fewer and fewer military officials would concur with that.... There might be some debate whether there is a security advantage to holding on to the Occupied Territories. You have almost full consensus that the settlements are a security liability.

RH: I don't think I've heard anybody frame it quite that way.

AA: Today most military people would say that the resources that we expend in the army to defend settlements actually deter our overall mission to provide security.

RH: I was in Hebron on Saturday. The military presence there is astonishing.

AA: Sure. To protect a very small number of settlers. And the other thing that is used is that "There's no partner for peace." There is no lack of workable peace plans.

RH: Jeff [Halper] has just come up with a new one.

AA: One of my debates with Jeff is that I don't think it is important to say that a plan is the only workable plan. The issue is the process by which Israelis and Palestinians come to agreement.

RH: Describe for me as best you can what that process looks like.

AA: I'll get back to it in a second. The point is that our [political] leadership has succeeded in convincing the vast majority of Israelis—and I think the vast majority of Palestinians believe the same way—to support parties and positions which are out of line with what they say they believe.... A process ideally would be authorized leaders sitting down and coming up with a negotiated agreement. Secondly, we know that too often leaders sign a piece of paper, to say that they signed a piece of paper and they can't back it up. Itzak Shamir was the prime minister during the Oslo process. In a rare moment of honesty for a politician, he said, "My plan was to keep on talking and talking and talking while we continued to populate the Occupied Territories until people would wake up and realize that there was nothing in writing to talk about."

RH: Can you think of six or ten people who have the stature and the trust of their own community, and you could get them around a table like this and have genuine dialogue?

AA: It's very difficult to imagine who we see on the scene on either side who can do that.

RH: First of all, they'd have to want to do that.

AA: Right. Similar to what happened to the Oslo Accords, if a group of people were to get together and present the results, that in itself could give them a certain stature. If we have another prime minister, another Palestinian leader, that would also confer a certain stature.

RH: Did you like that combination of officials and academics as cover for a secret process?

AA: Jeff told me once that the book *The Process* explains from inside what went wrong. There is always an inherent problem with political leaders because they're thinking about the next elections. But you have to have people with some kind of mandate.

RH: Do you have more hope for leaders from the nongovernmental community or process?

AA: I think we contribute a lot, but eventually we need the political leaders.

RH: Yeah. Eventually you have to pull everybody along, the grassroots, too.

AA: Right.

RH: Do you know Sahar Vardi at the American Friends Service Committee?

AA: Yes.

RH: She put more emphasis on the process and making the occupation unsustainable. She said, "It's not sustainable. It will have to end." What will make it unsustainable?

AA: I don't know. For many years I said that BDS is not workable, that it will not actually impact—

RH: Not enough critical mass?

AA: Right. If it were proven an effective tool I would have to re-evaluate it. It has gone much further than I expected ... to make Israelis wake up and say, The occupation is not sustainable.

RH: Can you think of other mechanisms or tools or tactics, or approaches?

AA: Jeff has often said, When is the PA going to stop cooperating with the occupation? One of the greatest nightmares of the Israelis is if the PA were to say, All right, we're shutting down; we're giving you back the keys. That would go a long way to making things unsustainable.

RH: It could be a strategy or a default. Abu Mazen has not groomed anybody to follow him.

AA: Nonviolence is a much greater threat to those who understand the occupation. Nonviolence can bring us to a very different place.

RH: How do you see the Gaza situation? Nonviolence is difficult to sustain, if you're being fired at by snipers. Will it just fade away, or might it build into some sort of nonviolent movement?

AA: [They need] creativity to do something which captures people's imaginations. One of the problems is that they didn't succeed in being entirely nonviolent.... I do not agree that the one-state solution is the only solution or that it's necessarily inevitable. Although the classic two-state solution is becoming less and less likely, there are other forms of the two-state solution which are still possible. But the success of the settler movement could prove its own undoing.

Whether or not we've already crossed the point of no return, when we do, you then have either the option of being an enemy occupation and having one democratic state or apartheid.

RH: Jeff was [saying] in 2003, 2005, that we're already in an apartheid situation.

AA: Yes and no. As someone who got my political start in the anti-apartheid movement, there are some things which are like apartheid, some things which are not. I generally don't find it helpful to call or compare the occupation to apartheid. Two years ago I would say the classic two-state solution of a clean return to the '67 borders and dismantling of settlements is less and less possible. There are other forms of two-state solutions such as border adjustments, Israelis remaining in Palestine as Palestinian citizens, or as extraterritorial citizens, the whole two states in one homeland.

RH: A final question about where we're at: Can you sum up your feelings about this moment?

AA: To twist a phrase, the only thing we have to despair of is despair itself. We have no lack of workable peace plans out there. The problem is that people don't believe it's possible. And just like with Sadat, if something would break through that and convince Israelis and Palestinians that peace is possible ... things would change overnight. [But] we are maybe in the worst situation right now that I can ever remember.

RH: I've heard other people say that.

AA: And that's because of the heights to which despair has reached and the degree to which people do not believe that a different future is possible. The other reason—we have a government which is the most radical [right] government we've ever had, a government which is not only ideologically run but believes that anything it has the power to do, it is permitted to do.

RH: That's dangerous.

AA: ... True democracy is about what the majority is forbidden to do. We've lost that. Our minister of injustice always says, You lefties just haven't accepted that we won the elections, and we're doing what we said we were going to do, what we were elected to do. We have a mandate. And if you don't like it, tough. Because we have the ability to do so.

RH: It sounds like the U.S.

AA: We are in a situation where some tools that were to some degree working are not working now. We see over the last 15 to 20 years, in a very strategic way the right wing, particularly the religious right, has taken over positions of influence in different government institutions ... and attacks on NGOs. All of this. The image that came to my mind two weeks ago was, as much as I hate to think of sides, a game of tug of war. At the point where one side has lost its balance and is being dragged across the line. It is not impossible, but it takes an extraordinary effort to get back on your feet and recover from that. That's the situation we're in. We're being pulled across the line.... I still have faith in the long term, but in the short term, things are pretty bad.

RH: It's political and personal and social and spiritual, I assume.

AA: It's all together. What allows it to happen more than anything else is despair. You to pray as if everything depends on God and work as if everything depends on you.... It would be much worse if you don't try, even if there's no promise you'll succeed. And therefore, despair is like a luxury resort that we can't afford.

RH: I agree. Thank you very much.

10 Peacemaking and Nation-building

Hanan Ashrawi

For decades, Hanan Ashrawi has been among the top legislative and peacemaking leaders in Palestine. After earning a Ph.D. in English literature at the University of Virginia, Ashrawi engaged in peacemaking at governmental, nongovernmental, and grassroots levels. In the 1990s, she founded The Palestinian Initiative for the Promotion of Global Dialogue & Democracy (MIFTAH), and she served as a frequent spokeswoman on American and European television. She was a member of the PLO Executive Committee until 2020.

Ramallah, May 2005

HA: I'm Hanan Ashrawi.

RH: I am researching the [work] of peacemakers in Israel and Palestine. Last night we went to a small restaurant in East Jerusalem, and when the owner asked us what we were doing, I said that we were talking to peacemakers. He burst out laughing at this absolutely absurd idea.

HA: An absurd idea in this context.

RH: I know from your literature background you are very familiar with tragedy and the whole range [of genres]. Help us locate what the various forces for peacemaking are at the moment.

HA: At this moment it is very hard to see any type of momentum for peacemaking. Most people are engaged in damage control and temporary quiet, and an attempt to try to create a situation where outside conflict is not viable. But to see a vision for peace, a process that is implemented for sustaining peace, a commitment – it is very hard to see. Palestinians are in an unenviable position of trying to relegitimize a peace language and peace behavior on their own without any reciprocal moves by the international community, by the Americans, or by Israel.

RH: [Prime Minister] Ariel Sharon said he had nobody to talk to.

HA: Which, of course, was fiction. Sharon claimed that he had no peace partner, but he was not interested in peace, so he found the easiest way was to find a convenient scapegoat and negate the Palestinian partner automatically. Many people swallowed that line without even bothering to look at the reality of the Palestinian leadership under President [Yasser] Arafat. Arafat did not abandon the peace agenda

DOI: 10.4324/9781003262817-12

at any time. The day [Sharon] was elected, he totally abandoned any type of negotiations and placed impossible preconditions. As far as the current situation is concerned, there is no peace partner in Israel. The peace camp is in disarray and has been undermined and excluded. The [Israeli] government is really a hard-line government with its own agenda based on unilateralism. My definition [of this situation] is power politics; the strong dictating to the weak, perpetuation of the occupation, land grabs, and the Wall.... So the Palestinian leadership finds itself in the unenviable position again of trying to create peace, which they cannot do; trying to move within a domestic situation of national unity, internal empowerment, nation building, and minimizing the damage of the occupation while, hoping for external changes in the political scene in Israel and the U.S.

RH: I have been quite impressed with a number of grassroots and NGO [peacemaking] efforts from Ramallah to Hebron. But it seems like these efforts can't flower because of the occupation.

HA: Of course. Any type of dialogue, any type of grassroots interaction, any type of even intellectual attempts at finding a different course or creating a new language or discourse for peace is always undermined, not just by the fact of the occupation, but by the deliberate practices of the occupation. For example, when you are in a state of fragmentation and you have no freedom of movement. The Israelis cannot come here [to Ramallah] and we cannot meet them there [in Israel]. The dominant logic is one of violence and negation. It is very hard to find the space to meet and to challenge this prevailing logic. That is why even the existing channels and bylaws are undergoing serious difficulty in that transformation, given the fact that the language of conflict is prominent, the language of extremism, and, of course, the isolation. There is a deliberate will to prevent like-minded Palestinians and Israelis from meeting and from exposing a sort of fraudulent agenda and the violent and dangerous agenda of Sharon and Israel. Sharon wants to claim ... the language of negotiations and peacemaking.

RH: At this point there is no official negotiation process at all.

HA: Of course. The issue has never been bilateral and cannot be bilateral; we need third-party internationals. You have an Israeli government that does not want to negotiate. Sharon's political agenda is very clear; he said he doesn't want to reach a peace agreement; he wants long-term interim arrangements that he can dictate unilaterally to the Palestinians. The only thing that we have to do is to provide security to the Israelis, even though we are the victims, the people under occupation. The Americans, of course, have fallen into the Israeli line, that unilateral disengagement is the only game in town. Therefore they have not provided any type of negotiating process, or channel, or prospect. They keep saying that even their own roadmap has been shelved pending Sharon's plan. The Quartet has also relinquished its will to the U.S., which has relinquished its will to Sharon, so we ended up with Sharon as the only decision-maker, and he doesn't want to negotiate. He doesn't want a peace agreement. He wants the freedom and the leeway to create facts on the ground that will destroy the chances of a two-state solution, that will satisfy his insatiable appetite for land and territory without demography, and that will lead to a long-term interim phase where you have an arrangement with the Palestinians to live in isolated islands or reservations while Israel continues to take our land and water.

RH: If the only way to unravel this Gordian knot is outside intervention, but the only one who can really do that doesn't want to play that role, then how do we create that space?

HA: It is very hard to create that space where you can reenergize and relegitimize negotiations and peacemaking with substance, credibility, and momentum, with a clear view of the outcome. Given the fact that a third-party intervention is not in the making, the nature of the ideology that dominates global relations now is not based on justice and peacemaking. When you have foreign politics like this, the ones who pay the price are the weaker side and the victims, which is what is happening to the Palestinians. The most that we can do right now is to try to work internally to build our institutions, to continue with nation-building, and to try to prevent Sharon and all other extremists from undermining the language of peace and the peace agenda among Palestinians.

RH: So that middle level [of] NGOs or democratic initiatives or non-violence training is the best—

HA: That is the best we can do right now, ... trying to maintain a commitment to peacemaking without falling into the trap of doing unto others what was done unto us, because that would encourage extremists and people who are violent. They see Israel as adopting the ideology of extremism and violence and they feel justified in doing the same. So we have to maintain a high moral ground, which is extremely difficult to do because you are accustomed to being shelled and battered. We have no freedom and our economy is destroyed. Lives, homes, trees – there is a systematic destruction of Palestinian reality and we are undergoing a serious de-development and aggression as a result of the occupation. Yet we are supposed to maintain our own sense of values and maintain a higher moral ground by not succumbing to feelings of revenge and not allowing pain to take over and become our motivation.

RH: Yesterday I came to a checkpoint [near Bethlehem] and I was utterly shocked that the Wall was almost [built] in a complete horseshoe. I am told by people here on the ground that the U.S. government knows this, the European governments know all of this and there is a lack of political will to change it.

HA: There is a lack of political will and there is a fear of confronting Israel, of using any type of accountability, whether legal, human, or moral. Somehow Israel is always accommodated. Israeli measures may be met with some verbal reprimands but there has never been the will to hold Israel accountable to carry out any type of sanctions or to even launch a viable peace process. A third-party intervention would transform realities on the ground and would curb Israeli violations. Right now Israel is engaging in a systematic humiliation of Palestinians, a systematic victimization of the Palestinians, and a devaluation of human rights and lives. They are getting away with it. Without international intervention, without subjecting Israel to the norms of civilized human behavior that should govern our state, we are not going to get anywhere. Right now, Israel feels that it can call the shots; it can do whatever it wants to the Palestinians with full security—because of the U.S. involvement on the one hand, and the sort of strategic alliance with the U.S., and Israel's being a domestic factor in the U.S., and the cliché of "might makes right."

RH: So things are stalled or even in regression at the top diplomatic levels. What are the grassroots [movements], either locally or internationally, that may provide a wake-up call? Divestments?

HA: Exactly. There are different ways in which we can face Israel's militarization and oppression, and it is not by adopting their methods, but by using our own methods. Among Palestinians there is a move to boycott Israeli goods and goods from the settlements, even though that is very difficult because we are captives and we are under Israeli control when it comes to our borders and even our internal mobility. Israel has destroyed our economy. So we have very few choices. But also there is nonviolent resistance to the Wall, along with solidarity movements. People [from] all over the world are unarmed and facing the Israeli soldiers and are demonstrating and protesting against the building of the Wall. There has to be this collective human spirit that will stand up to military might and will expose it. Again, internationals, grassroots organizations, others, NGOs, institutions of society can't take it all. Also we are launching campaigns of information, creating networks, and having the courage to tell the truth and to explain the realities of Palestinians—things that have been subjected to distortion, labeling, racist manipulation, trying to exclude Palestinians, blaming the victim, and vindicating Israel. We need the truth to come out. We need the facts to come out. We need a network of people with courage to stand up to the mainstream media to call Israelis on using media in an invasive way to distort reality. The American people and the international community as a whole [must move away] from government manipulation of politics. It is very important that public opinion be awakened to what is really happening so that people can take a stand. Divestment is one way, activism, churches, schools, and universities challenging the version that is in the media. We have been devalued systematically. All of these things can make a tremendous difference not just in perception but in policymaking.

RH: So all of these approaches are necessary. No single [approach] offers a magical solution?

HA: No, there is no magical solution, unfortunately. This situation has been in the making for decades, and for decades we have been excluded and distorted. People of courage and conscience and justice have either been intimidated or silenced. We need to speak up. We need to regroup. We need to challenge. To do this we have to have many different ways of addressing the issue, including going to [the U.S.] Congress regularly, challenging Congress. We need to act in a way that will dispel misconceptions and reenergize less biased policies.

RH: There are two more questions. One goes in the direction of the narrative. My undergraduate work was in English, like yours, and my graduate work was in theatre. Loads of information is available to anyone who wants to read it, but someone has to have the heart to look at it. Talk briefly about the role of narrative forms—films, novels, and oral history projects – to touch hearts and minds so people will come and see.

HA: Reading narratives is certainly the most effective way of not just humanizing the Palestinians but dispelling this whole cloud of misconceptions, distortions, dehumanization of the Palestinians. To present the Palestinians as recognizable human beings, with whom there can be immediate contact at the human level, is extremely important. The Palestinian narrative is told and directed by the Israelis. We were never allowed to do it ourselves directly, until recently, when we challenged [Israeli narratives], when there were people of courage who attempted to present [our stories] with honesty, and it takes a lot to do so. So it is very important to have oral history programs, immediate oral presentation of the moment. But at the same time this is the compilation of many individuals, personal narratives, and stories, and it goes a long way to present a human face. We become identifiable, not abstractions, and we have been abstracted in many ways, numbers, "Ten Palestinians killed today." It is OK. It is expected. We are not human. You don't see them; you don't relate to them, you don't get their names. They don't exist. They have no hopes, no dreams, somehow. The Palestinians are always presented as being reactive, as though we were born only in reaction to Israel, even though we are very ancient people with a centuries-old culture. We have a sense of pride of our identity. Again, we are abstracted. We are extracted from our context. We have to be recontextualized, and it takes a lot to correct prevailing depictions and distortions that have formed how most people think about the Palestinians. Having many different ways of dealing with narratives is very important.... For example, many Americans believe that *Exodus* is the story that really formulated their opinion. Nobody has bothered to present the Palestinian narrative and all of the visual reality that would dispel those convictions. We don't have the novel that will capture people's imagination, and make people say that this Palestinian novel is one that I can relate to, not just empathize [with]. I find myself in it because, after all, literature deals with awareness and awareness is not subject to boundaries and political realities, but it touches the human spirit. This is what we need.

RH: Perhaps this is one more task you will take on?

HA: [Laughter] I would love to have the time and luxury of just writing. I love writing. I love literature. I used to write in the wee hours of the morning because my whole day is taken up with so many other things. The world is too much for me. There are too many demands.

RH: So, talk to me about the central project you are focused on at the moment.

HA: [Laughter] I have many things that I am working on simultaneously. I'm working on democracy of the home. I am a member of the PLC [Palestinian Legislative Council]. So I'm dealing with legislation, and I'm looking at ways that will ensure women's rights, children's rights, and human rights, so that there are no violations. To ensure that we do have election laws and an electoral process is something that becomes constant and not just a one-time or sporadic thing. I'm working on women's empowerment as well. It is more internal, trying to support women to help them run for office and local government and legislative elections. Empowering women is a subject that is close to my heart. We have seen tremendous successes.

But I am also trying to maintain contact with the Israelis, to have a dialogue that is truthful. It is becoming more and more difficult to maintain the dialogue. Very difficult. We have had an ongoing women's dialogue, and it has been effective. I also believe in the power of the word, so we work on issues of information. We write, issue statements, deal with delegations; we meet with international leadership at all levels, from ministers down to grassroots groups and church groups. We constantly try to maintain contact with a network of people globally who have the same commitments, or we try to influence their thinking by presenting them with the real version. It is a challenge. I also work with the authorities to help them in terms of policymaking and… decisions that are needed. We are beginning to implement reform. I am a founding member of the Coalition for Accountability and Integrity. I am also a member of the National Reform Committee. There are many things dealing with reform, democracy, and internal nation-building.

RH: It seems to me the linkage for many of those different projects is a democratic process, building a democratic process.

HA: But also building networks that involve all sorts of conflict resolution based on justice.

RH: Your relationship is between peacebuilding and building a civil society.

HA: I believe nation-building, empowerment, and peacemaking are definitely connected and interdependent. For a while the international community dealt only with the peace process, and it became an end unto itself. So long as there is a peace process, we don't care about nation-building, democracy, human rights, or Palestinian rights as a nation. That destroyed the nation-building because the peace process suffered from a basic flaw, the fact that it did not have a human-rights component or a nation-building component. It dealt only with security, particularly military security addressing Israeli needs. So it became a tool for the destruction of Palestinian rights. We said that we needed the two processes, nation-building and peacemaking, to proceed simultaneously. We did not get that. The pendulum has swung to the other extreme now. We are being told that we have to pursue nation-building without the prospect of peace. We have to demonstrate that we are perfect, that we are reformed; we have no problems domestically, even under occupation. We can create democratic systems, accountable institutions, professional institutions, and rule of law, without the hope of ending this occupation, of having peace.

RH: It strips away the confidence.

HA: Exactly. It is not just decontextualizing; it is dealing with symptoms rather than causes. If you move on both fronts simultaneously, you will have in Palestine a democracy that is vibrant. We are committed to democracy. We are committed to rule of law. We are committed to good governing. The problem is that we have been prevented by the occupation and we don't have a state, for heaven's sake. We are enslaved by the occupation. So we have to work on freedom while we work on peace simultaneously. People tell us that it is a precondition: you have to demonstrate that you are worthy of negotiating with the Israelis....

RH: So the goal is really to end the occupation?

HA: Ending the occupation is crucial. But we are not saying give us a peace process and we [will] not work on nation-building. No, we will continue to work on nation-building. Help us do both. Give us hope. Let's see that there is a credible peace process, that there is international will—political [and] human will to deal with the Palestinians in an evenhanded way as human beings who deserve some sort of reprieve. We haven't seen that yet.

RH: Final question. We know that things are extremely painful.

HA: Yeah, very painful.

RH: Can you identify two or three places from which you draw hope, whether they are spiritual resources or family resources? Congratulations on your first grandchild.

HA: Thank you.

RH: Organizations, new innovations, vision from the nonviolence movement?

HA: There are many, actually. My strength comes from my commitment to the Palestinian people, to humanity. It stems also from my love of my family. My daughters are my life. Now that I'm a grandmother, it's amazing, it is incredible. I say that you cannot help others if you don't recognize that commitment, that humanity.... I can name rays of hope. Rachel Corrie – she didn't have to die. But she came here as a young American Jewish woman with courage and with vision. She didn't want to be a hero, but she became one. People who have the courage of their convictions, of their principles, of their beliefs to come here and say that we can do something about it. I see so many internationals that come here, unarmed, as human beings, stand [in front] of a bulldozer or a tank, trying to prevent houses from being demolished, people from being killed, the Wall from being built. It is tragic that some of them have died. Obviously we want people to live for a cause, not to die for a cause.

The cause of peace is certainly something worth living for. I see many ordinary Palestinians every day trying to rescue some sanity, some humanity. They are refusing to succumb to hate. To me this is an act of will and commitment. I will not give in to revenge. I will not give in to my daily humiliation at the checkpoint. I will not become a hateful person. I will not be vindictive.... I see people from all over the world who try to speak out, who write; quite often they are accused of all sorts of things. They challenge the prevailing narrative and the distortions. That is where I get my hope. I see many Israelis, actually, who also pay a very heavy price. There is an organization of parents, Israeli and Palestinian parents who have lost their children and who are trying to defy the occupation and to defy hate and to say, No. We will not dehumanize the other; we will stand for peace. These bereaved parents are the utmost in terms of courage, moral fiber, and human values.

It is so hard if you lose a child. It is so hard to maintain your humanity, and they have. And they refuse to dehumanize the others. I respect them. I love them. They are the real heroes. There are people like Rabbis for Human Rights; people like the Israeli Committee against Home Demolitions, people who put their lives on the line, who are also challenging the power of the occupation. These are the real unsung heroes. There are those who have refused to enter the war machine. The Israelis, the ordinary soldiers, the pilots, and the people who are now speaking out who were involved in some of the horrific acts of the occupation and who now feel that they have to expose them. Even from the heart of the Israeli military machine you have these rays of hope. So, there is no lack of people with such courage and integrity. They need to be heard. They need to be listened to. Eventually they will turn the tide.

RH: Thanks very much.

11 A Journey for Justice and Peace

Naim Ateek

In 1948, at the age of 11, Naim Ateek became a refugee. His family was forced from their village south of the Sea of Galilee, loaded onto a bus, and dropped off in Nazareth, where Ateek grew up. Later, he earned a B.A., a master of divinity degree, and a doctoral degree in the U.S. Returning to Palestine, Ateek was called to ministry in the Anglican church. While serving at St. George's Cathedral in Jerusalem, Ateek cofounded the Sabeel Center for Liberation Theology. His books focus on justice and reconciliation.

Jerusalem, July 2006

RH: Rev. Ateek, what is the translation or the concept of *sabeel?*

NA: *Sabeel* is an Arabic word that means "the way" or "the path"; it also means "a spring" or a "fountain of water." These concepts are meaningful from a Christian perspective because we believe that Christ is the Path, the Way, and the Living Water. So, Sabeel means we are on a journey of peace, justice, and reconciliation in the footsteps of Christ who is the Way. This basic theology is translated into programs ... with the Christian community, the Muslim community, and Jewish peace activists. We also work with Friends of Sabeel in different parts of the world.

RH: Central to your work here is the dynamic of liberation. What are your models of liberation?

NA: The model we have is Christ himself. He is the liberator, so we use the gospel as an important foundation for liberation theology. Christ began his ministry with words of liberation for the oppressed [in] his hometown of Nazareth. That is the foundation for all our work. We are preaching a message of peace and justice for all oppressed people in the land. This is how we approach the whole Israeli-Palestinian conflict.

RH: In *Justice and Only Justice,* what is the linkage between justice and peacemaking?

NA: It's very difficult to achieve peace if it is not based on justice. In this context, we are talking about international law and a body of resolutions that the international community has [agreed] on [United

DOI: 10.4324/9781003262817-13

Nations resolutions 181, 242, and 338]. If we implement those decisions, we will achieve justice. This doesn't mean Israel would be threatened in any way. [Before] 1967, the state of Israel was recognized by the international community, and will be secure.

RH: In fact, it may be much more secure with the 1967 borders.

NA: Yes. The justice we seek is … Israel's withdrawal from all the occupied territories, not impinging on the land which Israel took in 1948. We will make peace with Israel within the pre-1967 borders. Palestinians can then have their own state. Similarly, Lebanon … and Syria would take [back] their own territory. It's a comprehensive peace based on international law.

RH: So, describe the different dimensions of your work, the local work in Palestine and with Israeli peace groups, and your international work. Why is the international work so important?

NA: Israel is a very powerful, military country…. So, [we] work through our friends abroad in order to put pressure on their governments, especially our American friends, because one of the obstacles to peace today is America's blind support of Israeli policies … because of the U.S. Congress, … the pro-Israel lobby, the American Right, and Christian Zionists…. As long as these people support Israel and Israel does what it wants, peace cannot be achieved here.

RH: Are Americans surprised that U.S. foreign policy and Congress are major obstacles to peace?

NA: Our U.S. friends are very aware of Israel's influence on American foreign policy in the Middle East. Many of them say that it's really Israel that is leading American foreign policy and that American politicians are held hostage by pro-Israel groups. We are not able to work for peace without friends in different countries, especially in the U.S. I believe pressure is mounting on politicians [to resist] this [influence]. If America believes in democracy or justice, at some point the consciousness of people will be moved when they see what we are suffering here.

RH: Several people who work closely with you, Jeff Halper and Ghassan Andoni, declare flatly that a two-state solution is dead. So many "facts on the ground" work against that possibility.

NA: We're caught between these concepts of the two states and the one state, and I don't know the way out. I don't think the one-state solution is viable, and I don't think the two-state solution is viable either, in these circumstances. The more viable solution is the two states, but not the two states that exist as enemies. What we are working for is two states that somehow are connected eventually in a confederation. We still believe one state is the ideal solution but …

RH: With equal rights?

NA: With equal rights. But in the minds of many people, especially Zionists, you're immediately [considered] anti-Israel, once you pronounce a one-state solution with equal rights.

RH: Then you no longer have a Jewish state.

NA: Exactly. And that's why, when we talk about a two-state solution at Sabeel it's for the sake of those who want a Jewish state. Although, at the same time, we say a Jewish state is not a democratic state. You know, there cannot be a Jewish state and democracy.

RH: They're caught in a contradiction.

NA: The concept is self-contradictory. We believe that it is possible to think about two states, but not at any price. It's not the two states that Israel is working for today.

RH: [Palestine] as a little group of cantons.

NA: Yes, exactly. That cannot be acceptable. We are working for a two-state [solution] including all the occupied territories and East Jerusalem, every bit of it. If there are changes, they would have to be negotiated, changes of equal value. The Palestinian state has to be at least 22% of Palestine. The international community has to pressure Israel to give more than 22%, because the Palestinians, according to the [UN] Partition Plan, had over 45%. So 22% is the minimum.

RH: Things feel much worse this time.

NA: Things have been deteriorating quite rapidly since the election of Hamas. We hoped that the Western powers would honor the democratic election and that Israel would enter into negotiations with [Hamas]…. Unfortunately, Israel says Hamas is not a partner for peace. Israel demonized them totally, and America backed that up. Then things really deteriorated. Israel tried to break down Palestinian governments [with] incursions into Gaza, assassinations, and [other] pressures.

RH: Withholding tax monies?

NA: Yes, all kinds of things. The situation became much worse. It's very, very sad because we had an opportunity to open up and Hamas itself was beginning to see the importance of changing…. And then the incursion into Gaza made things much worse.

RH: Explain to me the Palestinian concept of "steadfastness."

NA: The Palestinian concept of *sumud* is of a person being steadfast, holding on no matter what. It is very much part of this culture. If things get worse, people adjust to it, and they're willing to withstand, waiting for the day when things would change. There is a conviction that they are in the right…. Because we are oppressed, we need to keep patient and wait. It is both the Christian and the Islamic view. It's very much based on faith in God. God will change this [situation]. If we are under occupation and under oppression, we should not give in. We must withstand all of this and ultimately God will come to our rescue. It's very deep, this [concept].

RH: Is the idea of resistance part of *sumud*?

NA: Yes, it's very much part of it. It's in the word itself. You withstand, so there is resistance.

RH: It's more than just being passive?

NA: Yes, it's not passive.

RH: And is there a linkage from this deep cultural dynamic to nonviolent resistance?

NA: Yeah. *Sumud* is part of the nonviolence we promote. We help people understand the power of nonviolence, that it is more powerful than the use of violence. To some extent [nonviolent resistance] is done all the time. We like to channel it and guide it because most Palestinians have been resisting nonviolently all along … to keep their farmland, or act against the Wall.

RH: Comment on the extent of the nonviolent movement.

NA: Throughout Jerusalem, the West Bank, and Gaza, there are plenty of organizations which do [nonviolence training] as part of their ongoing programs. It has opened the eyes of so many people about the power of nonviolence. They have been practicing it with the help of Jewish peace activists and people that come from outside. In some places it's ongoing every week.

RH: [What is] the crucial link between your international work and your local work here?

NA: We have a long list of agenda items within the Palestinian Christian community. It has nothing to do with politics. It has to do with the life of the Christian community—within its own relationships, its own hierarchy, the problems within the churches and the denominations. We have a very strong program for women, for young people, and for clergy. The most difficult is the clergy, because they have been educated or trained in different denominational ways and with a variety of disciplines. It's difficult to bring down the barriers among denominations. We work within the Christian community to bring new visions for ministry and to help people live their faith under occupation. We also have the Christian-Muslim program, to build respect and understanding with the Muslims. It's very important. The bigger program is the peace and justice program where theology and biblical interpretation come in.… [We] help people analyze the situation from a nonviolent perspective, encouraging people to have nonviolent resistance. It's a huge, huge area. We also speak to groups all the time, trying to educate them on what's really happening.

RH: Groups from outside countries?

NA: From France, Scandinavia, Europe, England, and North America. That's important to us.

RH: To [engage] the international community.

NA: As you know, we plan big conferences. Now we are preparing for the sixth International Conference on Palestinian Christians. Hopefully the situation will calm down....

RH: Thanks for your work.

NA: Thank you. It's always good to have you back here.

* * * * * * * *

Jerusalem, July 2008

RH: Tell me where you were born, and your growing-up experiences.

NA: I was born in a small town of 6,000 people, Beisan, south of the Sea of Galilee. The town was all Palestinian, largely Muslim, but we had three Christian churches. It's a very hot place, in the Jordan valley, but there are plenty of springs. I have fond memories of living there as a boy.

RH: Are those springs the source for the name of Sabeel?

NA: A couple of springs went through our garden. Water was our life, because the climate is very hot. Our life was disrupted in 1948, when the Zionists took over the town. I was 11 at the time. I remember how the soldiers passed through the town. There was no fighting, no violence. We were occupied, and that was it. This was days after the declaration of the state of Israel. We remained in Beisan for a few days. Then the military governor issued a statement that everyone had to leave [or] be killed. So, we had to leave. We could not take anything from our house or from my father's shop. He was a goldsmith and silversmith, and had a very good business. My father suspected that the occupation would not be temporary, [although] the soldiers said it was just for a couple of weeks, and then we would return. My father hid gold under the dresses of my mother and seven sisters. We smuggled out most of the gold, which saved us. Jewish soldiers rounded us up in the center of Beisan. The soldiers brought buses and trucks, sent the Muslims across the river to Jordan, and sent Christians to Nazareth, where they dumped us.

RH: Why the division?

NA: I don't know. They just divided us. They said, Muslims on one side, Christians on the other. They probably realized that Nazareth was a Christian town, although, because of the influx of refugees, it lost its Christian character in a few years. I went to primary school and high school in Nazareth. After high school, I worked for three years, then I received a full scholarship from Hardin-Simmons University in Abilene, Texas. After that I went to the Episcopal Seminary in Berkeley, California, and received my master of divinity degree. I returned home, was ordained, and started my ministry.

RH: Where was your first pastoral assignment?

NA: The first assignment was a small town close to Nazareth, Shefa-'Amr, a very nice town with a good-sized Christian community, together with Muslim and Druze communities. We had three religions living side by side. Those four years were some of the most beautiful of my life, serving the small Episcopal community in town. Soon, we [also] had an ecumenical ministry, a great blessing. Then I went to Haifa, a bigger city and a beautiful place. Haifa opened up my ecumenical ministry in a big way—[with] the Orthodox, Roman Catholics, Melkites, Maronites, Anglicans, and Baptists. One of my best memories. In between, I went for graduate work.

RH: This was doctoral work—

NA: At the San Francisco Theological Seminary, but I was living in Berkeley, and working there. And I had the family with me also.

RH: How many children did you have?

NA: I had two at the time. We did not have the youngest, a girl, but we had the two boys.

RH: Were you starting to work on liberation theology?

NA: My dissertation focused on contextual theology. Orbis Books published it as *Justice and Only Justice: A Palestinian Theology of Liberation* [1989]. That formed the beginning of a theology of liberation for Palestinians. I started my ministry in Jerusalem at St. George's Cathedral. The first *intifada* had started. So I took the book and started translating liberation theology into programs. We started discussions every Sunday after church about a grassroots theology of liberation. God started blessing this ministry, and it expanded. I left St. George's, and dedicated my ministry to Sabeel ... lifting up the voice of justice, a prophetic voice ... resisting the occupation.

RH: Outline the five or six primary areas that Sabeel works in....

NA: We're really building. We have a branch of Sabeel in Nazareth. Haifa would like to start a branch. Finances hold us back.

H: What are the primary areas of ministry here in Palestine?

NA: On the local level, we have a women's ministry that's going very well. The focus is on building up the faith of women and strengthening their commitment to nonviolence, mainly among Christian women. [Another] project is to collect stories of the Nakba in a book. We're asking people to write their own stories. It's important that they put them down on paper. We also have a very strong young adult program. We're hosting our third international young adult conference.

RH: From all over the West Bank?

NA: No, from all over the world, including people from here. We have around 30 university and graduate students who are coming. Most of them are in their early 20s, and some in their 30s. We connect young adults from this area with other areas. They are anxious and hungry for the faith.

RH: The situation is really difficult.

NA: It is. But when people from here and Nazareth get together, it meets so many different needs, the spiritual needs, and also the social needs. Now, it's so difficult to meet on the West Bank. Most of the West Bank people are not allowed to come to Jerusalem. So the only place that people can meet is Jericho.... Another program is for local clergy. But most of them cannot come to Jerusalem, so we meet in Bethlehem and Ramallah. And we meet with internationals.

RH: Getting the story out to internationals is crucial.

NA: Yes. Some know nothing. And some are shocked when they hear what's really happening. Some resist. They don't want to hear the truth.

RH: For theological or ideological reasons?

NA: Some politically cannot accept it, because they think Israel is a peace-loving country and Palestinians are terrorists. Biblically, they've been taught to interpret the Bible in a pro-Israel way, rather than a pro-justice way. We have big conferences, and we work with other peace and justice organizations, including Jewish organizations that are committed to peacemaking.

RH: Which are the primary Jewish organizations?

NA: The Israeli Committee Against Home Demolitions, Breaking the Silence, and Machsom Watch—any Israeli organization that dares to take a stand, to speak out against the occupation.

RH: What's the role of the Friends of Sabeel conferences, in the U.S. and elsewhere?

NA: First of all, education for those who do not know the situation. We always have people who are there for the first time. So education is very much a part of that.

RH: Education is one of your essential strategies as an organization.

NA: Yes, very much so. We also encourage people to move from education to advocacy.... You really need to prod, to encourage some people. But people who know the situation should help move the peace process forward, because the situation is becoming so much worse.

RH: Does the term "peace process" hide more than it reveals?

NA: Yes, it's a charade or game. People talk about the peace process, when there is no peace We hope we are building a foundational justice.

RH: Justice is really the platform, isn't it, for what can emerge?

NA: Yes, absolutely.

RH: Is it fair to say that *sumud*, or faithfulness, is in itself a form of resistance?

NA: Yes, absolutely. It means to withstand. It's a New Testament term. When St. Paul talks about resisting the "powers," and being able to withstand them, he uses the concept of *sumud.*

RH: Resisting the "principalities and powers."

NA: Yes. Being able to stand firm is very, very important [with] commitment to the truth.

RH: So, these are all forms of nonviolent resistance: speaking, writing, and telling stories.

NA: Yes. Sabeel is committed to nonviolence, despite the fact that we are increasingly accused of being violent and being anti-Semitic. If people look at all the things we write, our position is very clear. Everything is transparent…. So, we continue, in spite of accusations and attacks.

RH: Why do you receive so many attacks? Groups try to shut down your conferences in the U.S.

NA: Yes. People have said, You are more dangerous than Hamas. I think they want us to be violent so they can justify their attacks. But we are nonviolent. Loving one's enemy is part of our faith, but loving one's enemy means confronting the enemy's injustice. That threatens them. Opponents put defamatory statements on the internet against us. Thank God, more people are standing up for us. One of the strongest organizations standing up for Sabeel in the U.S. is Jewish Voice for Peace. On the internet, they say, "We have examined the work of Sabeel, and we don't see any anti-Semitism in it." Thank God for people who have the courage to speak up.

* * * * * * * * *

Chicago, August 2018

RH: How have things changed [in 10 years], and how much has *not* changed.

NA: It's becoming more difficult—if the Americans get by with what they want to do…. I think [Israel] intends to make Gaza the state of Palestine. This is the plan.

RH: And force [all Palestinians] out of the West Bank?

AN: Like home rule under apartheid. Historically speaking, Gaza was not part of Palestine.

RH: In your recent book, the interplay of justice, truth, and peace is [linked] with security. Israelis and Palestinians both say that security is [crucial]. How do you [see] security in a theological context? Lots of [biblical] terms [relate] to dwelling in safety.

NA: In Palestinian liberation theology, you begin with faith in a God of justice, a God of mercy, a God of love and peace. The problem is what human beings have done to their fellow human beings…. What's going on—divisions, oppressions, one against another—is totally away from God's expectations, God's love for everyone. Liberation theology is the cry of those who speak prophetically against injustice and evil.

RH: One of the reasons I appreciate your work is that liberation is not only for the oppressed; as Dr. King suggested, it's also for the oppressors, if they can appropriate it.

NA: Yes. Liberation theology is about taking what we know about God, trying to address the reality of life in Palestine-Israel, and embracing all people.

RH: I remember in the dialogue you had with Rabbi Brant Rosen, he said Jews focus on the Torah and not the prophets you and I are drawn to. Where's the Jewish liberation theology?

NA: Thank God for people like Marc Ellis and Brant Rosen, who are raising these questions.

RH: The Torah links the "promised land" [with] conditions. [People] want freedom but not responsibility. Does liberation theology consider what Jeff Halper calls "strategic thinking"?

NA: It's our responsibility to analyze [this] unjust situation, and to look for strategies that [resolve] the conflict.... We would fail in our ministry if we only analyzed the situation. We must find a strategy that [ends] the occupation. So I would be with Jeff all the way on this.

RH: Ilan Pappe says all of us are looking through a glass darkly; as long as the occupation is there, it's hard to think beyond that.

NA: Recently, we've been consumed with President Trump's declarations. He claimed he's a good negotiator. We did not see much negotiation. Then he says to Israel, Jerusalem belongs to you. It was a great shock. Palestinians would never accept a resolution without their share of Jerusalem. Jerusalem is as holy to Muslims and Christians as it is to Jews.

RH: On the radio today, you suggested that Jerusalem might be a way to a larger peace.

NA: Yes. We always said, Let's begin with Jerusalem. Find a resolution to the conflict about Jerusalem. It will make it so much easier to deal with the whole land issue. If Trump would've said *West Jerusalem* is the capital of Israel, we would've welcomed it. And if he had said, *East Jerusalem* is for the Palestinians, we would've said, Trump is the greatest.... Trump was flooded with letters from Christian Zionists who wanted the whole of Jerusalem for Israel. Now our people say we cannot deal with Americans. They cannot be trusted. It's very sad.

RH: Was that a mistake, do you think, on the part of the PA?

NA: Neither the Democrats nor the Republicans, on *this* issue, have a clear position on the basis of international law. It was a last effort before President Obama left office. I was optimistic when Obama became president. But then I found out AIPAC got to him.

RH: I think the first speech he made after he won the nomination was to AIPAC.

NA: When he spoke in Cairo and Istanbul, he said things that made many of us hopeful. But you could see that his heart is on one side, and his thinking is almost hypnotized by AIPAC.

RH: Let me come back to the question of how one [develops] a nonviolence movement.

NA: I don't know. With what happened about Jerusalem, it seems to me that in many ways, the need, the strategy has moved from Jerusalem to here [in the U.S.]

RH: Americans working on American politics.

NA: It's an American problem. Only Americans can undo the damage. Unfortunately, I cannot trust the British government. Although we have many friends who are with us in the U.K.

RH: What is the relationship between nongovernmental peacemakers like yourself and governmental officials? I argue that prophetic vision will come from nongovernmental people.

NA: The sides who want to work on real peace [must] accept the UN resolutions and international law.

RH: Whether it's one state or two states.

NA: Yeah. I don't mind if Israel has blocked a two-state solution by building settlements.... I would be very happy with a one-state solution.

RH: As long as it's not an apartheid state.

NA: Exactly. I still feel we can save the two-state solution; I'll tell you my idea. The United Nations and international law [call for] the two-state solution.... all of the West Bank, East Jerusalem, and the Gaza strip. Then you say, Oh, it's impossible because all the settlements are in the heart of the West Bank. I've negotiated this with Sabeel's board in Jerusalem, and some people were not very happy with this. We would say this is where the Palestinian state will be, and all settlements built on Palestinian land are part of Palestine. All people can stay.

RH: I know a couple of people who have agreed to that.

NA: Yes, I know a rabbi in Tekoa.

RH: I've recorded a conversation with his widow. His wife has picked up the work.

NA: I don't want them to do what they did to my family. I don't want Palestinians to act like Israelis, to throw them out. I say, Look, you are welcome to stay.

RH: It would be like areas in the U.S. like Chinatown, where people choose to be in those groups, but they're not discriminated against.

NA: It's called Palestine, so they would be Palestinians. If they don't like it, it's up to them. My fear with the one-state solution is it will be an apartheid state.

RH: A few days ago, journalist Daoud Kuttab said it's not likely to happen [since] the apartheid state is already here.

NA: Yes, exactly.

RH: [Are there] strategic ways to break this bondage through some kind of transformative process? You have this wonderful story of Pharaoh who "hardened his heart."

NA: That would be because Israel has hardened its heart.

RH: Yonatan Shapira, who [sailed] on the flotillas trying to break the siege of Gaza, said the only thing the Israelis can respond to is hitting them over the head … with a wake-up call.

NA: [And] cutting Israel's relations with as many countries as possible. They have to be isolated. Now it means that no country needs to move its embassy to Jerusalem.

RH: Americans might have some impact there.

NA: Yeah. Americans are as clever as the Israelis. They can always give incentives, millions of dollars, for these poor countries. And they will move their embassy….

RH: So, we have various political strategies, the economic strategy, other nongovernmental strategies that are there on the horizon…. In one of my dialogues with Jeff Halper, he calls out religious folks, people who make religious claims. He said, They've got to step up. Jeff is calling for prophetic voices—like Isaiah and Jeremiah—to step up.

NA: I wonder if he says that talking to you because he knows you're a religious person. Or is it something he has come to espouse, and it has a role. It could be both.

RH: You said that in one year things have changed so much. What else has changed for you?

NA: I think the issue of Palestine, the word Palestine became much more talked about globally, including in the United States…. There was a time, people would ask you where you come from, you say Palestine, and they think Pakistan…. There was a time I was always writing "Israel/Palestine." Recently I changed to "Palestine/Israel."

RH: That foregrounds the existence of Palestine more.

NA: I think it reflects also the common change…. Before 1967, for those of us who lived inside the state of Israel, it was taboo to use the word "Palestine."

RH: Track One diplomacy has failed. Is it too optimistic [to think] that nongovernmental peacemakers, Sabeel and other groups, will be able to hold on to that vision and translate it into the level where governments make decisions?

NA: Your question is so relevant now, in light of what Trump has done. I was really depressed. I started wondering, Is it over? If the [Israeli] policy is to force Gaza into becoming the state of Palestine, and Hamas is going to be in collusion with Americans, and the Americans are going to pour millions into Gaza to buy people [off], and they will force [Mohammad] Dahlan on the people there, and the Palestinian Authority will have home rule in disjointed pockets—if so, what do we do? I hope to God that many will continue to raise the voice of justice.

RH: The prophetic word. So, Track Two or nongovernmental diplomacy is crucial.

NA: It's becoming even more crucial!

RH: Estephan [Salameh] said that, too. He said that in the absence of a parliament, Palestinian NGOs are even more important in Palestine than in many other places.

NA: That's right.

RH: Thank you.

NA: Thank you! It's always good to see you. The testimonies that you have are essential.

12 Changing Public Opinion in Israel

Uri Avnery

Uri Avnery has been one of the most prolific journalists in the Israeli peace movement. Born in Germany and raised in Israel, he fought in the war of 1948, was elected to the Israeli Knesset, and advocated for a two-state solution to the conflict. In 1993, Avnery cofounded Gush Shalom. For decades, he published weekly columns, trying "to change Israeli public opinion." He died in 2018, just before his 95th birthday.

Tel Aviv, June 2005

UA: My name is Uri Avnery. I belong to the Gush Shalom peace movement (peace bloc).

RH: You are one of the cofounders.

UA: In 1993. You can find out all about me on the website of http://www.gush-shalom.org.

RH: Please tell me your personal history and what brought you to the Israeli peace movement.

UA: I was born in Germany. I came here immediately after Hitler came to power in 1933, and I've been here ever since. I was just ten years old when I came here.

RH: Do you remember that?

UA: I remember that very well. The last years of the so-called Weimar Republic and the beginning of the Third Reich are very vivid in my memory.... As a very politically conscious child, I remember the sights and sounds of the change in German history and in my own personal history. When I came to this country, Palestine at the time, I cut off completely any ties with my past. I used to say this was a second birth. Nothing which I had before I wanted to remember.

When I was 14, I joined the underground, which gave me a good education in terrorism.... There are two definitions of terrorists: freedom fighters are on my side; terrorists are on the other side.

RH: Did your training group use the term "terrorism"?

UA: Not at all. We were "freedom fighters," but we were officially defined as terrorists by the government of Palestine, which was under the

DOI: 10.4324/9781003262817-14

British Mandate. If we were caught, we would have been condemned as terrorists.

RH: Why was it necessary to pursue underground movements, if the British were helping out?

UA: The British gave the Balfour Declaration in 1917 out of purely British imperial interests—to win the Jews into joining the war against the Ottomans, and to win the Jews in Russia to induce Russia to stay in the war. The second reason, which is much more important, was that the French had designs on the whole Middle East, and the British needed a pretext in order to get Palestine, and it was the beginning of an alliance between Zionism and the British. Because the Zionist movement was antagonistic from the beginning toward local Palestinian people, the Zionists thought they needed a Western ally against Arab opposition. First they tried the Turks, then Germany, then Great Britain, then France, and finally they settled on America, which was the best choice they ever made. The British administration in this country became very quickly anti-Jewish, and Pro-Arab. On the eve of the Second World War we were more or less resolved to think about violent terrorist action. Like everything else that happened in the country in the past 120 years, it looks completely different to the Arabs. They are convinced to this very day that the British had set the Jews against the Arabs. Actually there was a joke at the time that the British high commissioner came into the colonial office in London and said, "I can't stand it any more. I'm cursed by the Jews and by the Arabs, and I want to resign." So the answer was, "If either side stops cursing you, you are fired" [Laughter].

The British involvement with this country is a very complicated thing. The book by Tom Segev gives quite a good description of this very ambivalent attitude the British had. By the end of the Second World War, after the Holocaust, Jewish people developed a very great bitterness against the British because the British did not allow the Jews to save themselves by coming here. At the end of the war, hundreds of thousands of Jewish refugees, who wanted to come here because they had nowhere else to go, were prevented by the British from coming here. So, all parts of the Jewish community here started a war against the British by different means. Some by violent action and terrorism. Others by illegal immigration, which became very dramatic. I joined the underground in 1938 and I left the underground in 1942–43. I became disillusioned. I did not like the methods of terrorism. The ideology was very right-wing and anti-socialist.

RH: So you were a member of the Irgun?

UA: I was a member of the Irgun, but I left when I was about 18 or 19. I became more convinced that we can and must make peace with the Arabs, and be on the side of the Arabs against the colonial powers.

People always ask, When did the change come to me? The answer is, there was no change at all. For me it was a continuation. I believe in the existence of nations. I believe in the right of nations to be free and independent. I joined the Irgun because they were a nationalist organization. But when I started to think about the problems of this country seriously, I came to the conclusion that there is a Palestinian nation here, and we shall never have peace if we do not acknowledge the right of the Palestinian Arab nation to have a state of their own, much like we want a state of our own.

In 1946 I founded an ideological organization which created a roar in this country. I proposed a union between the Arab national movement and our national movement. This has become the leitmotif of all my endeavors since then—there must be peace between two national movements ... to free the Middle East from foreign colonialist advances.... Two weeks before the 1967 war broke out, I published a booklet called *War or Peace in the Semitic Region*. In it I proposed the idea of an alliance between the Arab people and the Jewish nation. I did not call it Jewish; I called it Hebrew because we are a new nation. Later, we substituted word Israeli for Hebrew.

RH: How did your conception of the new state correspond to the Zionist movement?

UA: I called myself a post-Zionist, from the beginning of the state of Israel, long before this became an academic fad. The term is misunderstood because today post-Zionist is used as anti-Zionist. [But] post-Zionist means that Zionism has fulfilled its mission the moment the state of Israel came about. It was all about becoming a people like other peoples. It's a nation like other nations. A state like other states.... Within the Jewish community, we are different. We are conditioned by our own interests, our own culture, a new language, everything new.

RH: Once the community had gathered—before the state emerged—this new culture had arrived.

UA: Because it is a new nation. It's a new contract.

RH: So, Zionism had worked. It had brought you together.

UA: It's finished.

RH: So the term was no longer particularly useful.

UA: It was not useful at all. In our eyes, it was dangerous. Because the moment we considered ourselves as a new nation, a new state, we have new interests, national interests. One of our interests was to create an alliance with the Arab national movement, including the Palestinian movement. We are here. This is what our interests demand. Zionism automatically turns it around, looking at what a Jew is: American Jews, German Jews, Italian Jews – wherever Jews are, we are turning our backs on the Arabs with whom we have to live. What I advocated was to look at the whole "Middle East."

(Middle East is purely an imperialistic term. I called it the "Semitic" region. It is the only term that is common to Arabs and Israelis.)

Just before the war in 1948, I published a booklet called *War for Peace in the Semitic Union.* This has become my trademark. Everybody jokes about it, the term "Semitic union," when they talk about me. But, then the war broke out. We deplored it very much. It changed everything [because] this became a war of survival for both sides. So, I joined the army.

RH: How did you think about your goal of a national movement for two peoples during the war?

UA: By November of '47, it was too late to think about anything but war. It was a war of survival, full of atrocities from the very beginning. I wrote two books about it. My views evolved. It was an ethnic war. Ethnic wars are different from any other wars because they are not wars between two nations who want a piece of land between them. Here, both sides claimed the whole country as their historic fatherland. The term ethnic cleansing was not yet invented, but this is what the war was all about—for both sides.... We caused 750,000 Arabs to leave, but not one single Jew remained in the territories conquered by the Arabs. It was not a one-sided ethnic cleansing, but a general ethnic war. Fortunately for us, the Arabs conquered very small territories—the old city of Jerusalem, and several little enclaves. Where Arabs conquered territory, no Jew remained.

It started as a war between us and the Palestinian Arabs for about half a year. Then it became a general war with us and the Arab armies which entered Palestine ... the Egyptian army, the Jordanian army, the Syrian army. I was employed in the beginning of the war to fight for Jerusalem against the Palestinian Arabs and the irregular troops which were fighting on their side. From the middle of May, when the Arab armies entered the country, I was employed in the war against Egypt, against the Egyptian army. I was wounded close to the end of the war.

I came out of the war completely convinced of several very unorthodox ideas. One, there exists a Palestinian nation. The Palestinian nation must get a state of its own, and we shall never have peace if such a state is not created. Two, the state of Israel must find a place in a unified Semitic region and play a part in it. I wrote two books about the war: *In the Fields of the Philistines* is my war reports. I was not allowed to write and publish, but I did.

RH: So you've been a journalist most of your life?

UA: I've always been a journalist. Someone said I should publish my reports, from a soldier's point of view, as a book. It became a smashing success. But I realized that I really missed the point because there was severe military censorship; and, second, there are things during war that you cannot write. So I did not write about the atrocities.

I immediately wrote a second book, which came out a year after the first, about the other side. The book is called *The Other Side of the Meadow*. Because of the demons of war, it was boycotted almost immediately. So, one year after being immensely popular, I became very unpopular, and that is how I remain to this very day.

In the second book I did something that was literally forbidden. I added a political epilogue in which I set out this idea that we cannot realize our dream for the kind of state we want to have if the war goes on. We must make peace with the Palestinians and there must be a Palestinian state. I immediately set to work on propagating this idea of the state of Israel and the state of Palestine working side by side. I tried to create an organization for that purpose in 1949. At that time there were not 10 people in the whole country who were ready to accept this idea.

Ben-Gurion believed that the war with the Arabs could go on forever. Ben-Gurion did not believe in peace with the Arabs. It was Ben-Gurion who decided to drive the Arabs out in the second half of the war. In the first half they were pushed out by the war itself. People don't understand the real problem. What happened was, we would go up in our jeeps and shoot at a village. It always happened at night because we weren't equipped for fighting during the day.

RH: Was this especially around Jerusalem?

UA: All over the country. We would come with four or five jeeps, each with two machine guns, and shoot tens of thousands of bullets at the village. The people in the village, the wives and children, fled to the next village, where the same thing happened. We went from village to village, until one day we found an armistice line between ourselves and the village. This is part of the answer. The other part is that by the second half of the war, when it was clear that we were winning, there was a clear policy on driving the Arabs out; this was ethnic cleansing per se.

RH: There was a motive beyond survival in ethnic cleansing?

UA: We were winning and we could afford to. If you want to really know what happened, you have to read the books by Benny Morris, who now says it is a pity we did not drive out more.

The main problem is that Palestinians were not allowed to return. It would have been a completely different story if the refugees had come back, as refugees generally do after a war. It was Ben-Gurion's decision not to allow one single refugee to come back. I wrote this in my book, that we got orders to shoot any Arab that tries to come back to his village.

Ben-Gurion was convinced that the Arabs would not make peace with us. Not in our generation. Not in the remote future. Because we had taken their land and driven them out, they would not make peace with us, so we must live in a perpetual state of war. In order to survive, we need the support of one big Western power. First he tried with the British, then with the French, up to the war of 1967, and from then on, it became America. Ben-Gurion also believed that this was a Jewish state, and that we must induce all of the Jews of the world to come here. We cannot make any distinction between religion and state and religion and nation.

RH: It sounds like the things you opposed became the dominant direction of the state of Israel.

UA: We want a different kind of state of Israel from the beginning to this very day. In 1957, I cofounded the Semitic Action movement. We published a "Hebrew Manifesto" and proposed a Palestinian state. I was elected to the Knesset and served for 10 years. In the middle of the Six-Day War [1967], I published a letter to the prime minister, saying, Now that we have conquered all of the Palestinian territories, immediately offer the possibility of setting up a Palestinian state. He rejected the idea completely. I made 100 speeches to the Knesset against the first settlement. I had a running argument with Golda Meir. I told her, Every settlement is a land mine, and when the time comes, you will have to remove the land mines. That is a very unpleasant job.

RH: When did you begin Gush Shalom?

UA: In 1993. It is an optimistic movement. It is fighting against despair, which is very popular in certain circles in Israel.... I remember when there were not 10 people in the whole world who agreed that the Palestinian people must have a state of their own. Now that everybody in the U.S., Russia, Europe, the UN, the great majority in Israel, the great majority in Palestine recognize that this is the only solution, it is an immense progress. Even if on the surface it is always bad, things are moving under the surface. So Gush Shalom is an optimistic organization.

RH: Even though the "facts on the ground" keep getting worse and worse?

UA: If you compare bad today to bad yesterday, they are very bad.... In 1993, we decided that the peace movement which existed until then, Peace Now, was inadequate. We needed to create a radical Israeli peace movement. This movement became Gush Shalom. We formulated a detailed peace plan as a draft peace agreement. All the questions involved with our conflict had a clear proposed solution, a two-state solution. End the occupation and create a Palestinian state in all the territories of the West Bank and the Gaza Strip.

RH: On the 1967 borders?

UA: Yes, on the Green Line, with 1967 borders, Jerusalem as the capital, remove all Israeli settlements in the Palestinian Territories, connect the Gaza strip with the West Bank. And address the refugee problem, by far the most difficult problem. Assume responsibility for everything that we did in '48. Create a committee for peace and reconciliation of independent people, once and for all to set forth what really happened and who is responsible for what.

RH: Create a common narrative?

UA: Exactly. I'll come back to the common narrative because this is a very central part of the Gush Shalom. Secondly, there is a level of principle. Every refugee has the right to return and this must be recognized as a moral principle. Third is the practical solution. Israel is not going to take back four million refugees; it's impossible. On the other hand, we cannot stand on the principle that we shall not take back any refugees at all. We must agree upon a practical compromise which both sides will accept through negotiation, say 50,000 refugees for 10 years.

RH: Create a process that can be adjusted.

UA: A process which is psychological, economical, and so on. Gush Shalom's job is to change Israeli public opinion and to make peace possible. In the field, we conduct many actions.

RH: Do you mean demonstrations?

UA: Exactly. The objective of these demonstrations is to address Israeli public opinion through media coverage. You cannot propagate abstract ideas on television. You have to create events which can be and should be covered by the media in order to put this idea before Israeli public opinion. The Green Line had completely disappeared from all maps. We went to the supreme court and demanded that the Green Line be put back on maps, which was accepted. Seven years ago, we started the boycott of settlement products. We published a list of those products and distributed about 20,000 copies. At this moment, there must be 10,000 households who observe this. By not buying the water from the Golan but buying from Israel, we are trying to end Israeli settlements on Palestinian land.

RH: So the boycott continues?

UA: It goes on all the time. We work with Jeff Halper in building homes that have been destroyed by the army. We've had close to 400 demonstrations like this in 12 years.... The other part, which may be more important, is the common narrative. We can never have real peace if the ordinary Israeli is not able to understand the Palestinian narrative and vice versa. Therefore, we have published a concise history of the conflict of the last 120 years, to combine the narrative of the two sides. We have distributed 100,000 copies in Hebrew, Arabic, Russian, and English. We believe the people who read it change their minds. This is working under the surface.

RH: My [book] project is similar to that—to help create a new narrative for the American public.

UA: There are things here that touch on basic beliefs which every Israeli child is taught in school. This is absolutely axiomatic: "Before 1948, before the Arabs declared war on us and compelled us to conquer Palestine, we did not displace one single Arab. We bought the land with money, which we collected peacefully from Jews all over the world. No Arab was hurt." For Palestinians it looks much different; we bought land from absentee owners in Jaffa, Beirut, and Monte Carlo.

RH: So this narrative project is working at the deep structure of what people understand about their own history, and the other level of Gush Shalom is actions with very practical goals.

UA: In this respect I think Gush Shalom is unique. There are people who are very important in small movements who are acting in one particular niche, for example, the soldiers' movement, Courage to Refuse (Yesh Gvul), which encourages people to refuse military service in the Occupied Territories; Women in Black are extremely courageous; Rabbis for Human Rights—

RH: The Israeli Committee Against Home Demolitions....

UA: Of course. Each one doing excellent and important work. Gush Shalom is trying to activate a political pioneering force to break new ground in political thinking. We are publishing a weekly column for 13 years. We concentrate on one message every week dealing with a topical situation. I think it's a type of peacemaking for the whole peace movement, much beyond Gush Shalom. We are convinced that we can change Israeli public opinion. We completely reject despair, to give up on Israeli public opinion. We try to convince the world to change.

* * * * * * *

Tel Aviv, 2006

RH: I'm talking with Uri Avnery, one of the best journalists writing on conflict in the Middle East.

UA: I think so, but I'm not objective!

RH: We were talking about theatre as a metaphor for the ongoing drama here—the ongoing conflict. If a theatre metaphor is appropriate, which theatre metaphor—farce, tragedy, theatre of the absurd?

UA: All of it. All of it belongs to life, and life is all of it. It's a very tragic conflict we are living in; it sometimes borders on farce, and it certainly is absurd. So you take whatever you want.

RH: When I was in Jerusalem a week ago, most of the people I talked to seemed to move toward a sense of the absurd. Kafka's name came up very often as a kind of image or metaphor.

UA: Everybody is imprisoned in his own narrative, which consists of some truths, some lies, a lot of myths, and imprisoning terminology. In Hebrew you say, "Life and death are in the hands of the tongue." The words we use are the tyrants which direct our behavior....

If you say, "We are releasing Arab fighters for our soldiers," it's one thing. If you say, "We are releasing bloodstained murderers for our soldiers," this shows how morally superior we are to them, because they are base killers, cruel murderers, ghastly terrorists, while our soldiers are morally motivated fighters for our people.... The words we use are dominating our actions.

RH: Theatre also consists of actions and demonstrations, and I know that you are very much an activist. I marched with you in the streets of Tel Aviv two years ago.

UA: Demonstrations are theatre.

RH: Why is it important to go to the streets?

UA: A demonstration is a way to turn abstract ideas into a visible event. This is how the general public receives information. People see demonstrators moving toward the Wall, chanting, "The Wall must fall," and the armed soldiers attacking them—then they see the Wall in a different light.

RH: Especially Israeli-Jewish perceptions, or is it much broader than that?

UA: We concentrate on our own Israeli-Jewish public because we don't have to convince the Israeli-Arab citizens who are already convinced.... I don't have a good feeling about doing this in the U.S. I have Kafkaesque experiences with trying to voice our opinions in America.... In Germany and France and England, it's far easier. But it's fairly difficult everywhere because the official Israeli narrative is being accepted all over the Western world as a given.

RH: And your narrative is different. It doesn't fit into the dominant narrative.

UA: It's totally different! Therefore, it's rejected! People don't like it. But you need a mental pattern because you must organize the information somehow.

RH: Coherence. You can interpret things.

UA: There will be no peace for Israel, no peace in the Middle East if we do not change our perceptions—if we do not include and understand the hopes, aspirations, and fears of the other side. So this is the job we have to do. It has to be done and we are trying to do it.

And I must say I am very optimistic because, contrary to appearances, I think we have won a major part of the necessary victory. What we are saying is changing the Israeli perceptions quite a lot over the years. It's one of the privileges of old age—I'm going on 85—that you can compare it for a much longer span of time than young people can. We have won major victories.

RH: A year ago, you said many things are happening beneath the surface.

UA: I will repeat this. With even more certainty.... We are living in two worlds, or at two different levels, day-to-day occurrences—the situation on the ground, the subterranean streams. On the ground the situation is getting worse all the time—

RH: Much worse.

UA: By far, life in the Occupied Territories is becoming worse and worse. Settlements are expanding, new settlements are going up all the time. So you could say there are lots of grounds for pessimism on both sides. On the other side, it's now accepted in Israel by the vast majority that there will be no solution without a Palestinian state, and that Jerusalem must be divided.

RH: Mistrust.

UA: Most of all, fear and mistrust. An ordinary Israeli today will tell you, There isn't going to be peace because the other side doesn't want peace.

RH: You can't trust them.

UA: And you must be afraid of them. The other side says Israel has broken all its agreements with the Palestinians, with Arabs in general. There are enough facts on both sides that justify it. So this is the real battlefield. The battlefield is mental. The battlefield is psychological.

RH: So do you think the Wall was intended to be psychological?

UA: If on either side there had been a conspiracy, it would be better. If there is no conspiracy, if it's just a general consensus, it is by far more difficult. There is no conspiracy. Israelis believe—

RH: But to build a Wall like this, Uri, takes a great deal of thought and planning and effort and money. Somebody has thought about it and planned it.

UA: It's automatic.

RH: Automatic? They do it because they can do it?

UA: Political movements have genes—like a human being—maybe from inception. You do it automatically. You need a decision to change it, which is far more difficult.... It's far more difficult to make an operation and change the genetic code of a movement. This is what we are trying to do, metaphorically. On our side, the drive is an inherent drive, to take hold of as much of the country as possible and exclude non-Jewish inhabitants.

RH: Is it fair to call that ethnic cleansing?

UA: The expression ethnic cleansing has come much later. For Zionism, this great historic movement, which has done incredible things, good and bad, the basic drive was to have a state where the Jews can be on their own without fear. They suffered so much from non-Jews, the Gentiles, throughout the ages. At long last we want a place of our own where we could be masters of our own destiny and where we don't have to meet non-Jews. This is really the basic drive of Israel, of Zionism. If there's a clash between this basic drive and another drive, for example, to get all of Palestine, the demographic clash wins. This is why today the occupation is not popular and the settlers are not popular. Jewish people don't want to have a state where there are three, four, five million Arabs. They don't want to have a binational state. There's one thing about which Israelis are 99.9% unanimous: they don't want to have a binational state. They want to have a Jewish state.

RH: And would you include yourself?

UA: Including myself. I would not phrase it exactly in the same words, but basically, I want a state where our national personality will be dominant, where we speak Hebrew, where we make our own laws. I don't see any reason why there should not be Arab citizens or Japanese citizens. I don't think it should be an ethnically clean state. We have 20% Arab citizens in this country. I am quite ready to have another 5% Arabs if it solves the problem. Basically I want a Hebrew-speaking state where our national consciousness will be the dominant force.

RH: Is it possible that those cultural genes that you're talking about are so dominant and so unreflective that two states have been eliminated as a possibility; that all the Israeli governments have systematically ruined the infrastructure and made it impossible for a Palestinian state?

UA: It makes it difficult, but far from impossible.

RH: If there's a political will.

UA: If there's a political will, everything can be adjusted to this. If you want it. Like Theodor Hertzl once said, "If you want it, it won't be a fable."

RH: [Chuckles] Right.

UA: It's all a question of will, and the will is a question of perceptions and mentality. This is the basic drive of the whole thing. We have two peoples in this country; neither can be removed nor will go away. So the only solution is for the Palestinians to have a Palestinian state, a Palestinian flag, and a Palestinian face on the international map and membership in the family of nations.

RH: You've had extended debates with Ilan Pappe and others about this, yes?

UA: Yes, we had a public debate about this. His ideas run counter to the current of history, to the current of most people. Nationalism is a basic force in our world. Maybe in a thousand years, it will be overcome. But, in the last hundred years, anyone who ran counter to nationalism has lost.

RH: If your preferred scenario of two states would come about, would you advocate for equal rights and full citizenship for Palestinians who remain within Israel?

UA: Sure. At the same time, I hope there will be a region—united economically, militarily, politically and perhaps culturally—which includes Palestinian, Israeli, and Egyptian nations.

RH: Some kind of confederation.

UA: Today, we call it a union, as in the European Union.... Israeli Arabs are Israelis. They are used to Israeli democracy. And they like it. Therefore they are in a tragic situation. As one of them once said, "My country is at war with my people." There is a double loyalty here.... On one side, they are identified with the Palestinian people, and on the other side, they are Israelis; they have adopted from Israel many, many things. So, they are in a kind of limbo between the two things.

RH: When we started talking, you seemed concerned to keep a Jewish majority, so it remains—

UA: Hebrew. Not Jewish. We don't call it Jewish. Because the Jewish community, the worldwide community, belongs to many different nations.

RH: So as long as the Hebrew language and Hebrew culture remain "dominant"—?

UA: Majority, it's a majority, like Anglo-Saxon civilization in the U.S. How would an American react if somebody told him in another 20 or 50 years the great majority of the U.S. will be Hispanic and the language will be Spanish.

RH: There is a good chance that at least—

UA: How would you like it? Would you like it?

RH: Ethnically that will be the case.

UA: Would you like it?

RH: It won't matter whether I like it or not. It's likely to be the case.

UA: If the Arabs in Israel become the majority, I won't like it. Because I like what we've created here, our Hebrew language, literature, and theatre—in which there are quite a lot of Arab players.

RH: So how do we get from where we are now, with all of its confusion and suffering and fear, to what you envision? How do we get there?

UA: It's a struggle. It's a very messy struggle. Nothing is simple. Neither here nor anywhere else.

RH: There might be some sudden change that no one can anticipate, as in South Africa. So you keep the struggle going and nobody quite knows how it will happen.

UA: We know what we want to happen, but we cannot say how or when. I've seen in my long life so many improbable things happen.... [But] the comparison between Israel and South Africa is completely fallacious. But what could have been more unexpected than the collapse of the whole Soviet Union—without bloodshed? This is very unusual in history.

Two things you never can say—one is to fix a timetable. It generally takes much longer than you expect, and then it happens quite suddenly. And you never know exactly how it will happen—like a river from its source, striving to reach the sea. If there is absolutely no way to reach a solution, neither side can expect to take over all of

Palestine. It's impossible. [If] they don't want to live together in one state, and they've no other way to realize their national aspirations, by default it will reach two states. That will be a new beginning.

I expect these two states to go together very quickly [in] something like a federation. Yassar Arafat spoke to me many times about the need for a federation of Israel, Palestine, Jordan, and perhaps Lebanon. I believe this will happen because two totally sovereign, independent states in this little country are just not possible. There must be very close economic cooperation and freedom of movement. Palestinians need [these things] for their national healing. Israel wants it and needs it. Once we have two states, things will happen very quickly.

RH: Thanks. You've been very generous.

13 The Power of Nonviolence

Sami Awad

Sami Awad, the founder and former executive director of Holy Land Trust, is committed to support, train, and develop nonviolence in the Holy Land. Awad was influenced by the teachings of his uncle, Mubarak Awad, a Palestinian activist whom the Israeli government deported during the first intifada. *Awad holds degrees in political science and peace and conflict resolution. For Awad, it is very important that those who are working for justice in the Middle East "do not lose hope."*

Bethlehem, May 2005

SA: Holy Land Trust has a lot to do with where I come from, my personal information.

RH: Were you born here?

SA: I was born in Kansas City, Missouri, in 1971. My father was teaching in an inner-city school in Kansas City. He had come back here, married my mother, who is from Gaza, and then went back to the U.S. We returned here when I was six months old. I grew up most of my life in Bethlehem. In 1988, I returned to the U.S. after the Israeli military closed all of the schools and universities. I was a senior in high school, and became active in the nonviolent resistance movement. My father sent me back to the U.S., where I [finished] in political science at the University of Kansas, and my master's degree in peace and conflict resolution at the American University in Washington, D.C. I returned here in 1996.

A big influence on my life was my uncle, Mubarak Awad. In the mid-1980s, after living in the U.S., he came to Palestine [and] encouraged people to resist the occupation through nonviolence. He wanted to build more nonviolent strategies, and have the international community [learn] that Palestinians are resisting in nonviolent ways. I went with him to demonstrations and participated in protests on lands that were [threatened with] confiscation. I realized that this nonviolence really scares the Israeli government. Both sides rejected Mubarak; Israelis saw him as a threat and Palestinians saw him as an alternative to the

DOI: 10.4324/9781003262817-15

traditional armed-resistance movement. PLO leaders were not interested in nonviolence. He didn't get Arafat's blessing, [so] he was rejected.

Mubarak was seen as going against the flow of the resistance movement. In 1987, the first Palestinian uprising broke out. Local leaders took over the street and led the nonviolence movement. The Israelis arrested Mubarak and deported him to the U.S.

RH: Because of his work in nonviolence?

SA: Yes, because from 1984 to 1987, his ideas were implemented on the ground. He had a list of more than a hundred ways to resist through nonviolence—with strikes, boycotting products, closing shops, and disobedience campaigns. [When] he was arrested and deported, that was a turning point for me. I came back to Palestine in 1996 to work on [nonviolence]. Three of us continued Mubarak's work by initiating the Holy Land Trust in Bethlehem. Even though there was an official "peace process," we said that Palestinians should continue nonviolent resistance. The big eruption came in 2000, when the entire peace process failed, and the second Palestinian uprising began. Our role became stronger as an organization. Our mission is to strengthen the Palestinian community. As an organization, there are two main questions: What tools can we provide, and what comes after the occupation ends?

RH: Why is it so important to think about "what comes after," when day-to-day work is so difficult?

SA: It is difficult to end the occupation; it is going to be much more difficult to build a nation. We need to work on what it would take to maintain a nation. After the occupation ends, all kinds of groups and nations will target the Palestinian community and try to destroy it as fragile and weak.

RH: That is a lot to deal with—the occupation and the ripple effect on surrounding countries.

SA: That is where nonviolence comes in. It is a tool of self-empowerment. It is a way for the Palestinian community to take control of themselves and not to depend on others. We can't depend on Arab or Muslim countries to liberate us; we cannot depend on the U.S., the Europeans, or the UN to pressure Israel. The Palestinian community has to do this....

RH: Discuss nonviolence as both strategy and "weapon."

SA: We are engaged in warfare. We live under occupation and we resist this occupation. The weapons that we use are not the traditional weapons that armies have used, or that the Israeli military uses—F-16 fighter jets, tanks, and machine guns. We use the will of the people as the weapon of resistance. We do lack an overall strategy, and it is something that we work on.

Most Palestinians are just trying to survive daily hardships. When an individual asks if he is able to feed his family, or to shelter them, he is not thinking of large strategies. We do not have time to reflect on where we are, or [how] to reach [a goal]. We do not bring Gandhian teachings or Martin Luther King's teachings to Palestinians. We say, What is in our culture that we can build on?

RH: What [are] those traditional elements of Palestinian culture that you can recover?

SA: Palestinian people throughout history have engaged in nonviolence without even knowing the term and the concept. For example, in 1936, Palestinians engaged in a six-month, nonviolent strike against the British Mandate with two demands: that the British declare Palestine as a state and restrict the number of Jews coming to Palestine.... In the '70s and '80s, Palestinians engaged in nonviolent activities against the occupation through student councils, unions, and university students. This ended in 1987 with the first *intifada,* which was a great success—with recognition of Palestinians as a community, [with] legitimate leadership, a desire to negotiate, courage to raise the Palestinian flag, and courage to speak the word Palestine.

RH: Explain the Arabic word *intifada*. It is more than the translated word "uprising."

SA: *Intifada* is a wonderful term and a wonderful concept. It means to shed, to throw away, to get rid of.... We want the occupation to leave.

RH: Talk about the difference between your experience of the first *intifada* and what North Americans saw on television ... and other actions which were commonly called "violence."

SA: During the first part of the 1987 *intifada*, Palestinians lived a wonderful communal existence. We were united in the face of the oppressor, working together, demanding our rights.... We recognized that through nonviolence, we could achieve tremendous gains. We even saw transformations in the Israeli society; Israelis become aware of what their government and their military had been doing for many years against Palestinians. The media only showed the acts of violence. Palestinians who engaged in stone throwing realized it was a symbolic act.

RH: Wonderful work is being done, but how do you break through the occupation?

SA: We cannot wait on people to come and save us if we are not willing to fight. Most Palestinians are in the middle. They are not engaged in resistance, but they refuse to surrender.

RH: Talk about nonviolent resistance as both a power process and a call to conscience.

SA: We have two approaches: the pragmatic approach, which deals with tactics and strategies of resistance, and the principled approach, which is the communal approach, and the faith-based approach. As an organization, we focus on convincing people to get involved in the pragmatic side of nonviolence. If we engage people in the pragmatic approach, that brings them closer to the principled approach—how to live as a community, how to resolve internal issues.

RH: In Christianity, Islam, and Jewish history, people have justified fighting holy wars with weapons and structural violence. How do you call out nonviolent elements in these traditions?

SA: Many people think that resistance can only be done through the use of arms and traditional warfare. We challenge this, and channel nonviolence through religious Scriptures in Islam and Christianity. For example, the prophet Mohammad engaged in nonviolence or negotiations prior to engaging in violence. Violence was the last resort.

RH: In Christianity there would be strong parallels.

SA: Very much. The teachings of Christ are very clear—"Love your enemy." Some Christians manipulate these simple words ... to justify violent acts. With Christians, we talk about the need to resist oppression ... to use nonviolence as a weapon, a strategy, and a way of life.

RH: Summarize your approach to nonviolence as teaching and training.

SA: We are trying to change from a reactionary movement to a proactive movement. Our nonviolence addresses specific issues. The apartheid Wall is being built, so we demonstrate against it. Land is being confiscated, so we go and protest. It is a reactionary movement. For nonviolence to succeed, it has to be proactive, so the other side doesn't know how to react.

RH: To reframe the whole perception of the situation?

SA: In the first uprising, the world saw a [reversal] of David and Goliath. People thought, Something is wrong here. Look what the soldiers are doing to these Palestinian children.

RH: Can you give me another example?

SA: As an organization, we ... lead many protests and demonstrations in the Bethlehem area. At Easter, we did the first Palm Sunday demonstration. Christians and Muslims who live in Bethlehem are not allowed to go and pray in Jerusalem on holy days. So, this year, we organized a mass demonstration of Palestinians to go to Jerusalem and pray on Palm Sunday. Hundreds of people participated—with children, donkeys, palm leaves, and banners. We walked [several miles] to the checkpoint. Of course, we were completely blocked by the Israeli army and not allowed to cross into Jerusalem. We had a sit-in, and ... read a statement to the Israeli soldiers, informing them that they [could] refuse ... to be oppressors. The ripple effect was international awareness. We received hundreds of emails from churches around the world, saying they did not know [about the occupation]. They described the transformations in their lives.

RH: Does Christianity have a unique opportunity to work with Christian symbols in Bethlehem?

SA: I am proud that the nonviolent movement is a Palestinian movement. I am [prouder] that most of the participants are Muslims. Two months ago, when we organized the first conference for nonviolent resistance, we invited a hundred Palestinian leaders to participate. There were three Christians and 97 Muslims. So, it is a Palestinian movement. It is not faith-based here. We all suffer the same because we are Palestinians in the eyes of Israeli soldiers or settlers.

The role that Christians play is an important one because of the linkage they can make to Western churches. It would be much easier for the Israeli government to conduct a war against the Muslim community. They could create many justifications for a war against Muslims—as terrorists, or extremists—by saying "[Muslims] want to destroy us; their religion is a violent religion."

We want people to understand the conflict through their faith, to come and meet with Muslim leaders who are nonviolent. We want people to see what life is really like in Palestine, to see what the occupation does to us. Most importantly we want people to see the humanity of Palestinians.

RH: Your work includes programs for peace and reconciliation....

SA: Peace and reconciliation are at the heart of Holy Land Trust. All programs focus on building a nonviolent community. A second department is called Travel and Encounter. The third program is the Palestine News Network (PNN), for the news that happens in Palestine, and the news that CNN does not bring, such as news about nonviolence. PNN.org receives 400,000 hits per day.

RH: As someone committed to nonviolence, how do you work with television violence?

SA: The famous media statement is "If it bleeds, it leads." So, we engage in [lively] activities. For example, the Palm Sunday demonstration was eventful; it attracted a lot of media attention.

* * * * * * * *

Bethlehem, June 2006

RH: How have things changed since last year?

SA: Things have really changed—the redeployment of Israeli forces from Gaza, and the [2006] election within the Palestinian Authority. Hamas gained a majority of seats in the parliament and formed a government. The economic sanctions imposed on us caused tremendous suffering.

RH: So, it feels like a major sea change?

SA: It is. The situation has become worse and worse in Palestine, with Israelis refusing to negotiate with Palestinian leaders, blaming and punishing leaders for anything that goes wrong.

RH: So, these things not only affected people in Gaza but directly affected your own work?

SA: More and more people lose hope. People are afraid of the situation becoming worse if they engage in any resistance. For example, a village will lose 80% of its land because the Wall will be built around it, and people won't have access to their farmland. They tell us, "We are afraid if we do anything we will lose the other 20%. We can't even afford two shekels to come to a protest." We see more people accepting nonviolence, but there isn't [enough] capacity to organize ourselves nonviolently and deal with [our] economic and psychological situation.

RH: Which is more profound, the economic or psychological situation?

SA: The psychological level [is] more difficult because people feel that no matter what form of resistance we do, the occupation is going to remain and become more difficult. They say, There is nothing we can do to change this. It creates the sense of surrender, the biggest challenge.

RH: From the Israeli perspective, that's a central goal, to demoralize people and end resistance?

SA: I believe this. The Israeli government realizes that within the Palestinian community there is a serious challenge to armed resistance. The Israeli military fears nonviolence.

RH: How would restrictions on movement directly affect a nonviolent campaign?

SA: We are involved in a network of 19 villages in the southern and western parts of Bethlehem. When the 25-foot Wall is completed, these villages will lose up to 17% of their farmland. We are trying to organize these villages to work together....

RH: What's the interface between "self-sufficiency," a key term for you, and your strategy for going up against one of the largest military powers in the world?

SA: We need an internal approach to reorganize ourselves, to restructure the Palestinian Authority to focus on resistance. We need Palestinian leaders who are able to do very serious assessments. Then we take this to the people and say, "This is the situation we are in, this is the capacity we have, these are the difficulties we face, this is how we can challenge the occupation."

RH: Last summer, Jeff Halper said, "Israelis in the peace movement want to support Palestinian leaders but we're not getting clear signals about how to do that." So, you and he would agree.

SA: Yes, but nobody is talking about the occupation and a blockade of Gaza. It has been transformed into a big prison camp.... I will say this clearly, I am not a critic of armed resistance as a means to end oppression. History is full of examples where armed resistance was used.... But we have to make an assessment—is armed resistance working or not?

RH: So, your internal dialogue and internal conflict are nearly as large as the external conflict?

SA: It is a very difficult debate within the Palestinian community. We will not be able to address the bigger conflicts of the occupation if we fail to address the internal issues that we are facing.

RH: Is that dialogue beginning to happen now, since the 2006 elections, or is it still too soon?

SA: There have been many discussions between political factions. Recently the prisoners issued a document that was presented to all the political parties to discuss. That created a very serious debate within the Palestinian community. Hamas and Fatah came to some common ground. [But] we are far from political factions' addressing their internal strategies and their internal vision.

RH: Do you still think of a two-state solution or some really different model for a just peace?

SA: In our organizational documents, you will find [a call for] mutual recognition by each side of the equal rights of the other to be here. That, for us, is where the peace process begins.

RH: So, [you have] an internal strategy within the Palestinian community....

SA: Our focus now is going to the grassroots community in Palestine with an extensive training program. We just completed the training of 30 trainers, and the 30 trainers now are doing trainings in 10 districts in the West Bank. Soon, we will have about 800 individuals who are trained in nonviolent direct action all across the West Bank. These individuals represent different political factions, different organizations, even different components of the Palestinian Authority. We have been asked to open a dialogue with some Hamas communities [to do] trainings.

RH: Does that dialogue take place at the religious level, or is it primarily at the pragmatic level?

SA: It's a combination of both, but especially the pragmatic approach. But people also want to justify the acts that they do religiously. This creates a protected area for people to work with. They want to know if this is part of our culture, part of our religious teaching.

RH: Do you use the term nonviolence or do you use concepts around resistance?

SA: We really push the concept and the term of nonviolence. In Arabic this is more difficult, because nonviolence in Arabic is *la'ounf,* which means "no to violence." Many people see *la'ounf* as only a critique of armed resistance, and not as its own unique approach of resisting. So, we talk about nonviolent resistance, *"Allah muhawama Allah enfia."* But we put out all the terms from the first day. We say, Call it civil disobedience, nonviolent resistance, or popular resistance. You create the name you want for it. We are not looking for "dialogue" with Israelis. We are [trying] to create a mass resistance movement. Participants say, "OK, now we can start."

RH: Tell me about the nonviolence conference last December. Any observations?

SA: This event created a very serious discussion within the Palestinian community, raising it a notch and allowing it to grow. It was the first time that we had over 200 Palestinian activists come together, to meet each other ... to discuss different approaches and different strategies that they are engaged in. This internal discussion was a great success, and a success for internationals, such as Gene Sharp, to come here and recognize the Palestinian nonviolent movement as viable.

RH: In the mainstream press [in the U.S.], you hear absolutely nothing about this movement.

SA: Israel does not want this to happen, and they are trying to cut it at the root. It is important for those who work for justice in the Middle East not to lose hope. It is for the benefit of the world.

* * * * * * * *

Bethlehem, June 2008

RH: Assess developments in the nonviolence movement.

SA: Many militant and political factions realized that engaging in armed resistance was not achieving the results they wanted. So, a group of combatants asked for nonviolence training.

RH: Were you surprised?

SA: I was surprised.... I challenged them, because I want people to think about nonviolence as not the first option, but the only option. I asked if they were macho enough for nonviolence. We did an incredible training with them. It was all done underground.

RH: So, from your perspective, there were genuine transformations?

SA: There were. The guns have been put away—destroyed, actually.

RH: Tell me what the training components are.

SA: It's a four-day training.... We try to do it all together.

RH: Because it's not information as much as a transformation?

SA: It's transformation. We analyze conflict the first day. The second day we focus on violence as a means of responding to conflict, and the different types and levels of violence.... It's part of structural, psychological, social, and cultural violence, [including] violence that happens within our own society. It's good for them to see violence with new eyes. The third day we present different approaches to nonviolence, from the principled to the pragmatic.

RH: In our conversation two days ago, you used the word empowerment quite a bit....

SA: The first word I put parallel to nonviolence is empowerment—empowerment at the individual level [and] on the spiritual, emotional, physical levels. And then the family level, the community level, the organizational level, the national level, and the cross-national level.... More and more we're seeing less negative responses to the term nonviolence in Arabic. I can say I work in *la'ounf* in the community, and they won't look at me with criticism of *la'ounf* as a theoretical issue. The challenge is how to transform it into a practical issue.... Last year we trained 20 Hamas leaders in Tobas, in the north of the West Bank. Local leaders wanted to see what we're talking about when we say nonviolence.... They made positive remarks. At the grassroots level, we're seeing requests for training. We have 40 trainers, and thousands of people take the training every year.

RH: Both internally and externally?

SA: Mostly internally. If it doesn't start internally, nothing external is going to happen.... Once that starts, then we will see Israelis, internationals, and others joining in and supporting it.

RH: Jeff Halper says leadership has to come from [Palestinins].

SA: Leadership is the big program for us now.... This is not a traditional linear conflict or warfare, so we have to address it in a different way. People ask, Where is the Gandhi or Martin Luther King of Palestine? I say, We should ask, where is the salt or the Rosa Parks in Palestine?

RH: The spark.

SA: The spark. When people say, We want to be part of this, then we will have leadership.

RH: What's the relationship between your peace, nonviolence, and reconciliation work and the local committees, the popular committees?

SA: Very strong, especially in the Bethlehem area. We are part of the local committee, and we actively train and participate with them in their nonviolence work....

RH: Talk to me about needing breakthroughs, even if they are not grand solutions.

SA: "Breakthrough" is a big word in our leadership program.

RH: Do you have any recent breakthroughs?

SA: The 40 people that we did this training with, they started small projects, such as reading books at checkpoints.... not to get frustrated and mad.

* * * * * * * *

Bethlehem, July 2016

RH: I want to talk with you about dialogue between Palestinians and Israeli-Palestinian dialogue. After 2014 the war in Gaza, there was little dialogue between Israelis and Palestinians.

SA: A refusal to engage with the other, being attacked by locals if you engage with the other.

RH: Resistance within your own community.

SA: Exactly. Now we receive more pressure locally from Palestinians not to engage in any work with Israelis. People are labelled "normalizers," "traitors," and "collaborators" for doing this.

RH: You say both Israeli and Palestinian communities have to dig deeper for a serious dialogue.

SA: We Palestinians need to reevaluate everything—our vision, our motives, and where we want to go. Israelis need to do the same. Oslo is completely dead.... I distinguish between Oslo and a two-state solution. Oslo presented a framework for a two-state solution and that framework is dead. We can create another framework for a two-state solution, but not Oslo. We were convinced by Palestinian leaders to give up our fight for political rights. We were told by Arafat and the PLO, "This is all that we can get; we should accept this." We bought in to that argument.... The Israelis were told by their leaders, "It's all about security; it's not about reconciliation. They cannot be trusted.... The international community tells them that the only way to live in peace with each other is if you cut up the land—like the story of King Solomon and two women who claim one child. Both sides decided to cut up the land. So, we are living the failures of Oslo.

RH: How do you turn that around?

SA: By people coming together. This is where dialogue becomes important. I'm ready to engage in a serious dialogue with people ready to build a new vision for the future—for Palestinians, political liberation, and for Israelis, freedom from an obsession with security.

RH: Does that necessarily mean a one-state solution?

SA: No. It could mean a two-state solution, or two nations and one state, or a confederation. It could mean one state. Even a one-state solution will not be a Western-style democracy. It will be self-ruling, autonomous regions and identities. In a sense, what we have already—somewhere between tribal law, religious law, and civil law. We must talk about the foundation that we need.

RH: And what's the foundation for you?

SA: Human rights, civil rights, equal rights, full mobility, access to resources, not token dialogue.

RH: I completely affirm that. How do you get there?

SA: No matter how much Palestinians say they will give up the right of return, they will never give it up. Refugees must be acknowledged and given a real return or reparations.... From psychology we know inherited trauma is very present. The healing work for the Jewish community has not begun. The addiction to trauma has become fully embedded within the Jewish psyche.

RH: The addiction?

SA: Addiction to fear and trauma.... Any single attack becomes anti-semitism, anti-Jewish.

RH: Individuals can find a psychiatrist, or a pastor or priest or rabbi. But for millions of people?

SA: You need leaders to understand that, as a nation, we have experienced a trauma, and we cannot let this trauma lead us towards the future.

RH: But the leaders here in the U.S. and Europe now are leading with fear. And it works.

SA: Of course. Fear is the greatest modifier of human behavior: fear of separation, loneliness, or losing somebody. The whole world is motivated by fear.

RH: Halper says, Unfortunately, oppressed people have to assure the oppressor that they [the oppressed] will not give the oppressor what they deserve....

SA: We are developing a curriculum and programs for healing fear and healing trauma.

RH: And that's facilitated, you have facilitators—

SA: Yeah. One Israeli, one Palestinian facilitator, and a psychologist. We are bringing to our curriculum lectures on religion, spirituality, and psychology....

RH: How do you approach [this situation] as a spiritual problem?

SA: It's amazing. [Israelis] are secular until religion benefits their secularism, as in "chosen ones." ... A rabbi told me: The state has become our God and the Army has become our Religion....

RH: I see a deep connection between the prophets, the Sermon on the Mount, and human rights.

SA: There are prophetic voices asking, What does it mean to be a Jew in this land? They look into the Abrahamic Covenant and ask, What does it mean to be a light to all nations, including the Palestinian nation?

RH: Recently I went back and read those promises, including the conditions that go with them.

SA: These rabbis say, If we don't do [justice], the same thing will happen to us: God will kick us out, vomit us out of the land....

RH: So, along with the facilitated dialogues ...

SA: The second component is nonviolent activism, for exposing injustice and not perpetuating fear. To be honest, it's a struggle to see exactly what that looks like.... The question is how to [adapt] nonviolence from a Gandhian liberation movement, or the U.S. model of equal rights for all people in the land. That notion has not evolved yet, even within our organization.

RH: What gives you hope at this very moment?

SA: There isn't much, to be honest. [But] there is hope in the growing hopelessness.... You give up on what you were promised. You are letting go. But the more people give up on Oslo, the two-state solution, and our own leaders, this begins to cleanse the land for a new hope to be planted.

RH: Halper says this is a good moment to seize and turn things.

SA: We need a core group of people who are ready to launch a new peace process, with partners in the Orthodox religious community, and partners at the political level. If we can create a political vision of justice, equality, and human rights for all the people here, ... global conflicts would be resolved by creating a model. But we are in a dark, dark stage now. If we work really hard, it's still going to take a generation or two before we can say [we are at peace], because fear is so embedded.... We think, in our healthy, non-traumatized minds, that to maintain security you make peace. For Israel to maintain security, it must make peace with its neighbors. [But] for a traumatized mind, security means creating more mechanisms of security, and it's never enough.

RH: Facilitated dialogue, strategic dialogue, and relationship building take a long time. How do you translate dialogical and spiritual movements into a political program?

SA: Dialogue work cannot just occur in dialogue sessions, in rooms. This is where a nonviolent movement happens—What are the issues we want to address, what is the activism?

RH: These are complementary tracks—dialogue and nonviolent pressure?

SA: Both things are key for me. Dialogue alone has never liberated a country. There has to be activism and international pressure.... Otherwise, dialogue is just building nice friendships.

This could be a theory of change for me: leaders will always follow what people want. And the more you have a mass movement of people that say this is what we want, then either leaders have to step aside or leaders can emerge from the grassroots, and from that middle space. But the grassroots movements need to be there to support and launch such leaders.

RH: So, what is the spark at this time?

SA: I have no idea. We continue the trainings, and the dialogue work, but it could be an emerging charismatic leader.

RH: Ilan Pappé says the occupation is so pervasive, it clouds one's ability to see what's beyond.

SA: I redefine what it means to end the occupation. It is ending oppression. Until Jewish people realize they are oppressors and need to end this oppression, they will not see beyond it.

RH: If ending the occupation is only half of the job, the other half is defining an endgame?

SA: The political endgame is either one state or a binational state [with] full and equal rights for all people in this land, including the right to live wherever you want. You can have your own unique identity within that context. There has to be some overall structure, but completely decentralized. The old city of Jerusalem is a model for this, neighborhoods maintaining themselves and relating to the others. Or you could have areas of coexistence.

RH: Maybe Jaffa and Haifa could be models.

SA: The whole concept of nation-states is reaching its high point and it's going to [decline]....

Concern for our daily life is more about what cities provide than about what our nations provide.

RH: Comment on Jeff's insight that we have to spend as much energy on defining the future that we want as we do on ending the occupation; that gives us guidance for ending the occupation.

SA: Definitely, we need to know what we are fighting for. What is the endgame?

RH: Thanks very much.

14 The Business of Peacemaking

Sam Bahour

After the Oslo Accords were signed, Sam Bahour moved his family from the U.S. to the Ramallah area. He is a leading spokesman for Palestinian business interests. He focuses on telecommunications and informational technology. He earned an MBA degree in a joint program between Tel Aviv University and Northwestern University. He is a policy analyst with Al-Shabaka: The Palestinian Policy Network, a secretariat member of the Palestine Strategy Group, and chair of Americans for a Vibrant Palestinian Economy. He is a strong advocate for justice, nonviolence, and storytelling.

Ramallah, June 2008

SB: I'm originally from Youngstown, Ohio; born to a Palestinian father and a Lebanese-American mother. We used to come and go to and from Palestine to visit family, but I decided to relocate when we had one child, in 1995, immediately after the Oslo Peace Accords were signed. We arrived in Ramallah a couple of months before the PLO arrived. When we got here, the Israelis were still in control of Ramallah, but the process of handing over cities was going on. They had already given Gaza and Jericho to the Palestinians to administer. We were hopeful. We wouldn't have made a radical move if we didn't think that there was an opportunity here.

RH: You moved in large part because of Oslo.

SB: Absolutely. I had been active politically throughout college and my entire adult life. So I was very close to the Palestinian cause. However, the opportunity after Oslo was crucial. I read the Oslo agreement before I came, and I was convinced that this did not end the occupation. But it reshuffled the area on the ground, and I thought that it might open a different scenario. I had seen in our local Youngstown paper that Arafat had announced that he was going to privatize the telecommunications sector once it was transferred to him, because it was too complicated, and too much money was needed to invest government funds. In 1994 I recruited another Palestinian from the States, Dr. Mohammed Moustafa, who worked with the World Bank as a telecom expert. He led the effort and I helped him.

DOI: 10.4324/9781003262817-16

For me, coming back to Palestine was important. I had been married for two years to a Palestinian woman who wanted to come home. I wanted to be closer to the reality on the ground. I had always worked on the Palestinian issue, but I didn't live the reality. There was a gap in my own knowledge base, so coming here was filling that gap. Plus, I [could] make a soft landing. I came in my field of expertise, in my field of education, in a sector that's critical to state-building, which is telecom.... There was no company, only a sector that had been run by the Israelis for 30-some years, and Israel had transferred it to the Palestinians only months before. We negotiated with the Palestinian Authority for a license, and we created what today is the largest company in Palestine, the Palestine Telecommunications Company, with 2,000 employees. It's a very profitable company—too profitable.

I've been here ever since. I've gone on to establish my own business consulting firm here. I have earned an MBA degree in a joint program between Tel Aviv University and Northwestern University. I've also completed a project called the Plaza Shopping Center, which is a landmark retail development project here in El Bireh, next to Ramallah. That was a $10.2 million project that employs about 220 people. I have worked in various sectors, but telecom and IT remain my focal point. It's also a critical area for Palestine, because we need to tap our knowledge base, which is our people. Our resources are either limited to start with, or are being taken from us. This is not Saudi Arabia; this is not Iran; we don't have oil. We have smart people who are prohibited from accessing real markets. They have the academic skills to graduate, but they don't have the skills to be employed.

RH: You mean they don't have access?

SB: There's no access to real markets, because the military occupation has kept this community completely in a closed atmosphere. The only openness is trading products back and forth. But if you want to market knowledge-based products, you have to market your country before you market your company. Nobody will base a company's outsourcing in a country that's in upheaval. So a lot of times I find myself marketing not only my business opportunities but marketing Palestine. I spend a lot of time speaking to groups coming through here, because as a Palestinian American, I have a vantage point about this conflict that a lot of Americans and foreigners need to hear. A lot of people, even those on eyewitness tours, go through the motions of seeing, and either despairing, or being in great sympathy. But we are looking for actions to end the occupation.

RH: [Many] in the Israeli peace movement are quite Zionist. It prevents them from ending the occupation. They really want to make sure that a Jewish state remains. For access to blossom, the occupation must end.

SB: For the last 40 years, the focus on ending the occupation maybe has been overly stressed. I think we are at a point now where the occupation has been not only allowed to persist in full view of the international community, but the occupation is only part of the problem. The other part of the problem is how Israel is drawing its own lines in the sand. The Israeli side has a demographic issue. Israelis view the world in terms of who is Jewish and who is not. But that is an unsustainable equation for 10, 20, or 30 years from now. I'll give you an example. I had the opportunity to attend a lecture by Gadon Ezer, the minister of environment in Israel. He is a security guru.

RH: Which has been Israel's mantra forever.

SB: Absolutely. He represents a lot of Israeli thinking in a crude way. He is very blunt. I said, "Israeli statisticians are saying that within the next 20 to 25 years, there will be more non-Jews in Israel than Jews. Where do you see Israeli society at that point?" He said, "Jews have one country. It's called Israel. Arabs have 22 [countries]. They can go to any of them." He was talking about Palestinians [in Israel], who comprise 22% to 23% of Israel's population. He was telling his own constituency that they need to leave if they get to a certain number. That is shocking from a U.S. point of view.

RH: It's ethnic cleansing.

SB: Very much so. I call it sterile ethnic cleansing. What the Israelis were not able to achieve in 1948 and 1967—emptying the land of [Palestinian] people—they are achieving through administrative [policies].

RH: It's a slow, administrative strangulation.

SB: Exactly. The myth that Israel was "a land of no people for a people with no land," is the crux of this conflict: land and people. We see what's happening to the land: settlements, walls, road networks, and annexation.... We know what's happening with the land. People are less aware of what's happening to people. The last poll finds that 44% of the Palestinian population wants to emigrate. Almost half the population wants to leave Palestine! That's exactly what the 1948 and 1967 wars tried to enforce.

RH: Exactly what Israeli politicians want.

SB: Absolutely. But we have a misperception in the Palestinian community that those in solidarity with us need to be 100% in solidarity with us.

RH: Expand on that.

SB: When we find someone who, for their own narrow reasons, would like to support us in this or that campaign, we should embrace that wholeheartedly, hoping that the facts on the ground will be overwhelming enough to convince them to broaden their agenda. That does not mean that I cannot align myself with them in the part of the agenda that fits mine.

RH: That makes a lot of sense.

SB: We need to keep things in perspective. The numbers of people in Israel who are working to end the occupation are few. If those few are not incorporated into a national strategy of solidarity, then we have very little opportunity to make those numbers larger.... I look at those small numbers and think about how I can make them larger.

RH: For example, you can work with Rabbis for Human Rights as far as possible.

SB: That's my position. But I'll go further. [I engage] Israeli soldiers who serve in the occupation, once they see with their own eyes the discrimination and the racism and the battering of our people, and they go back into their communities and say, "I will not go back to serve in this occupation." Those are not pacifists. They are soldiers, and I speak frequently with them on the same stage because I think Palestinians have a perspective to communicate to the Israelis. As a community the Israelis are in denial, conditioned by a lot of political manipulation of Jewish history to make them fear....

RH: Two years ago, Jeff Halper [expressed] frustration, saying, We [Israelis] are helpers in this struggle, but Palestinians have to take the lead and articulate the vision, and they're just not doing it. A few days later, Ghassan said, "We're tired. We can't see where to go."

SB: Jeff is right; the Palestinians who are the owners of their own destiny need to define where they're heading. We have hit an area that's very confusing. We have been put into a corner from the international community. We have lost our leadership because of killing, imprisonment, corruption—a whole set of issues. In such an environment, it's not healthy for any single constituency to define an end path. Because unity is what will make that end path reality. We need to be clear, on the Palestinian side; we need to work harder, inside Palestine, within our own community, to bring unity back in. In relationship to the solidarity community outside, I don't think that the solidarity community should carry the burden of Palestinian confusion. The solidarity community, calling for the end of occupation, calling for the application of international law, has plenty to work on... while we work on solving our internal issues. It's a critical component to keep the ball rolling as we are working out our internal differences, and redefining how we view an endgame.

RH: You're talking about a platform. The solidarity community can help articulate an international human-rights platform to end the occupation.

SB: Absolutely. There are two systems of law in this world. There is either the rule of law (international human-rights law), or the law of the jungle: F-16s are OK; bombing residential neighborhoods is OK, because Israelis will cry for a couple of days, and then forget. That kind of environment cannot sustain itself. And the international community is allowing such an environment from both sides to be maintained. The other alternative is international law.

RH: It holds everybody accountable.

SB: Absolutely. The body of international law emerged in the 1940s because of the reality of the Jews in Europe. So, what was created as an international regulatory body to make sure such events don't happen again is now being brushed aside by those same people who were saved by it.... There needs to be yardstick that we can measure against. It's embedded within international law. The Fourth Geneva Convention is the law of occupation. It's up to third states, those parties that are signatories to the Fourth Geneva Convention, to ensure that international law is applied. The principles are clear. For example, moving a civilian population of the occupying force into the occupied territories and creating settlements is illegal.... Those clear principles are definitive....

RH: [Israelis say] it's just a response to this or that event.

SB: Some of my more enlightened Israeli friends will say, Sam, the Israelis honestly don't see this as an occupation. They see this as a silent transfer to get [Palestinians] off the land. They want to see Israel as extending from the Mediterranean to the Jordan River.

RH: Therefore, we're just in an extended transitional state, but not occupation.

SB: Which is very dangerous. Up until now, I have been calling for two states, in order for us to move forward.

RH: And then you move to a human-rights struggle.

SB: In my opinion, we're moving that way regardless of what the Israelis say.

RH: Because of what they've done.

SB: Their statisticians are clear that even in Israel—forget the West Bank and Gaza—they're going ... to hit apartheid as soon as the [ethnic] populations become equal. What [Israeli governments] have done in the West Bank and Gaza could dismiss the possibility for a two-state solution. The settlements are not haphazardly placed. They're placed on top of the aquifers of the West Bank, and water in the Middle East is the key to stability. The road networks are not haphazardly placed. They are put in places that disrupt Palestinian growth of their villages and cities.

RH: It's all [about] how to contain, how to control, how to surround.

SB: We need to look at what the Zionist movement is about. There were two philosophies: Jabotinsky talking about making an iron wall, similar to the separation wall that we have today. The other concept—from the beginning—was transfer. Today the Israelis have merged both philosophies, separating the populations via the Wall and colonizing all the Palestinian communities, while strangulating the economy, [so] people are leaving. That's dangerous.

RH: Right. It leaves no marks if people voluntarily leave. Not like torture.

SB: That's correct. What the Israelis are missing, though, is that under international law, if you bus people out as they did in 1948 and 1967, and force them militarily to cross the border, that's a war crime. An equal war crime is if you create the conditions that force the native population, the indigenous population, to exit the country. So, they may be getting away with it in the media. But from a legal perspective, they are committing not only a war crime, but crimes against humanity.

Bethlehem has lost its Christian population because of the strangulation. As I said, 44% in the last poll—half of the people—want to leave the country! I sit on the Birzeit University board of trustees. I used to be very proud that we were graduating a new class of Palestinian professionals. Today, I feel that we're giving people a ticket to leave the country. Because when they get their degree, they go into the community and there are no jobs. So, they end up leaving to be able to sustain themselves. At the end of the day, the situation will explode. There is no logic in saying that a policy of separation and transfer is going to reach a peaceful settlement.

RH: Here's the question, then. International law, the potential for criminal indictment for war crimes, doesn't matter unless it's enforced. That's been the dilemma for 60 years or so. They serve as a kind of moral compass, but without enforcement, they don't count for much; at least they don't count for enough. Who would prosecute? Who could deal with this? I've said to heads of NGOs, Who can help? They almost always say, A third party. And who is that? The Europeans are too divided, and the U.S. is too complicit.

SB: Absolutely. This is the problem that we're all facing. A couple of things. Although implementation of international law is at a roadblock right now, I have to continue to use it as my reference point. The day I drop international law as a reference point, anything goes, in terms of how these two parties fight it out. I cannot accept a world in which anything goes. If we drop international law from our toolbox for resolving this conflict, then we have done a disservice to humankind. And many more Israelis and Palestinians will die.

RH: This is important for the rest of the world. This is a benchmark for the globe.

SB: Absolutely. As an American who came here 15 years ago, I'm surprised the Palestinians are still holding on to international law. If what happened to Palestine happened to Youngstown, Ohio, I can guarantee you it wouldn't take 60 years before the Americans took up arms. The lights go out in New York for two hours during a blackout and all hell breaks loose. The lights have been out in Palestine for 60 years, and people are still saying international law must be applied. International law has an implementation mechanism built into it. Third states are obligated under international law to make sure that people under occupation are protected. Thus, the parties to this conflict are no longer Palestinians and Israelis. The parties to this conflict are every single country which has signed on to the Fourth Geneva Convention. With this community being donor-driven—underwriting the status quo, paying salaries, feeding people so we don't drop into a humanitarian crisis, all of those underwriters of the occupation—they have a role and a responsibility to see what they're doing.... We have become a dependent community. The governance of the Palestinian society is a governance led by donors, and not by indigenous Palestinian populations. We have all the trappings of a government, but we don't have the substance of a government.

The U.S. is playing the most dangerous role in this, because it has the most leverage. They don't put the most money into this—Europeans are contributing the most money—but they exercise the most leverage.

RH: It's a classic mixed signal.

SB: At the end of the day, one needs from the Palestinian side to be patient. We have been patient. As we promote international law, as we remain steadfast on the land, if the international community does not rise to its responsibility, and it hasn't for the last 40 years, or 60 years, then the reality is going to be changed by an act of civil disobedience or force. We saw it in the first *intifada*, we saw it in the second *intifada*. I would call the coming of Hamas our third *intifada*. I think we're heading for another breakdown.

I fear something worse than an *intifada*. An *intifada* is a civil uprising. It has a leadership. Ultimately, the Israelis, through third parties or directly, can be in touch with that leadership, to try to mitigate such a civil uprising. After the Israelis have killed or imprisoned the top leadership, and sometimes the second- or third-level leadership of the different parties—

RH: Or corrupted them.

SB: Or corrupted them, there's no leadership left. And when an uprising happens, I fear we're going to see acts of individual violence, such as the [Palestinian] bulldozer driver who went astray the other day and killed many Israelis.

RH: Just chaos. He snapped.

SB: He just lost it.... Genuine thinking about this conflict is embedded 20, 30, 40 years ago in the UN resolutions. There has been no genuinely new thinking about this. If you look at UN Resolution 181, it created two states; it talks about economic partnership and Jerusalem being an open city.

RH: [UN Resolution 181] is another example of a platform. It's the base from which a just [peace] could emerge.

SB: So, it is important for civil society to remain focused on a clear, internationally aligned goal, but civil society itself can't do it. Civil society is holding the ball. But other players have to come in and start doing the right thing.

RH: Eventually there will have to be some synchronicity and convergence of Track Two diplomacy—NGOS building civil society—and political leadership at the Track One level.

SB: That would be helpful. To be honest with you, Bob, I don't know how convinced I am of the Track Two track. I feel that all those may be helpful in terms of talking to each other and understanding each other's opinions, but I honestly think that both parties need to be held accountable to apply international law *today,* while we're in the conflict.

RH: ... We might be defining Track Two in two different ways. When I use Track Two, I don't mean unofficial people trying to do official business. I'm talking about people building colleges and universities, people building civil society.

SB: Ah. Track Two here is used for people negotiating behind the scenes.

RH: Ah, back-channel stuff.

SB: Institution-building is critical. Each society is doing it in its own way.

If we are moving toward a two-state solution, with Palestine and Israel living side by side, the next logical thing to say is that the capacity for state-building has to be built in Palestine. This requires key infrastructural items, telecommunications, water, electricity, and road networks. If we look at how Israel is dealing with those infrastructural items, it speaks volumes: Israel has no intention whatsoever to allow Palestinians to realize a new state.

When the Palestinians signed the Oslo agreement, the telecommunication sector, which was up until that time run by the Israeli military, was transferred to the Palestinian Authority.

RH: You're talking about radio, television, and informational networks.

SB: Yes, Article 36 of Oslo. The first sentence of that article is great. It says the Palestinian Authority has the right to build an independent telecommunications network. It sounds perfect. It's the next four pages that are the problem. The next four pages are all the constraints, and all the Israeli requirements and approvals you need before you can move forward, which completely undercut the ability to do it. That's why I think they were so surprised that we actually built a telecommunications network. Another example, a critical one: electricity. The Israelis have refused to allow the Palestinians to generate electricity. They force us to buy electricity from Israel at a premium to serve our market. Like everything else, that allows them to exercise leverage over all the utilities, whether it's telecom, water, or electricity.

RH: Which they can turn off at any moment.

SB: Anytime. For years, Palestinians have been asking to produce electricity. We have the money, we have the investors, we have the know-how. We're not missing anything, other than the occupiers' approval for us to do it. They only allowed it to happen a couple of years back in Gaza. They said the electricity generation plant can be built, but only to serve 30% of Gaza's electricity needs. And then they said, The fuel required to run the plant has to come through the

Israeli border. So OK, they said, we're going to give you the right to the plant, but not the fuel—and as you can see, one day they turn it off, one day they turn it on, to put pressure on Hamas. And then, beyond that, they actually sent F-16s and bombed the generators that were built. Even more recently, a couple of months back, in the southern tip of the Gaza Strip, the Israelis allowed Rafah to connect to the Egyptian electricity grid. And Jericho, in the Jordan Valley, was allowed to connect to the Jordanian electricity grid.

RH: This is not too subtle, is it?

SB: The Israelis were boasting in the media. "We're not that bad; we're giving them alternative means for utilities." The next step is to move the population there. It's very clear that the Israelis, in all the infrastructure items, have no intention to allow the Palestinians to realize the components required for statehood. Who is the international community fooling by saying there's a peace process, when everything points in the opposite direction?

RH: The term "peace process" is dangerous [in this context].

SB: It's insulting.

RH: It's dangerous and insulting. It covers up what's really happening.

SB: I'll give you one example of what's happening on the ground. I was born in the States. I came back here as a tourist, because Israel allows foreigners to enter only as tourists, and they give us three-month tourist visas. I've been in that situation for the last 14 or 15 years. I enter and exit every three months. I know everybody at the border by first name. But it's the only way I can stay with my family in Palestine. After Hamas was elected in our elections, some Israeli strategists made a decision to start denying entry to foreign nationals. So people like me, who would exit the country, as we've been doing for the last X number of years, when we try to come back into the country, the officials say, Too much. You've visited here too many times; you're not allowed back in. And they would separate families by doing this. We actually have a campaign now called the right to enter. You can find it at righttoenter.ps. We put ourselves in a campaign to challenge the Israelis and the international community, to make sure families can stay together. People who have been denied entry include teachers at Birzeit University. We lost half of our foreign teaching staff at Birzeit because of this policy!

RH: It's a good way to kill infrastructure, again.

SB: It's causing harm to the civilian population, something that's in blatant violation of international law. If you take that example of Israel denying entry, not only does it separate families, but Jerusalem has a more difficult problem. If you are an Israeli citizen, you can hold dual citizenship. You can be an American citizen and an Israeli citizen. If you are a Palestinian, the day you receive a second citizenship, or even a green card in the States, Israel will withdraw your Jerusalem residency. It's a way to force one family at a time out of Jerusalem.

RH: What's the best path to enforce international law, the [International] Criminal Court?

SB: There are many. We went to the International Court and got an advisory opinion about the separation Wall and the occupation.... It's a legal victory. An advisory opinion legally carries weight. It was taken to the General Assembly. The General Assembly voted in mass numbers confirming that that international advisory opinion should be applied. Then we engaged in civil disobedience. As you saw in Bil'in, civil society is acting.

RH: In fact, it's quite impressive.

SB: So we have nonviolent civil disobedience on the ground. But I believe it will turn violent if the international community doesn't do anything. No one should say, Why have the Palestinians turned violent? It's only a matter of time before we do.... We have information, lobbying, and diplomacy. Palestinians, within their limited capacity, are being battered, having their leadership killed. We use a multitude of approaches; it requires others to take action as well, specifically, constituents in third states. So the Palestinians are doing the most that they can, under the circumstances. If the international community continues to ignore applying international law here, people will take the law into their own hands. That's a dangerous path to go down. I'm part of a 40- or 50-person team of Palestinians, both inside and outside Palestine, right, left, religious, across a spectrum of politics, and we put ourselves through a strategic planning exercise. It was run by the Oxford Research Group. It's being edited now. We've come up with a strategy to define our options. We feel that Palestinians have many options. Some of our options are defining what kind of endgame may be available. And part of what we came up with is things we have to do to better articulate what are non-options. For example, the status quo is a non-option.

RH: At the policy level there's a status quo, but on the ground, there is no status quo.

SB: No. Israel is bulldozing [Palestinian houses] all along. Another non-option is the Jordan/Egypt option. Jordan can't become an alternative for Palestine, and Egypt can't become an alternative for Palestinian rule in Gaza. That is not an option. Acknowledging non-options is just as important as acknowledging the real options. We concluded that Israel will not accept a two-state solution.... Palestinians have a lot of options to move the international community forward. The Palestinians today should dismantle the Palestinian Authority. We need Palestinians to clean house in order to reunite their own house. The Palestinian Authority is now split.

We have two authorities, one running Gaza, and one running the West Bank. If the Palestinian Authority, as an administrative body, was removed, the fallback position would be the PLO, which is the only organization that represents the cross section of all Palestinians, inside and outside of Palestine. Hamas would have to be added. Reforming the PLO to be more inclusive is critical.

RH: Ghassan Andoni and many others are saying the Israelis have already eliminated the two-state option.

SB: I would say that as well. To be honest with you, it's a very fine line. Working for civil rights is going to be a long battle. But I think our society specifically, but both societies, need a cooling-off period. We need to be able to rehabilitate ourselves. And that's going to take tens of years....

RH: Gideon Levy said to me two years ago, If a U.S. president, any president, picked up the phone, he could end the occupation in a half-hour.

SB: He doesn't need to pick up the phone; he just needs to stop the funding and stop vetoing the United Nations resolutions.

RH: It's astonishing. The day after Barack Obama clinched the nomination for the Democratic Party, he went to AIPAC to pay his dues.

SB: Even so, there's a lot happening—for example, the [John] Mearsheimer book and the [Jimmy] Carter book. There are discussions happening in the States that couldn't be dreamed of 20 years ago. There's progress. The populace is ready to see positive movement, but those in power are working to be elected again, and the lobbies' influence is [highly problematic]. Every U.S. State Department report for the last four years talks about the violations of human rights by Israel against Palestinians. When is the U.S. going to link its foreign aid to its own State Department report? We have a long way to go.

RH: Thanks very much for your analysis.

15 What Reconciliation Requires

Eitan Bronstein

Eitan Bronstein founded Zochrot in 2001, serving as director for 10 years. In 2015, he and his wife, Eléonore Merza Bronstein, cofounded De-Colonizer to expose Israel as a settler colonial enterprise. In this dialogue, Bronstein searches for fresh terms to describe his work for "peace" and "justice." For Bronstein, reconciliation requires Israel to take responsibility for the Nakba, facilitate the return of Palestinian refugees, and accept that Jews can no longer live in Israel as occupiers.

Tel Aviv, July 2008

RH: [Tell me] some of your personal story. Did you grow up in Tel Aviv?

EB: No. I came to Israel when I was five years old.

RH: From?

EB: From Argentina. Yes, yes. I speak Spanish and Portuguese. When I was five I came to a kibbutz named Bahan, around 40 kilometers north from here.... My family all came to Bahan together ... and we all left Bahan some 21 years ago, when I was 27.

RH: So you're not Sephardi or Ashkenazi?

EB: I am mixed, because my mom is a bit Spanish, but we are Ashkenazi in cultural terms—not ethnic but political, because of the kibbutzim.

RH: How did you move from that background to do this kind of work? There must have been important, in-between turning points.

EB: [I have] a very important story. I was raised on a kibbutz near a village named Qaqun, near Tulkarm, north of Tel Aviv. As a boy, I knew it's a Crusader fortress.

RH: The Christian Crusaders?

EB: Yes. As you can see in my documentary, [there are] very impressive remains of something looking like a fortress.... It was a Crusader fortress hundreds of years ago. This is what I knew, a Crusader fortress. Then, some five or six years ago, when I became interested in the Nakba and the Palestinian places destroyed in 1948, I started to look for information on the internet. On one website I saw a map of the different districts of Palestine. I saw the district of Tulkarm, and at the center of that district I saw the name Qaqun. And I was

DOI: 10.4324/9781003262817-17

surprised. Qaqun, what does it have to do with me, with Palestinian history, my place, my childhood? I clicked on this Qaqun name and I was amazed to find out that this was a Palestinian village until 1948. A very big one. 2000 people lived there.... And there was a very important battle there in 1948.... Many Palestinians were killed and also Iraqi soldiers were killed trying to help them. I was amazed to find out that I didn't know anything. This is not from my childhood but it's from only a few years ago. This made me understand how little I knew. It also showed me how little information most Israelis have about where they live.

RH: A desire not to know, or a combination of people not telling you when you are a child, and maybe you don't want to know later.

EB: Yes, it's very mixed, of course.... But this history is there—the history of a destroyed [village]. But it's suppressed knowledge.

So it will not appear in books, in the curriculum in [Israeli] schools. Schools are not going to visit those places and listen to stories—what Zochrot tries to do in these places. It's not possible to say nobody knows it, because many Jews fought there and they know. You can go to other kibbutzim in the area that existed then—because Bahan is a rather new kibbutz. It's only established in 1956. If you go to other kibbutzim, they know the stories. But they don't talk about it much.... The knowledge is there, but it's rather suppressed for many reasons. To tell this story or to acknowledge what happened is to shake very much the establishment of this Jewish state. It shakes the moral basis of this state; it's challenging the possibility of continuing this project. This is not easy for Israelis. It is a main factor involved with [Palestinian] refugees. If you know about it and acknowledge it, ... you start questioning.

For example, let's say that in Qaqun there was a lot of resistance in front of the Israeli fighters. Let's say it was a battle between two equal sides, and the Israelis won.... Okay, it's fighters against fighters. But after the village was taken over, the civilians should return. People ran away because of shooting. But, by international law, after you take over a place, civilians should return. Nobody even [admitted] that women were there, old people, and people who didn't fight.... They didn't do any attacks on Jews. They should return. I don't know any moral argument against this.... If you acknowledge it, you have to ask yourself, Why did we prevent this return? If you want to ask hard questions, you have a problem in a Jewish state.

RH: In fact, many Palestinians were told, Just go away for a few weeks and then you will be able to come back. Many—

EB: Not so many.... The big leaders from Arab states, corrupted leaders, they all said, Very easily we take over Palestine. But not very many people believed them even then.... There was a lot of fighting but ...

the Jewish fighters were stronger, and the Palestinians understood in most of cases that they don't have any chance, and they ran away because they knew they were going to be killed or expelled somehow, so they left.

RH: And, of course, they're not allowed to come back.... So your growing up experience and what you discovered later was a turning point for you, but there must have been others to provide sufficient motivation for you to get into this kind of activism.

EB: When I was 18, I went to the army without any questions. I just did what I thought I had to do as a good citizen. I served three years in the army and many years in the reserves. My most crucial, political [development] was the [Israeli] war against Lebanon in 1992. When the war began, I was at end of my three years. I was afraid that we were going to be sent to Lebanon to fight. All the [other] soldiers wanted to go there. It was this man thing, a lot of testosterone. [Laughing.] It was terrible. I opposed this war from the beginning. I don't love any war. But for me, this war, as Menachem Begin said, was a war of choice. Usually Israel says, There is no choice. But Begin was honest enough to say that it was a choice. He explained why he chose it.

RH: To go after the PLO?

EB: Yeah. The main issue was to try to go after the PLO, to expel them. Suddenly they called us back from vacation and said, You go to Lebanon.... I didn't oppose it. I went. I just said, It's the end. I go for a few days, and then I come back, get released from the army.... Six months after I was released, I was called to [the war in] Lebanon. Then I had a very, very big hesitation, all kinds of complex thoughts. [Other] people refused to go.... I debated it a lot with myself, with my friends, with my colleagues, with my family. I decided ... to refuse, and I was sent to jail [for] one month.... In my life, this was the most crucial [event], because it was the first time that I draw the line and I say, I don't cross this line. I'm not going as a reserve soldier to Lebanon. This is not a war we need to have. It's all wrong. I refused and I was jailed. It was a great experience in jail—12 people who refused together, great people. I come from a kibbutz, and I am the only one who refused. I meet these people and suddenly it was a group.

RH: A family.

EB: Kind of a family, a group supporting each other. It was great. I was released and then called up again—

RH: So while you were in prison the soldiers didn't hassle you or punish you?

EB: No, not much. I tell you why, because in the prison, those soldiers in general don't like very much the system. That's why they are in jail. Usually it's people who run away from the army. Most of them are people who—how do you say it in English, people who are—deserters. They would say to me, Even if I'm not with you in your opinion, we respect you because you were brave enough and you went to jail. So they liked the fact that I went to jail.

RH: They give you credit....

EB: Before the first *intifada*, I served as a reserve soldier in the West Bank. I did terrible work, doing patrols and guarding at checkpoints. We broke up the first *intifada*. I said, If [Palestinians] uprise and resist the occupation, I'm with them. I'm not going to oppress their uprising. I refused and went to jail again. After six months, I went again to jail because they wanted to send me to the [West Bank]. I refused. These three times in jail were very important. Another most important point for [my] understanding the conflict was the experience I had in the School for Peace. I worked there many years. I was a staff member in the School for Peace, the institute in Neve Shalom. Have you heard about it?

RH: Yes. Yes, I have been there.

EB: I worked in the School for Peace.... Most of the time I coordinated the youth department. I organized, conducted, and facilitated many, many encounters between Jews and Arabs in Israel. By doing this work, I became very aware of ... the conflict. I understood much better that I am part of [the conflict]. I thought, I am for peace and I am for a Palestinian state and I was for the end of the occupation. But I thought, OK, I have to struggle against those who are opposing it. But working there, I understood that as a Jewish Israeli, I am part of [this conflict].

RH: Part of the occupation.

EB: Yes. Part of the occupation, but also in my behavior. Even though my statements are against it, in fact, I am part of it.

RH: You benefit from it.

EB: Yeah, I benefit, of course. But in many different ways I am really part of it. As a Jewish Israeli, I know nothing about the Nakba. I knew the word, but I never really knew what does it really mean ... and what are the details. The last breakthrough for me was the second *intifada* in October 2000. The Israeli government ... killed very many Palestinians here in Israel. It was the first time there were these big demonstrations by Palestinians in Israel.

RH: Palestinian citizens of Israel?

EB: Yeah. Israeli Palestinians. The Israeli forces attacked them and got the orders from Ehud Barak to open the roads in any—at any expense, you say?

RH: At any cost.

EB: Yeah, at any cost. It's amazing, you know? It's really amazing what they did. They shot 30 people and killed demonstrators.

RH: I was here in the summer of 2000, just three months before the second *intifada* began. Including going to Gaza.

EB: It was the best times. The feeling was very optimistic. We thought, Wow, it's really a chance. I was in Gaza, and I thought, Wow! The peace industry here is great, and we're going to have peace. But suddenly—like many colleagues and friends in what's called the peace camp, or the Zionist left—we understood there is an issue here. A very deep issue. Either you understand the essence of this state is to see the Arabs as enemies, even the Arab citizens of Israel. Or, I don't want to be enemies with them and I want full equality for them. Before that, when I talked about equality, I talked in terms of basic needs—a budget, schools, and money. But then I understood that the issues are much more than that; this state was established for Jews only! But the very basis of this state is that it's democratic.

RH: Was that a common point of view on the Left, people saw things your way, or were you unusual?

EB: Yes. No. After October 2000, there was a split on the Left. Unfortunately, most of the people are Zionists, so most of them became more mainstream. You could find many more or less Zionist leftists who condemned the behavior of the Arabs. They condemned them blocking roads and things like that. But they didn't condemn the shootings here. It was really unbelievable. But then there are also a few thousand Israeli Jews that were more or less in the same positions as the Meretz [Party], and all the leftist Zionists left, like me. We understood that here you are either a Zionist or you are not. And if there is a choice between Zionism and peace, I have to choose peace and democracy. What's on the table is Zionism; either we support it or not. This is the issue here. Zionism with peace and democracy doesn't exist. This cliché of a Jewish democratic state, of course, is only a cliché.

RH: After the second *intifada*—

EB: Yes. After it broke up, I understood more clearly that it's either Zionism or not. I said this in one project in Cyprus. I said it and people laughed. They were surprised….

RH: I remember being very surprised when Gila Svirsky called herself a Zionist, because I know how hard she works.

EB: When was it?

RH: This was 2003.

EB: So it depends. But we know that she is still a Zionist.

RH: Two years later, I asked her what she meant, and she said, The Declaration of Independence, that's what I mean—

EB: Yes, this becomes clear, depending whether you support the right of return of Palestinian refugees or not.

RH: Uri Avnery?

EB: For sure, he is a Zionist; there's no question.

RH: Does he support the right of return?

EB: Oh, no, not at all.

RH: No, because he wants to maintain a Jewish state.

EB: A Jewish state. He is a Zionist, of course. He is a very important fighter against the occupation, but he fights so effectively against the occupation he obscures the fact that most of the occupation began in 1948, not 1967. The year 1967 is the completion of the occupation, the completion of only 22% remaining of Palestine. Avnery says this, too. You know he was—

RH: He was a fighter in 1948.

EB: He was a fighter. He was wounded. And he participated in a very important event that we did in Rabin Square, commemorating the *intifada* two or three years ago.... We asked people to take the card with the name of a village or place that means anything to them. Some refugees participated with us. Some were Jewish Israelis. One of them was Uri Avnery. He took a card and he said, I was a fighter in Qaqun, and we expelled them. [He said,] We have to acknowledge the Nakba that goes with it. But he doesn't talk about the return of the refugees. His idea is to acknowledge the Nakba and to have some symbolic number of Palestinian refugees return.

RH: A modest number that is negotiated.

EB: Yeah. Something like that. But this of course maintains the Jewish state and the—

RH: That's his motivation really, isn't it? To maintain the Jewish state.

EB: Yeah. Of course, he says it clearly.

RH: Would you say that the [Israeli] peace movement is fairly small and most members of the Israeli peace movement are Zionists?

EB: It's difficult to say what is the peace movement today because Peace Now is part of your peace movement, but they are for a Palestinian state, also the Likud Party, and, of course, the Labor Party. So I don't understand exactly what's the big difference....

RH: For all of these reasons, you became passionate about helping Israelis understand the Nakba?

EB: Yeah. I must admit that it's ... not so logical—

RH: It's not a straight road.

EB: No. It's not. It was more coincidental or even a kind of luck. I'll tell you the story. The idea came to my mind when I was traveling. I was doing a lot of tours to a place called Canada Park. You've heard our reports about Canada Park.

RH: Yes. I know it was a very important project for you.

EB: Yeah. When I was working at the School for Peace, I organized tours to this place. It's a place that was built on the destruction of three Palestinian villages from the 1967 war. Not 1948. Canadians [donated] 15 million Canadian dollars from Jews, mainly, which is tax deduction money. One of the most important elements is the park on top of these destroyed villages. I take students to see the remains, and also to see the construction of space in Israel. It is an example of how space in Israel is being constructed as Israeli space. This park is in the West Bank. Most Israelis don't know that it's three kilometers inside the green line. People don't know because there is no sign. You don't cross any checkpoint, so Israelis [assume] this landscape is part of Israel. Thousands of people visit this park every year and they don't know about it.

RH: Israel is a state constantly under geographical transformation.

EB: Exactly. The structure of the landscape is part of Israel, and not something else. There are remains of those villages, and there are different signs around the park—10 different signs, telling some names and histories of the place, many histories. There are signs with two lines.

RH: Going way back.

EB: Yes, yes: Roman history, Crusaders, Byzantines, Ottomans, and the Jewish era, of course. But not one word about hundreds of years of Palestinians living there until 1967! But the remains are there. It's not just a recreational place. They put many trees for shade, but it's also a place to educate visitors. They educate them by not telling the truth. But the truth is there, in the ground. You can see the remains. If someone goes there and sees graves, they say, What's this? There is a cemetery here. What is it? I would show this again and again to people.... After one visit, in 2001, it just came to my mind to come here and post signs. So I posted signs—very simple signs—saying that this is the cemetery of the villages Yalu and 'Imwas. [Officials] removed the signs. And I would put them up again. My friends found it very inspiring.

RH: It's very low grade and very specific.

EB: It's very low grade, yes; very simple. Touching exactly to the point. When we started to talk about it, we said, There are three destroyed villages [with no signs], but there are hundreds of places [like this] in Israel before 1948. So let's apply this to 1948. That all fit together with what we said earlier about Zionism and the expulsions of 1948. So I went to a friend of mine, an editor of a kibbutz newspaper. The kibbutzim newspapers go to all the kibbutzim. He found it interesting and provocative. So, I wrote a short piece and they interviewed me for this idea. Also I made a list of different kibbutzim and the former Palestinians villages that they are living on. I suggested that each kibbutzim would post a sign, and say, In 1948, this village had this name. Of course the Israelis were all against this idea.

RH: Did they think you were trying to make them feel guilty? What did they think?

EB: No, no, no, they didn't like it. One of them said, The Palestinians in this village were all terrorists. But my friend published it. It raised a lot of discussions. Most of them were against the idea. When I saw an enormous reaction, I understood that there is something very strong here.

RH: You touched a nerve.

EB: Yes, yes; it's very strong. The idea raised such a big reaction, so I understood there is something very strong here. So that is why I am saying to you that [my work] is not all planned.... I had a good idea; I raised it, and the reaction was so strong that it made me say—

RH: This is powerful.

EB: Yeah, it's powerful. Now let's go to work for it. Then we started a group of friends. But, of course, Zochrot is much more than only posting signs. We do many other things now.

RH: So tell me about the variety of activities at Zochrot—advocacy, education, creative protest, work with tourists, and many other things!

EB: In Tel Aviv, we just had this conference on the return of Palestinian refugees.

RH: What's the relationship between, say, education and creative protest?

EB: Hmm, yeah, it depends.

RH: Commemoration can also be a creative protest.

EB: Yeah! Sometimes, [with] creative protest, we mean things that we do not so much. It's not a routine. It's more something that we do here and there, usually as a reaction to something that's going on. For example, when the JNF did an installation in the center of Tel Aviv, telling that they are making the desert bloom, and all of this ... bullshit, we had to do something.

RH: As though everything the Palestinians have created for hundreds of years is just desert—So, do you have an opinion about one state versus two states?

EB: Yes, of course. In general, here at Zochrot, we are for one state.

RH: With equal rights for everyone?

EB: Yes. For everyone. For people who live here now, and for people who were expelled from here and feel they want to live here. They should live here in equality and in all the territory between the Jordan Valley and the sea. So it means that if Jews want to live in Hebron, it's OK. And if Palestinians want to live in Jaffa and in Tel Aviv, it's OK—to have democracy. The two-state issue is not feasible any more. No power in the world could remove five and a half million settlers.

Zochrot in Hebrew means women who remember. It's a feminine form of remembering, because in Hebrew—like in Arabic—the verbs are either masculine or feminine. The Hebrew language is rather male chauvinist—the spoken language. We usually speak in masculine verb forms. So we intentionally chose the feminine form in order to imply that the language, Zochrot, is not the standard language. The memory that we deal with is not the standard memory of the independence war, the liberation war. [Israelis] forget about the Nakba, which is the other memory—the other side … the memory of 1948. Zochrot, as a feminine form … reflects the fact that we work very hard to have women's testimonies from the Nakba, memories with compassion for the other; the loss of the other is a feminine memory.

RH: Interesting. It's a compassionate memory.

EB: Yes. It is inclusive—the loss of the other and not only to our victories and our victors.

RH: Interesting. So, what's the new frontier?

EB: We are working on an educational kit to teach the Nakba in schools—in high schools. In Hebrew. We are working on this for more than two years. It is a very important project for us.

RH: It includes narrative, pictures?

EB: Yes! A lot of pictures, maps, videos, and different documents.

RH: I'm sure a few teachers will pick it up. But I'm also sure that many will resist.

EB: I think the minister of education would be interested in seeing it. She is from the Labor Party, and she is a professor of moral ethics. But we don't tell them, This is the only truth. We want them to be critical with the material that we bring….

RH: You have published in various places that Zochrot's work is essential to create a platform from which peace could happen.

EB: Yeah. I would say more than peace.

RH: So is this work crucial for creating a just peace?

EB: Yeah, yeah. It's even more than peace because usually when you talk here about peace, it became a very bad word because of the [Oslo] peace process.

RH: A charade?

EB: Look, perhaps there will be peace. I don't know. There might be international [actions]—Europe or the U.S. forces Israel to do something, to have peace with two states. Jerusalem they split somehow. They draw some borders. And they have peace. It may even be good as a stage—but this doesn't mean that we'll have reconciliation between people.

RH: It may not have enough justice in it.

EB: Justice, I don't know. Justice is a word that I wouldn't use, unfortunately…. It might even be dangerous…. If you really look for justice—

RH: Maybe restorative justice—

EB: Or transitional justice.

RH: Yes.

EB: Okay. I mean, not absolute justice. This doesn't exist…. So we suggest that in order to have reconciliation, we must have acknowledgment from our side, the Jewish Israelis, [of] the Nakba, and our responsibility on the part we are responsible for. We are not responsible for everything in the Nakba, but some parts, of course, we are responsible. This acknowledgment means many things.... One main thing is we have to work for the return of the refugees. There is a good chance that there might be a reconciliation here. This reconciliation means that we as Jewish Israelis can live here no longer as the occupiers or as colonizers.... We are the colonizers. So, this is more than peace. My vision is to live here in this area—not to continue being European—not like Barak said, that Israel is "a villa in the jungle."

RH: That tells you a lot, doesn't it? We [Israelis] made the desert bloom.

EB: Yes, exactly! Yes, and all along the people here are savage people....

RH: I know there was a long court battle [over Canada Park].

EB: Yeah, some five years ago, we commemorated 36 years of the occupation. We organized a big event together with Neve Shalom.... We had stories from refugees, and we posted signs to indicate the places [of destroyed villages]. They were removed two days later. And then we wrote a letter to the management of the JNF [Jewish National Federation] asking them to post signs. They delayed their answer for almost two years. We submitted a petition to the supreme court to ask them to answer us. They said, OK, we are willing to post those signs. A few weeks later, one sign was removed, and the other sign was painted black. It's a long story.

RH: So it's an ongoing struggle.

EB: The issue here is not to post signs. The issue here is to raise awareness.

RH: It's a basic issue between a Zionist consciousness and a non-Zionist consciousness.

EB: Yeah. In the Zionist way of thinking, there is no room for Palestinian villages. We ask them if there were people living there. Zionism is about expulsion all the way.

RH: It's about being exclusive.

EB: This is the point. This is only for Jews: the memory, the language, the history, the land, the water, everything! It's only for Jews. If there are still Arabs here, OK! They can say thank you every day, 10 times a day because they are still here. But the first chance, they are out. Renovate the language and Jewish culture; have a sanctuary for Jews, but not at the expense of someone else.

RH: Thank you very much.

16 5 *Broken Cameras*: A Film for Peace

Emad Burnat

A former student of mine arranged for me to go to Bil'in—20 miles west of Ramallah—to meet Emad Burnat, creator of the Oscar-nominated documentary 5 Broken Cameras. *I had gone to Bi'lin four years earlier to meet Emad's brother, Eyad, and to witness the ritual of Friday prayers, followed by demonstrations against the building of the separation Wall by the Israelis. During my earlier visit, along with other internationals, I had taken my sliced onion as an antidote to possible Israeli tear gas, but the wind shifted. Tear gas wafted over me. Running and gasping for breath, I retreated to a safer place.*

Bil'in, West Bank, June 2014

EB: This is a very difficult time; it's a very small example of what we live here and what you may experience here of the occupation and the bad conditions in Palestine. What happened to me in airports with my family, it was a very small experience. I was nominated to the Academy Awards [in 2013], and it was not respectful that they stopped me at the airport, and they questioned me. I went to the United States seven times before and they never stopped me. This was the first time.

RH: So why this time?

EB: I don't know. I told them I'm an Oscar nominee and I came to the Oscars. It was difficult for them to believe in a Palestinian Oscar nominee and they thought I was lying or I was joking with them.... They told me, "If you don't come with us—we have documents to approve—we will send you back." So, I called [director] Michael Moore. He was having dinner for all the nominees and they were waiting for me to arrive. So I called him and he called the Academy and he tweeted this to more than one and a half million people and it became the story of the day. After that, they held me for about one hour. It was very serious because they told me, "We will send you back." But after one hour, they released me. It became very hard work for me for the next three days to make interviews with TV and news people about this story. But this small story made publicity for the film.

DOI: 10.4324/9781003262817-18

RH: I remember. I've been to Bil'in one other time, four years ago. Near the mosque, I had an interview with your brother. I'm working on a book about cultural resistance, Palestinian resistance to the Israeli government, to the occupation. Now that *5 Broken Cameras* is done, what is your next project?

EB: I'm still busy with traveling around the world with that film. Next week I have another trip to Geneva, to the UN, and another one in Ecuador. I did a screening in New York a couple of months ago.

RH: How was that received?

EB: It was received well at the UN. I was really busy with showing the film at different events and everywhere around the world. But I'm still thinking about the future and the next project. I will continue to film, and I am teaching my son, 13 years old, to film. I'm following the same story and I'm thinking about another project. It all takes time. I don't have the ability to make it now—after watching and showing *5 Broken Cameras* around the world, how it was received, the reactions, the changes here on the ground, in the village, and the changes in my life, my personal life.

RH: Is it all positive or is there a difficult side to the success?

EB: Sometimes it's difficult, especially here [in the West Bank]. In Palestine, we live in the same situation and conditions. But the Palestinian community, it's very scattered around the world. It was very difficult for them to see the film in different cities—to see the Palestinian people, their mannerisms, their complicated lives, the many different sides of their lives, the political problems, and doing the organizing here. The politicians here, they don't care about my very strong, important, and powerful work. They never cared about it. And this is the surprise that will give you a very bad feeling. When I made this film, the idea was to make this film and show it to them and to the community. But I wanted to do something for Palestine; it's not for me, it's for all the Palestinian people. You should get respect from your side and you should pay attention to this work and you should get support and help from your government. But I feel that they never cared about this.

RH: And why is that? Is it jealousy or do they not understand?

EB: It's a little bit of jealousy and they don't understand. Some they don't care and some they only care about themselves. They care about if you follow the news, they care about if you become a singer, and they care about you because they look at you like a big project. If someone like an Egyptian or a woman dancer came here, they would give her a prize or respect.

RH: But we just came from the museum for Mahmoud Darwish. Is he the only one that gets praise—for his poetry?

EB: Because you have seen the film, I talk about these problems regarding the Palestinian authority and their relations and how to treat the situation. I'm not in a good relationship with them after showing this movie around the world, so if you want to do anything, you should pay attention to their guides. There are many ways to resist the occupation. I cannot reject your way and you cannot reject my way. We respect each other in many ways. We resist here and in other towns. They resist in other ways. I use my camera. My camera is my weapon; it's a very strong weapon and it's the truth; it's very strong.

RH: That's why it was so effective; it was connected to your personal story. Someone couldn't say, "Well that's not true."

EB: Yeah, this is why the film was very successful and very moving for many people around the world. Because it's my experience, my point of view; I live here. Nobody else could do that. If you don't live that experience and feel the same feeling, you will never understand how I feel. When you see the movie, you hear when I am talking; it comes from inside me to make a film.

RH: Your voice-over style was very effective.

EB: It's not like when someone comes from outside [the village]. There're many filmmakers who just come to film and get some footage and go to the editing room to make the film. The point is not just to make a film. The point is to tell my story to the world. This is why the film became very powerful and very strong. You have to talk to the people in their language. Our language in the world—my language and your language and everyone's language—is the language of humanity. We should keep our humanity.

RH: That was very clear, very effective. I'm glad to know that you are working on another project.

EB: Yeah. I'm focusing on building a small center with a small theatre in the village. To get more kids and more children to use the camera and to show more films, to show their work and to invite famous people. So my dream is to build this center in the village to teach more people and to focus more on films and documentaries.

RH: It's a great idea.

EB: I think this project will be part of my next film.

RH: Given the success that you've had, will it make it a little bit easier to raise money for a project like that?

EB: Yeah, this is the point of how to raise the money for this project.

RH: Best wishes.

17 Get Up, Move Ahead, Make Peace

Elias Chacour

Abuna Elias Chacour has an amazing ability to provide both pastoral care and prophetic truth-telling. In 2000, a few months before the second intifada *began, I coled a student group to Palestine and Israel. As we moved from Ramallah to refugee camps in Bethlehem and then to Gaza, students became more and more distressed by the suffering and stories which they encountered. When we arrived at Abuna Chacour's Mar Elias College in the Galilee, students were emotionally raw. Fr. Chacour invited us to the roof of his personal residence and embraced our distress with compassion. He has been nominated several times for the Nobel Peace Prize. In 2006, he became archbishop of the Melkite Catholic Church in the Galilee area.*

Chicago, April 2003

RH: Abuna Chacour, as you may know, I have been [recording] stories of Palestinians who were displaced in 1948. This is the first dialogue about peacemakers living in Palestine and Israel. Please provide some of the history which led up to the founding of the Mar Elias schools.

EC: It's important to know [my] background. I was born in a village in upper Galilee called Baram. It's an entirely Christian village. We lived very peacefully with much love and affection among all of us—so much so that we did not call our brothers "brothers" and our neighbors "friends." Everybody was a brother and a sister for everybody else.... I am a Palestinian. I am proud to be a Palestinian Arab. My middle name is Chacour. And I'm also a Christian priest, in the Melkite Catholic Church, the Byzantine branch. I'm also a citizen of the state of Israel. I have all these facets of my identity that are not exactly what I am. I was not born a citizen of Israel; Israel was born in my country and in me, at the age of eight or nine years old. And I did not choose to be a Palestinian. I was born around men who were Palestinians, [born] to speak Arabic, and what it means to be a Christian. I was baptized at the age of four years. So I had four other years that were not Christian in the technical term. I was not born Christian. I was born a babe.

I was looking for a priority in my identity, and I discovered that I was born a baby and created in the image of God. And all the other facets

DOI: 10.4324/9781003262817-19

that I mentioned took deeper meaning, especially my being a Christian. I discovered that I was born in the country where Jesus Christ, the man from Galilee, was born, and [where] he gave his teachings, not to Americans, the British, or the French, but to people from Galilee, who were my forefathers. I was attracted by what he said, and that's how I wanted to become a servant to that man from Galilee. I studied for six years in Paris to prepare for priesthood. I studied Bible, theology, philosophy, [and] psychology.

I returned to Israel, to Palestine, to my country. And as all young men when they finish their studies … they want to turn over the whole world, and to reform everything, and to make everything new…. You have to find your place, your way, your road, your path, what is going on, and try to make a small difference…. I was invited by the experience of deprivation, of belonging to a community that was stripped, literally stripped, of all its human rights. The Arab minority inside Israel—part of the Palestinian community—was scattered with the creation of Israel [in 1948], became refugees … or marginalized people, people with no rights, with no protection for their dignity. That stirred in me this determination to do everything possible to restore the self-esteem for my people, and to protect my human dignity. I became a priest in 1965.

RH: Did you see becoming a priest, working for human rights, and restoring dignity as the same thing, or at least as deeply linked?

EC: For me, it was the best way to do it. Others were not priests and they have done great things. But for me, this was the way.

RH: That was your calling—

EC: Exactly. So, I started my priesthood in a small village called Ibillin in the Galilee, where there was no electricity, and water we had [only] once or twice a week. It was very difficult starting, because I did not have even a room to sleep in, or an office to work in. That was a difficult time, but a time of grace, where you rethink your values, your assumptions, your attitudes. And you think, my goodness, I am so small. I discovered that the Arab community in Israel, the Arab minority, was very young. I discovered that 75% of our people are below 27 years old, and 50% are below 14 years old. I decided to give my life for these 50% of our community—the Muslims as well as the Christians. I consider the Muslims to be my community … because, like me, they were born babies. So, we started collecting books from everywhere that's possible in the village, and we distributed these books to children. And we started the first Arabic public library in Galilee. Now, I can pride myself very humbly by saying that we were able to establish eight public libraries in our villages. But [in] the other villages that we couldn't reach, each local authority tries to have a small library for the children in the village. From that I concluded that evil is contagious.

RH: Evil is contagious?

EC: Yes! And good is even more contagious, if you do it with conviction! Man is basically good; he is not basically bad. We need to give him the opportunity to manifest the goodness that God has put in human beings, and you can find astonishing surprises. We also organized summer camps in community centers. We wanted to start with 500 children, but we faced 1,127 children the first day.

RH: Because the need was so great.

EC: Yes, there was absolutely nothing for children to do in the long summer months. No school, nothing at all. They sat in the street, looking around at their land that was confiscated. Jews had surrounded it with barbed wire. Pools, green grass, everything they wanted, community centers, [our children] were deprived from accessing. This was a source of anger, of bitterness, of hatred, and a lot of violence. Unless you provide an alternative to violence, you are not allowed even to condemn violence. You have to give an alternative. You have to give hope, so that hatred can no more have its whole destructive impact.... At the last summer camp, we had over 5,000 children coming from 30 different villages and towns. To provide them with drinks, we invited all their mothers to send us from each village or town 10 mothers every day. We had 300 mothers to prepare sandwiches and drinks for over 5,000 children. The children were invited to sleep under the olive trees and fig trees, because that was the only place we had. These mothers were majority Muslims. They were beautiful mothers, generous, great, openminded. I'm happy to conclude that we do not have a monopoly over Holy Spirited Christians.... God is neither Christian nor Muslim nor Jew. God is God, creator of us all. The last project I initiated was the high school. There was no high school for teenagers.

RH: How far did students have to go?

EC: Sometimes 30, 40, 50 miles, every day. Out of 8,500 citizens, only 90 teenagers went to high school. It's too far away, it's too costly. And it's difficult. That affected many female students; five to seven girls went to high school every year. They were too poor. So, I opened a high school.

RH: The year would have been around—

EC: 1982. We opened the school despite all of the problems that were created by the state of Israel about giving us the building permit. So I decided to build without a building permit.

RH: I've heard you tell that story. Please tell it again.

EC: I applied for a building permit, [but officials] set us down as not have a building permit. I had to either give up on the children or to give up on an unjust law that prevents us from building schools, and build without a building permit, and that's what I did. I was summoned to court because the police came three months later to check on our building permit. They knew we did not have it. So they asked me, How can you build without a building permit? I said, It's very simple. I'm going to build it with sand, stone, cement, and steel. I was really afraid, but I was determined not to stop building. I was summoned to court 35 times, always for building permits. It was most unpleasant to go to court. We continued construction without building permits, and nine months later, the building was ready. I rang a bell on the first of September, 1982, to see in front of me 80 children, ages 14 and 15 years old. That project has been blessed by God and our friends and our determination. When I [came] to the States a week ago, I left behind me 3,500 students—from early age to over 50 years old. It's an amalgamation of different schools and institutions. We built it with the help of local volunteers. We were helped by international volunteers from the States, France, England, Germany, Switzerland, Australia, Africa, and from Israel. Even Jewish volunteers came to help. We were also able to do that through the income that I had from my books, *Blood Brothers* and *We Belong to the Land.* Everything was invested to develop that place.

RH: It's a beautiful campus. You had just finished a new building when I was there three years ago.

EC: Yes, since then we have started two other buildings—a big auditorium that can hold up to 2,000 human beings, after which we started a church. We called that church the Sermon on the Mount. It's in the form of a boat because I wanted to remind everybody that we are children of the desert. The other building is the elementary school, with two top floors as a dormitory for young girls. So we are still working very hard despite the drastic cuts in the funds subsidized by the government, a cut of 20%, which was a real catastrophe. Now my joy is that we have a start-up team preparing to open the first Arab Christian Israeli university, with accreditation from NCA and with the help of the University of Indianapolis. We took our accreditation papers to the Israeli academic authorities. We discussed with them for two years, writing back and forth, shouting, quarreling. We have two more meetings with them to obtain permission to make publicity and interest students.

RH: Excellent.

EC: And that will be a great big breakthrough in the relations between Jews and Palestinians inside Israel.

RH: Will that make it easier for Jewish students to come in some ways?

EC: Not in some ways, in all ways. We'll make it easy for Arab and Jewish students to come. No one will be guest, no one will be host.

RH: Because you'll have complete accreditation.

EC: Yes. So that's a little bit of the story of my life.

RH: Tell me more about the philosophy … that carries that vision.

EC: Our main goal is to prove to the Jewish people in Israel and to the Palestinians that the only way to solve the [ongoing] problem is to accept diversity and to make that diversity itself the community goal, where we all work toward accomplishing it. So unity within diversity is the key to solve the problem. Accepting diversity means sharing, and sharing means a minimum sense of justice, and out of that results acceptance of each other. When you accept each other on the basis of justice, then you are able to live in certain peace and security.

RH: Give me a story or an example of how that acceptance leads to reconciliation.

EC: The fact is that we are living together. We have 28 faculty members who are Jewish. That's very few, compared to the 290 members we have. So the fact that we continue to live together, and we have developed so many good relations with many other schools inside Israel and the Ministry of Education, that's proof that this is working. Otherwise, we'd continue to kill each other.... There are many examples. When a Jewish terrorist attacked the Muslims who were praying in the Hebron mosque, we all, Jews and Palestinians, wrote letters protesting, because we said that it was Nazi-like more than it was Jewish-like. But a few weeks later, a Palestinian from Gaza exploded himself in the middle of a crowded bus station in Tel Aviv, killing 16 Jews and wounding 86. We wrote letters to the Ministry of Education and to the families with our condolences. But my students wanted something more. One of them said, I want to donate blood for all the Jews. I said that I, a priest, would do that, too. I made a phone call and they sent us 15 Jewish nurses to pump our blood. I was afraid that only 10 or 20 would donate blood. Some 350 students were adults able to decide. Out of 350, 300 donated blood for Jews in Tel Aviv. So that's our dream. We do not distinguish [among] who is in the hospital. We only know that they need help, and we can give it.

RH: One of the many reasons why you are so widely admired is because of this vision. All of us need to learn this again and again throughout our lives, how the process of reconciliation occurs. You know very well we need this here in [the United States] as well.

EC: Not as well. As an outsider, I say you need it more than any other country in the world.

RH: That's quite possible. You risk being reduced to relying on your military power, on your money, but not at all on your constitution.

EC: That's evident with your attitude in the Third World with your foreign policy. It is amazing, the difference between the image that America exports of itself and the reality, the beautiful reality of America in America.

RH: That's why we take students outside of the country, so they can wake up and see. In *We Belong to the Land*, there are several places where you talk about your process of coming to understand the Beatitudes in the Aramaic. These "blessed" phrases aren't passive, right?

EC: It's better that people read what I have written because it's better organized, better done.

RH: But the point is, in your understanding, to be "blessed" is to become active in the world.

EC: Exactly. I don't think the Aramaic texts meant blessing or happiness. It meant, rather, a shred of hope. It means go ahead, get up, do something, move, get your hands dirty, feel you are hungry for visible justice. When you are hungry, you'll do everything to find food anywhere you can. Is that what we do when we see injustice in our society? Do we care when we write a letter to our congressman and say, I have done my duty; let the world go astray? The same is for peace. We all love peace, my goodness; peace is beautiful. We all like to contemplate peace. But in the gospel, it's never *contemplating* peace. It is *building peace, contracting peace, making peace*. And that's why, instead of just contemplating peace, we are to get up, to move, to go ahead, to do something, to get our hands dirty, to implement and pursue justice, from which peace and security will come.

RH: So the work of being faithful, the work of education, the work of peace and justice, they are all deeply related, and not separate from each other.

EC: They can't be separate from each other. Either you are or you aren't a person who believes in God, and does God's work. Or you select what pleases you emotionally, as many Christians do. They forget or they ignore or they don't want to remember that God's order is Kill not.

RH: In the West we have so many misconceptions about the Middle East and the Far East, and we have enormous misconceptions about Islam. [What are] the possibilities of nonviolence, and the possibility of recovering—for Christians, Jews, and Muslims—a nonviolent, reconciling spirit?

EC: I don't know if you [in the West] have a misunderstanding toward Islam or the Middle East, or you have misunderstandings about so many other things, because 56 years ago, you had so many misunderstandings toward the Jews.... And the same thing now; it is us Palestinians who are the dirty terrorists. Unfortunately, you care too much for all the Middle East. Not because we're Arab, men and women, children of God, not because we gave theistic religion to humanity, but because ... you want oil for your cars. So what is nonviolence? Can you become a nonviolent person? I don't think so. No one can become a nonviolent person. Only God is nonviolent. You are always tempted with violence; you are always tempted with evil, exploitation, with selfishness. You have to choose in every event the way you will work it. I don't like the term you have in the English language about nonviolence, as if you have to live constantly in reaction to something else, and you have no genuine initiative to take.

RH: It takes us back to the active form of peacemaking you were talking about.

EC: OK. So it's not a question of nonviolence as much as the conviction of the sanctity of life. It's much more important to consider the sanctity of life that you would sacrifice your life, save any life, that is endangered with violence.

RH: And resist any in-between measures that degrade life.

EC: Exactly. It seems that all those who believe truly in peace, and who refuse to use violence to reach their goals, refuse to use their arms and their military power to destroy this or that country, they are condemned to see their conviction in peace and the sanctity of life with their own blood. You have one in America who did that, Martin Luther King, in El Salvador, Oscar Romero, and a non-Christian, Mahatma Gandhi. For me they were all disciples of that man from Galilee, who did not hesitate to protest against violence and to affirm the importance of the sanctity of life.

RH: At Mar Elias College, your students, from all backgrounds, have encountered so much violence and difficulty. What is the process that you try to encourage in terms of curriculum development, to bring that vision into full flower?

EC: We do not need to discuss nonviolence in the school. We need to discuss the beauty of being together, of respecting each other. The enrichment that is there—we are different but complimentary. We do not need to decry the evil as much as to put on the good.

RH: Everyone can see the evil.

EC: Exactly; everyone already talks about the evil. But we are not soldiers who fight the evil. We are ministers to preach good news. And that's really a big difference between what we are doing and what the heads of state and presidents are doing, propagating fear, doubt, vengeance, and destruction.

RH: But even the affirmations are a kind of resistance. When you say we are all children of God, all equal, that is a resistance to the prevailing laws.

EC: If you want to call it resistance, I don't mind. But you are not resisting, you are not *fighting.* These people, presidents and others, who want to suffocate people, who want to kill people, who want to settle accounts, who dare say, The one who is not with me is against me. Only God can say that. We need someone now to say to humanity: Fear no more; I give you peace. It seems that our present political leaders do not know what that means.

RH: I agree; they're working out of fear.

EC: We are reducing poor nations to pieces. What are we to do? We are able to commit crimes and say, I'm killing this man; I'm liberating him. There is so much conscious and unconscious hypocrisy in our human attitudes today, mainly in politics. We create hypocrisy for ourselves and hide behind nice words, and mean completely the contrary.

RH: I agree. If you combine fear and weapons of mass destruction, it's about the most dangerous situation one can get.

EC: So you can claim that you are liberating a people from mass destruction, with weapons of mass destruction.

RH: You create the very violence you say you're trying to prevent.

EC: We need healing. We need to be healed.

RH: In the Israeli-Palestinian context, where do you see those healing streams that come alongside of your own?

EC: I am neither the only one, nor the more important one, nor the one who has a prophetic view. I am one among many who try to bring some hope.

RH: I understand. What I mean is, where else do you see some hope that gives you courage?

EC: That's what I mean. There are many Jews and Palestinians inside Israel and [Palestinians] in the Occupied Territories who are deeply disturbed by what is going on—this procession of funerals on both sides. When the Jewish lady cries over the loss of her husband, it's exactly like the Palestinian lady who cries and shouts, and they are both inconsolable. We cannot console a Palestinian lady who became widowed by using 10 Jews to become widows. And we cannot console a Jewish widow by destroying the houses of 10 families and killing 10 heads of families. It's an absolute example of "an eye for an eye, then we all become blind." And that's our situation. We need a charismatic leader who does not rely on military power.

RH: By charismatic leader, you mean—

EC: A prime minister, head of state, a decision-making person who believes in the sanctity of human life and the importance of diversity. To know who we are, and vice versa, to know somebody who is not like us—that's what we don't have. Unfortunately, the U.S. is shipping weapons here. And their weapons are creating only more problems.

RH: That's because we're not committed to finding a just peace, but to playing power games.

EC: One of the reasons, yes.

RH: I'm planning to go to Palestine in two weeks to record more of these [dialogues].

EC: People here [in the U.S.] need to hear these voices. And to rework their imagination from fear to a sense of a just peace.

RH: Is there anything that I've missed?

EC: Don't pray for Palestinians. They don't need your prayers. Don't pray for Jews. They don't need your prayers. I would like to help Americans pray for themselves, to have the courage to say the truth, no matter what the price is. But not to eliminate the other because he doesn't agree with you. This is the prayer we all need to pray, each for his own self.

RH: Thank you, Abuna.

EC: Thank you also.

18 A Comprehensive Solution

Mona El-Farra

Dr. Mona El-Farra is a medical doctor, development and human-rights worker, and storyteller. She is the director of Gaza Projects for the Middle East Children's Alliance (MECA), in Oakland, California, and a human-rights activist with the Palestinian Red Crescent Society. Her book, From Gaza with Love, *expresses her commitment to love all humanity. In her vision, the land can be shared on the basis of equal rights. She promotes health for women and children.*

Chicago, July 2007

MEF: My name is Mona el-Farra, and I'm a medical doctor. I'm not practicing at the moment. I promote health for women and children, and address human rights issues in the Gaza strip. I also work with health organizations at the level of administration. To be comprehensive, we cannot isolate health from other issues in the community. I have been traveling and giving presentations about life in Gaza under occupation. Thousands of women and children are vulnerable and suffering because of the war, and longing for peace. I noticed while traveling, there is a growing American movement toward peace in the Middle East.

RH: Talk about your early experiences, experiences that helped to shape who you are today.

MEF: There were two events. When I was 15, Israel took over the Gaza strip and the West Bank, 40 years ago, in 1967. Living in the horror and the hardship of war affected my life. As a child and as a teenager, I saw many people injured. We had no water. I was frightened. It was my first time to see the Israeli occupation. Later I took part in the nonviolent resistance.

RH: Even in 1967, there was a nonviolence movement?

MEF: Of course. I remember it very well; it was continuous. Students who wanted to say no to the occupation went out in demonstrations. It was a spontaneous movement in the schools.

RH: What form did it take?

MEF: It was peaceful. We shouted slogans against the occupation, "Get out of our land." The Israeli army was harsh, arresting and hitting

DOI: 10.4324/9781003262817-20

many of us. I was hit by Israeli soldiers. This engraved in my psychology the relationship between me and the occupier. We were hit, arrested, and put in jail. To get me out, my father paid $5,000, and he had to sign a document saying that I would not go to a demonstration again. This was my first occupation experience. Later on, I went to university in Cairo, Egypt. My experience was very harsh crossing the border all the time. We crossed at Rafah in the beginning, and evacuated in big vans. The vans were covered. These experiences also accumulated, coming across Jordanian borders, with all the restrictions.

After I got married, I was coming from the Allenby Bridge to Gaza, and I bought a doll in Jordan for my daughter. She was four then. She was dreaming of this doll. On the border, the Israeli guard searched the doll. He found nothing, but the guard said, “You cannot take the doll.” He confiscated it and threw it away. This is the first time I have mentioned this story in 15 or 20 years. I told the soldier, “You are throwing away my daughter’s doll. I am going to tell her that the Israeli soldier threw your dolly away. So, you are giving our children more reasons to hate you.”

He said, “I’m sorry, these are the rules.” I told him, “It is your turn to change the rules.” This happens everywhere I go; I have to repeat this line to guards. Another traumatic experience happened to me in the recent *Intifada*, in 2000. When the Israelis started home demolitions, they demolished my home, uprooted olive and orange trees, dug up graves and destroyed the well.

RH: Was it done because of your political activity?

MEF: No. It was collective punishment. This was the home of my mother. My mother was 80 years old and it was a small, modest home on our land. Because of her age and disability it was easier for her to live there. The Israeli army demolished it. This was a traumatic experience for me because all my memories were in that place, all our photos. I lost everything because my mother had moved everything to that place—pictures, papers—all our belongings were lost, besides the property. We couldn’t reach the property, because they built a bridge on top of that area to guarantee a passage for the settlers. It continued like that until the Israeli settlements withdrew from Gaza. They completely destroyed. It took a lot of effort to rebuild.

RH: How old were the trees?

MEF: Some were 140 years old; some of them were very ancient. This was the place where I played as a child. I remember when my father dug the well. I remember when I drank the water out of his hands. All my memories were destroyed in one minute by the Israeli army. That night, 26 homes were demolished. For many farmers, this was their living. After this incident I was really traumatized. I couldn’t sleep for days. I dreamed of the soldiers, the settlers, and what happened to me and the others. It gave me strength to defend other people's rights. This was in 2000.

It had nothing to do with security, because there was no militia movement in the area. They just wanted to destroy our history, and our future. The property was in Khan Younis, in Al Garara village. From that day, I was committed, besides my work with health, to issues of children and women, because I have seen how devastated the people were when homes were demolished. In my case, my mother has a place to stay in my home. But the poorest people have only their homes; now they had nothing. So, I was there to help them and to listen to their stories.

RH: Up until then you had been doing medical work, because that was your training?

MEF: Yes, but that was a turning point. I extended my work to include community development, and community empowerment. I focused on human-rights issues, because by talking to people and conveying their message to others, I was exposing the Israeli practices against human rights—what happened to me, and talking about what happens every day for us as workers in such difficult circumstances, where human rights are violated every day and where medics are literally working under fire. Many were killed; many were not allowed to reach patients. Ambulances and hospitals were attacked. It is my responsibility to keep talking about this.

RH: For you, listening and then retelling those stories is a crucial part of the work.

MEF: Listening to stories is crucial; so is my experience. I am a doctor; I live these stories.

RH: I visited at least one hospital in Gaza in 2000, and things were difficult then. I assume things are much worse now. How has your work evolved from 2000 until now?

MEF: Before 2000, I worked in refugee camps with organizations. I was a member of the board of directors of many organizations. I founded Al Awda Hospital, and I founded children's cultural centers in Jabalia and Rafah refugee camps. After 2000, my vision for work was to empower children, to give the children a chance of living without pain in places of their own, where they could paint and dance. I wanted to take away the culture of violence, and to give them a place of their own. I wanted to build bridges between those children and the outside world. This is my work—the promotion of health and children's cultural activities.

RH: Health is a much broader thing than just the body.

MEF: Exactly. In most centers where the children come and practice those activities, it is recreation for them. It keeps them away from the troubled life in the streets, and allows them to do something different. In other words, it is psychiatric support for the children. I've committed myself to this idea. Besides the idea of linking the children with the outside world, building bridges, so they don't feel isolated. They need to see the other side of the world, which is the peace movement. We need to regain children's and women's faith in the outside world. There is nothing more heartbreaking than when people lose faith, trust, and hope.

RH: Their expectations have been crushed so many times.

MEF: So, these centers are very important, because health issues are addressed indirectly. We entertain, keep the Palestinian culture alive, build bridges, and help children feel empowered.

RH: Many things are happening at the same time—crisis intervention, medical emergencies, dealing with cultural needs; Inevitably you're doing political work, human-rights work at various levels, resisting the occupation. That's exhausting, to work at so many levels at the same time.

MEF: There are many levels, linked to one another. They are all complete as a collective. They are all important. I am sometimes exhausted. But I have volunteers. I give ideas; I'm part of what's going on, I secure funds, and do relief work. But I don't work alone; I work with colleagues. We practice teamwork. This keeps me going because I am an activist who has to keep going. I have good friends who understand my pain and suffering. I wrote a book, *From Gaza with Love*.

RH: It's an unusual title.

MEF: Because, despite all the hardships, there's still love—not only family love or love between a woman and a man, but love in humanity. This is what I meant by "From Gaza with Love." And despite all the hardships, there's still peace and love.

RH: W.H. Auden, a British poet, wrote during World War II, "We must love one another or die."

MEF: That's what I meant. I love the world. I want to be happy to love my enemy—but on the basis of justice, or I would be stupid to give love, wasteful love. I believe in love.

RH: How did the concept of justice emerge for you across time?

MEF: It is modeled through my readings, my experiences, myself as a human being, seeing all people. Always the idea of the other was there for me, [including] the occupied forces. So, justice for me means justice for both Palestinians and Israelis.... I look at soldiers and I feel pity for them. They are victims of the system, the government, the ideology. On the other hand, I see our children as victims of this aggression. So I always have this vision of peace, but not at any price. I want long-lasting peace that does not neglect the political issues, nor people's inalienable rights.

RH: Without adequate security for everyone, no one is secure.

MEF: Aggression against my people will not bring security to Israel. Not war, nor being strong; it is *our* peace and satisfaction that will bring peace to them.

RH: Can you think of an experience in which you helped a soldier to see you as a human being?

MEF: Some of them are compassionate, but it is a small minority. They don't want to be there. In Gaza, during the first *intifada* I saw a soldier who wouldn't hurt a child. He had a gun, and he wouldn't shoot. Inside Israel now there's an emerging peace movement that believes in our rights, including the right of return. They recognize that what happened in 1948 was an ethnic cleansing of Palestinians. It was genocide. In Ilan Pappe's book, *The Ethnic Cleansing of Palestine*.... [soldiers] admit that they participated in the ethnic cleansing of Palestine....

RH: Do you see divestment as an important part of the peace and justice movement?

MEF: Yes, it's very important. At a conference yesterday, I was inspired to see all those people in the streets, part of a growing peace movement. I heard from my friend Jeremy Corbyn, a member of parliament in the UK, that the movement in Britain is growing larger. There were 20,000 people on the 40th anniversary of the occupation, saying no to the occupation, yes to the freedom of Palestinian people. So it gives me hope....

RH: Help us understand the current complexity in Gaza, especially since the election of Hamas. How has that changed ... basic needs for security, food, and drinking water?

MEF: Life became very difficult because of how the world responded. The sanctions keeping the Palestinian tax revenue money inside Israel—those measures already existed. But it went from bad to very bad to worse. That's why I told you people are losing hope.... Poverty reached unprecedented levels. In the hospital, we cannot secure our medical supplies easily. Aggression by the Israeli army continues. They stay in the village two, three, or four days, then leave. Air strikes continued. Many citizens were caught in these clashes. They formed a buffer zone, a new form of aggression, a sonic boom made by airplanes. This was amazing and terrifying.

RH: It was another form of collective punishment.

MEF: Yes. After that, electrical power plants were destroyed. Bridges were destroyed. People are hungry in the streets. Many families are living on aid. More than 70% of families live on international aid. The unemployed people number 40% or 50%. We are not safe inside our walls.

RH: Is domestic violence and ordinary crime increasing as well because of this pressure?

MEF: Domestic violence has increased inside the family and outside in the streets. People became more aggressive. And all this step by step with arms coming from abroad, for Hamas but more for Fatah. The U.S. wanted to support the mainstream and Fatah's Mohammed Dahlan. Out of a population of 1.4 million, 60% are children under age 18. They're living in hardship, poverty, and domestic violence. This is the outcome of the American policy.

RH: It's containment.

MEF: There is friction, lack of opportunity, and lack of resources. So, the clash was inevitable, and it happened. Now, instead of talking about a future for peace, we are talking about Hamas in Gaza, Fatah in the West Bank, talking about how to feed people, and forgetting about peace.

RH: Can you tell me stories of families that you've connected with in the past year or two?

MEF: Yes. I have a story from one family in Bureij refugee camp. A woman told me that they could afford one chicken every 30 days. You need meat, protein. There are no vegetables, no food. That's why there's anemia and iron deficiency. They subsist on bread, rice, sugar, and oil. Another story is a positive story. I am the Gaza project director for the Middle East Children's Alliance (MECA) [in Oakland, California]. We have 30 youths here to continue their education through a scholarship from MECA. I was told by the families how important it was for them to guarantee the education of their children. They were very pleased. Another story comes from women who do embroidery and we market it abroad. One woman came and kissed me and said, "Thank you very much; I was able to feed my family."

When the army withdrew, they demolished many houses. So people were homeless, with no clothes, no blankets, nothing. So we coordinated with them to get things for the children. A mother told me that 35 members of the family were all confined in one room for 48 hours, while the army commandeered the house. The army was on top, on the upper floor, and the family was below. The army came from the upper floor to use the toilet. One of the children was crying. He was four, and he was thirsty. The soldier offered him some water, and the child refused to take water from the soldier. He just flicked him away and said, "No, no! I don't want water from him." This for me is the occupied and the occupier. Occupation deprives people of their humanity.

RH: And to reassert his dignity he said no to the water, even though he was desperately thirsty.

MEF: Yes. This is the Palestinian people resisting occupation.

RH: That's amazing. So, tell me a couple of stories of hope, too.

MEF: Two years ago, in one of the refugee camps, the children were rehearsing for dabke, folkloric dancing. They were invited to perform in England. I visited the center during a big [Israeli] incursion into the refugee camp. I fundraise and I coordinate work for the hospital. So, I wanted to go to the hospital to see how the patients were. I stopped by the children's center to see how they were rehearsing and ask if they needed anything. The children were dancing, and the shelling from Israeli tanks was too close; it was only 200 meters away. But the children were dancing, dancing, dancing, and there was shelling. What is more hopeful than this? I love this story.

RH: And were they able to go to England?

MEF: Yes. After two months, borders were opened and they went to Britain and performed in many places. They conveyed a message that Palestinian people are people for peace, ordinary people who have to live. They play, they dance; they are not terrorists. You can see some of Israel's violence in the children's painting, because these are the circumstances they know. If they paint something, they paint what they experience. What they experience is violence.

RH: People outside of the peace movement in the U.S. do not link nonviolence with Gaza, because their views are so limited. What form does nonviolence take besides demonstrations?

MEF: People continue their steadfastness against the occupation. This is nonviolence. In Arabic, the word is *sumud.* They collectively endure such circumstances and continue to live. This is nonviolence. To walk to school, to endure, to persist, to be strong. This is nonviolence. They are fighting by living, helping each other, going to school. This is to resist. To work in the hospitals, to keep the community intact, in spite of domestic violence, I see that as nonviolence.

Last summer we endured difficult circumstances: no electricity, no water, closed borders, and continuous military operations. So, I went to visit one of the centers in the Nuseirat Camp of Gaza. It's called New Horizons for Children and Women. I was there in the center, and there was a group of girls playing, dancing, painting, happy. Again, the airplane was in the sky, the drone. I could hear an Apache helicopter. In spite of this, people who are responsible for the center brought the children to summer camp. The children couldn't go to the seaside because of the military operation in Gaza. It wasn't safe. So the organizers of the center and the children were there, trying to do something in spite of the circumstances. On my way back, the drone and the helicopters were in the sky. I was driving my car, subjecting myself to danger. But I *had* to go see the children and the organizers, and to empower them and to see what they needed.

RH: It's a continuum: to be steadfast, and to work.

MEF: Yes. Life is difficult. People have not adapted to the conditions, but they are coping. As I said earlier, it is very dangerous when people lose hope. It must come later.

RH: This is the situation now. Do you see any political solution to the Fatah-Hamas conflict?

MEF: At the moment, I don't have any predictions, because Hamas itself doesn't have any program. They don't know what they are going to do. They were dragged into this situation.

RH: They were surprised, at least.

MEF: They were surprised; they were happy to take over. So now they have taken over, but what will happen, we don't know. There are many expectations and analyses. But I don't have my own analysis because I am shocked. It's a big challenge now for Hamas to feed the people, because the West will continue its embargo, and reducing money for the West Bank.

RH: The people are caught in between.

MEF: And I blame both parties, Hamas and Fatah. They struck a big blow to our national goals. My vision is that this land, Palestinian land, can be shared by both Israelis and Palestinians.

RH: You believe that it can be shared?

MEF: Yes, of course. I still believe there's a place for a possible peace—for sharing resources, for living in one country, on the basis of equal rights, not on the basis of apartheid and racism and colonization. It should be based on human rights for everyone, sharing resources, and this will bring peace and stability for the area. The right of return for Palestinian people doesn't mean destruction of Israel at all. The place can be shared, if there is will and determination.

RH: Do you personally care whether it's two states or one state?

MEF: Not two states. It should be one state for everyone. The land can be shared.

RH: It's already shared, just not equally. [*Both laugh.*]

MEF: Let it be shared for future states. That will bring peace. We must say no to apartheid because what's happening in Gaza, in Palestine, now with the war—it is apartheid.

* * * * * * * *

London, July 2018 (via Skype)

RH: We met 11 years ago. What has changed and what has not changed [in] 11 years?

MEF: Many things have changed. For 11 years, Gaza has been under a siege which affected people's lives. It has affected their political situation as well; there have been three major Israeli assaults against Gaza. In between, every day there are attacks on the borders. You don't hear about it. There is a separation between Gaza and the West Bank. The Palestinian people contributed to this. Fatah did not have a strategic vision for our national goals.

RH: A political vision?

MEF: A political vision, yes. They didn't have a vision, and they didn't have the determination to end the division. The two parties have different ideologies. This affected our lives in Gaza a lot.... Instead of being one, we are divided. [During the] 11 years of the siege, Palestinian national goals [moved] to the back because the humanitarian situation has worsened greatly—unemployment, water, electricity. I am an activist working on the ground with MECA and the Red Crescent Society [to meet] these humanitarian needs.

RH: I've seen reports from the UN that by 2020 Gaza will be unlivable.

MEF: Gaza is unlivable now. This increased the severity of Palestinian suffering. The number of people who are dying in Palestine has increased. Children are dying from a lack of medication. Gaza patients cannot get the right treatment. Borders are closed. These factors encouraged more and more support for the boycott and sanctions movement against Israel.

RH: You would say that BDS has had some effect already?

MEF: Yeah, it has. For example, the Irish parliament a few weeks ago passed a motion to boycott the goods of Israeli citizens in the West Bank. It is not enough, of course, because military and economic power are linked between Israel and the American government. We must struggle, struggle until there is a comprehensive solution for Israel-Palestine.

RH: In our [dialogue] 11 years ago, you were certain that a one-state solution would be best.

MEF: At this moment, Israel will not give a chance for two states, and will [look at] the one-state solution in a sarcastic way.... But this is the right solution.

RH: I was in Hebron two months ago and it seemed like every two blocks had a barrier.

MEF: Yeah! Young Israeli girls and boys all the time have guns. This is the injustice of the occupation. I think that when people will be comprehensive, the resolution is coming.

RH: Will it take some outside diplomatic pressure, as well as economic pressure, and where will that come from? I'm not hopeful that the United States can do much.

MEF: The main issue is the United States—[its] political interests, military arms, the big corporations, and the politics. All is linked together. You can imagine what is the budget for the arms deals with different parts of the world and Israel. [Israel] is bombing Gaza. It makes me angry. I live there. I'm going back there. There was an attack against Gaza last week, which destroyed this big cultural center in Gaza.... We were shaken by it.

RH: People are afraid it might fall down.

MEF: With children [inside]. I understand the pain over the death of five children on the Israel-Gaza border. When Hamas hits Israel with rockets, it does not compare with the bombing of the F-16s.

RH: Are you able to talk more about the war in 2014, four years ago, "Protective Edge"?

MEF: Yeah, the Protective Edge [attacks].

RH: I know that you lost many family members, and this is very painful, but it's important for North American people to know what this is like. Can you talk about 2014?

MEF: Yeah, of course, but before I forget, you have asked me what has changed. I mentioned some political issues, some humanitarian issues. There's something very important that has changed. The psychological well-being of the children has changed.

We've gone through three attacks in the last 12 years. Doctors, social workers, and activists are facing children who are still suffering from the effects from the attacks.

RH: From four years ago—2014?

MEF: And before that. It is accumulating. In the same family [many] were killed. The kids are grown up now, but some of them are under treatment. The effects of that on the kids is long term. Not only physically and lack of basic needs, but also psychologically. The longest year of my life was in 2014. I was shocked and appalled when I heard about my cousin's family—nine were killed [by the Israeli army]. I felt that I am helpless. I have been dehumanized as well. I felt I couldn't go on or attend the funeral. My cousins are in Hanoun in Gaza, only 25 kilometers away, but I couldn't go. It happened to many people who could not bury their dead. It dehumanizes you. I was stuck and couldn't grieve properly. I was busy as a doctor with [trauma] in society. I have personal pain on one side; I cannot grieve, because I am doing other things. Lovely children were killed.... my cousin's beautiful grandchildren, like all Palestinian children. They were happy and doing well in school. They were in their pajamas at 2:30 in the morning. Their grandfather took them to a nearby [school] to escape from his building, and they were still hit. One of those kids lost a mother and brother and was unable to go to school for six months. She was afraid to be alone in the classroom. There were another 40 people killed in the same day in different parts of Gaza. My cousin's grandchildren are among 549 killed in 2014. It was very difficult.

RH: Over time, what is the collective effect of this trauma? How does one heal or go on?

MEF: We are trapped on a small piece of land [with] one deprivation after another. [Healing] has to be many things together. You need support, good atmosphere, good environment, and sports. Poverty is really difficult on their lives. At MECA, we are working to provide programs for children to heal, to enjoy, to normalize their lives. But our efforts are limited. The overall situation should end and there should be justice in Gaza and the West Bank.

RH: [Comment] on recent events and the March of Return. Do you know the background?

MEF: The background is the suffering of the people of Gaza because of the siege. The occupation is the cause of their cry for help. They wanted to express, "Gaza is under siege. Gaza is under occupation." It was a cry for help, and they thought they will do it in a peaceful, nonviolent way. It was a good action—balloons against Israel. Israel exaggerates to make it look violent when it was not violent. You could see girls and boys dancing dabke. You could see women making bread and [leading] cultural activities on the border, breaking the siege. It was an outcome of 11 years [of siege]. What has changed? A lot of violence in the school. You don't expect people to be peaceful in such awful circumstances. But a majority of the march was nonviolent. The message to the world was, "We are here." Somebody is trapped and knocking to remind the people, "I am here. Wake up, I am here!" It's a good way to struggle.

RH: What else would you like to say? Most North Americans don't have a clue.

MEF: The humanitarian situation, on top of the political one [is awful]. It is not good that the Americans still support Israel through their taxes. This is my message to ordinary American people who are unaware they are supporting unjust acts in Gaza. If it continues like this, Gaza will explode. I don't know how this explosion will go. [In the Great March of Return], what happened on the border in peaceful ways … is desperation. The world is silent, the government is silent. I think this is the worst year [for me] that happened in the Palestinian struggle. What happened with my people needs years and years of healing … not only [for] the assaults, the struggle, and hardships of life. [2014] was our worst time of struggle as Palestinian people.

RH: It's good to talk with you again.

MEF: Thank you very much. It was a great pleasure.

19 Struggles for a Just Peace

Jeff Halper

Jeff Halper grew up in Minnesota, earned a Ph.D. in anthropology, and became active in the American Civil Rights Movement. He moved to Israel in the 1970s and taught anthropology at Ben-Gurion University. In 1997, he cofounded the Israeli Committee Against House Demolitions (ICAHD) to analyze "facts on the ground," resist house demolitions, and facilitate strategic dialogue. In the early 2000s, Halper saw that a two-state solution was no longer possible, and proposed alternatives. In 2006, he and Ghassan Andoni were conominees for the Nobel Peace Prize.

Jerusalem, June 2003

RH: I'm talking with Jeff Halper. Tell me some of your personal history.

JH: I grew up in northern Minnesota. I was very involved in the 1960s. The Civil Rights Movement developed the view of human rights that I have now. The war against Vietnam led to my international involvement in the Middle East. I'm not religious, but being Jewish was important to me. So when I came to Israel as a student 35 years ago, the country spoke to me.... I came right after the 1967 war, and before the 1973 war. There were hopes for a just peace.... And I did accept there was a genuine tie between the Jewish people and this country.

RH: Historically.

JH: Historically, and the whole movement of the world toward nation-states. A nation has a need for self-determination, because it can't reduce its identity to an ethnic group.... Jews were a nation living abroad, but they did have a territorial connection. The vast majority of Jews continue to see themselves as ethnic, and where Jews had a choice, they usually didn't come here. Those who saw themselves as a nation came here. And there are persecution issues.

RH: Across a long period of time.

JH: It started in the 1880s—the combination of a positive nationalism, a homeland, and the push of persecution created a certain logic to Israel.... What ruined it all was the idea of exclusivity. Zionism had two types of nationalism it could adopt—the Western European model, like the American model, that says the nation is the state. The

DOI: 10.4324/9781003262817-21

state is the expression, and everyone in the state can be a citizen.... The framework is there for equal citizenship in a civil society. Eastern Europe was tribal. That's the kind of nationalism that Zionism adopts.... [If] they said, "We want to come back to this country for national reasons, and we acknowledge that there are already people living here, and we want to find an accommodation," something could have been worked out. Instead, they came with this tribal idea: "This is only our country, exclusively ours, there's nobody else here ... certainly not a Palestinian people." So, Zionism fatally compromised itself. The idea of Jewish nationalism—coming back to the land, developing an Israeli culture, using the Hebrew language—that was OK. But I don't think Zionism or Jewish Israel has a future. We'll evolve with a lot of bloodshed into one state.

RH: So, the dilemma is how to get from here to there.

JH: The problem is the ideologues that are in power. There are ways in which Israelis could see this as being one country. Palestinians have gone out of their way to accommodate Israel. In the Oslo process even until today, Palestinians will make peace with Israelis for 22% of the country, if Israelis give up the West Bank.... It's a generous offer. But Israel has refused it.

RH: We're looking at an extended period of apartheid, and an extensive human-rights struggle?

JH: Yeah. You have a lot of Palestinians, especially in the refugee camps, [who believe] that [they're] going to liberate all of Palestine.... That's not realistic. So, you're back to two states.

RH: Israel wins in the short run.

JH: Israel wins in the short run, but it's going to be a very short, painful, tragic, bloody run before we launch an anti-apartheid campaign ... like [in] South Africa.

RH: I spent yesterday in Hebron, under curfew, with Palestinian peacemakers. They say, If the U.S. roadmap fails, we will go on with the struggle for liberation and full human rights....

JH: The entire country would turn into something else.... Israel is what we call in social science an ethnocracy, not a democracy. An ethnocracy usually leads to conflict when one ethnic group privileges itself and says, This is our country and everybody else is marginalized.... Israel calls itself a democracy, but it's not real. A "Jewish democracy" is a contradiction in terms. You're either a democracy of everybody, or you're an ethnocracy. That has to change. Israeli Palestinians call themselves Palestinians with Israeli citizenship or '48 Palestinians.... This will have to emerge as one country. There are two very different options: one binational country, in a federation, keeping their own names: Israel and Palestine; or a union, such as the Union of Israel-Palestine. But the Israelis and Palestinians are all intermingled, so it would be very hard administratively.

Another option is a unitary state where everybody is equal, but that doesn't give either national group any self-expression. Palestinians could sign on to a binational state, but it's very hard to see how that could work, since the groups are so intermixed; a million Palestinians live inside Israel, and over 600,000 Israelis live in the Occupied Territories—a lot of things to work out.

RH: You're quite convinced about that?

JH: Israel is not going to do it voluntarily. It's going to be a bloody struggle. And in that struggle, the international community, the international civil society, has to play a key role. That's really where church groups, Jewish groups, NGOs, trade unions, universities, political groups—everybody's got to play a role, just like we all did with the anti-apartheid struggle in South Africa.

RH: Holding everybody accountable through international law.

JH: If Israel followed international law, the whole occupation would resolve itself. That's why Israel wouldn't allow international law to be the basis of the Oslo negotiations. We have to insist, internationally, for accountability under international law.... [Historically,] Jews were outside of ecclesiastical law, private law, and civil law. One reason why Jews were so prominent in the human rights and civil rights movements was because they saw that universal human rights includes the Jews. One of the most amazing Jewish figures, Rene Cassin, coauthored the Universal Declaration of Human Rights. He won the Nobel Peace Prize [in 1968]. Jews were at the forefront ... of human rights and civil rights—the only way Jewish rights would be recognized.

RH: Describe the complex interplay between Israel's "matrix of control" ... and "victimhood."

JH: The goal of Zionism and the Israeli elite is exclusive control of the land. How do you do that—militarily, politically, and conceptually? Most Israelis are good people. They don't see themselves as oppressors. So, provide an ideology. One way is to cast yourself as the victim.

RH: So this was a rhetorical battle?

JH: It's the way Israelis see themselves—as the victim. People ask me, Don't Israelis feel bad about bulldozers demolishing hundreds of houses, creating refugees? ... The answer is no, because, they say, Palestinians brought it on themselves. *They* attacked us; *they* deserve it. *We're* the victims. This is all security and defense. It's a very dangerous combination. [Israelis] have a combination of *tremendous power,* tremendous aggressiveness, and no accountability. They say international law and human rights don't apply to them. They're the victim. So, if you combine being the victim with being the fourth-largest nuclear power in the world, you've got all the freedom in the world to do anything you want to anybody: IMPUNITY, in capital letters, in their relationship to Palestinians. There's no responsibility.

Some conflicts are iconic. The world couldn't ignore apartheid [in South Africa]. If apartheid wins here, everything we're talking about—human rights, democracy, unilateral power in Israel—will impact everybody.

RH: Globally.

JH: Globally. It's not just a local Israeli-Palestinian conflict. Everybody loses. If occupation wins, apartheid wins. The implications are tremendous. What are we going to tell the rest of the world?

RH: Outline for me the "matrix of control," how one resists it, and ICAHD's contribution.

JH: My "matrix of control" highlights the broader Israeli control that provides a basis for the military.... Israel says, How can you occupy your own country? It's only administration. These aren't "occupied territories." They are "disputed territories."

RH: It's a rhetorical argument.

JH: That's right. That's the way Israel rejects international law and accountability, and the U.S. goes along with it. The matrix of control includes different levels of control: the military, since the iron fist is always there; creating "facts on the ground," and incorporating occupied territories into Israel in a way that they can never be detached—with one highway grid, one water system, one electrical system, erase the borders, and integrate everything. These "facts on the ground" make it impossible to establish a viable Palestinian state, with territorial contiguity, a viable economy, real political sovereignty, control of borders, control of water and other resources, control of its air and communication space, control of Jerusalem, and the ability to deal with refugee issues. There isn't a Palestinian grid, only Palestinian holes in the grid. There is no new infrastructure for Palestinians, only Israeli de-development, since 1948. Israel will allow certain projects—if…

RH: If the Palestinians capitulate.

JH: If they capitulate. That's the carrot which has always been held out to them. Israel tries to make things so miserable, so desperate, that Palestinians will say, "Forget a state; just let me live my life." The third level of control is administration: planning, zoning, and law. Israel sets its own legal and planning systems over the territories. It demolishes houses, prevents Palestinian development, expropriates land, and builds settlements—all illegal under international law.

RH: Does it also hide [political goals] for Israeli Jews?

JH: Sure. Since 1967, Israel has demolished more than 10,000 [Palestinian] houses. Of those, 95% had nothing to do with security. Israel hides the occupation, saying, "Palestinians are fighting us." [If] you eliminate the occupation, this is all proper administration. [Palestinians] are "terrorists" and Israelis are "freedom fighters." The matrix of control covers all those levels.

RH: How does ICAHD resist the matrix of control?

JH: We're an Israeli group that works with Palestinian organizations to resist the occupation. We resist the fallacy of house demolitions. We get in front of bulldozers. With Palestinians, we rebuild demolished houses, which is illegal, so that's an act of political resistance. Also, house demolitions are designed to confine Palestinians to little areas. We express solidarity with families that are traumatized and scared. We get at the essence of the conflict, which is displacement. A home is a primordial term, like mother, father, family, *home.* Denying Palestinians homes means "Get out." When we build, we acknowledge to Palestinians that they have a right to be here.

This is a grounded analysis. We take what we learn on the ground, what the lessons are, what the reality is, what the practices are, and take that analysis to the international community. We try to work with Israelis, but they won't talk to us. So, we take it to the international civil society—NGOs, church-based groups, and other groups, united with the internet, getting together with social forums, launching programs, supporting human rights and international law—to pressure Israel.

RH: This is called Track Two diplomacy—NGOs, churches, community leaders.

JH: That's right. The international community played a big role against apartheid in South Africa. It's important to mobilize internationals, to get people to understand that they're international citizens. Human rights and justice are universal. Violations are everybody's business.

RH: So, if you really want us to support Israel, hold it accountable.

JH: That's right.... Israel's real security is in peace and racial integration.... As a Jew and as an Israeli, I believe we need the support of the international civil society for a just peace we can't get ourselves; and Palestinians can't shake off the occupation by themselves. So, the international civil society is a key partner in this....

RH: Palestinians are saying to me, "We don't see any way forward until the occupation ends."

JH: We need a strategy to break the occupation. ICAHD has lot of experience and a lot of good ideas. But the Palestinians aren't at a stage to cooperate and think strategically with us.

* * * * * * * *

Jerusalem, May 2005

RH: Let's pick up your analysis of the matrix of control.

JH: The matrix of control is attempts to describe how Israel controls the Occupied Territories, and why that is relevant. Israel goes way beyond the military. They use administration and law, planning and zoning, the transportation patterns, urban patterns, and settlement plans—elements that are gray, dull, and boring to most people: infrastructure, planning, roads, and land-use patterns. This is the way occupation works, a matrix that controls Palestinians more than the military ever could. The matrix of control is intended to deflect attention from the occupation. And, if the control is bureaucratic, Kafkaesque, then it is invisible.

RH: A permanent fifth-class situation.

JH: That's right. It is no class. They don't even have citizenship. These people have no status in Israel. In international law they are considered "protected persons" living under occupation. Israel is responsible for their welfare. But Israel refuses to apply the Fourth Geneva Convention. It claims there is no occupation, so [Palestinians] have no protected status. Israel has come up with a whole new category of conflict. We want it to be a war so we can use all of our military means to fight Palestinians. But we don't want it to be a war because in war the enemy has rights. Israel wants to have all of the rights but none of the obligations. So it has declared that it is in a stage "short of war." There is no concept like that in international law. So [Israel] can use all of the military means at its disposal, but avoids every single category of status for Palestinians. They are not citizens, protected persons, enemies, combatants, or civilians. If they were civilians, they would be protected. They live in a Kafkaesque bubble, completely at the mercy of Israel.

RH: Why doesn't the larger civil society hold the people here accountable?

JH: That is really the question. Israel frames the conflict to never use the word "occupation." It talks about security and shifts the blame onto the Palestinians, blaming the victims. *They* are the perpetrators. We are simply defending ourselves.... Why does the Jewish community behave as it does, when the Jews have always had a stake in human rights?

RH: You begin your [recent] essay on strategic analysis and strategic choices by suggesting that facts on the ground have changed so much that in fact we are in a new moment.

JH: If the two-state solution didn't go away two years ago, it has vanished in the last year. Israel has consolidated its settlement blocs. [Prime Minister] Ariel Sharon has announced the building of 3,500 new housing units in Ma'ale Adumim. Behind it, a new city has been built for another 25,000 to 30,000 people. Israel has announced the building between Jerusalem and Bethlehem of a new city for 55,000 people in the first stage. It is building another city to the north of Jerusalem by Ramallah for 30,000 people. Israel has gone way beyond the point of no return.

RH: That involves cutting off and bisecting the north and south of the West Bank.

JH: Trisecting or quadrasecting the West Bank, [using] settlement blocs to make "cantons" for at least three encampments in the West Bank, plus East Jerusalem, plus Gaza, so [making] five or so cantons as Palestinian entities. Israel needs a Palestinian "state" to get rid of four million Palestinians. It won't give them citizenship. Like South Africa, Israel is setting up Palestinian Bantustans with half a million Israeli settlers living in the Occupied Territories. In the Bush-Sharon agreement, Israel does not have to go back to the 1967 borders, and it can keep its settlements. That is an annexation plan: control the borders, water, and land, and isolate Jerusalem.

RH: The West Bank is now a group of small population centers.

JH: That's right. The facts on the ground have been a project of the last 40 years. That has reached a climax and a point of no return. Facts on the ground have been established and internalized by both Israelis and much of the Palestinian leadership. For years we have talked about a one-state or a two-state solution as attempts to achieve a just peace and avoid apartheid. Maybe apartheid is inevitable. But I don't have access to Palestinian leaders. If they would say, "Jeff, have coffee with us and let's talk," that would be nice, but it won't happen.

RH: Near the end of your recent article, you outlined cultural shifts which have to occur, such as the shift from the perception of Israel as a victim to the perception of Israel as a superpower.

JH: There is a paradigm shift happening. Globally. Not locally. For Israelis, it is not political. It's a technical issue—what brings me personal security? I don't care if there is one state or 50 states.

RH: So, you need a clearer vision and you need—

JH: An endgame, a vision, a partnership. We are a grassroots organization that is critical of Israeli policies. We don't have resources, but we are articulate.

RH: Jonathan Kuttab suggests one reason why there is a of lack of [engagement] by Palestinian leaders: their cause is so clear that it does not need to be justified.

JH: They are right, in a way, but that is not the way the world works. Edward Said calls Palestinians "the victims of victims." For Jews, nothing trumps the Holocaust. Sympathy for Palestinians is part of the message, but if you wait for people to do the right thing, you lose.

RH: So one has to engage with power.

JH: That's right.

RH: So, along with defining an endgame, what are the strategies for engaging that power?

JH: We have spent the last eight or nine years going everywhere from Iowa to New Zealand, talking about peace, bringing my PowerPoints, slides, and booklets. But how do you get through to [the U.S.] Congress?

RH: So the progressive community really has to work at all different levels—

JH: We have to engage political leaders, but governments deal with governments.

RH: The diplomatic level is crucial.
JH: And the civil society, but there has to be a link. Civil society won't have access by itself.

* * * * * * * * *

Jerusalem, July 2006

RH: We have been talking about Israel's "matrix of control.... "
JH: Israel does want a version of a "two-state solution" because there are almost four million Palestinians in the Occupied Territories that Israel can't digest, and it can't give them citizenship in Israel because then Israel wouldn't be a Jewish state. Half the population of this country between the Mediterranean and the Jordan River is Palestinian. And Israel can't leave them in occupation forever.... So, it needs a Palestinian "state" that takes Palestinians off Israel's hands but leaves Israel in control of the entire country. That was the first stage. The second stage was to get U.S. approval, because Israel can't do anything without U.S. approval.
RH: The reason for that is both political and financial?
JH: Financial and military. The U.S. provides an essential political umbrella for Israel, or it couldn't pursue these policies. The Bush Administration recognized eight settlement blocs as a part of Israel, the most strategic places for Israel in order to maintain control. It's a nonviable ministate. The U.S. Congress ratified this by a vote of 407 to 9. That was the second stage. We call it apartheid because it's a permanent domination of one people over another, based on ethnic, religious, and national separation.
RH: While maintaining control.
JH: All the power is in Israel's hands, and Palestinians become a dependent, impoverished population, living on the whims and good will of Israel. So this really is apartheid. Now, how do we get out of it?
RH: While maintaining control.
JH: It's very Orwellian—a plan to "withdraw" in which Israel expands.... Then the international community can say, You tried, and now it's a unilateral thing.
RH: How do you avoid the sense of doing a tap dance while the Titanic sinks?
JH: You realize that you're confronting global forces of history, economics, politics, and national interest. It's not an easy struggle. On the other hand, we see ourselves as the people: the international civil society, trade unions, universities, political groups, human-rights groups, NGOs, churches, and other faith-based groups. We have our victories.... We have a twofold task: to fight injustice, and replace it with a just system. One advantage today is the concept of human rights.
RH: There is a kind of international consensus about that.

JH: Yes. Wonderful work on the environment, the rights of women, children, races, and political rights. Enforcement isn't strong, but it's growing with the International Criminal Court.... This was Rene Cassin's point as the lead writer of the UN Universal Declaration of Human Rights. It incorporated faith-based values of different religions, and the idea of human dignity—in Hebrew, *Selem Adam* is in the image of God. It's universal. It gives us a moral compass that anybody can follow, a floor below which you lose your human dignity.

RH: This suggests why you work with housing and resisting house demolitions....

JH: I go even further. Justice and human rights are big words. I just talk about fairness.... This conflict is part of a global conflict. Human rights and international law give me a handle.

RH: So, it's meaningful to talk about the ongoing work of the peace and justice community here?

JH: That's right; you have a vision of where you're going. You make corrections as you go along, new concepts emerge, things change, and you reevaluate....

RH: The vision would certainly include a multicultural community?

JH: Certainly. A world that runs by international law rather than by power and domination. We have a vision of human rights, human dignity, and multiculturalism.

RH: I talked to Sami Awad at Holy Land Trust. He and many others are still groping for guidance.

JH: We, as an organization, have earned the right to put in our two cents, constructively. We are part of the dialogue. But we're not Palestinian. We can't lead the national liberation struggle.

RH: Is it viable to think of stages in time as a kaleidoscopic model that will continue to shift? You get to a certain stage, you build trust, and then something else becomes possible?

JH: Exactly. I call it the *two-stage solution* instead of the two *states*.... First, a Palestinian state emerges on whatever land the Palestinians can get, with a parliament, citizenship, and representation at the UN. But the state is not viable; there has to be at least a second stage, and that's the endgame, the Middle East Union, a 10-year process....

RH: That provides many more resources.

JH: That's right. That's a *two-stage solution.*

* * * * * * * *

Jerusalem, July 2008

RH: Two years ago, the theme for you was a two-stage solution, and a regional approach....

JH: I still think it's the best approach. But it might be too early to deal with it because the Palestinian leadership hasn't given up the two-state solution yet.

RH: Ghassan Andoni did, a long time ago.

JH: Yes, but the PLO people, Fatah, and the Palestinian Authority people haven't given it up yet. Most Palestinians would still like a state, even if they've figured out that it's not going to happen.

RH: But the intellectuals are there.

JH: The intellectuals have adopted a one-state solution. But the problem is threefold: Palestinians give up the idea of national liberation for one national state, a binational or one democratic state, and start a civil-rights struggle. This isn't an academic exercise—this is life and death for them.... And binational states are not happy states.

RH: Are most of the people in the Israeli peace movement Zionist in some way?

JH: The peace organizations in the Jewish sector of Israel are mostly Zionist. That's why we're in a conflict today that doesn't seem to have a ready-made solution.... Two things are important for Palestinians: self-determination and sovereignty in their own state, with political identity, citizenship, a parliament, membership in the international community, and economic viability.

RH: What I sensed, in Bethlehem, is that the level of desperation is so high that lots of people will just capitulate in order for the boot to come off their necks—for relief of day-to-day oppression.

JH: That's Israel's strategy. That's why Hamas is so important. They won't settle. The Fatah leaders did already. Hamas keeps the game honest. Palestinians are exhausted. I'm constrained.

RH: You're part of the dialogue.

JH: I'm part of the dialogue. I suggest options like the two-stage solution and say, Let's have a discussion about it. I can help sharpen the debate, but.... Governments won't give money to us, because we're political. The EU wants partnerships, and they don't care if the Palestinians say no.

RH: Comment more broadly about civil disobedience or other symbolic actions.

JH: We're committed to nonviolence. But the main thing is to end the occupation. That's why we're political. We are trying to be effective, to work with governments, to work with civil society.

RH: Activism has to be linked to strategy.

JH: It has to be linked. Our job is to end the occupation, to bring about a just peace. The fact that my analysis is grounded, that I've gotten arrested, that gives me credibility. I have this argument with Arik Ascherman all the time. He runs around doing things. I say, "Let the 18-year-old kids plant olive trees. You should be writing articles on how the uprooting of olive trees is against Jewish law. You're a rabbi.

You should be doing advocacy." Activism is easy. You do an action, but nothing is really delivered.

RH: Are there other arguments?

JH: Naomi Klein's book *The Shock Doctrine* is amazing. She uses the concept of "warehousing" very effectively. She says in the world system of extreme *laissez-faire* capitalism, half of the population is superfluous. She says that Israel is developing a model of control and warehousing for the rest of the world. So, we went from occupation to apartheid, and from apartheid to warehousing. Klein says Palestinians are the first people to be declared "surplus humanity."

RH: This has implications for all of us.

JH: Israel is developing warehousing to apply to Americans. The implications are tremendous.

* * * * * * * *

Jerusalem, June 2010

After a brief dialogue in Jeff Halper's office, we meet a visiting Quaker group.

JH: The Israeli Committee Against House Demolitions is an Israeli peace and human-rights organization.… The bad news is that governments will not do the right thing, period. We look to governments to lead, to negotiate. But they're not going to do it unless they're pressured into it by the people. Governments deal in *conflict management*. They don't deal in conflict resolution. They've managed this conflict for 43 years, and could manage it for the next 43 years. So it's up to the people to stand up, like the Free Gaza Movement, say No, and force governments to act.

We work with civil society to light a fire under governments, to get them to act. Secretary of State James Baker called this conflict the "epicenter of alienation" between the West and the entire Muslim world.… The occupation is seen here as an American-Israeli occupation. Israel couldn't maintain it for a month without the political, economic, and military support of the United States.

So, this is a conflict you can't avoid. It's like when you've got a bone stuck in your throat. It can't be avoided; you can't bypass it. If you want to get on to the bigger issues—reconciliation with Muslims, oil in the Middle East, the Holy Land for Christians, Jews, Christians, and Muslims, you've got to deal with this conflict.

The problem is that between the Mediterranean and the Jordan River, you can look at this as one country. The Jews call it the land of Israel; Palestinians see this as Palestine. Internal divisions are artificial. Half the population is Palestinian. That's before four million refugees … come back. There will be a Palestinian majority. The question is, how do you resolve this conflict? There seem to be three solutions: the two-state solution—if a Palestinian state can emerge in the Occupied Territories alongside Israel, that would give the Palestinians enough sovereignty, enough self-determination to resolve this conflict. It's not fair, because the Occupied Territories are only 22% of historic Palestine. So, we're asking the Palestinians, who will be the majority, to accept a state on less than a quarter of the land. But the PLO, in 1988, accepted the two-state solution. That's still what the international community pushes for, but it doesn't look doable.

Israel's version of a two-state solution is apartheid, like you had in South Africa. Apartheid can be defined by two elements—separation and domination.... The third option is a one-state solution. But Israel will fight that tooth and nail, because it is anti-Zionist. Israel will not be a Jewish state anymore. It will be transformed into a state of *all* its citizens. The two-state solution seems to be gone, apartheid we can't accept, and the one-state [approach] isn't on the table.

RH: Comment on the BDS movement.

JH: A strong campaign is emerging in Europe and the States: Boycott, Divestment, and Sanctions ... campaigns against Israeli consumer goods, settlement products, [and] arms. Companies like Caterpillar and Motorola profit from the occupation. The Fourth Geneva Convention prohibits an occupying power from using the resources of an occupied territory.

We don't advocate a particular solution. I could accept a two-state solution, and many Palestinians do, if it was a real one. Or a one-state solution. The issue is getting to a just peace.

We're advocating an *approach to peace*, instead of a particular solution. Six elements have to be present in any peace process. If all six elements are there, a lot of solutions could work; if any of these six are missing, nothing's going to work. First, any peace has to be inclusive of Israelis and Palestinians—two national groups. We're advocating the South African model: everybody who's here is a part of this.... Second, peace has to be economically viable. Third, Israel has to accept the right of return, and Israel must acknowledge what it's done. Symbolic acknowledgment is really crucial. Fourth, peace has to be based on international law and human rights. Fifth, address the security needs of all the different parties. Sixth, there must be regional solutions to refugees, water, economic development, and security. With these elements, you can evaluate any plan.

* * * * * * * *

Jerusalem, September 2014

RH: In the recent Israel-Gaza war, thousands of people died and one-third of Gazans have been displaced. Was Operation Protective Edge a "game changer"? *Politically,* has anything changed?

JH: The war in Gaza put the PA on the spot. Now they are expected, by Israel and the U.S., to be the police over Gaza. If the PA collapses, there would be a vacuum. Israel will have no choice but to reoccupy all of the West Bank cities, and probably Gaza. Then things are clear—Kerry's POOF cleared the air. POOF. The PA is gone.... Then the one-state solution becomes relevant.

RH: Then it's either a permanent apartheid, or human rights.

JH: There's so much resistance to Israel's occupation. It's not sustainable. But our Palestinian partners are not talking to us....

RH: Dialogue is such a fraught topic between Palestinians and Jews. Some people say genuine dialogue is not possible.

JH: Ghassan [Andoni] got completely burned out with dialogue.

RH: He withdrew from ISM [International Solidarity Movement], right?

JH: Yeah. He was very involved with all the dialogues during the Oslo process. When the second *intifada* hit, all the Israelis he had talked to for years—WHOOM!—they cut him off completely, within minutes.... That's what drove him away from being involved.... I find it hard to be in a political struggle without an endgame. This is the biggest piece. The political process is gone, the two-state solution is over, the PA is on its last legs. If the PA leaves the scene, that's a game-changer.

We're stuck. If we don't articulate a vision of a one-state solution that's inclusive of both individual rights and collective rights of everyone living here, we're not going anywhere. In every political struggle, there's a tension between your ideology and what you can achieve....

We're not able to strategize. The Israeli Right and the Palestinian Right know where they want to go, and the Left doesn't. The Israeli military and Palestinian military talk to each other; security people talk to each other; business people talk to each; criminals talk to each other; but the intellectuals don't talk to each other.... In terms of the big picture, we're in this collapse. It's urgent that we develop a strategy and start to flesh out what the one-state solution means. We have to read the political moment, and we're not.... In terms of strategy or political meetings, there's nothing going on, zero. Not only with me, but with all the Israelis on the Left.

RH: There's no entity that can convene or create a common ground?

JH: We're in a collapse we weren't in four years ago—the collapse of everything—the two-state solution, the political actors, the occupation. We're headed toward a whole new situation, maybe a whole new occupation. Palestinians talk about being under two occupations. The PA can't keep a collaboration role forever. Once it collapses, Israel will have to come back in without a fig leaf.

RH: A nonviolent one.

JH: This conflict affects the whole international system. Israel is misreading this situation, and it's tough for Palestinians because [they had] a national liberation struggle for 100 years.

RH: Anchored in identity.

JH: In identity and in self-determination.... If that's gone, you're talking about a one-state solution, and Israelis are part of it, a binational state. It becomes a civil-rights struggle rather than a national liberation struggle. But Palestinians aren't there mentally or politically. They're exhausted. They would have to assure the world and the Israelis that Israelis will be safe.

RH: *Both* groups need assurance that they'll be safe.

JH: But the weird dynamic is that the oppressor—[as] in South Africa—before it gives up control has to be convinced that you're not going to get revenge on us. You're not going to do to us what we deserve. For oppressed people, that's very hard to do. The ANC did that for South Africa.

RH: But South Africa tried to go from truth-telling to reconciliation without going through justice.

JH: I belong to the critical peace movement, the critical Left that is *not* Zionist. It envisions Israelis' remaining here with Palestinians in one democratic state with meaningful expressions of self-determination for both peoples—a one-state solution. We're in a political struggle and a power struggle. In some ways, we're winning. There's a groundswell of support for Palestinians all over the world, in governments and churches, but we have no endgame to sell.

RH: So it's hard to organize.

JH: It's impossible to organize.... We're all against the occupation, but ending the occupation is half the story. The world doesn't wait for us. We're not sensitive to the political moment.... We're in the midst of a collapse of the political situation, more imploding than exploding. Then it opens up possibilities that don't exist now.... The Palestinian Authority is going to collapse. Abu Mazen is more than 80, and will leave the scene soon. It's the end of the two-state solution.

RH: Are there any hopeful signs or people?

JH: You never know how effective you are. You try to be strategic, but you don't know if it's going to happen in your lifetime. Sometimes collapses happen quickly, or it can take a while.

RH: Both things were true in South Africa.

JH: That's where hope misleads us; it doesn't read situations very well. Sometimes you're a lot further than you thought. So, I use the idea of struggle, trying to get your own people to be strategic and effective. If collapse happens without agency on our part, then we're not taking responsible roles. We have to be agents. We could resolve this conflict, but you have to struggle to do it. Apartheid in South Africa didn't just collapse. It was a lot of work! ... Palestinians in the *intifadas* and now in the Gaza resistance have been agents. The problem is that resisters can open things, but they don't negotiate, they're not decision makers, they're not the strategists. They have to pass the ball to leaders who take it further. We are part of the leadership, the educated; we have strategies, we have analyses.

RH: That's the focus of my book—leadership from the middle.

JH: That's right. People are trying to pass the ball and we're not there.... We are not talking to each other; we're not strategizing. The Left intellectuals are that agency that you're talking about. But they are isolated from political agency. They can create the ... alternatives that the higher political people pick up on. The higher political people aren't going to formulate solutions that are just. That's our job, and if we don't do it, there's a gap between the agency of the people and the agency of the political leadership, without that connecting link in the middle. That's where we have failed and where we can succeed.

RH: There must be positive models, which retain ... ethnic and national identities.

JH: Switzerland. A weak state and strong component groups.... I have [written] a number of articles on what a one-state solution would look like—in political science, it is a "consociational state." It means sharing power—a bicameral parliament, a system of checks and balances, where collective and individual rights are really respected.

RH: You can hang on to whatever identity is important to you.

JH: There's an ownership of the whole identity, because you're a part of it.... The ANC had the Freedom Charter and a kind of constitution *before* the end of apartheid. So, when the collapse happened, they could assure the whites that they're part of [South Africa].

RH: International mediator John Paul Lederach calls this a flexible platform that you can adjust [once] you've got the basic principles spelled out.

JH: There's no dialogue. Zero. Palestinian groups work with us abroad, but not here. We're not seizing the moment. We see exhaustion, fragmentation, Israel's negative role, the U.S., and the dead hand of the PA. Intellectuals are not contributing to the liberation struggle.

RH: Do you see any bright spots anywhere?

JH: The good news is that for Israeli Jews, the [central] issue is security, collective and individual. It's not the land. If Palestinians and Israelis, like the ANC, can come up with a freedom charter that says we want to go toward one democratic state, and it's inclusive of both people, sharing power, that could break through to Israelis, because that's their concern. As long as we keep talking about "occupation" and "violation of human rights," we're not signaling to Israelis that there's a future in which they are not the enemy.... Israelis have to hear this from Palestinians. Until they do, they're existentially threatened.... I always saw ICAHD as a political actor. We still have a role to play. We can develop plans and advocate; we can even work with governments. But I don't think the Left sees itself that way.

RH: You are a unique combination.
JH: I can bridge the academic and the activist roles.

* * * * * * * *

Jerusalem, July 2016

JH: We [need] three general principles: end of occupation, right of return, equal rights for Palestinian citizens. I'm starting to push a bit. All these years, I've been talking about one-state solutions, but I've always stopped short of advocating for it. More and more, I am starting to advocate. ICAHD has always been on the cutting edge, moving [ideas] forward—the matrix of control, apartheid and warehousing … way before anybody else. We have to do the same thing now. I am starting to say that BDS is a tool that has to be connected to an endgame—a binational democratic state. Israel has Judaized the whole country, so no more occupation.
RH: It is cultural, and it is also spatial.
JH: It is spatial, transforming Palestine into the land of Israel…. There is one Israel-controlled country, with borders, government, army, and currency. It is a Judean scenario, with little Palestinian islands. ICAHD is making a map that shows it is one country. I hope that will give us a vocabulary, concepts, and a direction. That's the first stage. The second stage is: How do we transform Judaization into something just? There is one state today. We are not ready yet for a solution. The Palestinians aren't there, so we can't just jump to that, though this is urgent.
RH: You have to focus on [a] platform and process.
JH: You could move Israelis toward a one-state solution, if they could see that the Palestinian concept is inclusive…. I would love to gather a group of Israelis and Palestinians from all different places—the West Bank, East Jerusalem, Gaza, inside Israel, refugee camps, and the diaspora—then sit down somewhere for a week or so, and try to forge a freedom charter. What are the principles? What is our vision? Binational is the big nut to crack. And not everybody has to agree…. [Israelis think] it's either two states or suicide. In a binational state, you remain Israeli Jews; your status, your national and collective rights are protected…. The issue for Israeli Jews isn't the "Jewish thing"; it is security, not the land. You can create a political system with a constitution, and build institutions comprised of two national groups—Palestinian Arabs, and Israeli Jews—[which] guarantees the integrity of each of those groups.
RH: And clear promises that revenge will not occur.
JH: A freedom charter says, "Let's think of a joint future." Then, the third step is, "Let's move on to a real detailed plan," and that is the binational state…. Once you accept the principles of a freedom

charter, there are different alternatives you can play with.... A platform.

RH: A platform, yes.

JH: The platform is the freedom charter. The process is developing the freedom charter. Palestinians have to sit with Palestinians, and work out what they want; and a parallel process with the Israelis sitting with each other. And then we could exchange.

RH: Who would convene that?

JH: You would have to bring Hamas into it. Probably it couldn't be in the U.S., or the U.S. couldn't sponsor it, because you are not allowed to even have contact with Hamas.

RH: To do peace work, you have to talk to your enemies, right?

JH: We have a plan, and nobody to talk to.... I don't think the Left believes it is an actor. The peace movement is marginal. We don't compete in elections. We do our analysis, we are very articulate, but we are not engaged.... I am saying to our Palestinian partners, "Unless we jump into this game, as advocates and actors, we will get an internationally sanctioned apartheid."

RH: So, Jeff, when will you convene this [working group]?

JH: An Israeli can't convene a group like this [unless] there is a Palestinian side, or organization.

RH: You need something vaguely like the Oslo process, a social-science group giving cover.... Track Two, citizen-based diplomacy....

JH: I have a good concept of where to go, but I have no mechanism, no program, no support group, no money, no venue; otherwise, we are doing great.

RH: Lots of people are doing good things, but they don't necessarily work at the [strategic] edge that you are talking about. It is a hard task: to figure out a deeply moral and political vision. To get there from here takes so many reaches of the imagination. Ilan Pappé said to me that "the occupation has created such a fog for all of us, it is really hard to see beyond that."

JH: Because the fog is the two-state solution. U.S. Secretary of State Kerry cleared the fog in a definitive way. He made this big peacemaking effort. He really tried. On one of his trips, he came with 130 advisors. In a defining moment, Kerry later testified before a senate committee. He said, "We are negotiating [with the Israelis], and starting to talk about the issues and agenda. [At the same time,] Israel declares it is building a couple thousand [illegal] housing units in the West Bank, and POOF!" That's what he said, "POOF!" That's it. POOF clears the air. POOF is it.... Kerry got us past the two-state solution.

RH: In at least half of the dialogues I recorded, people either say the two-state solution is dead, or they know it is on life support.

JH: I can understand Palestinians wanting a state of their own, but it's gone. "Poof" was the most accurate assessment. Where do we go from "poof"? We've evolved over the years.

RH: I had not planned to show that evolution, but maybe it is a good thing.

JH: It is a good thing; you have to constantly reevaluate your position.... The whole point of ethnographic research is that you're integrating yourself into people's lives.

RH: For years you've said, "I don't have people to talk to." Especially two years ago, that's the most down I have ever seen you. It sounds like it hasn't changed too much.... When I talked to Mitri Raheb, he was really clear: "We decided 20 years ago at Christmas Lutheran Church that whether the peace process won out or not, we would go ahead and build for the future."

JH: What future [do] the kids have? What future?

RH: Giving students skills. I guess they may have to leave the country to use them.... But it is not engaging in the political thinking that you are talking about.

JH: It doesn't have to be either/or.... We could do both.

* * * * * * * * *

Jerusalem, April 2018

In February 2018, Ilan Pappe convened a working group, including Halper, to discuss the concept of a One Democratic State Campaign (ODSC). Pappe hosted the group in Exeter, UK.

JH: I'm cautiously optimistic this might work out. It might be the spark that galvanizes things and they start to come together. We're in a very apolitical time, but I'm not unusual in the context of '60s people. We built our lives around commitment. That was our word.

RH: Every day we had to decide to go to the street or do our homework.

JH: So, the burden has fallen on us.... That's why our program is detailed. One of our projects is to draft a constitution, to show people how we work, how to dismantle power relations, to decolonize Israel, and set up an egalitarian society. If we can show that, we can address multiple fears. Palestinians don't believe that Israel would really give up control, or that it's possible. They're stuck between a two-state solution that's gone and a one-state model that's unattainable.

RH: Here's my suggestion. Along with a constitution, which is a conceptual framework, create a document for implementation. You need trust-building [steps].

JH: We'll have to work out a strategy. It's true what you're saying. Implementation is key. If you can show people that you address their fears, you have a shot at [transformation].

RH: Well, I'm pleased about this breakthrough.

JH: *Inshallah*. Or it could all collapse.... These proposals have to trickle up to governments. We need a concentrated, focused campaign. If we can lay out the win-win aspect, what the benefits are, the vision—and for me, the vision is building this new civil society—that's the exciting part.

RH: The two things you identify are going to be big: Israelis will have to give up a Jewish state, and Palestinians will have to give up the dream of sovereignty.

JH: Both groups will have to reimagine the country, to reinvent it.

RH: Lederach says the task is to imagine the future that includes your enemy.

JH: Exactly. That's right.

RH: As always, many thanks.

20 Universal Principles, International Law

Jonathan Kuttab

Jonathan Kuttab is a human-rights lawyer. He has practiced law in the U.S., Palestine, and Israel; cofounded the human-rights organization Al-Haq; and cofounded Nonviolence International. He has served on the boards of Bethlehem Bible College, Holy Land Trust, and other organizations. At the heart of Zionism, Kuttab identifies a contradiction between a democratic, progressive system and Jewish exclusivity maintained by law. Kuttab is the executive director of Friends of Sabeel North America (FOSNA). He recently published Beyond the Two-State Solution *(2021).*

East Jerusalem, May 2003

RH: When did your law firm begin?

JK: The Kuttab Holy Land Law Firm began here in Jerusalem in 1983.

RH: What were your early influences?

JK: We were taught to take very seriously one's commitment to accept Christ into your life, including your money, your politics, your career.... For me, Christianity also meant pacifism and loving my enemy. And Christ's commands about justice were always central to my Christian faith. It's strange that in the U.S., historically, churches have viewed that as a minority view. It is true for all Christians in the Holy Land. I am active in Sabeel, where there are people from different denominations—Greek Orthodox, Catholics, and everybody else. The predominant view is that to be a Christian does not include picking up a gun or a knife and trying to kill your enemy.

RH: Can you recall any early events that tested that severely?

JK: Yes. It's very normal in every culture for boys to have fights with each other under normal circumstances. But for me, I was always very clear that if I take my faith seriously I must obey God in this area of my life.... I lived through 1967, the beginning of the [Israeli] occupation.

RH: How old were you at the time, in '67?

JK: Fourteen or 15. My patriotic duty was very clear—to resist the occupation. But how can I love my enemy and at the same time stick a knife in his back? I realized very early that the fight with Israelis was not a military fight; that to resist the occupation, I had to work with

DOI: 10.4324/9781003262817-22

international law and international solidarity, and reject trying to defeat Israel with its technological superiority and weapons of mass destruction—nuclear, biological, and chemical weapons.

RH: And U.S. backing.

JK: And U.S. backing. But it was important to find other ways to resist and end the occupation.

RH: What form did that take for you as a 15-year-old?

JK: Very shortly after 1967, I went to the United States to study at Messiah College. There was a lot of [dialogue about] nonviolence and pacifism. I quickly realized that active, nonviolent resistance is a far better option for resisting occupation than violence. The Christianity I grew up with viewed politics as a bad thing. But the Sojourners group introduced me to the possibility of being socially and politically active.... After Messiah College, I studied human rights and I completed my law degree. When I came back here 10 years later, I studied Hebrew, joined the Israeli Bar Association, and tried to understand the system of oppression here in the West Bank. I was amazed to find how important a role the law played in that system. I helped set up the first Palestinian human-rights organization, Al-Haq, in Ramallah. I'm still a member of the board.

RH: What were your most important discoveries in being part of the Israeli legal system?

JK: I discovered that the Israelis invest a huge amount of thought, creativity, and time in maintaining a legal façade for what is a thoroughly oppressive, racist, and colonial system. The system was intended for very good and decent people to be able to participate in very evil policies with a clear conscience. And for the Western world to support an extremely oppressive system without knowing that it's so oppressive. I discovered a paradox at the very heart of Zionism and the state of Israel, a contradiction between a democratic, liberal, even utopian, progressive system and a racist, fascist philosophy and policy, based on Jewish exclusivity. They could maintain the contradiction through law. Law is simply what the letter of the law says it is.

RH: American history has many examples of this as well.

JK: But no system in the world rivals the Israeli system in the clever, manipulative use of law, because Israel doesn't have a constitution that you can appeal to. It's a pharisaic tradition like Jesus railed against—clever scholars using the law to defeat the spirit of the law.

RH: Based on the philosophical tradition of positivism from Europe?

JK: Exactly. But also based on the Talmudic tradition of interpretation. If you want to accomplish an evil purpose you never say, "I am powerful. I am taking your land." No! You ask, Is this land really *yours?* You don't take private land. But you redefine land so it's no longer called private; you call it public. If it's public, then Jews, who are the public, can take the land.

RH: By definition.

JK: By definition! So we can take your land for a public purpose, which is to help Jews. We're not taking *your* land—because it's public. In every country there's a public domain. So we take your land to serve the public, who are Jews, coming from Russia, Ethiopia, from all over the world. Once the Western world accepted the idea of Israel as a Jewish state, it had to accept policies intended to help Jews, even to the detriment of the non-Jewish population.

RH: For Jews, this was not only legal, but morally acceptable?

JK: My mission was to expose this. By taking Israelis at their word, I wrote and explained how law becomes an instrument of oppression. How a military authority can take the existing legal situation toward an end that is very oppressive, very fascist, very controlling, and very racist.

RH: Did your mission emerge in law school, or when you came back?

JK: After I came back. I became aware of the great dissonance between official Israeli narratives that prevailed in the West and the reality on the ground. How can Israelis be so oppressive to Palestinians on the one hand, and enjoy such a wonderful reputation in the West?… I saw the importance of shedding light on the subject. We had to learn the language of the West, to stop believing the justice of their cause is self-evident. Nothing is self-evident. You have to show it.

RH: Alex Awad [told me] that Palestinians have not told their stories. They think oppression is self-evident, so they don't need to tell their stories.

JK: Exactly. It's not obvious. The system has hidden the reality even from Israelis. Foolishly, the Arab public fed into that. Palestinians, 20 years ago, did very little to militarily resist Israel, other than to protest in very graphic terms…. From 1948 through the '70s and '80s, until the Oslo process, Palestinians perfected the language of armed struggle, but not the practice. Palestinian rhetoric and sense of exaggeration fed into that. They would yell and scream about how they are going to destroy the oppressors and make the ground boil and burn under their feet. Israelis said, Look at those people; they are going to burn us alive. This reminds us of the ovens of Auschwitz.

RH: So, Palestinians [appear to be] hateful people.

JK: They're hateful, violent, and vile. Meanwhile, Palestinians are saying, We're doing nothing. We're not even lifting a knife, much less a gun or a bomb. Jews said, Oh, they are bent on annihilating Israel. They were very clever. They gave us the rope to hang ourselves. They let us get excited, then they'd tell the world, See what they want to do to us?

RH: And [Jews said], We're just trying to survive, as we did in Europe.

JK: It's shalom, shalom, shalom. Every other word is shalom. We are the peace-loving people. And out of [Palestinian] rejection of Israel and

Israel's oppression of the Palestinians, it was [perceived] that we are against peace and Israelis are for peace. So, the first thing that I did in setting up a human-rights organization here was to train our field researchers in the need to be very, very accurate, very objective, very understated, not to use emotionally loaded terms.

RH: No hyperbole.

JK: No hyperbole. Let the facts force whatever conclusion you want to reach. During the first *intifada*, I was extremely gratified that Palestinians were very careful and accurate in the numbers. If they said four people were killed, they would give you names and ages. Before that, they would exaggerate and say, 20 people were killed. They were talking about their sense of devastation, but to the Western world, that sounded like lies.

RH: So [Westerners saw] trustworthy [Israelis] and untrustworthy [Palestinians].

JK: Exactly. The Israeli army general would stand there neatly dressed in a well-pressed uniform, speaking English fluently, and he sounded very believable. But the Palestinian would be pulling his hair, saying, They killed our people in the thousands. They killed 17 people, not thousands.

We saw an example of this in Jenin, where Israelis did horrendous things. They leveled the middle of a densely populated refugee camp. They prevented the medical workers from coming in for days after the fighting ended. My wife was one of the first outsiders to come into the Jenin camp after the Israelis lifted the closure, and she talked about people crawling from under the rubble and little kids running up to her, begging for a bottle of water. But all the war crimes that took place in Jenin were wiped away by one Palestinian official who came from outside, who talked about a "massacre" and hundreds of people killed. It was closer to 60 people killed, not hundreds, and there were people buried under the rubble. Two days later, they were still digging people alive from under the rubble. But because that Palestinian official exaggerated and talked about hundreds killed and used the word massacre, the Israelis made the whole conversation center on was it a massacre or wasn't it? Many other significant issues got snowed under. The Israelis prevented an international investigation. People still don't know what happened in Jenin.

RH: They just moved on.

JK: They moved on. So one of the first things that I did in my human-rights work is emphasize bringing light—the weapons of light that St. Paul talks about—against the forces of darkness, which meant observers, objective documentation, and an appeal to neutral, universal principles of international law rather than politics. I connected my training as a lawyer, my interest in human rights, and my Christian faith and commitment.

RH: Estephan Salemeh suggested to me that one of the reasons why the Israelis are so afraid of Palestinian autonomy and a Palestinian state has to do with truth-telling. There would be a free flow of truth-telling and information, international observers, and peace activists.

JK: Twenty years ago Israel was still arguing that they are desperate for peace.... Israel says it is willing to be in [dialogue] with anybody anywhere and it's just Arab rejection that prevents peace. Now, Israel rejects peace and anyone who is a peacemaker is no longer welcome.

RH: So the nonviolence movement calls their bluff.

JK: That's exactly what happens. Israel can deal very well with any military threat. They can out-gun, out-shoot, out-kill, out-violence Palestinians and Arabs any day. But how do they deal with people who won't carry guns or bombs but who still insist on their rights, their freedom, their independence, their dignity, and their equality with Jews? That is totally unacceptable to Israel.

RH: Why has it been so difficult for a nonviolent movement to gather support?

JK: There is a lot of support for nonviolence. The problem again is with the narrative. Palestinians have perfected the *language of violence* and have a hard time giving up *the poetry of violence.*

RH: The heroic struggle.

JK: [Giving up] the bombastic language of violence in favor of nonviolence. Also, "peace" has a bad name. "Nonviolence" in Arabic, *la'unf*, sounds so passive rather than being an active, vibrant method of fighting the occupation. People who advocated for nonviolence were viewed as being passive, who are against suicide bombings and armed resistance, who don't want to fight the occupation. For many Palestinians, nonviolence meant playing dead, accepting the occupation.

RH: So, some other term is necessary.

JK: Exactly. Exactly.

RH: Are there other, better Arabic terms for progressive, active response [to oppression]?

JK: Not so far.... Gandhi also had this problem. He had to create a contest to come up with the word *satyagraha.* Everyone has used the word peace so much, it's gotten a bad rap. The so-called "peace process" was a cover for continuing the occupation with Palestinian cooperation.

RH: And corruption.

JK: We really need a different word. That's why Christian Peacemaker Teams were so important as an active model, which is why Israel feels so worried about CPT. They deported Mubarak Awad before the first *intifada* because they sensed how powerful nonviolence can be.

RH: Probably more threatening than violence.

JK: Far more threatening.

RH: Where does the [peace] movement go from here and how does it connect with your work?

JK: Right now Israel is going all out to crush [peacemaking]. They will try to discredit it first; they will try to cut it off from international participation and solidarity. They would like to brush the whole Palestinian people with the paintbrush of suicide bombers, fanatics, and terrorists. But the movement has tremendous potential.

Mubarak Awad was here recently. Everywhere he went, people told him, You were right [about nonviolence]. These were people … engaged in armed struggle who are saying, Our way has failed. What you said [about nonviolence] is the way to move forward. There is a recognition in the Palestinian community that violence has not helped us, but I don't know if we have the leadership, the commitment, the resources for a sustained nonviolence struggle. It takes much more effort than to throw a bomb or strap a belt of dynamite around your waist and kill yourself and everybody else around you. It takes much more work and discipline for a nonviolent struggle.

RH: Therefore training and education will be crucial.

JK: Absolutely.

RH: Are there good Muslim resources for this?

JK: Yeah, there are many Muslims who are committed to nonviolence.

* * * * * * * *

East Jerusalem, 2005

RH: The last time we talked about a deep connection between your faith and peacemaking.

JK: My central point was that I am a committed Christian and my peace and nonviolence grows directly out of that tradition and faith. By a wonderful coincidence, the peace strategy and the nonviolence strategy are what makes the most sense for Palestinians living under occupation. We stand no chance of "out-violencing" Israelis, of outgunning them, of coming to any kind of resolution in military terms. They can't come to military terms with us, either. It makes no sense for Palestinians to turn to guns, bombs, and violence to achieve peace with the Israelis. It makes much more sense for Palestinians to use nonviolence to deal with this occupation.

RH: For you it is a philosophical, religious, and a practical strategy.

JK: Very true. Not just for me but for all Palestinian people today, regardless of their fear.

RH: You took your law degree in the U.S.

JK: Yes, at the University of Virginia.

RH: So, you know the North American mentality very well. You know that nonviolence sounds contradictory to American mental images of the Palestinian community.

JK: That's true because there is a lot of negative stereotyping and because we Palestinians also have not perfected the language, the narrative of peace and nonviolence. To the contrary, we have been utterly foolish, always speaking in hyperbole about guns and fighting, when in fact we have not been *practicing violence* as much as we've been *speaking and preaching violence.* Violent images are immediately captured in the West. The style of language in Arabic is very violent. You don't speak about spanking your child, you speak about breaking his neck or killing him with a beating. The language is much more violent than the actual practice and action.

RH: So, the Israelis were brilliant in literally translating that language.

JK: I don't want to blame it totally on the Israelis. There was [Palestinian] violence, there was terrorism, and that is horrible. All violence is horrible. But we ourselves promoted that [violent] language when we were not very violent. We practiced a lot of nonviolence without calling it that. On the other hand, Israelis were extremely violent, but they were always speaking "shalom." Shalom this, shalom that. Good morning in Hebrew is shalom, good evening is shalom, hello is shalom, goodbye is shalom. So, while they have a most violent, totally militarized society, they speak the language of shalom. At the same time, we who are oppressed and largely nonviolent speak the language of violence and war. So, I will give us as much blame as Israelis.

RH: In our earlier dialogue, you called it the "poetry of violence." How does one change that?

JK: It is very hard since we don't have much access to international media. No matter what we do internally, the West will always view us as violent. Islam is a very peaceful religion, by and large. The concept of jihad in Islam is largely an internal jihad, the higher jihad. Actual fighting is minuscule. The word Islam is part of Salaam, of peace, of submission to God and the sanctity of life. In Islam, peace is greater than in Christianity or Judaism. We Christians are taught to be faithful till the end to obtain glory. The Christian church was built on the blood of martyrs. Faithfulness to one's belief till death, till martyrdom, is a Christian value, not a Muslim value. Islam, by contrast, teaches the principle of *taqwa*. Islam values the sanctity of life so highly it permits the faithful Muslim to deny his faith and to preserve his life. In the West, images of Islam are militant and violent—the curved knife between your teeth—stereotyped images. The reality is totally different.

RH: On my last visit, one of the things that impressed me was the number of people and towns doing nonviolence training. Is it possible to turn that passion into a [movement]?

JK: The problem is that the language that goes with it is not there. The media awareness is not there and even if it was, the media isn't interested in people sitting and meditating, or people praying in front of an army checkpoint which is preventing them from coming to

Jerusalem. We've seen those images again and again, but they are not news. My brother, a journalist, tells me that "if it bleeds, it leads." The media looks for violence, for bodies and destroyed vehicles.

RH: After you got your law degree, you decided that your project was to learn how the Israeli system works, how the system of oppression works. What did you discover?

JK: The Israelis are not only brilliant in trying to convince the world that they are righteous, upright, seeking peace, believing in democracy and human rights, but they are also experts in convincing themselves. For them, it is important that they consider themselves good. That's why they have to create the total myth—that the refugee problem is not of their making; that the Palestinians left [Palestine] on their own [in 1948]; they left out of a nefarious motive to clear the way for the destruction of the state of Israel. But the reality was that Palestinians were driven out at gunpoint, pushed out of their homes, and loaded on trucks.

But Israelis don't want the world to know that. They don't want to live with the reality that they pushed the Palestinians out in order to create the state of Israel. So they created this myth that [Palestinians] left on their own, that they left at the direction of their own leaders. There is never any [admission] of We took this land. No, no, no, no, [they] attacked us. It was a defensive war; it was forced upon us. We don't want to rule over another people.... Even among liberal Israelis you hear that. How others see them is more important than the reality of what they are doing. They need to be extremely creative to deceive the world and to deceive themselves. Law is one of the best instruments to do it.

RH: So, talk about how [Israeli] law works....

JK: First, you keep the legal system the way it was before. This way [Israelis] can use all the bad elements of the law and say, This was the law we inherited. Zionists inherited the British Emergency Defense Regulations when they were fighting against the British. Menachem Begin called them worse than Nazi laws. The minute the state was created, instead of repealing these laws, they said, No, no, these laws are very useful. They are now in our hands and we need them. So whenever [Israelis] do something that is really terrible, they will say, This is the law. We are only applying the existing law. On the other hand, they change the law to suit their purposes for military orders. These military orders on their face will appear very neutral because they will give total discretion to the military governor to act in a certain way. They will prohibit something without a license or without a permit and then they will retain the power to give or deny that permit so, in reality, they are prohibiting the activity outright. They will say, No we are not prohibiting it; we are just saying it is subject to a permit, and if you don't get a permit you can even appeal to the court. You can even go to the high court, where it's very liberal, open. So, the "rule of law" actually means it is "rule by law." Laws provide them with the tools to continue oppression. The courts play a very, very negative role, by giving the appearance that there is recourse to a neutral, objective body. But "the neutral objective body" is objectively Zionist, racist, and committed to goals that favor Jews at the expense of non-Jews, the indigenous population. The courts are independent of government interference, but they have already internalized the Zionist ideology of preference to Jews at the expense of non-Jews.

RH: So there is a fundamental paradox or schizophrenia to talk about a "Jewish democracy"?

JK: There is. That schizophrenia is real and integral to Zionism and the state of Israel.... At the heart of Zionism are very positive, progressive, modern, even utopian ideas. But at the heart [of Zionism] is the idea that that the state should be for the Jews and that that goal must be achieved at almost any price; that the creation and survival of the Jewish state, serving all Jews [but] not serving [all] its citizens, is a paramount value: that you should be able to do anything, including having weapons of mass destructions, nuclear weapons, even genocide, if needed, to achieve that. So, you can have your idealism, fascism, and racism at the same time. This combination of utopian progressiveness and fascist racism is the true schizophrenia, and it's embedded in the very heart of the ideology, the creation, and the practice of the state of Israel, the Jewish state.

RH: So the project that you set for yourself as a young lawyer was to expose and contest....

JK: First, to understand, and then to expose and contend with it. I come across many Israelis who are wonderful people, who are really, truly, and genuinely decent believers in human rights and human dignity. And I can believe that these people would also be my oppressors. When I talk to them, they hate oppression, they hate injustice, and they hate all the things I hate. So, how can they live with themselves and be my oppressors? This is where law becomes important to understand the procedures that allow them to [support oppression] and to live with themselves.

RH: What are the primary ways that you work at understanding and exposing Israeli law?

JK: The fact that you went through the Holocaust does not exempt you from the Fourth Geneva Convention. It does not exempt you from rules that apply to the rest of the world. The fact that you are Jewish does not give you special status.... You may think you are the chosen people, but that's an internal faith. In terms of human rights, you are not chosen. You have to abide by the same rules as everyone else. Then come all the excuses—The other side does this, the other side does that. You have the right to retaliate, but there is the principle of proportionality in retaliation and there are some things that are totally prohibited.... Some things are crimes against humanity, and if you commit those things, you are subject to law, just like everybody else. You cannot exempt yourself from the International Criminal Court just because you are in Israel or the U.S. You cannot exempt yourself from international law. I appeal to reason, I appeal to law, I appeal to objectivity. I try to understand the other side, but then I go back to objective principles.

RH: What happens in the interface where Israeli law is not consistent with international law, and the Israeli law is [applied] but international law is not supported?

JK: I present my case to the world. I translate the decisions so that people can read what the court is saying. I expose it to Israelis, to Jews worldwide, and to the Christian community that is so supportive of Israel. If you appeal to neutral principles, you have a fighting chance.

RH: This sounds difficult. Do you need a staff of thousands to make a significant difference?

JK: You just need to speak the truth. You force people to hear the truth and deal with it.

RH: Give me an example how this worked out in a specific case you worked on.

JK: Craig Rollins, a Canadian Mennonite, worked with Christian Peacemaking Teams [CPT] in Hebron. He was committed to nonviolence and peace, a really wonderful person, totally against violence, even totally against the violence of Palestinians and rock-throwing. At one point he jumped in front of an Arab woman who was trying to knife an Israeli soldier and took the knife away from her. The Israelis decided they didn't like these meddling peacemakers. (This happened after Rachel Corrie was run over by a bulldozer trying to prevent a house demolition.)

Craig Rollins was arrested in Hebron and [faced] with deportation because he was at the edge of the Palestinian territory. To deport or deny entry to people for no other reason than that they work for peace ... was so contrary to the Israeli image of "We want peace." I convinced CPT to bring that case to court. We went to the Israeli High Court and we challenged the policy of deporting individuals for no other reason than that they favored peace. And, of course, it was embarrassing for them. Well, Israel claimed secret evidence related to security. In the end they backed down and they cancelled the deportation order. They said that he could come and go as he pleases. But the minute he left the country, they wouldn't allow him back in.

RH: In the last two years, there have been politically significant events—Arafat's death, the [Fatah-Hamas] elections, and the creation of the Wall. Have new approaches evolved for you?

JK: It is now harder and harder for Israel to maintain a facade that it favors peace when it is clear that it rejects every attempt at peace. It is now becoming less important for Israel to maintain that facade. We sense a tremendous arrogance. Israelis are powerful as long as the United States is backing them. They have used the events of 9/11 to jump on the bandwagon of fighting Islamic and international terror. Everything is allowed, and the Fourth Geneva Convention is not applied. When the International Court of Justice ruled against the Wall 14 to 1, Israel totally dismissed it. They dismiss every attempt by the Arabs to make peace.

RH: For you personally, does day-to-day living require a dance back and forth between legal strategies, and a faith stance that says, finally, the divine must intervene in some way?

JK: Yes, I think that has always been the case. When I was much younger and more foolish, [I thought] the fate of anything depended on me. I don't anymore.

RH: Why is it so difficult for established principles, UN principles, to hold people accountable?

JK: Because you have very strong, very powerful forces from well-organized sources who are totally dedicated to their cause, who are systematic, who are influential, who operate at the military, political, financial level, who are in the media, who are in Congress, who are in the churches, who are everywhere, and who are consistently active against these principles.

RH: Tell me more just about the role of language and narrative in this conflict. I remember years ago Alex Awad said to me, We have not been so good at telling our story.

JK: Edward Said first alerted me to this. He said that a narrative is an authoritative story that people need in order to make sense of their lives. And any item of that that doesn't fit into that narrative gets dismissed, even if you see it with your own eyes. He gave the example of the bombing of Beirut during the Israeli invasion of South Lebanon, which was supposedly to get rid of the PLO who were attacking Israel. That fits within the Israeli narrative. And there was the siege of Beirut that also fits within the narrative somehow. But then there was the massive bombing and destruction of Beirut on the 78th day. Everybody saw it on television, but it didn't fit within the narrative, and so it was totally dismissed and ignored. We need a narrative to understand what is happening. If a particular narrative captures the minds and hearts of the media, it will prevail.

The Palestinian narrative has never been told or accepted in the West. So all the daily suffering of oppression has to be explained within the Israeli narrative, which says, Because Palestinians resist the occupation, we have to do this. Because they hate Israelis, that's why we have to assassinate and kill them. Because they want to kill us, that's why we have to put up the Wall. Because they hate us, that's why we have to turn Gaza into a prison and make life totally miserable for them. They have to accept the Israeli narrative that we are innocent, we are the good guys, we are decent, we want peace.

RH: We [Israelis] are the victims?

JK: [Palestinians] are terrible people who want to attack us. But the Palestinian narrative has never been heard. The Palestinian narrative is that Jews came from all over the world, jumped on us, took over our land. We [do] understand that Jews wanted to come here, but to tell us this place is only a Jewish place can only be done at our expense. It is only natural for us to resist. In fact, we wouldn't be human if we didn't try to resist. Our resistance is totally legitimate, because this is an oppression, a military occupation, denying us the right in our own land. This is the Palestinian narrative that has never been heard. Our desire for peace is never heard. Our resistance is [called] terrorism; our existence is a problem for the Israeli narrative. When our narrative is heard and understood, we will be able to make [progress toward peace].

RH: So storytelling is quite crucial along with resistance, peacemaking, and legal work?

JK: The legal work is actually a small part of the narrative. It says, Don't buy the [Israeli] narrative, and don't buy ours. Let's have a neutral set of standards and laws that apply to everybody.

RH: What are the next strategic steps?

JK: The progressive community needs to reevaluate where it stands, what it believes in, what it is willing to say and do, the myths that it has accepted that it now must reconsider—everything from the Oslo process to a two-state solution, the concept of a Jewish state and Zionism, the whole concept of nationalism and the relation with the rest of the world, the concept of military might and armed struggle, the issue of nonviolence and rejection of armed struggle, and divestment and economic and cultural boycotts. All these things become very important to consider as legitimate and necessary tools for fighting against oppression.

RH: Thank you very much for your insights.

JK: You are so welcome.

21 Telling the Whole Truth

Gideon Levy

The intense security that confronted me throughout much of Jerusalem seemed generally absent in Tel Aviv. The offices of Ha'aretz *newspaper are located on a quiet street in a plain, unremarkable building. A friendly receptionist sent me upstairs to Gideon Levy's office. I worked my way through halls covered with modern art. Because of the current (2006) Israeli war in Lebanon, Gideon Levy was intense, preoccupied, and frequently interrupted by phone calls.*

Tel Aviv, 2006

GL: I am Gideon Levy and I am a columnist for *Ha'aretz*.

RH: How long have you worked here?

GL: About 25 years.

RH: What brought you to this work? Have you always been interested in journalism?

GL: Yes, journalism and politics. For four years I worked with Shimon Perez, then League of the Opposition, and ever since I left Shimon Perez, I'm with *Ha'aretz*.

RH: What was your university training? Did you go to journalism school?

GL: No, I got bachelor's and master's degrees in political science and international relations.

RH: I've had ongoing conversations, especially with people on the Left, about whether or not Israelis understand what's going on in the West Bank, in Gaza. People say that you think Israelis do not know.

GL: Israelis do not know. Israelis do not want to know.

RH: Israelis do not know?

GL: Do not know and do not want to know. It's a rare condition in which the publishers are not too much interested, the people are not too much interested, the writers are not very much interested, and the leaders are not too much interested in knowing. And it's a rare, rare coalition, without any kind of government censorship whatsoever, just self-censorship of many, many years, mainly ever since the second *intifada* broke out, in which information is prevented from [reaching] the average Israeli reader. Though I must say that those

DOI: 10.4324/9781003262817-23

who really want to know can very easily know because I am here and other [writers] are here. If you really want to know, you can know. The problem is that if you don't want to know, you find your way very easily of not knowing. The outcome is that the vast majority of Israelis have no idea, not the slightest idea of what's going on. And how do I know? I know when I take somebody with me from time to time how astonished they are, and how they change their minds when they see, because it is about changing minds.

RH: That is, when you take someone to the West Bank or to Gaza?

GL: That's right. It's very direct. It's very rare, but if it happens, people are amazed.

RH: Can you give me an anecdote or an example of taking a friend or an acquaintance?

GL: No, because it happens so little, so little. Even if you think about something like the separation Wall, which was so well covered all over the world, by documentaries and news programs and everything. I am sure that over 90% of Israelis don't even know how it looks. No idea, never saw the separation Wall, the famous separation Wall. They have no idea how it looks. They don't know. They never saw it.

RH: It's difficult to hide; it means that they don't go anywhere close to those borders?

GL: They don't go anywhere close. Most of the Israelis don't go to the Occupied Territories.

RH: Well, there are [Israeli] laws that restrict that sort of contact or that exposure.

GL: Sure, because it became dangerous; it became closed many times, and there is a big, big separation between Israel and the Occupied Territories. The Israelis don't go there anymore. There were times in which they used to go for shopping, but they don't do it anymore. It is a total, total separation in which only the [Israeli] settlers are in the Occupied Territories.

RH: It's both a [physical] separation but even more profoundly a cultural separation.

GL: No doubt. The settlers are separated by separate rules, almost a separate state.

RH: Settlers are even separate from the wider Israeli culture?

GL: No doubt, no doubt.

RH: Elaborate on that.

GL: The settlers are living in total [separation]. Things that are implemented here are not implemented there. Small things like foreign workers. Here, officials are hunting every one of them. There it's normal to find some. I give it as an example of a different set of laws, a different way of behaving, a different culture. It starts with a different language. They give different names to their children. It's a very different society.

RH: From your perspective, is that problematic to have two different Israeli societies, aside from all the questions of occupation?

GL: No, I am very much for a multicultural society, and even multinational. I don't care about it. I just think that this group of people is creating such damage that separated or not, I would like to see them just disappear from the place where they live. So, it's not about having another people or another culture; it's about the damage that [settlers] create.

RH: If Israelis have generally no idea about what's happening on the West Bank and Gaza because of the occupation, are Israelis also ignorant about the impact of the occupation on their own culture?

GL: Sure. First we must understand that ever since the second *intifada*, Israeli society became apathetic and indifferent as never before.

RH: Since 2000?

GL: Since 2000, since Camp David, since the enormous success of the lie that Israel has "no Palestinian partner for peace," since the exploded buses—something happened in Israeli society, a cloud of indifference that we never faced before. So this way nobody bothers himself too much with collective national questions. Everyone is in his own corner. We can see it now [2006] in Lebanon. There is a war two hours away from here. [But] life in Tel Aviv is uninterrupted; it's exactly as it was before. If people don't know somebody there, don't have a son there, they don't care. They continue their lives. There is a sense of disintegration and above all, apathy. So all these questions about occupation, nobody does anything about it.

RH: Would you characterize it as a turn toward individualism?

GL: Yes.

RH: The concern is for the self and one's immediate family.

GL: And apathy. Apathy to anything which happens, even terror. If you didn't happen to know somebody, ... so another bus exploded....

RH: How would you explain it?

GL: It's very sick.... It's a very bad sign for society.

RH: It's a withdrawal into oneself?

GL: Yes, in a way, withdrawal, being tired ... a sense of apathy.

RH: In one of your recent columns in *Ha'aretz*, you used very strong language, such as "vengeance," with regard to the war in Lebanon right now. It had the tone of the Hebrew prophets. Tell me how you see your role as a writer and as an analyst.

GL: I was very flattered to get the other day an e-mail from Noam Chomsky, whom I've never met, who compared me to the prophets. He used this term. It's not for me to judge my role. It's too early to judge. Many times I feel that I am working for the archives.

RH: That you are writing for the future?

GL: I think so, because I don't see a real influence right now. If there is an influence, there is a cumulative influence. I have written so many years, week after week, Sunday after Sunday, Friday after Friday; it must have some kind of cumulative influence, but I can't really estimate it. One day it will be much clearer.

RH: You certainly influence people outside of Israel, because many of us read you on a regular basis and find a kind of solace, of hope, of profound truth-telling. How do you see the interplay of telling the truth and its connection to justice, to the health of society, and building a just peace? What's the role of the truth-teller?

GL: First of all, it is not about the truth-telling; it's about the whole truth-telling. The main problem of Israel is there are many lies which are being spread. But it's not about the lies; it's about the partial truth, the one-sided truth, being so concentrated on ourselves and not seeing the other at all. They don't exist. One of the roles of the Wall is to make it physical, that you will not see Palestinians. It's about hiding half of the truth, at least half of the truth. They believe that every intelligent human being's first step must be knowing, and then you can make your conclusions, your point of view, your philosophy. But first of all, just know the truth. I don't care if after people read me they say, The Palestinians deserve this brutal occupation, or The Arab states are to be blamed for this brutal occupation. I just want you to know how brutal the occupation is, because it is there on your behalf. Every one of us is a checkpoint soldier. All of us carry this stain. Therefore, my main role, my journalistic role, is to try to put a small light on the very, very dark backyard of Israel. It's very dark, it's very hidden from the Israeli eyes, and this will be my biggest contribution, if I could put some light there.

RH: Why do you refer to it as a backyard? Because it's out of sight, out of mind?

GL: In the front yard, you've heard that Israel is the only democracy in the Middle East. It is Western and liberal. For Jews it is by far very liberal and the best proof is.... Excuse me. And the proof that it is really liberal—freedom of speech, freedom of movement, a free press—is in the front yard. Then in the backyard, there is the occupation. See if you can be half-pregnant, then see if you can be half-democratic.

RH: That is the conundrum, isn't it? The difficulty of a Jewish democracy or a democracy for people of only one background.

GL: Right. Israel is a real democracy for Jews, no doubt, but this is not in [keeping] with our demographics, ... not real democracy. If it is democracy, it is all over, for everyone.

RH: We in the United States know this paradox as well, the long struggle for civil rights for everyone. The struggle for liberation is really a universal one. Are you ever harassed when you try to go to the West Bank to see and report?

GL: Physically, no, and I don't go to the settlements. I almost never go; there are enough reporters who will tell their story, and I have no interest to be there.

RH: You might be more in danger there than you are in Palestinian communities.

GL: That's for sure. It's dangerous everywhere. I'm not physically attacked, but you can imagine how my e-mail looks, especially now in the days of war where everything becomes much more sensitive, extreme, radical, violent. But I am so much used to it that I couldn't care less.

RH: If Israelis, in general, do not understand the impact of the occupation on Israeli society, what, if anything, might help to liberate Israelis from this burden?

GL: I can see only three ways, and all of them are not very promising. One, a very courageous leadership in Israel, but I don't see it happening. The other one, a very courageous leadership in Washington, which I don't see. I truly believe that an American president would bring an end to the Israeli occupation within months, but really months.

RH: Any president who had the courage?

GL: Any president, especially with the last prime ministers we had, like Sharon and Olmert. If Olmert got an instruction to evacuate the West Bank, within the hour it will be evacuated. No doubt about it.

RH: So we really have a complicity here?

GL: The United States could put an end to this occupation much easier than it seems, but we lack that leadership. So, the third way, the only other way, is another cycle of bloodshed. But this time a terrible bloodshed, because history tells us that Israel, usually after bloodshed, is ready to make compensation which it doesn't before. We have this terrible example of the Yom Kippur war. We could have had peace with Egypt before the Yom Kippur War and we refused. After 2,600 soldiers were killed, all of a sudden Israel was able to make peace with Egypt. And the same we can say about the first *intifada* in recognizing the PLO. We needed the first *intifada* and the bloodshed to recognize the PLO. It was a small bloodshed with a small outcome. A bigger bloodshed will bring a big outcome. As terrible as it is, that's the history of the policy of Israel. Never will you find any kind of....

RH: Initiative?

GL: Initiative or giving up lands, anything before bloodshed. It's always after the bloodshed.

RH: What is the cultural dynamic that makes this so?

GL: If you think you have other choices, you go for the best option instead of taking the first one. Take now peace with Syria. It's now 40 years since the border is silent, but the Israeli government says,

Why should we make peace with Syria? We have a silent border. After the next war with Syria, I can assure you that we'll be at peace with Syria. But we need another war. Why? All this conflict now would have been prevented if we had had peace with Syria.

RH: It would cost so much less to make peace proactively than to do it after so much loss of life.

GL: People don't realize it, don't recognize it. Maybe there is a very deep need to have a war every few years. Maybe it's a physiological need, a national need; I don't know. It seems that there is a real need for war.

RH: There is an American theologian, Walter Wink, who writes about the myth of "redemptive violence"—that through violence somehow we can achieve some kind of salvation. It is certainly true of American culture and it would appear to be true in Israel....

GL: In Israel it's very true because it's a source of something that unites the people, something that makes the leadership always very heroic. It's very important for the weapons industry; not only the weapons industry but the whole....

RH: Military-industrial complex?

GL: Sure. I don't blame the army.... They are just waiting for the next war. An oversimplification, but from time to time we get this feeling that there is also a basic need for a war. Every three years. It is like a ritual that comes back. This [war in Lebanon] is one of the most foolish wars that Israel has ever had. Nobody will be able to claim that it's not a war of choice. Israel wanted a war.

RH: Uri Avnery, in one of his weekly email letters, recently said he had a conversation with [former Prime Minister] Sharon a few years ago. In that conversation, Sharon said that the planning for this war was done a long time ago, and that the government was just waiting for an inciting incident to trigger it, to get it started. Is that your sense as well?

GL: No, the military planning was for sure there, but this doesn't mean that the politicians were waiting to do it. I think there were the maps, the plans in the army. Then came this provocation and [Prime Minister] Ehud Olmert was the one that introduced [taking war] to Syria in 15 minutes. When it comes to the battlefield, we are very quick to react. When it comes to negotiating, always it takes postponing and postponing and conditions and preconditions. When it comes to war, 15 minutes and there is a new war.

RH: Fifteen minutes?

GL: Fifteen minutes.

RH: Is this a local or regional conflict, or part of a much larger imperial project?

GL: I can tell you that Hezbollah is playing the Iranian game. Israel is playing the American game. Israel was encouraged to go to this war but the United States discouraged Israel from continuing it. Same as the war against Hamas. Again, a big push from the United States.

RH: The U.S. is urging Israel to do the dirty work.

GL: No doubt. Mostly against Hamas and Hezbollah, and, God forbid, maybe also against Syria. And this brings me to very, very sad thoughts about why are we here and what is the level of independence we have. What's the difference between us and Hezbollah? They are playing the Iranian game and we are playing the American game. What is the difference? And both have also local interests. Hezbollah has local interests and Israel has local interests. But I still think that if the local actors will want to get to peace, they can make all the agreements [needed] in the Middle East. If the local actors want to have peace, they will have peace. It's not like we need so much dependence. It takes courage.

RH: A final question of clarification. If I understood you correctly, peace could happen one of two ways?

GL: Three ways: Israeli leadership, American leadership, or another bloodshed.

RH: Which way will it go?

GL: As I don't see the first two coming, it's very easy.

RH: So you anticipate a third *intifada*?

GL: Yes; I don't want to say, No doubt, but I don't see who is going to help us avoid it. Either from Washington or from Jerusalem. I don't see anyone. It is in our hands.

RH: I assume that you agree with the analysis of many people on the Left that a two-state solution died a long time ago.

GL: No, I think we have to go through it. Maybe it's too late, but I don't see another solution because a one-state [solution] will be an apartheid state.

RH: In spite of all of the facts on the ground, the Wall, the closures, the cantonization?

GL: Still reversible.

RH: Still reversible?

GL: On the edge, but still reversible. Yes, because once one state is the best form … it will become an apartheid state.

RH: But it's that now, is it not?

GL: It is now, but if you make it one state, do you not get any better? It will not get any better. And with all the emotions that there are between the two peoples, it will not work. We need really two states. They deserve a national, independent state. And then maybe it becomes, one day, a confederation or whatever. But that is so far away, I don't see it.

RH: A two-state solution?

GL: End of the occupation. That's the first thing. I don't care about any solution—one state, two states, three states. End of the occupation.

RH: That's the first priority.

GL: That's the first, immediate [step]. This should have taken place without any conditions.

RH: And that would have huge implications for relationships with other governments, with external relationships.

GL: The whole status of Israel would change. And it's the only way to guarantee the security of Israel. The only real way. Anything else … more weapons and more weapons. They will get more weapons.

RH: Security based on international human rights and self-determination?

GL: And justice, and justice. And with the issue of the Wall, it is so much more than any "wall." A state which covers itself with walls is really in bad shape, very bad shape.

RH: Thank you very much.

GL: My pleasure.

22 A Mandate for Human Rights

Jessica Montell

B'Tselem is one of the outstanding human-rights organizations in Israel. Jessica Montell worked there for 19 years—six years as development director and 12 years as executive director. After that she developed a research project at Hebrew University to assess the effectiveness of human-rights organizations. Currently, she is executive director of Hamoked, a legal-aid organization for Palestinians.

Jerusalem, June 2005

JM: My name is Jessica Montell, and I'm executive director of B'Tselem, The Israeli Information Center for Human Rights in the Occupied Territories.

RH: That's a very long name. How long have you been here?

JM: I've been at the center since 1995, so for 10 years, and I have been director since 2001.

RH: Let me start back with just a little bit of personal history and then we'll come back to the present. Were you born here?

JM: I was born in California, in the U.S., I grew up in a Jewish family, a liberal family, not a Zionist family, in northern California. I was active in a Zionist youth group in Young Judea through high school, and at the same time was part of a liberal family. Northern California is quite a liberal, politically active place. I worked on behalf of Jewish causes and on behalf of Soviet Jews who weren't allowed to leave the Soviet Union. I also [worked for] broader causes—for farm workers and against nuclear weapons. I came to Israel a few times in high school and college and then came here for a year when I finished college. That is when I first got involved with human-rights organizations here.

RH: What brought you in the direction of human rights?

JM: It's true that American Jews and Israelis can spend time here and not come in contact with issues of justice for Palestinians. It's the reality of the occupation for Palestinians. There is a parallel universe that you can live in without understanding that reality.... I came to Israel after college and wanted to be involved with social justice here.

DOI: 10.4324/9781003262817-24

RH: What is the connection between human rights, doing justice, and peacemaking?

JM: Human rights is very narrow, almost technical. We are not involved in the big issues that are the root causes of those human-rights violations. Although we are all suffering from the Israel-Palestinian conflict, and human-rights violations are necessarily part of that conflict, we are not involved in those bigger political issues—one or two states. Jerusalem as a united city. Our mandate is focused specifically on those rights as defined by international law, and to Israel's commitment to the right of every individual to basic human dignity as it is phrased in Israeli law—the right to work, the right to housing, the right to be free of mistreatment and torture, the right to life. In some ways it is a very legalistic approach. I would argue that that is the approach that enables us. There is a minefield here, and this approach enables us to keep true to an ideology of justice without getting tangled in that minefield. Also, it's a way to appeal to a larger Israeli public.

RH: What is the disjunction or tension between the strong ethical tradition that runs through Judaism, and negative "facts on the ground"?

JM: There is a certain schizophrenia in Israel. We Israelis see ourselves as part of a liberal democracy, and Israel defines itself as a Jewish democratic state. There is certainly tension, some say, "a tension we can live with," and some would say a contradiction between a Jewish state and a democratic state. One-fifth of the population is not Jewish. Issues of human dignity [and] human rights can be found both in the Jewish tradition and in the core values of democracy. We would say that we are committed to those values; and yet, for 38 years, we have maintained a military occupation of two million Palestinians. It is very hard to reconcile those two realities of a liberal democracy and a military occupation. For most Israelis, maybe that explains their ignorance about the occupation. In general terms, Israelis know what it means to have a military occupation, checkpoints in the Occupied Territories, a separation barrier, and demolishing houses. But of what that means in the daily life of Palestinians, Israelis are quite ignorant. In the internet age, it can be described as a willful ignorance.

RH: Because the Jewish tradition is steeped in ethics, knowing would make you responsible?

JM: Well, the Jewish tradition can be understood in a wide variety of ways. I'm not an expert, although I have an undergraduate degree in Jewish studies. [There are] rabbis for human rights who advocate that the Jewish tradition obligates us to respect the human rights of Palestinians. You can also, from the Jewish tradition, take the most extreme, nationalistic, us-against-them values as well. For me, human rights is rooted in faith, but it's not necessary as an organization.

RH: I understand what you are saying. The range of understanding—

JM: The possible interpretation of—

RH: Of being Jewish—

JM: The [current] disengagement from Gaza is violently opposed to removing the [Israeli] settlements from the Gaza Strip, which are a source of so much suffering for the Palestinians.

RH: So human rights for you is international law and UN [resolutions]....

JM: Right. Although we are not a religious organization, the name B'Tselem comes from the book of Genesis. B'Tselem means "in the image of God." In modern Hebrew it is used as a synonym for human dignity. This is the connection between the human-rights language of the Universal Declaration of Human Rights, which says that all people are created equal in dignity and rights, and the Jewish tradition that says that since we were all created in the image of God, we all have an equal right to basic dignity.

RH: So, many Jewish Israelis would [accept] that basic premise, but others would not.

JM: Most Israelis would say everyone is entitled to human dignity, but then would say, in reality, a criminal has to be punished, arrested, and put in jail, even though that is a violation, theoretically, of their rights to liberty. If someone comes to kill you, you are allowed to use lethal force even to kill them, to defend yourself. So that is the framework. I participate in regular discussions in the Connective Law Committee about human rights in the fight against terrorism. The military occupation of the West Bank and Gaza is now seen through this prism and the "war on terror." Everything that the Israeli government is doing in the Occupied Territories is justified in the name of the war on terror.

One principle says all human beings have a right to human dignity. The second, also a principle from the Bible, is that if someone comes to kill you, you kill them first. It is the basic principle of self-defense. Then there is a gray area in between. What is self-defense? What is necessary for self-defense? What is an overreaction or a manipulation of the legitimate rights of self-defense? Most of our discussions with the Israeli public are in that gray area of what the Israel public thinks is essential to defend us from suicide bombings, to protect me and my family when we get on a public bus, and what is frequently a manipulation of our fears for security.

RH: Is there any granting of the possibility that suicide bombers or other forms of resistance, even nonviolent resistance, is a response to the occupation rather than the other way around, that the occupation itself is a provocation?

JM: No, very little willingness to explain, to engage in understanding the other side. In a very famous statement a few years ago, Ehud Barak, when he was running to be prime minister, said, "If I were a Palestinian,

I would join the resistance." From a human-rights perspective there is no legitimacy for suicide bombings. It gives no justification, no leniency, that a murderer had a hard childhood, in terms of a criminal-justice perspective or human-rights perspective. That in no way absolves a person for their crime. You need also a strategic plan for how you are going to stop that, and you do want to understand what is making these people tick. But, from a human-rights perspective, suicide bombings are war crimes, and it doesn't matter to me that the person has suffered in their childhood, for whatever reason.

RH: To what extent do you consider all the manifestations of occupation—from outright violence to house demolitions—to be war crimes under international law? Are those all war crimes?

JM: The phrase "war crimes" comes from what are defined as grave breaches of the Geneva Conventions. There is a relatively short list of what is considered a grave breach, and that has been given greater legal weight with the establishment of the International Criminal Court; the Rome Statute of the International Criminal Court has a very lengthy list based on the Geneva Conventions and other international humanitarian laws of what is considered a war crime. These include willful killing, the intentional killing of civilians, extensive destruction of property that is not necessary for military operations, and torture.... Every bad thing taking place is [not] a war crime. The words "war crimes" and "crimes against humanity" need to be reserved for the most egregious, horrific crimes being committed against human beings.

RH: I quite agree with you. What I'm trying to explore is ... in the world of political realities, we're left with interpretation. When someone says something is "necessary," is it up to whoever has power to define what is necessary?

JM: You mean in terms of property destruction?

RH: Any element of this.

JM: Yeah, we are applying two different standards here. One is a human-rights standard, which is the right to life, the right against torture. It is a very clear-cut, well-defined standard, what is permitted and what is prohibited. The United Nations is not comprised of politicians, but is comprised of experts for determining what is permitted and what is forbidden. In the case of torture, the guidelines are very clear.

When you talk about humanitarian law, laws of war, the guidelines are much less clear. The question [arises] of destruction of property that is strictly necessary for what is justified as military necessity. Of course, the military says everything we're doing is military necessity, and then where do you draw the line between what is nice to have from a military perspective and what is absolutely essential to defend troops, which you are allowed to do? You are right that in some cases there is a gray area where we say, This is not strictly necessary, and the military says, Yes it is. Then it is up to the courts to decide. I have to build my case, and they build theirs.

RH: Where do human-rights research and advocacy intersect with political realities? It sounds like you are left in [need of] persuasion—building a legal case, making an argument. What is the tension between what it is in international law and what actually happens here on the ground?

JM: I would say even where the cases are clear-cut our main tool is persuasion. You can call it lobbying, or public education. We are not a legal organization. We rarely turn to the Israeli high courts. Most of our work is documenting, what is called in the international community as "naming and shaming." We publish reports that document what is actually taking place, give the relevant international law, and render a judgment. This event, that took place on this and this day and caused this and this suffering, is a violation of laws that Israel has taken upon itself to uphold.

RH: What is the level of human-rights distress? You can call it shaming and blaming if you like, but [in this conflict], are you talking about an occasional breach or massive levels of violations?

JM: Right now, we're in a relatively quiet period. Since January, the situation in the Occupied Territories is much calmer than it was last year or the year before.... Today the numbers have gone way down, not only in terms of casualties, but also in terms of house demolitions, and in terms of restrictions in movement. In almost every parameter the situation is a big improvement, [but] the situation is [not] good. Over the past five years, we have seen a very severe deterioration.

I think I would make a distinction between "fire-brigade issues," what occupies the headlines, people who are killed and injured, house demolitions, even checkpoints that are preventing people from getting to urgent medical care—urgent issues that we have to immediately respond to; then there are those human-rights violations that are the basis for all of this suffering. Consider the establishment of settlements in the Occupied Territories, a violation of international humanitarian law. A military occupier, an occupying power, is not supposed to bring its civilian population into occupied territories. So, we're in violation of international humanitarian law. Settlements result in all sorts of human-rights violations against the Palestinian population, both in terms of expropriation of resources of land and water, and serving as the basis for the justification of restrictions on movement, house demolitions, and a flashpoint for violence, both clashes between Palestinian soldiers and then settlers themselves are very much exposed to violence by armed militant Palestinians.

"Fire-brigade" issues have improved very dramatically. Palestinians would say that daily life is better than it was six months ago. These infrastructure issues have not improved, and in some cases have maybe intensified. Israel is building a separation barrier inside the Occupied Territories along a route that is blatantly political, a route that has nothing to do with Israeli security. Israel is increasing settlement expansion around Jerusalem and along the route of the separation barrier. That is also resulting in human-rights violations against Palestinians.

RH: How does one reverse that process? For example, if the government wanted to, it could finance settlers to move back into Israel.

JM: Right.

RH: They could find money. They could find international money for that.

JM: Even if Israel maintains a military occupation, Israel has to behave according to the rules that have been established for a military occupation. You cannot engage in collective punishment. You can't restrict movement within the Occupied Territories. You can't move your population into occupied territories. So, all the things that Israel is doing today have to be stopped. That means not engaging in collective punishment, not restricting movement.... Israel has violated humanitarian law and has to dismantle the settlements, regardless of the political process. Of course, those questions are very connected to the political process. Our perspective is that once there are negotiations, negotiations have to take human rights into account.

RH: Is it appropriate at this moment to talk about what Jeff Halper calls the endgame?

JM: Again, we are not involved in the political issues. The resolution of this conflict is not my job. As long there is a military occupation, there are going to be human-rights violations. My job is to make sure that the military occupation is conducted in as humane away as possible. With a bit of cynicism, we are working within the contradiction of terms. On the other hand, a military occupation cannot be reconciled within the basic standards of human rights; it has to be ended. How it is ended is not part of my mandate.

RH: Implicitly there is a strong sense that the occupation needs to end.

JM: I would say that it's even explicit, [but] we are not involved in proposing one specific resolution, negotiating with this or that party, [or] these borders.... There are all sorts of possibilities, but it is quite explicit in our work that we cannot have full recognition of human rights as long as we have a military occupation.

RH: The people with power determine what they are going to do, right? What difference does it make if an international organization says the separation barrier is a major violation of international law?

JM: I'll give a macro answer and a micro answer. The International Criminal Court of Justice gave an advisory opinion, so it is not obligatory for Israel. It is sort of educational, stating the fact for the enlightenment of the international community without necessarily obligating Israel legally. That is not to say it doesn't have implications for Israel. Israel's high court, which ruled 10 days before the ICJ advisory opinion to reroute the separation barrier, of course was influenced by the judgment hanging over their heads. I don't think Israel's court would have issued what is a courageous judgment regarding one specific route of the barrier but then has implications for the entire route of the barrier without this judgment by the ICJ.

But your question is a more philosophical question about power. Governments are the ones in control. They are the ones with power to violate human rights, the ones with human-rights obligations. Take the issue of violence by settlers against Palestinians. There, too, the [responsibility] belongs to the government from a human-rights perspective. The settler who perpetrated violence, and a Palestinian criminal who uses violence—the authorities have to arrest them and prosecute them [both]. The human-rights committee must keep people from using violence.

RH: I assume that your work is not only here in the office but that you travel and move in the West Bank and Gaza....

JM: Not in Gaza. Israelis are not allowed to go to Gaza. We have two field workers, Palestinians from Gaza who are not allowed to come to Israel. A technical difficulty.

RH: So you have Palestinian field workers?

JM: Yeah, we have nine field workers who today, because of restrictions on their movements, are Palestinian residents of their areas. They are responsible for taking testimonies from Palestinian victims and eyewitnesses. We also take testimonies from Israeli soldiers and Israeli civilians. This work has a dimensionality to it that is much more than simply technical.

RH: When you are dealing with eyewitness accounts, you are dealing with narrative and oral history to some extent and all the subjectivity of that experience, yes?

JM: Yes, although again, the ideology of human rights has quite a moral, philosophical basis; the practice of human rights is quite technical. We have human-rights standards. I take a testimony; I want to know the facts, and it is my job to take out all of the subjective narrative. I may take testimonies from three different people who saw what happened from three different directions. I want to get to the truth. Is somebody lying to me? If so, I disqualify that testimony. If they are telling the truth, I cross-check what did the army say, what did the eyewitness say, what did the victim say? This will get it down to a pure truth.

RH: I understand, but if three different narratives about an incident of beating wildly contradict each other, how do you get to the truth?

JM: That is our job to know, and our fieldworkers are very carefully trained and supported on an ongoing basis to do what is a very difficult job. Of course they are sympathetic to residents of their area who are victims. They themselves are victims of human-rights violations. It is very important for all of us to understand that aside from any sympathy with the victim, our job is to get at the truth, even if victims, for a variety of motives … fabricate stories. [We compare] the same way any investigator knows to check from three different sources that don't know each other or haven't spoken to each other to hear what the official version of events was. They know to go to the scene and conduct a reconstruction of events. We also use forensics, video, and other technical processes to get at the truth. We are well aware that we are operating in a minefield, a propaganda minefield as well. Palestinians are in some cases manipulating the facts to better serve their cause, in terms of winning international sympathy. Israel is also involved in that propaganda battle, and we are very careful not to get caught up in that.

RH: So trustworthiness is really crucial to the work that you do?

JM: Yes, being able to trust our staff and to give our staff the professional tools to know who to trust in terms of taking testimonies.

RH: My final question has to do with the intersection of your personal experience and your professional work. Can you identify significant experiences, perhaps turning points, in your own process along the way, some moment in which this work became clear for you?

JM: In terms of how I got to where I am, it is much more of a process than a formative moment when I turned a corner. A few experiences brought to me the significance of our work and the disparity between the reality on one side of the border and on the other side of the border.… I talked about the schizophrenia of Israeli society and in Jerusalem. Once you see the reality on the other side you return to your life and are seeing the world as a split screen. I live in West Jerusalem in a liberal democratic society, have water for as long as the faucet is on, as opposed to the Palestinians, who don't have running water during the summer months.

I'll give another example. My daughter had a very high fever one day, nothing life, threatening, just a fever of 103, but a panicked mother. I put her in the car, and it is a 15-minute drive to get to the doctor. The whole way, running through my head is the [experience of] a mother who is living in the Beit Foreek village near Nablus, a trip that could take three hours. You would have to take her out of the car and carry her over a checkpoint, have soldiers let you pass or not let you pass. It is such a banal example of the obstacles of daily life, and added to that the layers of daily life for Palestinians. How do you go about daily life with all of the added humiliation and obstacles?

I'll give the flip side of that. We took the testimony of a father and his 11-year-old girl, who had appendicitis. In my neighborhood that is not life-threatening. In this case the father tried for two days to get his 11-year-old girl to the hospital, and she died. So, the juxtaposition of life five miles down the road from my house ... what it means for my daughter to have appendicitis and for a Palestinian is the difference literally between life and death.

RH: Your work is not only collecting the data but publishing it. What do you do with a narrative like that in terms of local governments, national governments, and international organizations?

JM: It is a real challenge to Israeli society to understand, to sympathize. First, to know the facts about daily life for Palestinians and to care, when we ourselves feel that we are the victims. That we are the ones targeted for willful killings, in the language of human rights. I think a testimony like [that of] the father of an 11-year-old girl with appendicitis, something we can all identify with, anyone who has a child. We can identify what it means to be a worried parent when your child is sick. That is a way to break through the wall of denial about the big picture, Israel's policy on freedom of movement. It has a very cold, euphemistic sound to it that prevents us from coming face to face with the father of an 11-year-old girl with appendicitis.

My job is to take that story to the Israeli press and say, Maybe you want to do a story about this case. You put out a press release. You take a journalist to meet the father. You give a briefing to diplomats: any source of public work, publishing reports alongside the facts, how many checkpoints there are, all of those sorts of dry statistics, to bring this human face that I think is very important in reaching people.

RH: So you would see your work here as deeply connected to the approaches and work of others in the peace and justice community?

JM: Yes, we are working very closely with other human-rights organizations. Our work serves people who are working for dialogue between Jews and Arabs, people who are working on peace, fostering negotiations, all of the issues we are not engaged in but ... we produce a map of settlements in the Occupied Territories that is essential to a bunch of other initiatives.

RH: Thanks. You have been most generous.

* * * * * * * *

East Jerusalem, April 2018

RH: The central question is, What is the relationship between human-rights work, your research, and peacemaking?

JM: I was at B'Tselem for 19 years, an organization that I love and feel really proud to have been a part of building. I left feeling like it was time to look for new adventures on a personal level. I was lucky to get a fellowship the year after I left at the law school at the Hebrew University. I did research on the impact of the Israel-Palestine human-rights community. What were the tools that were effective and what can we learn from that? I identified 14 concrete achievements of the local human-rights community and significant changes: a 10-year moratorium on punitive home demolitions, stopping what was systemic torture by the Israel security agency, rerouting the separation barrier, and on and on. And a small anecdote that I think reveals the larger tensions. I presented a draft of this research to the local human-rights community and the response, rather than being gratified to learn that in fact our work is effective and that we have had an impact, the response was indignant: How can you say that we have had any achievements at all when the occupation is stronger than ever? And then I said to them, What are your goals; what are you working on; what do you aim to achieve in your three- or five-year plan? Nobody says, End the occupation. You want to stop punitive home demolitions and abuse of minors in detention.

RH: Very specific things that are immediate needs now.

JM: Yes. And are within the tools of a human-rights organization. This led me to think about this gap between promoting human rights as opposed to ending occupation. This led me to think on the theoretical level about what are the tools and strategies of ending occupation and also for me personally, [since] I see occupation as the number-one issue that needs to be addressed.

RH: I must say, there is a consensus about that in the [peacemaking] community.

JM: Yes, of course. There are people working on refugee rights and gay and lesbian rights; maybe they don't see occupation as the burning existential threat to all of us.

RH: I've heard more this time than ever before about intersectionality. So that's interesting.

JM: Yes. After having left B'Tselem and doing this research that shows that human-rights organizations have really important work to be done and are impactful, I still wanted to look for ways to be involved in the political efforts to end the occupation. For two years, I did all sorts of things, and last Fall I took this position, executive director of Hamoked, which is a legal-aid office assisting Palestinians who are victims of the occupation. That trajectory says something about my understanding of where we are now, in terms of the occupation and the likelihood of political organizing that can successfully move something right now. To my mind, the urgency is to be helping people who are suffering, both in terms of the very dismal political situation inside Israel and within Palestinian politics. This is the reality for the near future. Given that that is the case, human-rights organizations have a really crucial role to play.

RH: You have also commented on the interplay of immediate resources, whether Jewish Israeli or Palestinian and outside resources, to make the occupation less sustainable.

JM: Yes. On the level of human-rights advocacy, my research made clear that every achievement that we managed to make was the result of a combination of domestic tools and international tools. That in most cases, you need high-court litigation. Inside Israel, the high court is accused, rightly so, of entrenching the occupation. The high court has not been willing to take a stand on the building blocks of occupation. And yet, on the level of making changes in terms of human rights, the high-court has been the most effective tool when combined with international advocacy, pressure from the international community of jurists, but also political pressure or general popular criticism of Israel. That plays a positive role in influencing also domestic high court judges, or other domestic channels. There's no way you're going to make change here if you are only focusing internationally. And there's no way to make change if you ignore international tools and you are only looking at domestic tools.

RH: Part of the theory of peacemaking is that there are various levels: the grassroots level involves the most people. That middle layer some people call Track Two diplomacy, which you are doing, intellectuals and NGOs and community activists. And then the political elite, which is the smallest group of people. Talk about that interplay for you.

JM: I wouldn't put human-rights organizations as part of Track Two diplomacy. I see our role as informing and feeding into all three of those levels. Human-rights groups, in addition to actually helping people on the ground, also provide information, the documentation framing the issue. If we understand this broader problem of occupation, information and analysis feed into grassroots protest, Track Two [leadership], and diplomacy and negotiations.

RH: So, you're part of several streams, all of which are needed.

JM: Yes. Human-rights organizations are part of this broader ecosystem.... We're part of this bigger puzzle but also our role is limited in terms of promoting political change. It's important that we not attempt to fill the vacuum in terms of the political stage that could be better filled by other actors.

RH: That's the purpose of my book, to show a mosaic of players or actors contributing to a just peace.

23 The Only Nonviolent Alternative

Ilan Pappe

Ilan Pappe is one of the Israeli "new historians" and an activist for a just peace. At the time of our first dialogue, he was the senior lecturer on the Palestinian side of Haifa University (1984–2007), and chair of the Emil Touma Institute for Palestinian and Israeli Studies in Haifa (2000–2008).

After receiving death threats, Pappe joined the College of Social Sciences and International Studies at the University of Exeter (UK), and he became director of the university's European Centre for Palestine Studies, and codirector of the Exeter Centre for Ethno-Political Studies.

Washington, D.C., November 2004

RH: I want to find out how people and groups can change. So, tell me your family background.

IP: I was born in Haifa, in Israel, and grew up in a segregated Jewish community. I learned Arabic in high school, which was rather exceptional. And I served in the army until I finished my undergraduate studies. I had a typical Israeli life.

RH: Where did you do your undergraduate work?

IP: At Hebrew University in Jerusalem. It was not very dramatic. I was like any other Israeli Jew.

RH: What was your field?

IP: Middle Eastern history and international relations. I chose a topic which combined my interests, convenience, and what I did in the army.... My real interest in the Middle East began when I left Israel and started to do postgraduate studies in England, at Oxford. I became involved in both the history of Palestine and the history of the Middle East to a much deeper extent than most of the academics I know—where the social, political, and cultural implications came into play. The turning point was leaving [Israel] for four years.

RH: But many other people leave the country and don't go through what you did.

IP: I agree. It is a question I find difficult to answer. It has nothing to do with my family, my school, or my university. It is a combination of

DOI: 10.4324/9781003262817-25

several processes: I chose to look at 1948, a year which the Palestinians regard as a catastrophe and the Israelis regard as a miraculous year; my decision to be supervised by an Arab supervisor. He introduced me to a community of Arab and Palestinian scholars, something you couldn't do in Israel in the late 1970s or early 1980s.

The combination of what I found in the archives about 1948 and what I heard from new Palestinian and Arab friends were eye-openers. But, to your basic question, I know of several other Israeli Jews who had that combination and it hasn't changed them. So, there must be another key, which I cannot find. I would assume that anyone who saw what I saw in the archives and anyone who had the supervisor I had could only have gone on the course which I have chosen. But I know that [other] people didn't. So that is a good question.

RH: No matter what is in the archives, people bring their beliefs to it.

IP: Absolutely. [But] why was I liberated from my Zionist glasses and people with a similar education were not? Why was I such a flawed product in the Zionist industrial plan? I have no good answer. People, especially in the Arab world, are dying to know if there is a formula so they can clone me. I really don't know. My good friend Gideon Levy, probably the most courageous Israeli journalist, comes from a very similar background as I do. He also can't explain why exactly he went to the West Bank and saw with his own eyes what goes on there. Why we at the same age, and at the same time, were dramatically transformed. This is not changing a position. This is almost changing your identity.

RH: Another key would be relationships. Relationships change your way of knowing.

IP: I fully agree with you. I think about the other new historian, Benny Morris. Benny and I worked in the archives at the same time, and we were both shocked by what we saw, compared to what we knew. He developed very differently, not by challenging the picture—we both were the first ones to bring the full picture to the Israeli public of the ethnic cleansing of 1948—but in how we coped with the picture.... He eventually said that what happened [in 1948] was not too bad, and what [Jews] did [in 1948] was the right thing to do. As years went by, I said it was even more horrible and more despicable than what I thought. We had very different ways of coping. I decided to devote my life to asking for restitution and compensation, true reconciliation....

RH: So, what was the narrative that you had lived inside of until reading in the archives?

IP: In 1948, the common Israeli mythology was that you had a Jewish community seeking to live in peace with the next-door Arab community. [This Jewish] community was outnumbered in military terms, compared to the Palestinian community and the Arab world. That community was willing to share the country with the Palestinians, and therefore accepted the [UN] partition plan. The

Arab world sent massive forces to destroy the state of Israel. The [Arabs] ordered the Palestinians to leave and make way for the invading army so that they could conquer the country.

I challenged this depiction. First, we questioned this myth of the Jewish David against the Arab Goliath. We showed that in military terms the Jewish forces were much bigger, and better equipped and trained than any of the Arab volunteers. There were hardly any proper Arab soldiers. Arab soldiers were sent as a token to show that they had some sort of commitment to the Palestinian people. More importantly, we showed that the only Arab force that could have somehow undermined the Jewish state was the Jordanian army, but the Jordanians had colluded with the Jewish leader to annex the West Bank in return for not invading the Jewish state.

The whole Arab military effort was neutralized and not a very serious challenge to the Jewish community, which was not, for one moment, under any danger of annihilation. Secondly, in the archived material I found that Israel was master planning the expulsion of the Palestinians regardless of the Arab neighbors. Long before the Arab countries entered Palestine with a token force—to show the Palestinians that they cared about them—the Israelis began a massive expulsion, which today we would call ethnic cleansing. With it came atrocities, massacres, and rapes, which were totally erased from the Israeli collective memory and national narrative.

Finally, we debunked the typical Israeli myths that Israel was looking for peace after the war. In fact, we saw that the Arab world, the Palestinians in particular, were seeking a solution, but Israel refused. People went back to the early years of Zionism and analyzed Zionism as a colonial movement. This was not accepted by the hegemonic Israeli narrative. We looked at the 1950s and exposed a very discriminating policy toward the Palestinian minority that was left in Israel and toward Israeli Jews who came from Arab countries.

RH: Uri Avnery says both Israeli metanarratives and Palestinian metanarratives make it difficult for people to create a just narrative. Is that valid?

IP: It is difficult to judge. Basically he is right. Israel is still a very indoctrinating state. People still suckle, from cradle to the grave, a very clear narrative, a Zionist metanarrative.

RH: Is this by design?

IP: Oh yes, it is by design. It is very systematic. It is very calculated. It is very difficult to deviate from it because it is based on deep fears of the Jewish people and their history. It is not difficult to get acceptance of that [Zionist narrative]. The interesting case is how did they [instill this fear] in Jews from Arab countries, Jews who did not share this collective fear, and definitely did not share the anti-Arab feelings, which is a very important part of the metanarrative. Yes, it is a planned indoctrination. Therefore, if you want to challenge it from within, it is difficult. If you want to challenge it from without, it is difficult. It is a long process to deprogram people.... In the 1990s, Israeli television, textbooks, playwrights, and filmmakers all adopted the new narrative and found it conducive for the peace process. During the second *intifada,* a majority retracted [the new narrative] and fell into the warm embrace of the Zionist metanarrative once more. Now we are in a restless layer with the occupation above us, Israelis and Palestinians alike. How far can people move? As long as the occupation is there, who can talk about 1948 and deeper chapters?

RH: I understand Palestinian exhaustion with the occupation. What is the Israeli exhaustion?

IP: It is not even exhaustion. It is a numb feeling because of suicides, the Wall is so high you don't see anything on the other side, and you can live in Israel without knowing about the occupation.

RH: Therefore, [a suicide bombing] is not seen as a political gesture.

IP: Not at all. We live in a sealed bubble. It is a feeling that became an integral part of the accepted life ... a taken-for-granted reality. That is the good news, maybe—the fact that those who are active against the occupation are very crystal-clear about what it is all about. When we had the mass movement against the occupation, led by Peace Now, they had no idea what the occupation really meant, and suggested solutions which were not leading to the end of the occupation. We have now a much clearer group. So things may change.

RH: Organizations such as Gush Shalom, the Alternative Information Center. The Women in Black, Gila Svirsky, Neta Golan, they are doing an excellent job.

IP: They might herald a different period. We are not there yet....

RH: In the U.S. and in Israel, I see general narrative summary, "We are the victims. We resist being a victim again." To what extent is that a psycho-political phenomenon?

IP: That plays a very important role, the reality in which you are the victimizer and yet you still have the self-perception of being a victim. I would say that the main feature of this phenomenon, the home of the pathology, is a fear of losing the role of the ultimate victim of the 20th century.

It is clear to [me], someone liberated from that [fear], that everything that the state of Israel has done to the Palestinians disqualifies it for representing the survivors and all of the victims of the Holocaust. Israel never wanted to represent the survivors. Survivors were an antithesis to what Zionism is all about. If you were a Zionist, you couldn't survive. You would have fought against the Nazis. So, Israel has manipulated and exploited the memory of the six million victims rather than the survivors. That is why the survivors are treated very badly in terms of welfare and positions in society. You choose something important by this question of victims. On the one hand, [Israelis] are not the same Jews that survived. They are also not the same Jews that were victims. They represent the brave Jews who rebelled in the Warsaw Ghetto and places like that. This allows Israelis to be both a victim and a powerful victimizer at the same time. The worst nightmare for the Zionists is that Palestinians are becoming the ultimate victims of this century.

RH: As world opinion shifts.

IP: Exactly.... Had it not been for 9/11, I think we would be at a very different place today. But you are right in general; it is a kind of bank account ... the bank account of victimhood that is actually empty. The reason neoconservatives, Christian Zionists, and the Jews around the world support Israel has nothing to do with representing victimhood; it comes from different motives.

RH: It is about the future place for Christian Zionists.

IP: Also for neocons. The bank account is empty and the Palestinians' bank account is growing. It would be very difficult to assess how significant it is, but it definitely plays a role.... I have a different theory about it. I interviewed Jews around the world who told me what happened to them after the 1967 war. They held no affinity with Zionism until the Six-Day War. When Israel became a mini-empire, suddenly Jews felt it compensated for their own history. They have a state that is a safe haven; it should be protected, and it should be powerful, a state [with] the fifth largest army in the world, the largest army in the Middle East. This is what is so wrong with Zionism. It started as a movement to save Jews, but it turned into a movement that makes Jews feel like they are a powerful people, the "New Jews." It has a dialectical and complex relationship with the concept of victimhood. It is compensating for years of being a victim. You needed the victimhood to begin with, to recruit and to get some money into this bank account, but you don't need it now....

RH: Unfortunately, it parallels the American will to power, which seems to be inexhaustible.

IP: Mutually they are feeding each other.

RH: So how does one break through this?

IP: As I said before, there is a precondition for allowing any serious grassroots work or conceptual work to really succeed—ending the military presence in those parts of Palestine which are under direct military occupation. Prior to this, breakthrough efforts go in two directions. One is definitely the conceptual field of knowledge production and trying to expose, especially to the Israeli Jews and Jews around the world, the manipulation and the abuse of collective memory. Some good work has been done. No less important are small enclaves which we are trying to nourish in Palestine and Israel, joint kindergartens, joint school systems, groups of joint artists and joint academic dialogues—not in the Oslo concept of dialogue between two segregated partners, but dialogue based on a de-Zionized and denationalized understanding of the situation, and creating small enclaves that allow people to do that.

We have to get out of the occupation. You could create models in the Galilee where there is no occupation, and people are doing it. These enclaves could serve as models in the future. It is trying to convince Jews, not just Palestinians, that Zionism is working against their interests.

Secondly, enable them to get over their fears in order to accept an alternative way of thinking. Most of them only say, There is something morally wrong with the way we ensure Jewish survival, but … what you suggest to us, for example, a state where Jews and Arabs would be equal, is the end of Judaism. We cannot accept it. We would rather occupy and oppress, even if you are right…. Sure, we will be immoral, but we will be alive." They are utterly wrong, but it is not easy to show them the way.

RH: It would certainly be the end of a Jewish state. Israel might exist, but it would not exist…

IP: Not as a *Jewish* state. Is it a Jewish state now? It depends on how you understand the precepts of Judaism. I claim in my recent articles that Israel is not a Jewish state.

RH: No?

IP: No, it is not a Jewish state at all. I'm a Jew and my heritage and my civilization oblige me to take positions which put Jews at a very important place within the civil-rights movement in the U.S., against apartheid in South Africa, and should put Jews in the same place where most of the supporters of the Palestinians are today. If they don't do it, they are not Jewish, to my mind. It is even less Jewish to claim that you are doing that in order to ensure survival of the Jews as a whole. It would be much more Jewish to not allow certain Jews to do what they do to Palestinians, ensuring a Jewish majority by all means and at all expense.

RH: That is what Jeff Halper calls an ethnocracy.

IP: Every moral precept has to succumb to that. But don't sell it to me as a Jewish thing.

RH: For many who are not Jewish, this is puzzling, that the Jewish tradition, is so profoundly ethical. I understand the historical traumas, yet ethics would seem bound up with survival.

IP: I completely agree with you, but every identity is constructed by knowing not only who you are but also, who you are not. The other side of the coin is no less formidable in liberating Jews from their prejudiced ideas about Arabs, which is as difficult as convincing them that Israel is not a Jewish state. And, so much blood has been spilt.

This is where Edward Said is so helpful in trying to show that the Arabs were packaged in a certain way that made you feel the way you feel toward them, and telling in a more focused way the story of the Arab Jews and how *they* were de-Arabized. I am an initiator for several workshops inside Israel which take these two tasks very seriously. These are educational strategies, so the powers that be do not interrupt us too much.

RH: What form do the workshops take?

IP: There is the energy that challenges the reality; people say we are Arabs and Jews and we want joint kindergartens. This is part of a major effort. I funded a private institute to push forward these projects, which allows intellectual thinking as well as help and advice to people.

RH: What are some of the other strategies of the institute?

IP: We focus a lot on what Christianity refers to as original sin. You can start untangling the manipulation of the story of 1948 through the visible remnants and oral histories of 1948.

RH: Palestinian oral histories?

IP: Yes, but also Jewish histories.

RH: Soldiers?

IP: Soldiers who confess.... It is a very Christian thing—confession and original sin. It is interesting as a kind of theology of liberation. It is essential and urgent because this generation is going to disappear pretty soon. We are less successful with the Arab-Jewish community. The Israelis have succeeded in making people hate their own culture, because that is the only ticket to being integrated. We try to be in touch with Russian Jews and challenge their education.

RH: So this has worked outside of your university?

IP: Oh, you can't do these things in the university. The academy in Israel is totally in the hands of the establishment and will not allow anyone to deviate seriously from it.

RH: Do you yourself get threats or accusations of being a self-hating Jew?

IP: Oh yes, it comes and goes. I even make it to the newspaper headlines as public enemy number one, which I did in April 2002 and April 2004. Every two years I get the heat. Constantly I have death threats. But once there is an intimate dialogue, these accusations [go away].

RH: One of your current projects is attempting to create a common narrative?

IP: A bridging narrative. This is a project I started with Palestinian friends in Ramallah in 1997, and we call it the bridging narrative group. We have 20 historians, 10 Israelis and 10 Palestinians who are trying to create a joint curriculum—an educational curriculum, and a joint textbook. First we located the areas of disagreement and then we started to work toward an agreed narrative. It is fascinating work because you think that politically, given that group, it would be very easy, but it is very difficult. Secondly, the divisions are not between Israelis and Palestinians but between positivist historians and relativist historians, nationalist ones and anationalist ones. There is a calling to national origin, which is very hopeful. You open these metanarratives and disintegrate them; then people recollect them differently than the day before.

RH: It creates a space in which rethinking can occur.

IP: Absolutely, in a very unpredictable way, but yes, definitely.

RH: Is it still a problem that for one cultural group the [1948] events were a matter of liberation and celebration, but for another group those events were a catastrophe? How do you bridge that?

IP: There we have had very considerable progress. The narrative of 1948 is a narrative of two very different wars. In the "real war," there were Israelis in isolated settlements who felt that the Arab world was trying to take over the state of Israel. Prior to that, there was the "phony war," the war of ethnic cleansing. In the Jewish collective memory, that part of that year [1948] would be a history of heroism. But it does not contradict the fact that while these heroic acts were taking place and Jewish national sentiments were so high that a state was created, something else also happened. We don't challenge the real war; we want to absorb it into a more complete picture.

RH: How do you think of your own work as an academic, activist, and initiator, someone who is working at bridging projects of various types? Would you accept the term of peacemaker?

IP: I'm not sure that it is useful; my work is much more fragmented, several things rather than just one thing—a dissenting voice that is missing in Israel. That is an important function. There is peacemaking and reconciliation. I think of myself as more of a facilitator between groups and people who think that they have nothing in common. I'm a constructive facilitator who shows people that their narratives, identities, and cultures are not that different; therefore, their future is not that different. They have similar problems in terms of who manipulates their lives.

RH: Would you consider yourself hopeful at this point?

IP: Hmmm. Again, it is a difficult question. It is kind of a Leninist approach on a good day, which is, "The worse it becomes, the better." I'm not hopeful for the short term. I'm very afraid and apprehensive about what is going to happen. But I have faith in the people who live there for the long term. I think that they will eventually overcome their politicians. They have the power to do that. Unfortunately, they will not discover this potential before more destruction and bloodshed is inflicted on them or they inflict it on someone else. But, in the long run, yes. I don't think that I could do what I'm doing if I had no hope at all.

RH: Nobody could have anticipated precisely the turning point in South Africa.

IP: Exactly. You never know how quickly in one case it will work and how slowly it will work in another, but it shows you that positive change is possible. You need inner resources for this. I don't think that you can take it from anyone else. You have to have it inside you. It is essential to meet other people who have similar feelings, but I don't think I work with people who are necessarily as hopeful as I am. You are alone in it, rather than lonely. You need inner strength. If you don't have it, nobody can give it to you.

RH: When I spoke with Gila Svirsky, she said she had changed over the years from a traditional Zionist to "being in the mold of the Hebrew prophets" and Israel's founding principles.

IP: You have to be careful not to castigate people. I am confident with the definition of an anti-Zionist, though I try not to use it very often because it really has a bad effect on people in Israel. For me it is clear that however you define Zionism, it is a disincentive for reconciliation and peace. But I can work with people like Gila. The tags are not important.

RH: A final question: within the American context, perhaps Europe, too, there is an overwhelming investment of energy for a just peace. How are you reading this energy?

IP: The energy is there. It is very clear. There are very good people in different sections of the civil societies in the West in particular who have had enough and are trying to find more effective ways of putting pressure on Israel. These energies are not grounded in any efficient structures yet. Secondly, this is the only way that we can bring about an end to the occupation. The diplomatic effort has failed. The armed struggle, whether one likes it or not, is a failed project as well. After 38 years, you can say it doesn't work. A just peace is the only nonviolent alternative. Thirdly, now that the Palestinian civil society under occupation has voiced a very clear support for this, it depends on the organizational skills. It depends on a political structure like the ANC had in South Africa, which we don't have. That is a very serious problem. It is going to be very difficult to push it forward without restructuring the Palestinian leadership.

And it depends on how the world deals with Israeli accusations of anti-Semitism. I've seen churches standing firm on their commitment. I don't think that anybody will be able to stop it. Will it help? We wish to create something similar to the anti-apartheid movement. I don't see any other way of doing it, but … it is very difficult to see where it is going at this stage.

RH: Over the last two years, there seems to be a rise in the Palestinian nonviolence movement.

IP: It is an essential part. This will be such a turning point in the history of the Palestinian resistance if they get international legitimacy for a nonviolent ideology, I would even say theology, because the Islamic movement is so deeply involved in the violent resistance. If the world says to the Palestinians, This is as good as the stones that you threw in the first *intifada*; this allows us not only to support you but also to stand firm against the accusation of anti-Semitism. People are waiting for nonviolent support to convince the young generation that there is an alternative to violence.

* * * * * * * *

Exeter, UK, May 2021 (via Zoom)

IP: There's something to be said for the passage of time. Much has changed in the way we look at history, Zionism, and the nature of Israel. A nice addendum ... would be to look at the way I and others have been thinking in the last 10 to 15 years. [Earlier] I did not tend to use the word colonialism, which I use now, because there's a change of paradigm.

RH: It's really important to see how your insights have changed.

IP: Three things have changed since our last [dialogue]—the political and ideological changes, our application of "settler colonialism" to Israel, and third, how the new perspectives on colonialism changed activism on the ground in and for Palestine. Regarding political developments.... I was aware that the Israeli political system was moving to the right. But I don't think we ever predicted the Netanyahu era....

RH: Would you call this primarily a will to power or primarily pragmatism?

IP: It's an obsessive will to power. He's like Trump. It's the same kind of obsessions. He convinces himself that he's saving Israel.... This political development has a few implications. It drives the message that there is no hope for change. If you care about changing the reality on the ground for the sake of justice, freedom, and reconciliation, you will have to do it on the outside. The Palestinians will have to lead the way on the inside.... The second implication is that the Palestinians are subject to even harsher policies of oppression [and] killings.... There is also a positive side to this approach. It harnesses the unity of the Palestinians further. It allows them to overcome previous factionalism and fragmentation.

And the last one.... until Netanyahu came to power, [liberals] could say, You can be a universalist, a liberal, even a leftist, and a Zionist in a very brittle way. Identifying with Israel now and the way Netanyahu developed makes it is very difficult to justify his sense of crisis. Among the younger generation of American, British, or Latin American Jews, you can see the beginnings of uneasiness.... How do you square your basic belief in a democracy and your support for the state of Israel? Some of them have changed from being in the Hillel organization to join the Soviet Jews for Justice, or Jewish Voice for Peace.

RH: It does feel like a new beginning for liberal Jews.

IP: In the last 10 or 15 years, I and others were reminded of an old idea ... put forward by Palestinian scholars in the '50s and '60s: it's important to distinguish between colonialism and settler colonialism.... Suddenly you saw people teaching and researching Israel within the studies of colonialism, imperialism, ethnic cleansing, even genocide studies, because of the settler colonialist movement, what Patrick Wolfe called "the logic of the elimination of the native."

In the long run, it undermines the scholarly scaffolding that Israeli academia provided to Israel over the years. It protected Israel from international scrutiny. We are at the end of an era.

Another paradigm [shift]—part of the third development—is how the world of activism and solidarity with the Palestinian people changed all around the world, but particularly in the U.S. Activists went further than the academics. They said, [Israel] is not just a settler colonial entity; it is also an apartheid state.... There is now a new identification and solidarity between oppressed groups, in domestic situations around the world. A strong example of this is the new tie between Black Lives Matter and Palestine.

RH: It's really fascinating. It comes from the ground up.

IP: It is also connected to ecology, which wasn't there in the '60s. We're facing something that is far worse than capitalism. There's new solidarity there. If I look at all these three issues together, we have to be aware of the gap ... between the clock of destruction on the ground and the much slower clock of ways of seeing on the more positive side. It behooves all of us to do even more; it's very clear. Palestinian politicians and leaders have to do much more in terms of unity and clear purpose for the future. Maybe we need to increase our pressure from the outside. Maybe the academics should be even more active in politics....

RH: As you know, President Biden is getting pressure from within the U.S. Congress, including Jewish senators. That seems new to me.

IP: We see pressure from society begin to tip into the political system. Bernie Sanders is also an example; a re-networking of international solidarity that connects oppressed minority groups around the world; and BDS. This kind of solidarity brings a lot of hope, and does not allow anyone to be forgotten.

RH: Are there other paths opening up that you think are efficacious, including ODSC?

IP: The ODS, a One Democratic State initiative, is one of many groups of people on the ground who think that the two-state solution is not going to work anymore.

RH: I agree.

IP: ... We are beginning to succeed in creating the dialogue we want with the Jewish society. Of course, not in great numbers. And there is the international community. We don't call it a movement. We don't represent anyone apart from ourselves. We are the initiators of a dialogue, of a discussion. We think this discussion should be led by the Palestinians, and should be offered also to Israeli Jews. Palestinians are beginning to talk about this—democratic movements, pluralist movements. They all have something in common. They want to decolonize the whole of Palestine.

RH: I've had many conversations with Jeff Halper about this. He is always frustrated. At least through 2016, he said there just is not sufficient Palestinian leadership.

IP: I have a different take on this. It's a fact of life that I'm not a Palestinian. And among young people, there is a lot of disdain toward organizations, movements, and parties. This is the world of the young people; they have a lot of mistrust toward hierarchies, toward organizations. They feel that if you are a party to this, the cause itself is being left out. On the other hand, it's impossible to do these things without some structure. It will take time. I think solidarity is waiting for the Palestinians to tell us what we can do for them, not telling them what they should do.

RH: Right.... Is there a genuine dialogue about the one-state campaign? At least within the groups that are talking with each other.

IP: Yes, yes. There is a dialogue. Like so many things on the Left, sometimes they hate each other more than they hate anyone else. [Both laugh.] The most important dialogue is with the people who represent the Palestinians right now and seem to stick to the two-state solution as if it is a religious idea, while they themselves know it isn't working.

RH: In 2014, as you know, the existing channels of dialogue seemed to dry up. Jeff Halper said not only did he not have any Palestinians to talk to, but he didn't have Jewish dialogue partners, either.

IP: I see very fruitful dialogue. There is concern for normalization, so people like myself and Jeff might not be invited to talk in Ramallah. I think the dialogue is really open. It is true, I don't have a clear referee. This is not easy. Even the most oppressed Palestinian has a referee. We don't have a referee. The Jewish society doesn't accept us; the Palestinian society doesn't see us as an organic part of them. So we decided to leave the zone of privilege. It is the price that we are willing to pay for doing this because we believe in what we do. Now is the time to look at the cause itself, and ask, What can I do more than ever before? I can be part of the joint activism. Sometimes it's easy; sometimes it's not very easy. But this is my mission in life; this makes my life meaningful.

RH: Thank you very much. It is always a privilege to talk with you.

IP: It's good to talk with you.

24 The Infrastructure of Hope

Mitri Raheb

Rev. Dr. Mitri Raheb served as pastor of Christmas Lutheran Church in Bethlehem for 30 years. For Palestinians, who contend with Israeli checkpoints and other forms of occupation on a daily basis, Raheb suggests that cultural forms, such as theatre, media, and music, are crucial for teaching people "how to breathe, how to survive." Refusing to see oneself as victim is also vital for survival. He is the author of many books. In 2006, he founded Dar al-Kalima University College of Arts and Culture to embody "the infrastructure of hope."

Bethlehem, June 2006

RH: It is good to see you again, Mitri. Tell me the many responsibilities you carry.

MR: I am senior pastor of Christmas Lutheran Church and the director of the International Center of Bethlehem.

RH: Explain various parts of the International Center.

MR: The International Center of Bethlehem is an outreach ministry of Christmas Lutheran Church. The idea started in 1995 when we said, We don't want to be spectators in this conflict and we don't want only to cater to our members. But for Christians, God is calling us to reach out to the society at large and to try to empower the people to become actors rather than spectators.

RH: Describe the Media Center and the other departments.

MR: The International Center of Bethlehem started very small 11 years ago—one room, eight chairs, one desk, and one old typewriter. This ministry has been growing for 11 years. We have now around 77 employees in the different departments. We have three main centers. First of all, we have a cultural and conference center which includes a state-of-the-art theatre where we have plays, concerts, international conferences, and local workshops. In the same compound we have a guesthouse with 13 rooms, a restaurant, and a coffee shop. We have a computer center and a media center. We do lots of training in [computer systems], in arts and crafts, ceramics, glass, mosaic, and jewelry. The computer section has 66 students, and in arts and crafts we have 88 students right now. With the

DOI: 10.4324/9781003262817-26

conservatory we have a joint music program with around 140 students coming in the afternoon to learn to play instruments. We have several projects in the Media Center. For example, one year ago we finished a DVD on the Wall around Bethlehem and its impact on the community.

RH: This is something I want you to talk about more.

MR: Another center, the Health and Wellness Center, has several clinics, including a psychotherapy clinic dealing with trauma. Now we are opening a metabolic clinic for diabetes, high blood pressure. The Wellness Center includes a swimming pool, rooms for exercise, yoga, and meditation. Part of it will be a park area with trees and flowers so that people can go and be in an environment that is green, that is colorful, playgrounds which the kids and young people can enjoy, and where the parents can relax. The last unit is the school with 264 kids right now—58% are Muslims and 42% are Christians. Altogether we serve 50,000 people every year.

RH: From a cultural or theological perspective, explain how all these ministries are linked for you, why they are important in the current context.

MR: We have a holistic approach to human beings. We are here to provide a holistic ministry for the spirit, the body, and the soul. It is very important for us to create our own "facts on the ground." As Palestinians, we don't want to feel comforted in the role of victim. Israel has been doing that for so long, and they try to pretend as if they have a monopoly on suffering, which allows them to inflict so much suffering on Palestinians. We don't want to become like the image of our oppressors, as our oppressors became like the image of their oppressors. For us it is really important to provide a sense of hope. This is why, in all of our projects, creating infrastructure is very important—schools, an auditorium, conference center, guesthouse, and park. All of this creates something constructive in a context where everything around us is very destructive.

RH: North Americans who only see mainstream television have no understanding of what things are like here. Stereotypes still persist. What are the primary traumas which oppress people here?

MR: I think it was Johns Hopkins University that did a study which showed that over 80% of the Palestinian people have some kind of traumatization.

RH: Eighty percent?

MR: Eighty-two percent, I think. Life here is not easy at all. For example, right now in Bethlehem the Israelis are building this Wall. Once it's completed it will go 35 miles around the city. It is 25 feet high. I think Israelis are competing for the Guinness record to have the highest number of open-air prisons in the world, because each of our cities will be a kind of prison. The West Bank is being transformed as we speak into something like a Swiss cheese, where Israel gets the cheese that is the land, and the Palestinians are pushed into the holes. Bethlehem will be such a hole. In terms of freedom of movement, it is very, very difficult. For the last eight years, I haven't had any permit to go and visit Jerusalem, although it is just five miles away from Bethlehem. Really, you cannot plan anything in this country because things might just get out of control. This is why many people emigrate. They say, Why should we stay here? Each year you think things will become a bit better, and the fact is, they are becoming worse. It is really not easy.

RH: So the different ministries within the church all address some of aspect of human need, whether it is dance, theatre, cultural events, medical needs, or physiological needs?

MR: Exactly. We try to plan something which will really make a difference in terms of the needs in our society—for young adults who have studied abroad, to come back and to want to live here.

RH: You did your graduate work in Germany, so you are familiar with [Holocaust history] as well as the situation here [in Bethlehem]. As a pastor, can you analyze the important dynamic of victims becoming victimizers—or traumatized people becoming insensitive to the suffering of others—and perhaps learning the wrong lessons? For individuals there is therapy. How do you address a whole culture that has been traumatized, whether Israeli or Palestinian culture?

MR: It is clear that people who have been persecuted often become persecutors themselves. Although people hate their oppressors, sometimes they fall in love with them because there is some kind of admiration. This is what happened with the Israelis regarding Nazi Germany. And I think this is what's happening to Palestinians regarding Israel. To know about it is difficult, but to see it in practice is even worse. It is very important that we do not understand ourselves as mere victims. We are victims, yes, but we are much more than victims. This is why it is important that we become proactive actors. If you feel you are a victim, you feel you are an object and other people are making decisions for you.

RH: You feel that they have power; I have no power.

MR: Exactly. So for us it is very important to change this kind of thinking; and this is why our center is something unusual. We emphasize how Palestine should and could look 10 years down the road, if there is real faith and the right management of resources.

RH: How many programs do you have that work explicitly with conflict resolution, nonviolence training, or justice awareness as part of bringing about that vision for Palestine?

MR: Most of our programs have that [focus]. For example, in the arts and crafts, our students went out to look for the broken pieces of glass that the Israeli invasion left in Bethlehem. They transformed these pieces into art pieces that talk about celebrating life in the midst of death. This is our ministry—to transform the lives of those who feel broken into something that is whole.

Think of our summer academy. This year we had over 550 applications and we were able to take a maximum of 350. We have 350 kids coming five days a week, five hours a day, learning karate, which is really self-defense, doing painting on human-rights issues, and learning how to do theatre. Sports are very important in a context where our young people under 17 years old are over 55% of the population. Kids paint and comment on human-rights issues. The bulk of our work is geared toward this goal.

RH: It is inevitable because people are working out of their lived experience?

MR: Yes, exactly. And we help them to process it.

RH: So it becomes both therapeutic and artistic at the same time?

MR: Exactly, exactly. Therapy is important but also creativity is important, because Palestine doesn't have any resources, such as oil. We don't have lots of land for agriculture, so the only thing we have is the human brain and human resources. Unless we upgrade those resources, we will not have any future.

RH: So is there an adaptation process or a transformation process—traditional forms combined with European forms? Has there been an indigenous theatre movement for a century or more?

MR: No, not a century, but I would say for the last 40 years.

RH: Adapting European models or creating really indigenous forms of theatre?

MR: I wouldn't call this an Oriental form of theatre. I don't think so. They are adapting but also working on [new works].... Next Wednesday, we have the next theatre performance. There might be a translation. It has to do with women's issues.

RH: Since I did graduate work in theatre and film, I am deeply interested in everything that comes from Ramallah [and from here].... I have seen your theatre space. It's spectacular. Tell me about the conference on narrative, because clearly the work that I am doing is centered in people telling stories about their own lives. In my earlier Nakba project, I adapted oral history narratives for a theatre performance.

MR: Right, I actually saw it one time.

RH: It's a very simple technique, and can be done anywhere. People asked, Where did you come up with this experimental technique? I said, this is very traditional, the storyteller speaking to the community.... I assume that the conference on narrative came from your imagination?

MR: The problem is that there are basically two main narratives in this country.

RH: Competing narratives?

MR: I am not talking so much about the Palestinian narrative and the Israeli narrative, but even within each, you have to outline those. On the one hand, you have a narrative of land, people, and nationhood as one narrative—you have one land and one people, and they are a nation. And you have the other narrative of land, people, and God in one unity. This is really the narrative of the two national movements—Zionism and Palestinian nationalism. And on the other hand, you have a religious, fundamentalistic approach which you find in Israel, Palestine, and the U.S.

RH: I am very familiar with that.

MR: It's important to see that we should be talking about land, people, and identities, multiple identities. We are not really dealing with facts and claims but with narratives, perceptions, and perspectives. There are multiple identities evolving. Unless we see it in this way, we will be very simplistic and fundamentalist in our understanding. It could be nationalist or it could be religious, but in the end it's the same.

RH: Because they get combined in really powerful ways that don't allow for pragmatic moves or compromise or dealing with the current situation.

MR: Exactly. This is the most difficult thing—if you blend nationalism with religion.

RH: It leaves no room for negotiation.

MR: No, it doesn't. And unfortunately, this is what is happening in many places.

RH: Both within Israel and in Palestine?

MR: Yes. Even within the United States.

RH: Talk about struggling with these narrative paradigms and the implications for creating a just peace.

MR: If you understand that these are narratives, then we are not talking about national or religious claims. One [should] start asking, Why is this narrative so important? Then you start looking into the context. How is the context shifting, and when it shifts, why is the identity changing? So it becomes very dynamic, which means that the future is very much open. Our identity is not set once and for all. Like Paul said in First Corinthians, "We don't know yet."

RH: "We don't know yet what we will be …"

MR: Exactly. We don't know what we will be, which means it's open. So there is movement because you can think of something which is not there yet, so it gives you a different perspective.

RH: This has profound implications for conflict transformation. A fundamentalistic [or nationalist] approach says our identity is complete; we have to [defend] it.

MR: Exactly. Our identity is here and the other identity is there, and you have a clash. But these narratives—and within each group there are different narratives—are always changing, ever-changing. So [the situation] is dynamic and political.

RH: What are the practical implications of the understanding of the narrative situation in terms of programming, in terms of what you do on a daily basis or as an organizational structure?

MR: For us it is very important to help our people articulate their story. Again, not as victims, because in Palestine we always see what Israel is doing to us.

RH: It's a temptation because the occupation is so overwhelming.

MR: It's overwhelming. It's good that some people are [telling victim stories]. But for me, it is so much more important to think, Who am I and what do we want? Where do we want to be 10 years down the road? Where do we want to be 100 years down the road? And this is why we are not interested in most projects, in producing paper tigers, but producing infrastructure which will help people find jobs, become creative, see that they can make a difference in the life of people around them. They can be [more than] a number; a somebody, a someone.

We want to invest in creativity and beauty to show the potential of our country. One of the biggest problems here is that our narrative is becoming so much a narrative of the victim. People are forgetting who we are and what the options are for us. So here, you can see [our vision] in terms of infrastructure and also in terms of the staff we have, including dynamic, very well educated, articulate women. We try to set a model of how the whole liberation should and could look. Basically we are trying to provide a model of what is to come. A model of the kingdom [of God]. And this is something totally different than to be absorbed with all the craziness around us.

RH: Apparently there was a great deal of surprise even for Hamas when they won the election. To the extent that Hamas is anchored in the kind of narrative that you find problematic, how do you work with the new reality? What sort of dialogue do you have for working with the people who were elected democratically and work at a different narrative than the kind of narrative that you think is crucial for opening up the future?

MR: First of all, one has to realize that Hamas doesn't have one narrative but several narratives. Once you expose that, that is already a very important starting point. Hamas is not so much about theology and dogma as people might think. For example, 10 years ago when we had our first legislative elections, Hamas said, We will not participate in the elections. If they would have participated, they might have gotten 15% of the votes. This would have showed them being a very weak party, on the periphery. This year they were sure that they would be getting at least 30%. They still were thinking that Fatah had a bigger [vote]. So 10 years ago they found a verse in the Quran saying, Don't go to vote. This year they found another verse saying, Go to vote. So it's not about theology; it's about something else, pragmatism. Once you expose this, then Hamas doesn't become so [problematic].

RH: It's not monolithic.

MR: No. There are lots of possibilities for a dialogue, because within Hamas there is a big dialogue going on. And the question at the end is, Who will win in the dialogue? Which narrative within the Hamas narrative [will win]?

RH: It's not unlike the diversity within Israeli society. Unfortunately, the progressive narrative hasn't won out yet at this point.

MR: No, and I have to say it will not win out as long as outside forces are interfering.

RH: And where does that come from?

MR: It comes from the U.S. on the one hand, and from Arab countries on the other. Basically this [U.S.] Administration doesn't have any clue of how society is formed. Look what is happening in Iraq, in Palestine, in Lebanon. They don't know what they are doing. Or if they know, then …

RH: Then it's criminal. So, what's the next project? What are the next steps? How will you follow up on the conference on narrative?

MR: We said during the last conference that for the coming 10 years we will work on this topic [of narratives] with some different perspectives.

RH: This [focus on narrative] is really crucial because it gets at the infrastructure of consciousness, the paradigm out of which we work individually and collectively, and whether we are working in a way that provides freedom toward the future or closes it up. I don't hear of many people doing this work.

MR: No, it's a new approach. I think also it's part of a disciplinary [problem] because usually each discipline in itself is stuck. So, we are trying to bring together different disciplines—theology, anthropology, sociology, and so on.

RH: There isn't a single discipline that deals with a complex situation like this.

MR: Exactly. One of the most impressive things at the first conference was a professor from Germany who did a one-woman show. She read the story of Jericho, not from the perspective of Joshua, but from the perspective of a young girl in Gaza who was killed when the walls came down. That was very moving. We would like to encourage theatre and audiovisual productions. Our biggest project is starting a college that will focus on the arts, multimedia, communication, and tourism-related studies. We are offering two-year degrees now, and maybe soon, a four-year degree. This year we are offering documentary filmmaking.

RH: That's a good place to begin. It is not terribly expensive, and with new [digital] cameras you can do amazing work. You can put the camera under your shirt and go through a checkpoint.

MR: We did that, actually. Hopefully we will offer degrees in theatre in two years.

RH: Were you always interested in the arts as a young person?

MR: No, actually I was not. It came [along] the way. Culture is important for people who live under oppression and occupation. Previously, people were thinking that the Israeli-Palestinian conflict is like a 100-meter sprint. During the 100 meters, you have to have full power. But what if the Israeli-Palestinian conflict is more like a marathon of 30 miles? Then you have to learn different techniques, even how to breathe. Otherwise you will kill yourself. We think that culture teaches people how to breathe, how to survive, and how to control oneself in order to reach the goal and not die on the way.

* * * * * * * *

Bethlehem, April 2018

RH: Hello again, Mitri. Tell me where you were born and what your family circumstances were.

MR: I was born in Bethlehem. My family has been living in Bethlehem for centuries.

RH: How far back can you go?

MR: There are written documents beyond the Middle Ages.

RH: Most people can't go back three or four generations. And was your family involved in the church? Was your father a pastor?

MR: No, he wasn't a pastor. He was a businessman, and my mother worked at social-relief organizations and worked for the blind. I don't have anyone in my family who was a pastor. Maybe way, way back, because our name, Raheb, means monk.

RH: What drew you into the church, into ministry?

MR: My father and my mother were connected with the church, maybe my mother more than my father, but it was the youth work that drew me into the church. As a teenager I was looking around to see which church was responding to the questions of the youth at the time.

RH: This would have been the 1980s?

MR: Mid-1970s. I went church-shopping. I looked at five, six, seven churches, got involved for a few months in each one of them, and ended in the church where my family were members. It was the youth work that drew me in, and it's the youth work that also drew me to study theology, because at that time none of the churches had adequate answers to the questions of the young people. At that time we were studying the relation of science and faith, which today is no longer that hot, but back in the '70s that was the topic we were struggling with.

RH: It's not particularly a problem or a challenge anymore?

MR: Not anymore, because I see science and religion both as dynamic, and nothing is set in stone. What we know in religion is not the last answer, and what we know from science—everything is contextual.

RH: You did an undergraduate degree—here or in Germany?

MR: I did both my master's degree and doctoral work in Germany.

RH: The Lutheran Church association was strong.

MR: I got a fellowship from the Lutheran World Federation. I wanted to choose what to study and where to study. I chose theology and I chose Germany.

RH: Tell me about several of the changes that you've gone through in the last two years. Is it mostly just leadership reassignments, or more major than that?

MR: Three years ago, I decided I'm going to step down from being senior pastor at Christmas Lutheran Church, because I'm doing three jobs at the same time. And we get older all the time. I said, I cannot do justice to all three; I had to give up something. I thought that after being 30 years at Christmas Lutheran Church, it was time to step down from there. I was looking for a successor, to train him, and then to hand that ministry over, so that I can concentrate on two things: college [administration] and international speaking.

RH: Tell me about your achievements. Two years ago, you gave me your annual report from the year before. It was quite impressive.

MR: I am focused on the college. We keep expanding. Last year we opened the newest building which is a new library.

RH: I was there when it was in progress.

MR: Now it's finished and open; a great building. So we keep working on accrediting new programs. Right now we have seven bachelor's programs, nine associates degrees, two special diplomas and two special continuing education certificates. Basically we have 20 programs.

RH: That's a lot.

MR: Yes, that's a lot.

RH: Who accredits your programs? A local body, or an international body?

MR: It's a local Palestinian national body.

RH: And how many students do you have?

MR: We have exactly 500 right now. We also have several initiatives. One initiative is reaching out to a new generation of Christian academic leaders at Middle Eastern universities, who are together at research conferences [asking] what would be a wider way that Christians in the Middle East [can address] everything that's going on.

RH: Do you see that as just Palestinian or broader?

MR: This is regional—Egypt, Iran, Syria, Jordan, Iraq, and Palestine, at this time. We started an initiative last year, which is eventually to create a network between Christian theological faculties and Muslim sharia theological faculties in the Arab world; right now we have 18 faculties to work on new curricula and curricular reform to combat religious fundamentalism.

RH: Two weeks ago I went to a dialogue between Naim Ateek and an American rabbi about liberation theology. I'm curious about the extent to which that is part of your work.

MR: I don't call it liberation theology, but contextual theology is what I'm doing. Definitely.

RH: It was very interesting; I'd gone to a similar conversation between those same two people about two years ago and was surprised when the rabbi said, "In our weekly services, we don't read the prophets. We read the Torah," which is much more nationalistic and even genocidal in some places. That was just stunning to me. I'm less familiar with liberation in the Islamic faith.

MR: There are Muslim liberation theologians, definitely.

RH: Can you name a couple?

MR: The most famous is Farid Isaac. He's a South African Muslim of Indian background. He has written extensively about that. I think he has a book about Islamic liberation theology.

RH: Excellent. So people are working at it.

MR: Yes.

RH: The first time we had this sort of conversation, you told me that you decided a long time ago that your project would not be political; that it would be much more spiritual. Can you fill that out for me? In my own mind it seems difficult to separate them.

MR: It is political in the sense of caring for the polis; it's political in the sense that you have to do political analysis. But it's not driven by party politics. I don't belong to any political party and I never will.

RH: At the end of the second *intifada*, Jeff Halper lamented that there's not enough strategic thinking going on, especially in Palestinian communities. He said, "We Israelis can't lead." Can one be strategic without necessarily getting caught up in the machinery of politics? Is there a connection between liberation theology and identifying some kind of end goal or solution?

MR: I guess yes; the problem here is twofold. One, the situation is always volatile and changing all the time. When you do strategy, are you doing long-term analysis and are you thinking what are the chances that outside forces will intervene? You can more or less control the internal things. A second is that we have so many players in the game; some are Israeli and some are Palestinian, but you also have the whole international community, neighboring countries, Arab countries, and everything is shifting quickly. Even a strategy is out of date quickly.

RH: So many things happen that are totally out of your control.

MR: Right. I think the only two strategies that I see are de-facto strategies. One is for the Israelis; they can accept killing the two-state solution and go toward an apartheid system. I think that is their strategy. The Palestinian strategy is *sumud*, or steadfastness. We are not going to emigrate; we are here to stay; we continue to survive as much as possible, and this is our strategy. I think these are the two de-facto strategies

RH: *Sumud* is really central, isn't it?

MR: Yes. I think this is its function. This is one thing that definitely functions.

RH: When you're talking to North Americans, how do you define that for them?

MR: The best description in English is resilience.

RH: I like resilience, because it seems active, participatory.

MR: Yeah, I also like resilience more.

RH: In terms of your own work, would it be fair to say that education is also a central strategy?

MR: Not education per se, but it's what kind of education. We focus on arts and culture, because this is what we need to educate the new generation of creative leaders for Palestine.

RH: Yes, the storytelling in all of its forms is absolutely necessary.

MR: Absolutely. Film, drama, music—these are new, important, creative communication tools to communicate our story. If I tell it the old political way, I go there and give a political lecture.

RH: It has to be creative and excellent.

MR: And human.

RH: Not just true; it has to be human. I remember years ago you told me, It enhances the capacity for people to breathe. A very nice phrase.

MR: Yes, exactly.

RH: Another elegant phrase of yours is your idea of the infrastructure of hope. Building something that you can see and it has principles and people—that's the infrastructure part.

MR: That's important, because people in Palestine especially need to see functioning [models]. There are so many dysfunctional models on the political side, on many sides. They need to see Palestinian inventions in spite of all the difficulties. And not just talk; they are fed up with talk.

RH: They need role models so they can say, "We Palestinians can do things. We can achieve."

MR: Exactly. And not something that is short-lived, but something that has a long duration—

RH: Institutional depth.

MR: Exactly.

RH: The dialogues that you participate in, are they primarily within Palestinian communities, or is there a calling for some people to work with Israelis like Jeff Halper or Ilan Pappe? They are among some of the most [dedicated] people I know in terms of their commitment to justice and fairness. How do you see the role of dialogue? Where is it meaningful or possible?

MR: I think all dialogue is somehow good. But you cannot do everything. You have to choose your focus. We chose to focus on the intra-dialogue. And not necessarily Christian-Muslim interfaith dialogue.

I was one of the founders of an initiative back in the '80s, but I think now it's a cultural challenge: what is the Palestine that we envision? And what kind of future leaders do we need? What about the role of women? What about the role of law and social justice? What about the form of government? It's these issues that we decided to focus on in dialogues.

RH: In terms of an endgame, what do you hope Palestine will become?

MR: Our vision of Palestine is already what we have embodied through the college. It's an open space. It's a space for creativity.

RH: Does it include both sets of people?

MR: Oh yeah.

RH: Jeff tells me that there are still some Palestinians who say, "We like the Algerian model. We need to push out the people who have oppressed us."

MR: No. At the end of the day, there are three religions here. They have to learn how to live together. It's not acceptable for one religion to have more rights and other religions fewer rights.

RH: For a long time, the general [peacemaking] formula was land for peace. Have Palestinian communities shifted to the struggle for human rights rather than land for peace?

MR: I don't think so. It's not enough; there are national rights. So human rights alone is not working. But a rights-based approach is what many Palestinians would choose.

RH: Based on international law. But no American president, including Obama, really worked for human rights and justice in Palestine.

MR: Some tried. I think John Kerry, under Obama, was serious. Clinton tried and James Baker. So there are a few people, but the Israelis have just preempted all these efforts.

RH: What's going to break through—a kairos moment, a miracle, or an implosion?

MR: I don't see breakthrough in the short run. Sometimes, it's the darkest hour just before the dawn. The Israeli government and society have become so entrenched in their arrogance that they have become racist, and they are proud of being racist. This is a good recipe for the end.

RH: It's not sustainable.

MR: No, it's not sustainable.

RH: Then what do you prefer to happen—two states, some form of one state or a one-state process? Lots of intellectuals are saying that the two-state solution is dead.

MR: Yeah. It's true that ... it's too late for a two-state solution. The problem is, it's too early for a one-state solution. We are in that limbo; that's the danger of it.

RH: That is a dangerous place.

MR: Exactly. So [we are] living with a system of oppression, comprised of three tools—the walls that Israel copied from eastern Germany;

apartheid, copied from South Africa; and the Indian reservations, copied from the U.S. This unholy trinity they are cooking together. This is a three-in-one. [But] it's not sustainable. I don't know when the egg will break. Once it breaks, we will see what kind of new solution will come out, maybe a two-in-one formula, a bit like British and French Canada—

RH: Switzerland, maybe?

MR: Switzerland is another route. I think two in one might be roughly what we'll end up with.

RH: And how do you sustain your own hope?

MR: By being around students who are creative and innovative. They keep me going.

RH: Thank you so much.

MR: I'm most grateful.

25 Work for the Common Good

Estephan Salameh

Estephan Salameh is called to public service, including mid-level, nongovernmental projects, government responsibilities, and grassroots work. The first dialogue occurred soon after the 2014 Israeli-Hamas war ended, while he was no longer working for the Palestinian Authority, and while he was teaching at Birzeit University. The second dialogue occurred in 2018, after Salameh resigned as a senior advisor to the Palestinian prime minister. In 2019, the current prime minister asked Salameh to serve as the senior advisor for planning and aid coordination. For Salameh, all these efforts are "for the common good."

East Jerusalem, August 2014

RH: Estephan, it's good to see you again. Among the people working for peace and justice here, there's a consensus that without getting rid of the occupation, nothing else is very possible.

ES: True. Most people believe that development or even improving the life of people under occupation is unsustainable. At the individual and household levels, people are worried like everywhere else in the world. All of a sudden, we have enough funding, and the banks are giving a lot of loans. So, everybody is taking loans and worrying about how they can secure jobs [and] pay off loans. In other words, Palestinian interests are changing.... The financial burden of the people has taken priority over resistance....

RH: They find ways to negotiate this burden.

ES: Yeah. There is enough outside funding, which creates less urgency to resist the occupation.

RH: They're not going to the streets.

ES: Much less than before. They say, "If we go to the streets, there is a lot to lose now." In the first *intifada*, it was different; people didn't feel like they had much to lose. Although people were only making enough to survive, they felt they were fighting for something that deserved the sacrifice. But now, some are feeling comfortable under occupation.

RH: In the West Bank?

DOI: 10.4324/9781003262817-27

ES: Especially in the West Bank….

RH: Rabbi Arik Ascherman was talking to me today about Jewish trauma from the Holocaust. If [it lingers] for Jewish children, then it will likely be true for Palestinian children as well.

ES: Oh, yeah. We have a whole generation that probably has stress disorders. I have friends in Gaza that tell me their children, if a door slams, they start crying, and they don't sleep at night. That level of bombing is affecting everybody…. Entire families were just annihilated.

RH: I know a medical doctor, Mona El-Farra, doing development work [in Gaza]. She sent an email letter to friends, saying she lost nine family members in one day.

ES: As a result of the last war, there are around 1,400 orphans who lost both parents. It's huge. We have over 10,000 injured, 2,100 killed, over 100,000 houses were damaged, and 12,000 houses were destroyed completely.

RH: … I can't imagine that anyone can beat the Israelis with military power.

ES: Maybe not, but not everyone believes that….

RH: So why not think of some [other strategy]?

ES: Exactly. I'm like you, I reject violence in principle. I also reject violence because it doesn't make sense, especially in our case. Israel has one of the strongest militaries in the world.

RH: … I've been asking people if military victory isn't possible and the Israelis are determined not to yield anything—not two states, not one state—does that leave only apartheid?

ES: Unfortunately, it looks like this is the direction we are going.

RH: Easy political solutions don't seem available. So, how do you bring about some kind of transformation in which fear subsides and it is offset by trust? Everybody I talk to says that this [war] in Gaza set [peace] back five or 10 years, but prospects weren't good before that.

ES: I'll tell you, Bob, for years the world has been focusing on the Palestinian people, thinking we've got to tame them so we can create the right environment for peace. But they ignored the Israelis. Sadly, the Israelis have been turning more violent and more radical.

RH: Other people have been saying the same thing to me.

ES: The things we have been seeing are unprecedented. It wasn't like this 20 years ago. Now the level of prejudice inside the Israeli society is very alarming. The hate is especially among settlers…. The Israeli government has incited violence, and the Israeli educational system is not contributing to peace and coexistence. This is why nonviolent solutions, which take many forms, could be much more effective than any other forms of resistance. The international community could go to the Israeli society and educate them about accepting Palestinians.

RH: But that assumes that they want to change the situation.

ES: They feel no urgency to change the situation on the ground.

RH: The current [Israeli] administration doesn't want a just peace.

ES: I'm not sure they are even interested in ending the conflict.

RH: At the very least, they could stop settlement building ... but they have no interest in that.

ES: No, not at all. However, another effective form of nonviolence is the boycott. One of the effects of the Gaza War is that Palestinians have decided to boycott Israeli properties. They have been using the motto, "Don't fund the military that kills our children."

RH: Maybe that would get the Israeli attention even more than rockets.

ES: Right; the economy is always effective. And we are probably the biggest or second biggest importers of Israeli products. We import almost $5 billion a year. That's huge.

RH: And if Europe would start to boycott, that combination would be very effective.

ES: Of course. It's far from happening in the West, although the European Union is taking some modest steps in that direction.

RH: It's something that everyone can do.

ES: Everyone can do it, absolutely.

RH: And it's easy; you don't have to go to the streets; you can do it privately.

ES: I see it now. Businesses don't buy Israeli products. Grocery stores in Ramallah cleaned out all of the Israeli products. Imports have gone down 50% already over the past two months. That form of nonviolence is legitimate; it was used in other places and was effective, [along with] boycotts, and other forms of nonviolence, peaceful demonstrations, education, and mobilizing international solidarity. We have seen significant changes over the past three or four years. Especially after the recognition of Palestine as a non-member state in the UN. That form of nonviolence could be expanded.... If you want to continue the negotiation, that's fine; but don't make it the only way of resisting the occupation. You've got to have other, nonviolent ways.

RH: Last night on the Mount of Olives, a UN deputy director said the UN still supports a two-state solution. I said, Most of the people I'm talking to say that Israel killed the two-state solution long ago, but [Palestinians] haven't quite given that up. I'm surprised the UN keeps using those terms.

ES: I was a longtime supporter of the two-state solution. However, the two-state solution is losing momentum and is approaching death rapidly.

RH: They're not going to reverse the settlements.

ES: It's not likely, ... not without serious international pressure. I put that in one of my articles—six or seven steps that the PA could take to change their strategy from a two-state solution to a one-state solution, including calling for equal rights for everyone.

RH: Which everybody in the world can understand.

ES: I believe so.... I always thought that for the two-state solution, everybody thinks that Palestinians want to take something from Israel. But in a one-state solution, you're asking for your rights. Americans could relate to that....

RH: Jeff Halper has said that for years.... Last Sunday, he seemed very discouraged. He said [after Israel's] latest fight with Gaza, his Palestinian friends won't talk to him. People in the peace movement won't talk strategy with him. He said, "We have slid back five years." He feels really isolated. He doesn't have conversation partners.

ES: It's unfortunate.... Communication between the two peace camps is necessary....

RH: Creative minorities typically change things, and the majority eventually has to ratify things. But creative, smaller groups initiate change.

ES: They make change, absolutely.... Are you going to Aida Refugee Camp on Saturday? We partnered with Abdelfattah Abusrour to put our last library there. He uses drama as a form of resistance. He has an organization called Al-Rowwad. He calls their work "beautiful resistance."

RH: If I don't go there this time, I'll go there next time.... You're teaching at Birzeit University?

ES: I teach at Birzeit and I do a lot of consulting. We are developing a new school of government.... This school is going to be very challenging and very good. As for the Seraj Library Project, both my wife and I are volunteers. In nine years, we are close to finishing the seventh library.

RH: How did you discover that the need was so great?

ES: There are no public libraries in the villages, and we have hundreds of villages in the West Bank. People contact us. We have a waiting list, and we try to do one or two libraries every year.

RH: Once you start a library, do you have independent boards or leadership?

ES: We partner with a local organization. We provide them with everything they need, and they run it. Now we have an advisory board for all the libraries. Laurie and I have a lot on our plates, so we do it on a voluntary basis. We have a wonderful board in the U.S. You know most of them.

RH: Give me examples of whom you would consult with. Mostly nonprofits?

ES: No, I consult with a wide range of organizations, including the government, international organizations, UN organizations, and, of course, nonprofits.

RH: And who sets the priorities in the Palestinian government?

ES: The minister of planning, together with aligned ministries and agencies. That's why this job was very demanding. Aligning donor funding with national priorities is much harder than people imagine. A lot of politics is involved....

RH: Everybody has a different set of expectations?

ES: And agendas. It is always challenging but rewarding....

RH: In this book, I argue that the Israeli government can't or won't create a just peace, and that NGOs and civil-society will have to create and lead this transformation for a just peace.... The vanguard will be [nongovernmental] peacemakers and mid-level leaders....

ES: Interesting. I share with you this point of view. In Palestine, we have some of the most active civil society organizations, even in comparison to the rest of the Arab region. Their role is even more important [since] Palestine doesn't have a functioning parliament. After the general election of 2006, Israel arrested one-third of the parliament members. Add to that the split between the West Bank and Gaza in 2007; the parliament is completely paralyzed.

RH: Do they still meet sometimes?

ES: In the absence of a legislative council, which is supposed to monitor the executive branch, who [provides] checks and balances? The role of civil society in Palestine is even more important than in other places.

RH: Which means your new program [at Birzeit] is very much needed. Hanan Ashrawi said to me, "We get much pressure to either work on peacemaking or to build civil society. We have to do both at the same time. We can't afford to do only one." She moves back and forth between civil society and having official roles in the government.

ES: Now she's on the executive committee of the PLO, the highest committee in the Palestinian political system.

RH: Hanan Ashrawi has had an amazing life. Did you have a chance to work with her?

ES: No. My brother did; when she was the minister of higher education, he was in the ministry working with her.... I'm on the board for Sabeel and two other nonprofit organizations. My volunteer work is equivalent to my full-time job. It's a way to give back to the community.

RH: Those are important things to do.

ES: Sabeel and Seraj are taking most of my time for voluntary work. Sabeel is going through a transition and I'm on the new board.... I believe we have 10 Friends of Sabeel organizations, and the most active ones are in the U.K., the U.S., and Canada.

RH: So far [the strategy] has been mostly educational, right? Raising awareness.

ES: I urge them to do more. It has unrealized potential, especially for lobbying and advocacy.

RH: You mean lobbying Congress, in Washington?

ES: Actually, I pushed them to do more work at the state level in the U.S. The national level is pretty much controlled by the Israel lobby. At the local level, we have a better chance....

RH: What gives you the most hope?

ES: Palestinian resilience ... children going to school under fire, crossing checkpoints, and mothers trying to provide for the well-being of their families, despite the hardships of the occupation. This is what gives me hope.

* * * * * * * * *

Chicago, July 2018

RH: What are some of the key events that brought you into the kind of work that you do?

ES: In 1948, my dad was 12 years old. His family lived in Jaffa and in Jifna [near Ramallah]. Family members had taxis and a bus, and they used to commute. When the war happened, he was in Jaffa. They had to walk all the way to Jerusalem and then from there to the family in Jifna.

RH: That's a difficult walk; it's very mountainous.

ES: Yes. It took a few days. It's wartime, so along the way there were people walking, escaping.

RH: Did the family own property in Jifna?

ES: Yes. We owned a big house for the whole family in Jifna. It's a big, beautiful house. It was [for] my grandfather and two of his brothers as well.

RH: They were commuting to Jaffa for work?

ES: For work. Mostly they were in the car business, like a dealership.... But my family comes from Jaffa. Our house is still there. So, every time we go to Jaffa, we stop by the house. When we were children, my dad used to take us to see the house. There used to be a Greek family living on the first floor. I remember going inside once. They offered us coffee. My dad told them the story. And now I take my children. I show them the house and tell them the story. We came from a Catholic Christian background, with pacifist teachings. We repeat Dad's phrase, "We have to forgive, but we cannot forget." So we have tell the story. We hope that at some point people will come to apologize for the injustice that has happened to so many families. Facing this requires a lot of courage from the people in Israel. The government of Israel has to say, We also did wrong.... That links who you are as people. Whether you are the occupier or the occupied, it affects who you are as a human being. So, my family ended up in Jifna.

RH: Did they keep selling cars?

ES: No; that's something my dad talks about—the loss of the house in Jaffa, but also the cars. Basically they lost them. At that time, my family was wealthy.

RH: This was a transportation business?

ES: Yeah, to go to Gaza, Jerusalem, and Jifna. My dad was a boy. He tells me, "This house was for our family. This is where we used to play." He remembers the neighbors, every house. The biggest loss for him is the emotional loss—the attachment to the place and the property, but also attachments to the people. He never saw them again. It's very sad.

RH: Was that a change in identity from wealth to moving away? Those are huge losses.

ES: Huge. When he talks about it, yes, but he steers the conversation to talking about people more than the money and the property. Indeed, they had to start over. His father refused—and my dad, too—to register as a refugee. We are refugees, in a way, but we are not registered as refugees—out of pride. Funny enough, later on my dad worked for UNRWA, the agency providing support to Palestinian refugees. We became Jerusalem ID holders.

RH: Where's the emotional core for him? The loss of relationships?

ES: Finding himself out of place—where he grew up, the loss of people—Israelis captured 78% of the land. Almost 90% of the population at that time became refugees and scattered. It was a complete change. The loss of people and property, the loss of identity, who we are—what we were before is not what we are right now. That puzzle that looked like a beautiful picture with a 1,000 pieces—all of sudden, somebody comes and throws these pieces around. There is no way you can put this puzzle back together the way it was. For my dad, it felt [like] a complete loss of this whole picture—who he is, who he was as a person and part of a family, and who he became. Every time he talks about it, it's an emotional event.

When I was 12, because of the family connection to the church in Jifna, I wanted to become a Catholic priest. I went to a Catholic seminary near Bethlehem for four years. This experience changed who I am forever and planted in me the life of a public servant.

RH: Do you remember why you wanted to become a priest?

ES: We were very devout; we loved the church; we were very, very committed. We were part of the children's group and the youth group—any group that existed.

RH: I've been to your church; it's a beautiful church.

ES: I was in the school in Jifna and a priest came, telling the students about the seminary [in Beit Jala] and about becoming priests. I got excited. I went home and I told them that I wanted to be a priest. My parents expected it, but it was tragic. I was a child, incapable of making that decision. [But] they respected my decision. It was in 1987, the year the first *intifada* started.

RH: And that was a really active area, too—Beit Jala, Bethlehem and Beit Sahour.

ES: I decided to go, but I was very emotional. I was a child, away from my family. I stayed there for four years, the years of the first *intifada.* The first *intifada* was run by people my age.

RH: Yeah. It was very grassroots and community-based.

ES: Everybody was involved: children, young people, mothers, elderly, everybody. But people my age were the most affected. When I left the seminary, the reality of the first *intifada* was a big shock. That was the first time Israeli soldiers came into our house in the middle of the night. My brother was a student at Bir Zeit University. Soldiers came to the house around 3:00 a.m., and knocked with their rifles on every door and window in the house. This was absolutely the scariest moment I had ever experienced in my whole life. They came in. They knew where my brother was sleeping. They took him outside barefoot. My mom was crying; my sisters were crying. My dad followed them, barefoot as well, begging the soldiers to keep him in the house. My brother wore a jacket with 1,400 shekels in the pocket for his university tuition. It was frightening. In the seminary you learn how you should love everybody, and you go home and see this stuff and you start questioning....

RH: You were 16 at the time, more or less?

ES: Probably 15. You start questioning what the seminary is all about, what the church is all about. My brother was a peaceful guy; he's active in the church, in the choir, in the youth groups, and yet, he's not safe. He was arrested. And I don't think my brother did anything [wrong].

RH: It's collective punishment.

ES: It is. They terrorized us. It's very tragic. I think there were one million Palestinians who were in Israeli jails since 1967. One million. That moment really started changing me, thinking about the peaceful world I believed in, from the church teachings in the seminary.

RH: How would you describe the internal change?

ES: I struggled [with questions] for a year or two—What are these peaceful teachings all about? Why should we continue to be peaceful? It was a real struggle. I decided to leave the seminary.

RH: There was too much dissonance?

ES: It was too much for me to reconcile what I had experienced that night and what I had been hearing and learning in the seminary, as if you live in a bubble inside the seminary. Outside, a lot of young people were being killed and arrested and injured. In the first *intifada*, everybody was involved, everybody was in the streets.

RH: How did you understand what was going on—as resistance to the occupation?

ES: The daily events of the occupation were our educators. You hear people's stories, you see soldiers everywhere, you see them shooting everywhere, you see people being thrown in jail. All were part of our daily life under occupation.... You didn't need a college degree to understand it.

RH: It was the air that you breathed.

ES: Exactly. And the occupation distorted our view of Jewish people. This is why the occupation is bad not only for us but also for the occupiers. Soldiers or settlers, that's all you see. So, you grow up with enmity inside you. Once you know a different group in the Jewish community, you say, The occupation is different than Jewish people; Jewish people are different than the Israelis.

RH: Identify other turning points that brought you into your current identity and work.

ES: Kids left school in the middle of the day to throw rocks at soldiers, then came back to school to finish the day. Some never came back. They were either shot dead or badly injured. My dilemma was, What type of activism should I be involved in?

RH: You had to do something.

ES: But I didn't know what to do because I still believed in peaceful resistance. I didn't think we collectively should ever be involved in violence. Also, I did not want to have the same experience my brother had. He was jailed for four months. Our life changed as a family. We didn't feel we could be happy anymore.

RH: It's another loss.

ES: It's another loss. When we came together around the dinner table, one of us was not there. My dad's mission every day was to meet with the lawyer who was defending my brother. Every day we needed to hear the report, and we asked, Is he going to be released? Our life as a family turned upside down in just one evening. It's hard to think about it now after all these years.

RH: Multiple losses.

ES: Multiple losses. The same year, my oldest sister got married, and my oldest brother left for the U.S. So, all of a sudden, my parents had one child at home—a family of five down to one. Our life, especially when my brother was in prison, was never the same. I couldn't reconcile with my old world, so I searched for a new life outside of the seminary. The hardest part was when classmates went to demonstrations and didn't come back. I had that trauma like everyone else.

RH: You had friends who were killed?

ES: Yeah. And friends got arrested, too. I couldn't handle the struggle. I left the seminary.

RH: When was Birzeit University shut down?

ES: Soldiers shut it down multiple times during the first *intifada*. Once, they closed the university for three years. My brother took classes in churches, mosques, and teachers' homes. Students got arrested if they carried books. This generation we call the steadfast generation, especially those who spent eight years in undergraduate studies.

RH: So, the concept of *sumud* was really palpable.

ES: It was strengthened during the first *intifada*, in every aspect. Carrying a book, that's *sumud,* a kind of resistance. Going to school, that's a form of resilience.

RH: Just existence is resistance.

ES: Exactly, being there and handling the hardships of the occupation. The level of solidarity during the first *intifada* was unprecedented. The first *intifada* was the peak of Palestinian resistance. I was in a band that sang political songs. I organized people. It was fun. You feel proud. There's meaning and hope.... But, when the [Oslo] peace process started, all of this began to fade. From '93 on, things went downhill. The situation now is going from bad to worse at all levels. There is no hope for peace or even reconciliation among Palestinians.

RH: It's a charade?

ES: Yeah. We didn't only lose the peace process, we lost everything that we built during the years of resistance, the solidarity, the social cohesion between the society, the values that we had built, the sense of belonging, and the identity that we built. All of this, unfortunately, is lost. We are at the worst possible moment in our history, a moment of complete loss.

RH: I've heard quite a few people say this. What made you decide to do graduate work? For some people, activism and academic work are opposite things.

ES: We are a family who likes public service.... After college I continued church and other community work. I went to work for Sabeel. In 2000, I thought, I'm stuck. I need to leave the country to continue my education, to improve myself so I can help my community better.... Don Wagner invited me to come to North Park University in Chicago. He opened the door for me to receive my higher education. When I arrived in Chicago in the Fall of 2001, I had very little money—for education, or for rent. But after a church service, somebody came to Don and said, I have a wealthy uncle who may be able to help! From an unknown source, I received help for three years. This was important—to reflect on who I am and what I want to do.

RH: Leaving a tough situation was important for you as a time for reflection.

ES: It was very important.... The second *intifada* [began] in 2000. I came to the U.S. in 2001, three weeks after 9/11. In 2003, I met Laurie Millner at North Park University. She became my wife in 2004, and my best friend. Now I could go back with new energy.

RH: The second *intifada* was very different from the first *intifada*.

ES: Very different, more of an armed struggle; fewer people were involved. In Chicago, I did my master's degree in community development, and my Ph.D. in planning and public policy at the University of Illinois at Chicago.

RH: Which Palestine desperately needed.

ES: I didn't know that. I didn't know what to expect. But urban planning was developmental planning, how to create policy, very useful [skills] for my country. When I returned to Palestine in 2006, all doors were open to me. I didn't know that the natural place for me was working for the government, where policies are created. I didn't know I would love government work. I had lost my desire to be a diplomat. In 2007, I started working for the ministry of planning and loved it. I found my place. I could make change at the national level, faster and quicker. I was fortunate because all I had was my education. I worked on two main projects: helping Palestine create new strategies at the national level, and [working] on the relationship between Palestine and the international community. I practiced diplomacy while also using my public policy training. I was involved in development projects worth hundreds of millions of dollars.... I made sure donor money came in and was used according to our national priorities. I brokered a lot of agreements between donors and Palestine. I was involved in the design process and the agreements for implementation. This is the first time I get to talk about it. Thank you for that.

After 1993, Palestine had one strategy, a two-state strategy, based on the [Oslo] peace process. Options A, B, and C were one option. What are the alternatives? What are the resistance forms?

RH: Israel has completely blocked the possibility of a two-state solution....

ES: We spent so much time convincing Palestinians to believe in a two-state solution. Frankly, it is better for Israel than it is for Palestine, because they get to lock in control of 78% of the land. For us, it's a much bigger loss. It took a long time to convince our people of the two-state solution, and yet Israel has systematically destroyed it.... I'm not saying we should leave negotiations, but there have to be other strategies and alternatives in case negotiations fail.

RH: What Jeff Halper calls an endgame.

ES: What is the endgame we want? What will take us there—negotiation, nonviolent resistance, armed strugglee, or all of this? It's way past time for a new strategy. People talk about one state, two states, as if they are mutually exclusive. I've tried to introduce a new strategy which I call "one homeland," which preserves the rights and demands of both sides. Leaders on both sides tried to convince us that the best way forward is to be separated.

RH: It's the official [Israeli] policy of separation. The Hebrew word and policy is *hafrada*.

ES: I don't know the Hebrew word, but separation never brings peace. It's just separation.

RH: There are so many ways in which that policy is expressed. The Wall is just one example.

ES: Of course ... military checkpoints are another.

RH: [Negotiation is] for the sake of whatever the endgame turns out to be.

ES: Absolutely. Israelis will negotiate for the next 100 years, to make themselves look good. [They say,] "We want to talk, and the Palestinians don't want to talk." We *are* interested in meaningful talks, talks that will lead to something, … a meaningful negotiation process.

RH: In terms of your own identity, how would you describe it?

ES: It's a hard question. But I like it, because it challenges me again. I love to use government tools to make change, to help people achieve the change that they want to make.

RH: Is social justice at the core of that?

ES: Yes, social justice. Government, universities, Seraj, and other community organizations are tools [for] change. I am a teacher, diplomat, and politician, with the ability to work in a highly complex political environment and with the international community. My identity requires skills of diplomacy, politics, knowledge of policy and development. I love teaching. I love community work, because you connect with the grassroots. Often in government work you are detached from the community. You think at a high level; you meet high-level people. Then community work brings you down to the ground, to the real world. It's all of this.

RH: Can you comment on [the role of government]?

ES: Governments do things the way they do because of reasons the general public is usually not aware of.… This is what we call political pressure.

RH: The PA is under pressure, terrible pressure.

ES: Extreme pressure. It's not always easy to make the right decisions.… We should always work to make sure the right people are in the right place.… To make the right decisions, you have to have exposure to everyone.… When good people are involved in government, we know we have good government and vice versa.

RH: Eventually government has to ratify what civil society works out.

ES: Yeah. And civil society is not all angels, either. They're not all doing the good work and the right work, either. They have issues. They have good points to raise. I was always in the middle of this, always the convener. In the prime minister's office, I worked with civil society to bring them closer to the government, and the government closer to civil society. The same for the private sector, the donor community, and for UN agencies—unique positions that I held for 10 to 12 years.

RH: You have special gifts.

ES: You can never please everybody, and you have to make sure that you can reach a consensus to a certain degree. You have to work with everybody; you have to listen to everybody; you have to make sure that you can find a middle ground for everybody. We have 80 to 84 donor countries and UN agencies and thousands of NGOs; we have international civil-society organizations; we have local civil-society organizations; the government, the private sector, all of that. When you have to work with everybody and bring everybody together, it's hard.

RH: I certainly think of you in terms of peace and justice. Those are the qualities you care about.

ES: But peace and justice are too idealistic for the work I'm doing. That's what the issues [are].

RH: Of course. That's why I'm asking you.

ES: Why? It's for the common good.

RH: If they want to, they could all work together, and win, including Israelis and Palestinians?

ES: Yes. Including everybody. The world makes people feel like there has to be a winner and a loser. This is why it's so hard for moderates to function in our society.... Peace and justice are a spillover effect of our work for the common good. If we work for the common good, peace [will come]—justice, I'm not sure. Justice is a very difficult thing to achieve. I don't think it's possible.

RH: But some aspects of justice certainly inform your idea of what the common good is.

ES: Definitely. This is my idealistic motivation. I want to see peace and justice. Definitely.

RH: That should be the goal of government.

ES: Exactly.... [We have] to evolve to meet the aspirations of the Palestinian people. The alternative is to have winners and losers. Winners and losers create injustice.

RH: And lots of conflict.

ES: Lots of conflict. So this is why I'd like you to use this dialogue. If we work for the common good, the ultimate effect, the spillover effect, is peace and justice. The absence of work for the common good creates winners and losers; that creates a lot of conflict, which means no peace. This is why I admire what you're doing.

RH: Thanks very much.

ES: I want to thank you for talking about my life. This will help me to write my story.

26 Three Sails for Gaza

Yonatan Shapira

Born on an Israeli air-force base, Yonatan Shapira grew up in a Zionist family. On Memorial Day, he celebrated the people who died in the wars, reading their names and singing. After high school, Shapira became an elite air-force pilot. When a friend invited Shapira to participate in an encounter group with Palestinian students, the experience changed his life. He left the air force, co-founded Combatants for Peace, and became a facilitator at the School for Peace.

Tel Aviv, August 2014

RH: [Describe your] early family situation.

YS: I was born in an air-force base next to Beersheba, where my father was a fighter pilot and a squadron commander. It was a year and a half before the Yom Kippur War in 1973. My mother was a biology teacher and researcher in botany. We moved from one base to another. During the Yom Kippur War, my father was the commander of Squadron 105 that did the famous bombardment of the head of the armed faction of Hamas in 2002.

RH: How old where you at the time?

YS: I was already a pilot in the air force. That was one of the things that led me to organize pilots later. But going back to the childhood.... I grew up on air-force bases and in a neighborhood of air-force officers and veterans. Most of the kids in my class were connected to the military. We had very strong Zionist values at home. Not religious, but traditional—sabbath dinner; celebrating holidays; and very, very strong values of helping the community. But the community was always our immediate community, or Israel, or the Jews. My parents adopted several people that lived with us. When I was a child we were five children plus several kids or grownups that joined us.

RH: That takes a big heart.

YS: Yeah, my parents gave us the best, loving environment, not criticizing the Zionist narrative, not saying bad things about Palestinians.... They said, We need to be nice to them and make peace with them. I always was against the settlements. During the Lebanon war my mom

DOI: 10.4324/9781003262817-28

was in the big demonstrations in Tel Aviv against Israeli attacks on the Sabra and Shatila refugee camps. It was a Peace Now background. My father was the opposite. He was for Prime Minister Sharon. After his military service, he worked for the arms industry.

RH: Did your parents fight a lot about that?

YS: Yeah. It was a good relationship and quite a good family with lots of love and warmth. But ... I remember after elections the kids would have to intervene sometimes....

RH: To calm things down?

YS: My mom was so much against Sharon. She said that he was a murderer and if he ever becomes prime minister, we are leaving the country. She was still super-Zionist. So the typical, liberal Zionist lefties didn't like the right-wing Likud party or the settlers. [They] put all the bad stuff on settlers—*They* are grabbing land, *they* are doing the injustice; *we* here in the center, we are good, and want peace. And the Arabs don't miss any opportunity to miss opportunities.

RH: It took me a long time to understand liberal Zionism.

YS: The liberal, leftist Zionists, in my view, are the core problem.

RH: More than settlers?

YS: The settlers at least are clear. There's a problem when we see ourselves as pure and the others, more right-wing than us, as the source of all problems. We don't see that we are living here, on grabbed land, on [Palestinian] villages that were totally wiped out.

RH: I talked with Gideon Levy about that.

YS: It's easy to sit in Tel Aviv and criticize settlers when you are doing the same thing, just 20 years before.... I believed that we were good and I totally identified with the state [of Israel]. Friends laugh at me today, saying that I was the typical Zionist poster boy, reading the names of people who died in the wars in the Memorial Day ceremonies. In high school I sang all those songs in the ceremonies and played violin or flute. I was in the center of the Zionist narrative, with bereavement songs, beautiful songs with a Russian melody weaved into the storytelling, and with songs of the first year of the country, or the beloved son who died in the war. Everything is weaved together, penetrating your heart and recruiting you to the Zionist narrative, and recruiting for the military. As the son of a fighter pilot, I wanted to be a fighter pilot.

RH: It's a high honor, right?

YS: Yeah, I wanted to do the most courageous, high-class [thing]—everyone looks up to a pilot—having a good profession and protecting my country. I was [hugely] Zionist, believing that, if there are problems, I'm going to fix them. I should climb as high as possible in the system so I can fix those cracks of immorality like the massacre of 1966–1967, during the Six-Day War. It's part of the ...

RH: Mythology?

YS: You learn ... the reason this massacre happened, but you don't learn about the Nakba. You don't learn about the expulsion; you learn that [Palestinians] ran away, thinking that the Arab militaries will come and clean [things up], and then those [armies] can come and take over. So, when I joined the military, I was a Zionist lefty with critical views towards the war in Lebanon. It was already going on for eight or nine years. I still believed that I have to be there. I didn't know if I should become a pilot or a commando soldier. I did all the training for those units, and I was accepted to the most elite unit, like the one that [Prime Minister] Netanyahu, Ehud Barak, and my older brother [belonged to]. That was my dream.... At the same time, I was very much against the right-wing government. But once you go into the air-force system, you try to survive, pass the course, [and] reach the top. You push aside things that bother you.

RH: I wonder if you have ever gone into the West Bank.

YS: Maybe I drove through with my parents once.

RH: You were how old when you entered the air force?

YS: I finished high school, did one year of community organizing, and volunteered to work with people in villages that are less privileged than where I grew up. Then I went to the air force. I was 19. In 1993, I finished the helicopter course. It was good luck that I was put in a squadron doing helicopter rescues, because I was not attracted to killing. I always dealt with questions of morality. I wanted to do good work. I told people how proud I am to be part of the military and I just saw [rescue work] as good luck, because most pilots want to fly Apache helicopters, or F-16s, or F-15s and to be the shooters. I was happy to do rescues, but I still didn't see my naiveté. Both are eventually taking [Palestinian] land and taking their freedom....

RH: Were there key turning points?

YS: One was the bombardment of Salah Shehade ... a few weeks after I became a reservist.

RH: So, you had been in the air force ...

YS: From 1991 till 1999. Then I had time off to travel the world and do music studies. I returned for a half-year to transition to Blackhawk helicopters. I was in the United States, with the U.S. Army in Alabama, in Fort Rucker, and all these Bible-belt places.... After I started my air-force career, I was invited to participate in a dialogue at the School for Peace at Neve Shalom/Wahat al-Salam.

RH: I've been there.

YS: I had a pop-rock band and one of the guys invited me. I didn't want to go. [The dialogue] included Israeli students from Tel Aviv and Palestinian students from Nablus. I was already upset with the air force and the army. and I thought I knew everything about the situation. But my friend convinced me to go. I tell this story many times because it grabs the essence of my change.

RH: The second *intifada* was still going on?

YS: Yeah. It was sometime between the killing of Salah Shehade in July 2002 and the release of the pilots in September 2003.... In this first meeting, we sat in a circle—one Israeli, then one Palestinian. Our group had eight Israelis and eight Palestinians. We had to present ourselves and answer three questions—who we are, why we are here, and what we do.... I planned to say, my name is Yonatan, I'm an air-force helicopter pilot, I'm against the occupation, and I'm for peace. The event that led me to come here is the bombing of the house of Salah Shehade, and the killing of so many innocents. In my view, this is a crime.

The guy sitting next to me, a Palestinian from Nablus, said the big event for him was that his younger sister became paralyzed because an Apache helicopter shot a missile that hit his sister and their neighbor's house.... I said, I'm in the force and I want peace. Suddenly, flying this machine and that machine ... didn't seem important. When you sit next to a guy whose sister is paralyzed because of someone shooting a missile at their house.... I simply couldn't say the word "pilot." So, I said everything I had planned, except that part.

RH: The pilot part.

YS: Yeah. And I'm *still* a reservist pilot in the air force. For the whole weekend, I participated a lot, represented a group, and did a simulated "settlement" peace agreement—blah, blah, blah. But I didn't say, I'm a pilot. I spoke for everyone and said we were going to do everything we can to stop the occupation. It was a promise. Even though I partly lied, the promise was a hell of a promise. One of the guys in the group was a reservist who refused [to go into the military] again. He is willing to go to jail.

RH: He called himself a refusenik?

YS: Yeah, from Courage to Refuse. I remember how he was accepted by the Palestinians. They legitimized him, gave him a blessing and forgiveness, because he was brave, because he stated that he's not going [to the army] anymore; he's going to jail if needed. I remember two strong feelings, jealousy for his boldness, honesty and bravery, and a feeling of shame. I was ashamed of being what defined me—one of the most important things in this period of my life. The idea that I want peace and I'm against the occupation suddenly felt so irrelevant. My political opinions are not the issue here. Every week I serve one day as a reservist and do anything that they tell me, even if it's not rescuing [someone]. Sometimes you fly commando troops and land them in the [Palestinian] Territories....

That was a big change, but it was just one story in a collage of many moments. There were six or seven things that led me to do something [for peace].

RH: You achieved some consistency.

YS: Suddenly all my Zionist ideology, like wanting to contribute to my nation, everything found a door. I could steer all my energy towards something that I thought, "This is right." This Zionist poster boy, who sings on the Holocaust Memorial Day, and the Memorial Day for the wars, suddenly found where I can invest all this energy to do something that, for the first time, I completely believe in. I found something that I know it's true, it's just, and it's clear; I know I have to refuse. I know I have to shake the hell out of this, shake the system, the biggest shake I can think of. I totally believed in my honest, nonviolent will, and my commitment to benefit everyone around me. That's an amazing, strong feeling. You get a buzz of energy from somewhere. It gives you the power and the energy to cope with anyone who will call you names, or shout at you....

Ten days later, I met with the commander of the air force. He had a big Israeli flag and a big air-force flag behind him. He had newspaper pictures of all the people who were killed in a [Palestinian] suicide attack a few days before. He tried to show me that I was protecting [Palestinian] monsters. But I felt so confident. Suddenly I was a channel bigger than this moment.

RH: We can identify 10 reasons why this conflict goes on and on, a toxic combination of fear, history, and ideology. When they are combined, you can't see with compassion. How do you turn that around?

YS: For others?

RH: Yeah, how do you help others go through [what you went through]. If you invite a friend to go to Neve Shalom, one person at a time, will it take a thousand years [for collective change]?

YS: First, you translate your ... conflicts and a solution for yourself. [Then] translate it to something that is connected to your society, or your surroundings.... People write poems, do art, or other things to meditate. You can do many things in order to cope with internal conflicts. Then translate it to something that has a political or social context, that influences events around you.

RH: How do you do that?

YS: This is the big question. I use everything that we have, including the prestige of pilots and fighters in the Israeli society. I speak the language and nuances of the Zionist people. We are seen as people that they can trust.... They investsed a lot in us and gave us the responsibility to fly expensive machines; now listen to what we say. Some were influenced; some were upset—

RH: And felt like you had betrayed them?

YS: Yeah. Betrayal. Totally.

RH: How did your parents respond?

YS: My mother was supportive. She asked me what she can do to help, and I gave her a number for Machsom Watch. She called them and today she is more active than the whole family together. She's 72 and she is like a 16-year-old activist, with many new friends.

For my father, it was harder. He still goes to the meetings of air-force veterans, and listens to lectures by security personnel. He supports me as a father, but he doesn't agree with my political views....

Once you stay and live in this society, with family and friends, you have to act. We are agents of change that have a very, very strong mission. I appeal to my family. For a long time, after my refusal, people thought I was crazy, but I didn't want my cousin to join the army. I took him to meet Palestinians, people that refuse, people that don't refuse.

RH: So he could compare....

YS: It's irresponsible for me to try to change the world, but not to change the hearts of my beloved cousin who is about to go [to the army]. Eventually he went through training, and at the end of the training he refused. My younger brother [refused], and my older brother... organized a group of commando soldiers that refused publicly, and that made a lot of noise.... A lot of the family now are in the business [of peacemaking]. When I turned 40, I decided to do a birthday party. I said, if you want to make me happy, come to a picnic and tour of Canada Park.

RH: I've been there.

YS: So you know the story. Everyone listened to a Nakba narrative, and saw pictures.... It was really a gift. I saw that you can organize something for yourself that really is a present....

RH: Tell me about the *Mavi Marmara* flotilla [trying to break the siege of Gaza].

YS: Israelis used Blackhawks that I [had been] flying to drop commando soldiers who massacred the people on the *Marmara*. I saw on TV the participation of my own squadron. The helicopters brought [commandos] to slide down the ropes [to the deck]....

RH: How does one person in a family go in one direction and someone in the same family goes in a different direction? You may need a psychotherapist to answer that.

YS: Translate the need into action—act together with those that you used to fight against. Instead of therapy, talk to the people that you oppressed; work with them to stop oppression. This is an emotional, psychological solution. I'm for psychological treatment, but the real treatment is correction. Correct your wrongdoing and heal those parts in yourself that are problematic.

RH: That was the message of the Hebrew prophets: "Do the right thing."

YS: Once you understand it's not about you, it's about Palestinian liberation, you can join the struggle. You don't think any more as a Zionist, wanting a Jewish majority and other tribal things. Now you can experience the struggle, the decision making, the hopelessness—

RH: And the joy!

YS: And the joy. You're together with those who are struggling for liberation. And it cannot happen without the big initiative around the world, the boycott movement.

RH: Are you most hopeful about that?

YS: On that front, we are moving forward.... So, back to the flotilla boats. A couple of weeks after [the *Mavi Marmara* events], I was asked to participate. I said, I can sail yachts. Count me in.

RH: You weren't scared because of what had happened on the *Marmara*?

YS: We still have this feeling, because we are Israelis, we are a little bit more protected. We still benefit from being in this apartheid [state]. That sometimes gives us false [protection] and sometimes real protection. But that's our job, to push it as far as we can. And in that situation, I felt that that's where we can push it. Two months later we got into high gear.

In September 2010, we sailed from Greece with four people—my younger brother, and a British and a Scottish guy. With lots of adventures, lots of technical problems, we brought the boat to Cyprus. In Cyprus, a group joined us, including a Holocaust survivor, and a bereaved father whose daughter was killed in a suicide attack. We sailed with 10 people to Gaza.... We were intercepted, taken to prison for a few hours, and then released.

RH: No trial?

YS: No, although I still have an open file for that, and now I have problems getting jobs because of that. I'm trying to close [the file]. There are many things that happened. One of them is that we were singing "We Shall Overcome".... They shot me in my heart with a stun gun.

RH: Was it quite painful?

YS: That one was, but it wasn't real bullets.

RH: What's the sensation?

YS: Like an animal being slaughtered. Everything jumps. I say that they tried to resuscitate my Zionist heart. That's what the whole country needs to make their hearts beat again.

RH: That's the basic question we've been circling around.

YS: A year later there was the *Audacity of Hope*, the American boat.

RH: That's a great political title.

YS: That second flotilla had many other boats. Most of us were stopped leaving Greece.

RH: Did the Greek government collaborate with the Israelis?

YS: Oh, we know that. We were still in Greek territorial waters, but they were getting their orders from [Israel].... There are many funny stories about that. The last [sail] was in 2012 with the Swedish boat the *Stelle*, with a group of international activists, mostly from Sweden and Norway, and three Israelis. About 15 warships, small and big, stopped us 40 miles from Gaza.

RH: Explain your philosophy about this symbolic act. Why does Gaza need to be liberated?

YS: It sends a very strong message. Some of the boats actually made it.... Previously, in 2008 and 2009, some got in. I think that Jeff Halper was on one of them, Gideon Levy, and Amira Hass. Even if you're stopped, it's a strong message to the world and to the people in Gaza.

RH: That they have not been forgotten.

YS: Yeah! That some people are willing to throw themselves into this [situation] and get arrested.

RH: And not just any people, but Israeli people.... So these Gaza stories are quite important.

YS: There's a lot of stories, funny and sad and interesting.

RH: I often think in terms of this whole conflict as tragedy.

YS: But you have to weave in some comedy to make it all the time.... The fact that I was pushed out from working as a pilot gave me the freedom to join any [peacemaking] initiative.

RH: We don't often think about being freed up to do things.

YS: In the last several years I joined three sails to Gaza, which is super-important for my spirit, for me as a human being and an activist. I couldn't have done that if I had not been fired....

And now I have a little daughter; she's a year old in a couple of weeks, and I've started to think, I need to find a job. I can't go again and again to the States to work like I used to. Now I have to find other ways to manage both things. In the next year I will still come to the States to do intense periods of flying for a private company. Because here [in Israel] I'm not able to work.

RH: Thanks for giving me a title for this chapter, "Three Sails for Gaza." It's beautiful. It changed your life, right?

YS: [Laughs].

* * * * * * * *

Oslo, November 2018 (by Skype)

YS: Since last summer, my base is in Oslo, where [my daughter's] mother is from. I do work in the U.S., do music and activism in Israel and Palestine, and raise a daughter here. She [is] almost five.

RH: Four years ago, we were just getting to the stories of sails that you took to Gaza.

YS: On Wednesday I'm going to participate in one more sail to Gaza. [Others] left two months ago from different places in Scandinavia—four small boats, three sailing boats, and a second fishing boat. The fishing boat has international members. I will join the fishing boat crew in Italy.

RH: What do you think will happen?

YS: Probably the usual.

RH: Do you think they will stop you while you are still in international waters?

YS: Yeah. It's not totally relevant if we make it or not. It's a long journey and the boats go from port to port in Sweden, Norway, Spain, Portugal, France, and Italy. [At] every place, there's an event and people come. The idea is to make a platform to raise awareness and gain momentum.

Many people along our route take part in it. We know that we don't have the power to take over the Israeli navy. They have their wannabe-dictator-military-fascist guy and they have the backing to do whatever they want. If they want to kill 120 civilians in the unarmed defense of Gaza in the last few months, they will do that. If they want to sink our boats, they will do that. But they make calculations, and they know that Europe and its mostly hypocritical leaders will only tolerate [them] up to a certain line. If they kill Muslims, mostly Palestinians, that's okay with some countries in Europe. But if they sink a boat belonging to Swedish and Norwegian activists, that will be more problematic. Likely we will be tasered, taken ashore, and detained. Or, they could just shoot us, like they do the fishermen in Gaza.

RH: Is the March of Return [in Gaza] still going on?

YS: Yeah. Their idea was to do something this month. Just last Friday, Israelis killed a 14-year-old boy by the fence in Gaza. They feel that they can do whatever they want.

RH: When I was in the Middle East this summer, I was surprised at the number of people who used the word despair. Most of them—committed for the long haul—said things are worse than they have ever been, or worse than they can remember. There was a very somber mood.

YS: Yeah; sometimes when people are very hopeful it may be based on some illusion. These illusions are sometimes super-important to keep us going. When you feel that you are not being heard, and the leaders of the world [don't] hear your voice, that's when people feel weak and they can resort to things that don't promote their cause. It's so important, especially when leaders all around the world are becoming more right-wing, anti-immigrant, Islamophobic, everything is becoming worse and worse. That's why it's super-important … to do symbolic things like trying to break the blockade. It's also important *not* to think that doing that will solve a problem. You may give some sense of solidarity to people that have to cope with a really difficult time, and maybe your action helps to maintain the energy that keeps them struggling…. If I can encourage [them] a little bit by trying to break this evil blockade, I'll do that. But I don't want to convince myself that I'm doing something super-important that will affect the situation in a big way.

RH: Do you have any sense of what the relationship between suicide and nonviolent protest might be, say, in the recent events in Gaza?

YS: I don't want to differentiate between violent and nonviolent protest; a protest is a protest. One may throw stones or fly a kite with fire. We can discuss whether this is violence or nonviolence. It's a struggle, and I support them, whatever they do in this situation. What helps people everywhere is doing something together with other people for a cause. Write, and give a social, political context to the thing that made you suffer. Then struggle against the root cause of it.

RH: Four years ago, I liked what you said about a form of reconciliation in which you go and work with the people that you had hurt. You get involved in their lives. What's your sense of why the March of Return happened now? Many of us were surprised at the scale of participation.

YS: I think the popular resistance there, the committees, the people that brought up the idea and made it happen realized that this is the strength they have. Militarily they have no chance; they shoot one little missile built of agricultural pipes. Israel will hit it in the sky. They build a tunnel and Israel will bomb the whole [thing]. Militarily they have no chance. But they have the courage, and the millions who are determined to leave. It's a struggle. The question is how long you can survive. Will the world still be silent? Because protest like that can work only if it's being heard. Gandhi was doing his actions for decades, but if people in England hadn't listened and created pressure as a result of seeing the actions, India would still be a colony. The oppression [here is] an occupation of more than 70 years [and has been] mostly met by nonviolent resistance.

RH: Right, including the 1936 strike.

YS: Yes. At this point in my life I'm for nonviolence because that's how I can be most useful. But I'm not criticizing. I will join the nonviolent struggle. The Gaza people are locked in a ghetto and have the legitimacy to fight against us, against the Israelis.

RH: Under international law it's permitted. But it may not be practical.

YS: One of the plans they had a few weeks ago was to wear striped uniforms, prison uniforms, to remind the soldiers and snipers what all of us think of when they see people with striped uniforms behind fences. Suddenly four big countries in Europe are pressuring the Israeli government, even if they do it in a hypocritical way, [while still] continuing to do arms trades with Israel.

RH: Pressure can work.

YS: These techniques can sometimes work. But … the struggle is long. That's what is important to understand. The sail is a long sail, not just one or two events. Do you want more examples?

RH: Yeah; that would be great….

YS: In 2010, after I was arrested on the first boat, the Jewish boat, an officer tasered me in the heart and handcuffed me and my brother as well. We were the younger members of the crew and they took us away to the headquarters boat of the navy. When we were in the belly of that big warship, with Navy Seals guarding us, they took our handcuffs off, and we just sat there for many hours.... Then I remembered that I had a harmonica in my pocket. I brought it as a symbolic gift to the kids in Gaza. A company had donated musical instruments.... I asked the soldier if it's OK if I play. I started playing "The Sea of Death." The song is super-romantic and poetic. My brother sang along. More and more soldiers came down to that room. Officers and soldiers, and men and women came down. It looked quite ridiculous. We were recovering from tasering, handcuffs, and being hit by soldiers. We both felt that we need to build up our souls.

RH: Right.

YS: We thought that that they would sink our boat, or kill us, or maim us. You know how much you can push it, and then you can push it a little more, and so we did. We sang and played ... and the whole situation became more and more surreal. Then the commander came down ... and said, "Take the harmonica from the guy", and they took the harmonica away.

RH: Well, it's such a threatening instrument, you know.

YS: Yeah. I remember smiling at some point. At that point we had done what we should have done in order to relax from that experience. It was kind of humorous.

RH: That's a great example of nonviolence, of coming up with an unexpected idea, a surprise.

YS: If I [had been] a Palestinian activist, I would be dead with a bullet between my eyes. As far as possible, we take advantage of the fact that we are still members of the occupying side.

RH: Right. You have special privilege. I ask everybody this question about identity. Name for me the different parts of your own identity. How would you identify yourself today?

YS: I'm a human being, a man, with a deep connection to a certain place in the world, and a certain community. A Jewish upbringing connects me to a Jewish tradition and Israeli culture. Being a non-Zionist is a strong part of my identity, a connection to people who struggle against injustice around the world. This is the strongest part of my identity now—connected to [people] wherever they are in the world, women, LGBTQ—struggling for justice. My connection to my roots and to the journey I made from being a typical Zionist leftie Israeli to where I am now is also part of my identity. The change I went through is a building block in my identity. That's why whenever I meet someone in the world ... what I connect with immediately is something in them that went through some process of transformation, of widening identity to include other views, other ways of seeing things not the way they were born. The change of my identity became a big part of my identity.

RH: That makes complete sense to me. These are really transformation stories.... You talked about hope versus despair. What keeps you going? What are you hopeful about?

YS: We cannot go back to the past and correct things.... We have limited abilities to influence all the bad stuff that happens around us. So, wherever we live, wherever we are connected to, that's where we should try to alleviate the pain and be part of something that is bigger than us. In order to both be sane and not to lose it and not to live in a constant feeling of despair, we must connect with other people and struggle together with them.... If we do that, we will be fine.

RH: A final question. Do you anticipate more sails after Wednesday?

YS: As long as people want me to participate and use my skills as someone who can hold the wheel and then sail, I will go anytime. I'm trying now also to dedicate more time to doing music and things on the soft side. There's the hard side of struggling with the soldiers in these kinds of actions. The soft side enables me to communicate with some people who will not listen otherwise. A year and a half ago, I released a music album of songs, part of a concert I'm doing, and I'm telling stories. Some of the stories are stories that I told you.

In the last year and a half, I did 30 concerts, some of them by myself with a guitar, some of them with a band of one or two other people. Some in concert places, and many of them in houses and backyards. I can meet people that I would not meet otherwise. After one of my last concerts, a mother came to me, asking me to help her son refuse. He's an officer and a pilot. It's important [for me] to keep a softer side.

RH: Are you finding more employment within Israel? Or do you still have to fly to the U.S.?

YS: In Israel it's difficult for me to find employment in my situation as a pilot. I facilitate at Neve Shalom-Wahat al-Salam, but it's mostly volunteer work. I facilitate workshops there. I go to the States every few months and fly. I'm sent every time to a different place.

RH: It's constructive work rather than the army.

YS: I can't say that the company I fly for is not connected to all the things I am against. But this is my way of making a living, not being dependent on other things, and having the freedom to sing whatever I want.

RH: It's a real honor to have this dialogue with you. Thanks.

27 A Better World for All of Us

Gila Svirsky

I have met Gila Svirsky several times—at busy intersections in Jerusalem for Friday demonstrations by Women in Black, and at B'Tselem—The Israeli Information Center for Human Rights in the Occupied Territories. She identified herself as both a "Zionist" and a leader in women's organizations working for a just peace. She connects her Zionism to the Hebrew prophets and Israel's Proclamation of Independence.

Jerusalem, May 2005

GS: My name is Gila Svirsky. I'm with the Coalition of Women for Peace.

RH: Tell me about the many organizations that you are part of, their relationship to Women for Peace, and your role in helping to create them.

GS: The Coalition of Women for Peace was founded six weeks after the second *intifada* broke out in November of 2000. We bring together nine different women's peace organizations. At the time that the *intifada* broke out, all hell was breaking loose all over, and we knew that there were peace organizations of women working in different places. My friend Hannah Saffron and I said, "We have to work together." So we called a meeting in Tel Aviv, and there was tremendous enthusiasm for doing work together. What we have now is minor organizations working in their separate areas. For example, Women in Black is a vigil and that takes place every Friday throughout Israel. Women dress in black and stand in a busy intersection holding signs that say "End the Occupation." Those signs are shaped like a hand for a stop sign.

There's Bat Shalom, a political organization, which means "daughter of peace." It brings together Palestinian women and Israeli women. Together the joint group is called the Jerusalem Link. On the Jerusalem side it is called the Jerusalem Center for Women. The women of the Jerusalem Link work on specific political issues that divide us and try to come up with pragmatic solutions to those issues. A third example is New Profile which looks at how Israeli society has become intensely militaristic and has moved from

DOI: 10.4324/9781003262817-29

being a society with a vision of becoming Athens to resembling Sparta. So, New Profile helps us understand how the shift has occurred and how to see the militarism pervasive in our society. Sometimes it's difficult for us to see it because it is so much a part of the lenses that cover our eyes.

RH: Before the second *intifada* you were deeply involved with these issues, so we'll go back to why you came to Israel and the process that got you involved with this work.

GS: I moved to Israel in 1966, one year before the Six Day War, as part of an upbringing that led me to feel very fervently Zionist and staunchly Orthodox. A lot of that has changed over the years, but I certainly was part of the Orthodox ethos throughout my first years in Israel. There is something that people miss. The Six Day War was very much a survival war for Israel, perhaps not with respect to Jordan and Syria, but certainly with respect to Egypt. Israel felt very defensive, and rightly so. Egypt was angry at Israel for its involvement in the 1956 Sinai campaign and it was planning to retake the land. As a preemptive strike against Egypt, Israel went overboard and also entered the Palestinian territories and the Golan Heights, things that were not required for survival. As a result, we ended up with a good deal of land that did not belong to us.... We all began the war fearful and in terror that we were going to be captured or killed. We ended the war five days later with a sense of euphoria, of having gotten through this impending doom. That euphoria took many years to wear off. Many of us assumed that the Palestinian territories would be a bargaining chip of land for peace. That option was precluded by the actions of the settlers who, throughout the 1970s, very intensely set up settlements throughout the territories.

My own personal shift happened sometime during the course of that settlement heyday, when I began to dislike the things I heard from the Orthodox community of settlers. Their arrogance and triumphalist spirit shocked. It looked brutal. It did not appear to be in keeping with the values that I had been raised in. Slowly but surely, I stopped voting for the religious party and started voting for parties on the Left. Over time, I shifted more to the Left. I have to say that it was gradual. I wasn't the only one. Today I meet friends that I haven't seen for 20 or 30 years and who shared my nationalist views in the '60s and '70s. I am surprised when they say, "You are not the only one who has changed"!

RH: Would you identify some significant turning points in your process?

GS: It's hard to point to milestones along the way. It was very gradual, the product of reading and talking to people and hearing things on the media. I recall the sense of betrayal that we had at the time of the Sabra and Shatila massacres, when it was revealed that the Israeli government had done something awful, and had allowed the killing of so many innocent Palestinians.

RH: In refugee camps in southern Lebanon?

GS: In southern Lebanon. The entire Lebanon war was traumatic for many of us. I would also mention the Yom Kippur War in the early '70s. That was the first time that many of us noticed that the government was lying to us, telling us untruth about what was happening in the field. Perhaps that was the first big shock for me. Then it deepened through the Lebanon war and the brutality of the last 15 years.

RH: It is one thing for you to have new information and new insights but you probably know many people who have access to the same information and have said, it's not my business. What is the correspondence between what you are reading and what *you* bring to the reading?

GS: Well, as we sit and talk here at B'Tselem, I'm looking over your shoulder and there is a photograph on the wall of a settler who is aiming his rifle and shooting it. That is my cousin. He is the head of the yeshiva in Hebron. That famous photo appeared on the front page of many newspapers in Israel. It shows him at the moment of killing a Palestinian. Later, he was not interrogated, not prosecuted. Like many settlers, he got away with murder. He's a good example of the opposite of what happened to me. We were a fairly close family for many years, and then, over time, we drifted to two separate extremes. I have gone to the extreme of saying that I can't tolerate the actions of my country; it is behaving horribly and I'm ashamed of it. He's drifted to the extreme that says my country is not behaving brutally enough with the local occupation. There has been polarization throughout Israel and both sides have gone to the extremes.

RH: Identify the various strategies or approaches to peacebuilding which you are involved in.

GS: There are many approaches by the women's movement for peace in Israel. There are vigils and witnessing. Women do excellent witnessing, reporting, and documenting what takes place at checkpoints. Women raise awareness through all sorts of demonstrations inside Israel. There are all sorts of acts of solidarity with the Palestinians.

At this stage, five years into the second *intifada* and having participated in most of the previous forums I mentioned, my feeling is that the best strategy is to do outreach inside Israel to groups that don't agree with us. That is what the Coalition of Women has been doing for quite some time. We have done outreach to Russian-speaking Israelis, who comprise 17% of the Israeli population and are generally right-wing. We have done outreach to the poor in Israel, who are generally voting for Likud and don't understand the connection between their own economic plight and continued funding of the settlements.

Oh, let me mention one more. We do outreach to centrist Israelis. We take them to the Wall, the separation wall. We take them to checkpoints and we show them what happens there, hoping that they'll put two and two together and understand that you can't steal someone's land and expect him to sit quietly and take it.

RH: Recently I've had several discussions with Jeff Halper, who is frustrated because he says the end game is not clear. He needs for Palestinians to identify what the end game is. Others in the peace movement say that's not up to us to decide what the end game is. Our job is to help end the occupation and then let Palestinians go from there. Is it fair for those who are not Palestinian to talk about the end game or to demand that it is clear? What is your own sense of what you are after?

GS: As Israelis we are allowed to talk about how we view an end game that would be good for us. Palestinians are certainly entitled to talk about it for them. My goal is to hold both sides in that conversation so they can come up with an end game that works for both sides. My specific responsibility is to make sure that the Israeli government is negotiating with integrity and responsibility. I underscore the Israeli role in making the end game so difficult and complex.

I have often heard Jeff talk about the Israeli "matrix of control," which I call the "patrix of control." I've heard him make a case that there is no way we *cannot* have a one-state solution. I think that is utopian. I think that there is no way we *can* have a one-state solution. The situation now is that Israelis desperately need a sense of safety, and they will never have it if they are part of a bigger state in which they are just one of many, or even a minority. I'm not saying that is good. I'm saying that that's the inevitable product of 2,000 years of persecution and the Holocaust. Israelis simply feel the need for a state of their own. The Palestinians have been gracious enough to say that they will make peace with Israel if Palestinians have a state of their own. So let's grab that opportunity. Let's figure out how we can live side by side. We keep our state and do a good job in it and they have their state and do a good job in it.

RH: So, you are committed to an eventual, two-state solution?

GS: I'm completely committed to a two-state solution. I believe that it is the only pragmatic way to go. I believe that in 100 years, when we break down all the borders of the world and nobody has state borders, we can talk about a one-state solution or a non-state solution. But in the current constellation of fears, the two-state solution is the only practical solution.

RH: Because, from your perspective, keeping Israel as a Jewish state is crucial and politically necessary given Jewish history?

GS: Given history, Israel continues in its 1967 borders. I very much hesitate to use the word Jewish, a Jewish state. Because that implies an element of racism and xenophobia and keeping out others. But if we define the borders as pre-1967 borders, then we'll figure out how to make it a proper democracy with no discrimination for anyone. But, above all a place where Jews can feel safe.

RH: I know that on a daily and weekly basis you put your body on the line, you put your spirit on the line, and you put your resources on the line, especially around occupation issues. What is the relationship between ending the occupation and the larger goals that you are talking about?

GS: Ending the occupation is all part of an entire fabric that talks about justice in the Middle East. I wouldn't separate occupation from gender equality or economic justice, from ending nuclear arms. All of that is part of striving toward a just state. Certainly, when we talk about the basic values of justice and equality, living together in peace—all of that has to be part of the picture. If one element is missing, that is a problem and that feeds into instability in all the other elements.

RH: From your perspective, would it be fair to say that without an end to the occupation none of the larger goals can be realized?

GS: I would say more broadly that we have to work on all of the goals at the same time—ending the occupation, providing economic justice for the poor in the region, providing gender equality, overcoming homophobia, working on environmental concerns—all of that is part of the same thing. I don't want to say let's end the occupation and then we'll attend to everything else.

RH: That is a really huge agenda. So I assume that coalition building is crucial.

GS: We are very concerned with coalition building. For example, Women for Peace is very deeply involved in something called the Forum Against Unemployment. We have women who are active in that, and they feed into what we do in the Coalition. We don't focus on that but that is certainly an important element of what we do.

RH: In North America as you know, a powerful block of voters support Christian [and Jewish] Zionism. When we talked two years ago, you referred to yourself as a Zionist and it was a real surprise for me because I wondered how you combined that with your activism for a just peace. Could you tell us how you define Zionism for yourself? Where you part company with other Zionists?

GS: It often surprises people when I say that I'm a Zionist because Zionism has been identified with land grabbing. That is not what Zionism was intended to be. Zionism was intended to be the liberation movement of the Jewish people. It was formed before the state of Israel was ever formed and it looked for a way to give Jews a home where they could be safe in the context of anti-Semitism around the world. Now it goes without saying that Zionism lets you justify injustice to the Palestinian people. In 1948 when the United Nations said let's partition the land, the Zionist view said yes let's do that, some Palestinians said yes, some said no. A war broke out between Israel and other countries and when the dust settled, Israel controlled an even larger territory than the U.N. had been willing to assign it. Israel was born in sin, and that is why I'm grateful to the Palestinians for saying, Let's live with that fact. Let's see how we can make peace, with a Palestinian state side by side with an Israeli state.

Today, *my* Zionism is manifested, not in grabbing more land in the Occupied Territories, but in working on the character of the state of Israel; in trying to develop the state according to its original vision as annunciated in the Proclamation of Independence for Israel. That includes the vision of the Hebrew prophets. They talk about equality for all and justice for the poor. That vision is what I want very much to work on. For me that is being a Zionist, working on developing the character of Israel to be the kind of state that we envisioned when we founded it.

RH: That is very eloquent and helpful to me. The tradition of the Hebrew prophets is also very close to me, a guiding star in my own life as well.

GS: Israel's Proclamation of Independence talks about the vision of the Hebrew prophets. It is in one of the first sentences. For me that is Zionism.

RH: It really is a global vision.

GS: Absolutely! It is a global vision of justice for all.

RH: Tell me about your experience of the last two years, how "facts on the ground" have changed, the infrastructure of the occupation, taking Palestinian land, building settlements and the Wall. Can you give us a reading of this moment from your perspective?

GS: Things have gotten worse over the last five years. Part of it has been the institutionalization of the occupation. Checkpoints are no longer random or half-baked. They are now building terminals between Jerusalem and Ramallah, between Jerusalem and Bethlehem, which will be a full-fledged security apparatus for examining everyone who moves through them. The Wall has created a reality that is reversible but will take a great deal of effort and hardship and pain to reverse.

For me, the single most problematic thing that has happened in the last five years is that the occupation of the West Bank is becoming entrenched in the minds of Israelis as a result of giving back Gaza. Israelis believe that paying the price of returning Gaza to the Palestinians is high enough so that we will never have to pay a similar price for returning the West Bank. That is the most problematic part. That is getting many of us very upset. There is very little world opinion providing a major critique of what the Israeli government is doing.... Returning Gaza could have been the scenario for a wonderful step forward, a significant leap forward in peace.

Arafat died and we have Abu Mazen who is clearly a peacemaker. If we only had a peacemaker on the Israeli side who was his equivalent, we could have had a window of opportunity. Instead, we are stuck with someone who believes that the return of Gaza is a tactical move in order to entrench the West Bank. These are not optimistic times for me.

RH: So rather than the first step in a larger disengagement process, it is a clever move to seal the fate of the West Bank.

GS: Yes, the Gaza disengagement is a clever move by Sharon so that he will not have to do it again in the West Bank. Israelis will say, Oh my goodness we don't want to go through this again, in respect to other settlements in the West Bank. The scenes that I'm concerned about are not the scenes of violence, some settlers shooting. The scenes I'm concerned about are the tear-jerker scenes where people will be embracing their terrorist roles and swearing that this is the land that God gave us. Or, children will be pried away from their mothers who are about to be arrested. Those are the scenes that are going to be etched in the minds of Israelis and very hard to get rid of when the next step should be taken.

RH: Tell me about your hopes for the conference in August.

GS: In August we are holding an international conference that has been organized by Women in Black. There will be hundreds of women from every continent and from many different countries. They will share the kinds of things they are doing in their own country to prevent war or end war. There will be women from Chechnya, Rwanda, and the Ivory Coast, many places where there has been war, and many places where war is no longer the dominant event. We hope to learn from each other, not just about the strategies but about the vision. How to create a world that is not based on solving problems with violence. Deliberations will be held in our meeting space and others will be held in the Occupied Territories. The name of the conference is Women Resist War and Occupation.

It will be planned and implemented jointly by Israeli and Palestinian women. It is an opportunity for us to cross lines and break down some of the power dynamic that exists between us. It is going to be happening the same time as the disengagement from Gaza. That is very significant for us. We are trying to make the statement that leaving Gaza is step one; it is not the end of the line. I don't know if we will be able to create a better world through this conference, but we will certainly be taking steps to promote a better world for all of us.

RH: Thank you very much.

GS: Thank you.

References

Abunimah, A. (2006). *One country*. New York: Henry Holt.

Abunimah, A. (2014). *The battle for justice in Palestine*. Chicago: Haymarket.

Abu-Nimer, M. (1999). *Dialogue, conflict resolution, and change: Arab-Jewish encounters in Israel*. Albany, NY: State University of New York Press.

Abu-Nimer, M. (2003). *Nonviolence and peace building in Islam*. Gainesville: University Press of Florida.

Abu-Nimer, M., Khoury, A., & Welty, E., (Eds.). (2007). *Unity in diversity: Interfaith dialogue in the Middle East*. Washington, DC: U.S. Institute of Peace.

Abuzayyad, Z. (2018). President Trump's decision on Jerusalem lacks international legitimacy and strategic vision. *Palestine-Israel Journal, 22*(4) & *23*(1), 4–6.

Akhter, T. (2020, June 22). Bangladesh's garment workers are being treated as disposable. *The Nation*. https://www.thenation.com/article/world/bangladesh-garment-workers-covid-19/

Aljamal, Y. M., & Alcott, B. (2018, August 4). "Which one democratic state?" *Mondoweiss*. https://mondoweiss.net/2018/08/which-democratic-state/

Alon, C., Citron, A., (Ed.), & Zerbib, D. (Ed.). (2014). Dismantling road blocks: Non-violent resistance of the Palestinian-Israeli group "Combatants for Peace." *Performance Studies in Motion*. London: Methuen.

Anderson, R., Baxter, L. A., & Cissna, K. N. (Eds.). (2004). *Dialogue: Theorizing difference in communication studies*. Thousand Oaks, CA: Sage.

Andoni, G. (2001). A comparative study of Intifada 1987 and Intifada 2000. In R. Carey (Ed.), *The new intifada*. New York: Verso, 211–218.

Armstrong, K. (2001). *Holy war*. New York: Anchor.

Armstrong, K. (2004). *A history of Jerusalem: One city, three faiths*. New York: HarperCollins.

Ashrawi, H. (1996). *This side of peace*. New York: Touchstone/Simon & Schuster.

Ateek, N. (1989). *Justice and only justice*. Maryknoll: Orbis.

Ateek, N. (1997). A Palestinian theology of Jerusalem. In N. Ateek, C. Duaybis, & M. Schrader (Eds.), *Jerusalem: What makes for peace* (pp. 94–107). London: Melisende.

Ateek, N. (2008). *A Palestinian Christian cry for reconciliation*. Maryknoll: Orbis.

Ateek, N. (2017). *A Palestinian theology of liberation*. Maryknoll: Orbis.

Avishai, B. (2021, May 21). Even with a ceasefire, Israel must face a changed reality. *The New Yorker*. https://www.newyorker.com/news/daily-comment/even-with-a-ceasefire-israel-must-face-a-changed-reality

Bahour, S. (2011, June 16). Arab-Jewish dialogue: Is there a purpose? sbahour@palnet.com

Bahour, S. (2018). Israel at 70: A darkness unto the nations. http://thisweekinpalestine.com/israel-at-70/

Bahour, S. (2020a, June 18). America's Intifada must dig deeper. https://medium.com/@sbahour/americas-intifada-must-dig-deeper-8b0a64a689e4

Bahour, S. (2020b, July 12). European countries need to recognize the Palestinian state before it's too late. *The Guardian.* https://bit.ly/EU-Palestine-now

Bahour, S. (2021, April 27). Israel called to account. *Le Monde Diplomatique.* epalestine-request@lists.riseup.net

Barghouti, O. (2008, October 1-2). Palestinian dance education under occupation: Need or frill. *This Week in Palestine*, No. 102.

Barghouti, O. (2011). *BDS: Boycott, divestment, sanctions.* Chicago: Haymarket.

Barron, R. (2019, June 25). Palestinian politics timeline: Since the 2006 election. United States Institute of Peace. https://www.usp.org/palestinian-politics-timeline-2006-election

Barsamian, D. (1994). An interview with Edward W. Said. *Z Magazine* (Feb. 1991), 90. In S. Lynd (Ed.). (1991). *Home Land: Oral Histories of Palestine and Palestinians.* New York: Olive Branch.

Bauck, P., & Omer, M. (Eds.). (2016). *The Oslo Accords.* New York: The American University in Cairo.

Ben-Eliezer, U., & Vardi, S. (2019). *War over peace: One hundred years of Israel's militaristic nationalism.* Oakland, CA: University of California Press.

Bennis, P. (2002). *Understanding the Palestinian-Israeli conflict.* Orlando, FL: Trans-Arab Research Institute.

Braverman, M. (2010). Fatal embrace. Austin: Synergy.

Bright Stars of Bethlehem. (2020, June 19). A solidarity statement from our board. Communications@brightstarsbethlehem.org

Brueggemann, W. (1978). *The prophetic imagination.* Philadelphia: Fortress.

Brueggemann, W. (2014). Foreword. In D. E. Wagner & W. T. Davis (Eds.), *Zionism and the quest for justice in the Holy Land* (pp. xiii–xvi). Eugene, OR: Pickwick.

Brueggemann, W. (2015). *Chosen? Reading the Bible amid the Israel-Palestine conflict.* Louisville: Westminster John Knox.

B'Tselem. (2010, September 27). 10 years to the Second Intifada—Summary of data. https://www.btselem.org/press_releases/20100927

Bunton, M. (2013). *The Palestinian-Israeli conflict.* Oxford: Oxford University Press.

Burgess, H., & Burgess, G. (2010). *Conducting Track II peace making.* Washington, DC: United States Institute of Peace.

Butler, J. (2020). *The force of nonviolence.* New York: Verso.

Carey, R. (Ed.). (2001). *The new intifada.* New York: Verso.

Carey, R., & Shainin, J. (Eds.). (2002). *The other Israel.* New York: The New Press.

Carter, J. (2006). *Palestine: Peace not apartheid.* New York: Simon & Schuster.

Chabon, M. & Waldman, A. (Eds.). (2017). Kingdom of olives and ash. London: 4th Estate.

Chacour, E., with Jensen, M. E. (2001). *We belong to the land.* Notre Dame: University of Notre Dame Press.

Chacour, E., with Harvey, A. (2008). *Faith beyond despair: Building hope in the Holy Land.* London: Canterbury Press Norwich.

Chomsky, N. (2003). *Middle East illusions.* New York: Rowman & Littlefield.

Chomsky, N. (2016). The Oslo Accords, 1993–2013. In P. Bauck & M. Omer (Eds.), *The Oslo Accords* (pp. 1–11). New York: The American University in Cairo Press.
Chomsky, N., & Pappe, I. (2010). *Gaza in crisis*. Chicago: Haymarket.
Chovanec, S. (2018, May 15). The massacre in Gaza: A deliberate and calculated policy. http://www.truth-out.org/news/item/44486-the-massacre-in-gaza-a-deliberate-and-calculated-policy
Churches for Middle East Peace. (2018, October 1). Tell Congress: Pressure the Administration to immediately restore critical humanitarian assistance to Palestinians.
Cohen, R. (2009). *Strangers in their homeland*. Portland: Sussex Academic Press.
Cole, A. L., &. Knowles, J. G. (2001). *Lives in context*. Walnut Creek, CA: AltaMira.
Conquergood, D., & Johnson, E. P. (Ed.). (2013). *Cultural struggles: Performance, ethnography, praxis*. Ann Arbor, MI: University of Michigan Press.
Cypel, S. (2014). *Walled: Israeli society at an impasse*. New York: Other Press.
Daiute, C. (2014). *Narrative inquiry*. Thousand Oaks, CA: Sage.
Dajani, M., Baskin, G., & Kaufman, E. (2006). Israeli-Palestinian joint activities. In E. Kaufman, W. Salem, & J. Verhoeven (Eds.), *Bridging the divide: Peacebuilding in the Israeli-Palestinian conflict* (pp. 87–110). Boulder: Lynne Rienner.
Davies, J. L., & Kaufman, E. (Eds.). (2002). *Second track/ citizens' diplomacy: Concepts and techniques for conflict transformation*. Lanham, MD: Rowman & Littlefield.
de Certeau, M. (1984). *The practice of everyday life* (S. F. Rendall, Trans.). Berkeley: University of California Press.
Diamond, L., & McDonald, J. (1993). *Multi-track diplomacy: A systems approach to peace* (rev. ed.). Washington, DC: Institute for Multi-Track Diplomacy.
Dutta, M. J. (2011). *Communicating social change*. New York: Routledge.
Ellis, C., & Bochner, A. P. (Eds.). (1996). *Composing ethnography*. Lanham, MD: AltaMira Press.
Erakat, S., & Raheb, M. (Eds.). (2020). The impact on international relations during and following the Coronavirus pandemic. *The double lockdown: Palestine under occupation and COVID-19* (pp. 8–39). Bethlehem: Diyar.
Farber, S. (2005). *Radicals, rabbis and peacemakers*. Monroe, Maine: Common Courage Press.
Finkelstein, N. (2018, March 6). "Gaza: An inquest into its martyrdom." Speech. www.thejerusalemfund.org/events/upcoming/book-talk-gaza-inquest-martyrdom
Fox, S. (2020, June 17). Now would be a good time for the ADL to stop arranging police exchanges with Israel. https://outlook.office.com/mail/deeplink?version=2020060802.13&popoutv2=1
Framke, N. (2013, March 15). Israel's "Plan Dalet": The green light for Zionism's ethnic cleansing of Palestine. http://www.globalresearch.ca/israels-plan-dalet-the-green-light-for-zionisms-ethnic-cleansing-of-palestine/5326140
Freire, P. (2017). *Pedagogy of the oppressed*. New York: Penguin.
Frisch, H. (2011). *Israel's security and its Arab citizens*. New York: Cambridge University Press.
Gerner, D. J. (1994). *One land, two peoples* (2nd ed.). Boulder: Westview.
Godfrey-Goldstein, A. (2014). Dialogue with R. Hostetter.
Goodall, H. L. Jr. (2000). *Writing the new ethnography*. New York: AltaMira Press.
Gordon, N. (2008). *Israel's occupation*. Oakland: University of California.
Greenstein, R. (1995). *Genealogies of conflict*. Hanover, NH: Wesleyan University Press.
Greenstein, R. (2014). *Zionism and its discontents*. London: Pluto.

Halabi, R. (Ed.). (2004). *Israeli and Palestinian identities in dialogue: The School for Peace approach.* New Brunswick, NJ: Rutgers University Press.
Halbfinger, D. M., & Kershner, I. (2018, July 19). Israeli law declares the country the "nation-state of the Jewish people." *The New York Times.* nytimes.com/2018/07/19/world/middleeast/israel-law-jews-arabic.html
Hallward, M. C., & Norman, J. M. (Eds.). (2011). *Nonviolent resistance in the second intifada.* New York: Palgrave Macmillan.
Halper, J. (2004). Paralysis over Palestine: Questions of strategy. *Journal of Palestine Studies, 34*(2), 55–69.
Halper, J. (2005). Israel in a Middle East union: A "two-stage" approach to the conflict. *Tikkun, 20*(1), 17–21.
Halper, J. (2014). *Obstacles to peace: A re-framing of the Israeli-Palestinian conflict* (5th ed.). Jerusalem: Israeli Committee Against House Demolitions.
Halper, J. (2015). *War against the people: Israel, the Palestinians and global pacification.* London: Pluto Press.
Halper, J. (2019, May 23). The Palestinians: Warehousing a surplus people. Israeli Committee Against Home Demolitions. https://icahd.org/category/news/
Halper, J. (2020, October 1). The progress of the one democratic state. Israeli Committee Against Home Demolitions. https://icahd.org//category/news/
Halper, J. (2021). *Decolonizing Israel, liberating Palestine.* London: Pluto Press.
Hammack, P. L. (2011). *Narrative and the politics of identity.* New York: Oxford University Press.
Hammad, S. (2017, December 10). Stories from the first intifada: "They broke my bones." *Al Jazeera.* https://www.aljazeera.com/news/2017/12/stories-intifada-broke-bones-171210111414673.html
Handelman, S. (2011). *Conflict and peacemaking in Israel-Palestine.* London: Routledge.
Herbst, R. (2019, January 28). After years of study and discussion, Jewish Voice for Peace rejects Zionism. https://mondoweiss.net/author/robert-herbst/
Hirschfeld, Y. (2014). *Track-two diplomacy toward an Israeli-Palestinian solution, 1978–2014.* Washington, D.C.: Woodrow Wilson Center.
Hostetter, R. (2001). *The Longing* (unpublished play).
Hostetter, R. (2014). Passion: Scenes adapted from dialogues with peacemakers in Israel–Palestine. In L. Friesen (Ed.), *Center for Mennonite Writing Journal 6.1: Contemporary Drama.* http://www.mennonitewriting.org/journal/6/1/contemporary-plays-mennonite-writers-anthology-par/
Hovring, R. (2018, April 26). Gaza: World's largest open-air prison. Norwegian Refugee Council. https://www.nrc.no/news/2018/april/gaza-the-worlds-largest-open-air-prison/:
Human Rights Watch (2021, April 27). A threshold crossed: Israeli authorities and the crimes of apartheid and persecution. https://www.npr.org/2021/04/27/990993903:
Israel/Palestine Mission Network of the Presbyterian Church (U.S.A.). (2009). Kairos Palestine: A moment of truth, 13–24. www.kairospalestine.ps
Jabareen, Y. (2017). Controlling land and demography in Israel. In N. N. Rouhana (Ed.), *Israel and its Palestinian citizens* (pp. 238–265). New York: Cambridge University Press.
Jamal, B. (Moderator). (2021, June 3). Palestine rises: The ongoing resistance. A webinar by the Palestine Solidarity Campaign. https://outlook.office.com/mail/deeplink?popoutv2=1&version=20210524004.16
Jarbawi, A. (2014, August 4). Israel's colonialism must end. *The New York Times* https://www.nytimes.com/2014/08/05/opinion/ali-jarbawi-israels-colonialism-must-end.html

Jegić, D. (2019). *Trans / intifada: The politics and poetics of intersectional resistance.* Heidelberg: Universitatsverlag.

Jones, P. (2015). *Track two diplomacy in theory and practice.* Stanford: Stanford University Press.

Kahanoff, M. (2016). *Jews and Arabs in Israel encountering their identities: Transformations in dialogue.* Lanham, MD: Lexington.

Kassis, R. (2009). Kairos Palestine: A moment of truth. Israel/Palestine Mission Network of the Presbyterian Church (U.S.A.), pp. 13-24. www.kairospalestine.ps

Kaufman, E., Salem, W., & Verhoeven, J. (Eds.). (2006). *Bridging the divide: Peacebuilding in the Israeli-Palestinian conflict.* Boulder: Lynne Rienner.

Kaufman-Lacusta, M. (Ed.). (2010). *Refusing to be enemies: Palestinian and Israeli nonviolent resistance to the Israeli occupation.* Reading, UK: Ithaca.

Keaten, J. (2021, May 27). UN rights chief: Israeli strikes in Gaza may be war crimes. https://www.pbs.org/newshour/world/un-rights-chief-says-israeli-strikes-in-gaza-may-be-war-crimes

Kellett, P. M. (2007). *Conflict dialogue.* Thousand Oaks, CA: Sage.

Kellett, P. M., Connaughton, S. L., & Cheney, G. (Eds.). (2020). *Transforming conflict and building peace.* New York: Peter Lang.

Kelman, H. C., Mattar, P., & Caplan, N. (Eds.). (2020). *Transforming the Israeli-Palestinian conflict: From mutual negation to reconciliation.* New York: Routledge.

Khalidi, R. (2005). *Resurrecting empire.* Boston: Beacon.

Khalidi, R. (1997, 2010). *Palestinian identity: The construction of modern national consciousness.* New York: Columbia University Press.

Khalidi, R. (2014). *Brokers of deceit.* Boston: Beacon.

Khalidi, R. (2017, June 5). The Israeli-American hammer-lock on Palestine. *The Nation.* https://www.thenation.com/article/archive/israeli-american-hammer-lock-palestine/

Khalidi, R. (2020). *The hundred years' war on Palestine.* New York: Metropolitan Books/Henry Holt.

King, M. E. (2007). *A quiet revolution: The first Palestinian intifada and nonviolent resistance.* New York: Nation Books.

Klein, M., & Malki, R. (2006). Israeli-Palestinian track II diplomacy. In E. Kaufman, W. Salem, & J. Verhoeven (Eds.), *Bridging the divide* (pp. 111–134). Boulder: Lynne Rienner.

Klein, N. (2007). *The shock doctrine.* New York: Picador.

Kolbert, E. (2014). *The sixth extinction.* New York: Picador.

Kouddous, S. A. (2018, May 17). Palestinians engaged in nonviolent protest. Israel responded with a massacre. *The Nation.* https://www.thenation.com/article/archive/palestinians-engaged-in-nonviolent-protest-israel-responded-with-a-massacre/

Kovel, J. (2007). *Overcoming Zionism: Creating a single democratic state in Israel/Palestine.* Ann Arbor, MI: Pluto.

Kubler-Ross, E. (1969). *On death and dying.* New York: Simon & Schuster/Touchstone.

Kuttab, J. (2021). *Beyond the two-state solution.* Washington, DC: Nonviolence International.

Kuttab, J., & Kaufman, E. (1988). An exchange on dialogue. *Journal of Palestine Studies, 17*(2), pp. 84–109.

Landy, D. (2011). *Jewish identity and Palestinian rights.* London: Zed Books.

Lederach, J. P. (2002). Truth and mercy, justice and peace. In C. Schrock-Shenk (Ed.), *Mediation and facilitation training manual* (4th ed.) (pp. 39–40). Akron, PA: Mennonite Conciliation Service.
Lederach, J. P. (2003). *The little book of conflict transformation.* Intercourse, PA: Good Books.
Lederach, J. P. (2005). *The moral imagination: The art and soul of building peace.* New York: Oxford University Press.
Lederach, J. P., & Appleby, R. S. (2010). Strategic peacebuilding: An overview. In D. Philpott, & G. F. Powers (Eds.), *Strategies of peace.* New York: Oxford University Press.
Lerman, A. (2014, August 23). The end of liberal Zionism. *The New York Times*, pp. 1, 5. https://www.nytimes.com/2014/08/23/opinion/sunday/israels-move-to-the-right-challenges-ddiaspora-jews.html
Levy, G. (2007, April 27). Israel doesn't want peace. *Ha'aretz.* www.haaretz.com/hasen/spages/846420.html
Levy, G. (2010, March 7). There has never been an Israeli peace camp. *Ha'aretz.* www.haaretz.com/hasen/spages/1154539.html
Lovato, R. (2021, June 9). The kids are reimagining international solidarity. *The Nation.* https://www.thenation.com/article/activism/millennial-genz-solidarity/
Lowenstein, A., & Moor, A. (Eds.). (2012). *After Zionism: One state for Israel and Palestine.* London: Saqi.
Lynd, S., Bahour, S., & Lynd, A. (Eds.). *Home land: Oral histories of Palestine and Palestinians.* New York: Olive Branch.
Madison, D. S. (2020). *Critical ethnography* (3rd ed.). Thousand Oaks, CA: Sage.
Maltz, J. (2019, March 24). Two states, one, and other solutions to the Israeli-Palestinian conflict. *Ha'aretz*, pp. 1, 21.
Marantz, P., & Gross Stein, J. (Eds.). (2017). *Peacemaking in the Middle East.* New York: Routledge.
Matar, D., & Harb, Z. (Eds.). (2013). *Narrating conflict in the Middle East.* London: I.B. Taurus.
Matar, H. (Moderator), Alnaouq, A., Friedman, L., & Iraqi, A. (2021, May 26). A pivotal moment for Israel-Palestine: A joint webinar by *+972 Magazine,* The Foundation for Middle East Peace, and Just Vision. https://fmep.org/event/a-pivotal-moment-for-israel-palestine/
Mattar, P., & Caplan, N. (Eds.). (2018). *Transforming the Israeli-Palestinian conflict.* New York: Routledge.
Matthews, E. (Ed.). (2011). *The Israeli-Palestinian conflict: Parallel discourses.* New York: Routledge.
McDonald, J. W., & Bendahmane, D. B. (Eds.). (1995). *Conflict resolution: Track two diplomacy.* Washington, DC: Institute for Multi-Track Diplomacy.
McDonald, J. W., Davies, J., & Kaufman, E. (Eds.). (2002). The need for multi-track diplomacy. In *Second track/citizens' diplomacy.* New York: Rowman & Littlefield.
McRae, C. (2015). *Performative listening.* New York: Peter Lang.
Merryman-Lotze, M. (2018, March). When dialogue stands in the way of peace. *Friends Journal*, pp. 18–21.
Montville, J., (1993). The healing function in political conflict resolution. In D. J. D. Sandole & H. Van der Merwe (Eds.), *Conflict resolution theory and practice* (pp. 112–127). Manchester: Manchester University Press.

Munayyer, Y. (2014, June 23). Civil society takes the lead on Palestinian rights. *Al Jazeera.* www.aljazeera.com/indepth/opinion/2014/06/civil-society-takes-lead-palest-201462/6/23/2014

Munayyer, Y. (2020, July 7). A summer of reckoning—for American racism and Israeli aggression. *The Nation.* https://www.thenation.com/article/world/palestine-blm-protest

Nadler, A. (2004). Intergroup conflict and its reduction. In R. Halabi (Ed.), *Israeli and Palestinian identities in dialogue* (pp. 13–30). New Brunswick, NJ: Rutgers University Press.

Najem, T., Molloy, M. J., Bell, M., & Bell, J. (Eds.). (2017). *Track two diplomacy and Jerusalem.* New York: Routledge.

Nichols, J. (2021, May 25). More than 500 of the staffers who elected Biden demand that he defend Palestinian rights. *The Nation.* https://www.thenation.com/article/world/biden-staffers-letter-palestine/

Pacheco, A. (2001). Flouting convention: The Oslo agreements. In R. Carey (Ed.), *The new intifada* (pp. 181–206). New York: Verso.

Paffenholz, T. (Ed.). (2010). *Civil society and peacebuilding.* Boulder: Lynne Rienner.

Pappe, I. (2004). *A history of modern Palestine.* Cambridge: Cambridge University Press.

Pappe, I. (2006). *The ethnic cleansing of Palestine.* Oxford: Oneworld.

Pappe, I. (2014). *The idea of Israel: A history of power and knowledge.* New York: Verso.

Pappe, I. (2016). *The biggest prison on earth.* Oxford: Oneworld.

Pappe, I. (2017). *Ten myths about Israel.* London: Verso.

Pappe, I. (2020, Oct. 11). Israel's peace process was always a road to nowhere. *Jacobin.* https://jacobinmag.com/2020/10/israel-peace-palestine-oslo-accords-plo

Pearce, W. B., & Pearce, K. A. (2004). Taking a communication perspective on dialogue. In R. Anderson, L. A. Baxter, & K. N. Cissna (Eds.), *Dialogue: Theorizing difference in communication studies* (pp. 39–56). Thousand Oaks, CA: Sage.

Pearlman, W. (2003). *Occupied voices.* New York: Nation Books.

Pearlman, W. (2011). *Violence, nonviolence, and the Palestinian national movement.* New York: Cambridge University Press.

Peleg, I., & Waxman, D. (2011). *Israel's Palestinians.* New York: Cambridge University Press.

Philpott, D. (2012). *Just and unjust peace.* New York: Oxford University Press.

Philpott, D., & Powers, G. F. (2010). *Strategies of peace.* New York: Oxford University Press.

Prior, M. (Ed.). (2004). *Speaking the truth: Zionism, Israel, and the occupation.* Northampton, MA: Interlink.

Puddephatt, A. J., Shaffir, W., & Kleinknecht, S. W. (Eds.). (2009). *Ethnographies revisited.* New York: Routledge.

Qumsiyeh, M. (2004). *Sharing the land of Canaan.* London: Pluto Press.

Qumsiyeh, M. B. (2011). *Popular resistance in Palestine.* New York: Pluto Press.

Raheb, M. (2012). *The biblical text in the context of occupation.* Bethlehem: Diyar.

Raheb, M. (2014). *Palestinian identity in relation to time and space.* Bethlehem: Diyar.

Ramsbotham, O. (2010). *Transforming violent conflict: Radical disagreement, dialogue and survival.* New York: Routledge.

Ramsbotham, O. (2017). *When conflict resolution fails.* Malden, MA: Polity.

Ramsbotham, O., Woodhouse, T., & Miall, H. (2011). *Contemporary conflict resolution.* Cambridge: Polity.

Roach, C. (Ed.). (1993). *Communication and culture in war and peace*. London: Sage.

Rosen, B. (2019, Jan. 31). Republicans are using shameless tactics to split Democrats over BDS. *Truthout*. https://truthout.org/articles/republicans-are-using-shameless-tactics-to-split-democrats-over-bds/

Rotberg, R. (2006). *Israeli and Palestinian narratives of conflict*. Bloomington: Indiana University Press.

Rouhana, N. N. (1997). *Palestinian citizens in an ethnic Jewish state*. New Haven: Yale University Press.

Rouhana, N. N. (2017). *Israel and its Palestinian citizens*. New York: Cambridge University Press.

Roy, S. (2011). *Hamas and civil society in Gaza*. Princeton: Princeton University Press.

Roy, S. (2016). *The Gaza Strip*. Beirut: Institute for Palestine Studies.

Roy, S. (2021). *Unsilencing Gaza: Reflections on resistance*. London: Pluto Press.

Rubenberg, C. A. (2003). *The Palestinians: In search of a just peace*. Boulder: Lynne Rienner.

Sabbah, H. B. M., & Kassis, R. (2020, July 1). Cry for hope: A call for decisive action. www.cryforhope.org

Sabeel Ecumenical Liberation Theology Center. (2004). *The Jerusalem Sabeel Document: Principles for a just peace in Palestine-Israel*. Jerusalem: Sabeel.

Said, A. A., Funk, N. C., & Kadayifci, A. (2001). *Islam and peacemaking in the Middle East*. Boulder: Lynne Rienner.

Said, E. W. (1978, 1994). *Orientalism*. New York: Vintage.

Said, E. W. (1979). *The question of Palestine*. New York: Vintage.

Said, E. W. (1993, October 21). The morning after. *London Review of Books*, *15*(20–21), 3–5.

Said, E. W. (1999). The one-state solution. https://nytimes.com/1999/01/10/themagazine/the-one-state-solution.html

Said, E. W., & Viswanathan, G. (Ed.). (2001). *Power, politics, and culture: Interviews with Edward Said*. New York: Vintage.

Salameh, E. (2013). A one-state solution for Palestinians and Israelis. http://www.suntimes.com/news/otherviews/26904704-452/a-one-state-solution-for-palesinians-and-israelis.html#.U1Ce-PldXVs

Salameh, E. (2014). What's next for Israel and the Palestinians. http://www.suntimes.com/news/otherviews/27299242-452/whats-next-for-israel-and-the-palestinians.html#.U2xlWoGSzjQ

Salem, W., & Kaufman, E. (2006). Palestinian-Israeli peacebuilding: A historical perspective. In E. Kaufman, W. Salem, & J. Verhoeven (Eds.), *Bridging the divide: Peacebuilding in the Israeli-Palestinian conflict* (pp. 11–38). Boulder: Lynne Rienner.

Schaefer, E., Halper, J., & Johnson, J. (2006). *Counter-rhetoric: Challenging "conventional wisdom" and reframing the conflict*. Jerusalem: Israeli Committee Against Home Demolitions.

Schirch, L. (2004). *The little book of strategic peacebuilding*. Intercourse, PA: Good Books.

Schirch, L., & Campt, D. (2007). *The little book of dialogue for difficult subjects*. Intercourse, PA: Good Books.

Shalhoub-Kevorkian, N. (2015). *Security theology, surveillance, and the politics of fear*. Cambridge: Cambridge University Press.

Shalhoub-Kevorkian, N. (2020). Gun to body: Mental health against unchilding. *International Journal of Applied Psychoanalytic Studies*, *17*, 126–145. 10.1002/aps.1652.

Sharp, J. M. (2016, August. 7). *U.S. foreign aid to Israel.* Washington, DC: Congressional Research Service. fas.org/sgp/crs/mideast/RL33222.pdf

Shavit, A. (2013). *My promised land.* New York: Random House.

Shomali, A., & Cowan, P. (Directors). (2014). *The wanted 18* [Motion picture]. National Film Board of Canada and Kino Lorber.

Smock, D. R. (Ed.). (2002). *Interfaith dialogue and peacebuilding.* Washington, DC: United States Institute of Peace.

Spangler, E. (2019). *Understanding Israel/Palestine.* Boston: Brill.

Stratfor. (2018, April 23). Israel confronts its changing demographics. https://worldview.stratfor.com/article/israel-confronts-its-changing-demographics

Suleiman, C. (2011). *Language and identity in the Israeli-Palestinian conflict.* New York: I.B. Taurus.

Svirsky, G. (2001). The Israeli peace movement since the Al-Aqsa intifada. In R. Carey (Ed.), *The New Intifada* (pp. 323–330). New York: Verso.

Taylor, G. (2020, June 14). What Hamlet can teach us about Black Lives Matter. https://www.tampabay.com/opinion/2020/06/14/what-hamlet-can-teach-us-about-black-lives-matter-column/

United Nations Foreign Policy Association. (1998, Winter, No. 318). *And justice for all: The Universal Declaration of Human Rights at 50.* Chicago: The Great Books Foundation/Foreign Policy Association.

United States Institute of Peace. (n.d.). Step 5 – Encourage Track II dialogue. In *Managing a mediation process.* Washington, DC: www.usip.org/managing-mediation-process

UN News. (2021, May). Ceasefire can't hide scale of destruction in Gaza, UN warns, as rights experts call for ICC probe. https://news.un.org/en/story/2021/05/1092482

van Teeffelen, T., with Biggs, V. (2011). *Sumud: Soul of the Palestinian people.* Bethlehem: Arab Educational Institute.

Wagner, D. E., & Davis, W. T. (Eds.). (2014). *Zionism and the quest for justice in the Holy Land.* Eugene, OR: Pickwick.

Waldron, V. R., & Kelley, D. L. (2008). *Communicating forgiveness.* Los Angeles: Sage.

Watson, G. R. (2000). *The Oslo Accords.* New York: Oxford University Press.

Weizman, E. (2007). *Hollow land: Israel's architecture of occupation.* London: Verso.

Wildangel, R., Scheller, B., & Paul, J. (2013, December). 20 years since Oslo: Palestinian perspectives, *Perspectives, 5*, 4.

Winslade. J., & Monk, G. (2001). *Narrative mediation.* San Francisco: Jossey-Bass.

Wood, J. T. (2004). Foreword. In R. Anderson, L. A. Baxter, & K. N. Cissna (Eds.), *Dialogue: Theorizing difference in communication studies* (pp. xv–xxiii). Thousand Oaks, CA: Sage.

Yoder, C. (2005). *The little book of trauma healing.* Intercourse, PA: Good Books.

Zak, M., & Halabi, R. (2004). Cofacilitation: A symmetrical dialogue in an asymmetrical reality. In R. Halabi (Ed.), *Israeli and Palestinian identities in dialogue* (pp. 141–158). New Brunswick, NJ: Rutgers University Press.

Zehr, H. (2002). *The little book of restorative justice.* Intercourse, PA: Good Books.

Index

Abu-Nimer, M. 10, 53, 68, 69
Abusrour, A. 21, 47, 49, 58–59, 83, 84, 91–101, 292
Abuzayyad, Z. 32, 40
activism 14, 18, 21, 58, 67, 68, 86, 128, 168, 169, 184, 273, 275, 297, 318
activists 4, 8, 11, 14, 19, 24, 28, 29, 36, 50, 51, 63, 64, 68, 115, 133, 136
actor transformation 13, 83
advocacy 11, 14, 18, 20, 57, 67–68
agonistic dialogue 63, 66, 70, 86
Aida Refugee Camp 21, 58, 91, 292
AIPAC 141–142, 181
Al-Aqsa *intifada* 7, 44
Aljamal, Y. 87
Allenby Bridge 204
Al-Rowwad 292
Al-Rowwad Cultural Center 58, 91
Alternative Tourism Group (ATG) 102, 109, 110
American Civil Rights Movement 214
American Friends Service Committee 102, 112, 122
ANC 80, 86, 227, 228, 272
Anderson, B. 32
Anderson, R. 32
Andoni, G. 7, 15, 21, 26, 32, 41, 42, 43, 46, 47, 54, 58, 60, 62, 64, 83, 88, 102–112, 134, 181, 214, 223
anti-apartheid movement 56, 113, 272
anti-apartheid struggle 8, 55, 216
anti-Semitic discrimination 25
anti-Zionism 35, 47
anti-Zionists 26, 33, 47, 48, 65, 147, 225, 272
apartheid 56, 82, 225
Appleby, R. S. 23, 24, 81
Applied Research Institute 107, 109
Arab-Israeli conflict 5
Arab-Jewish community 270
Arab peasants 6
Arabs 6, 34, 146, 147–149, 152, 154, 156, 185, 186, 191, 243, 269–270, 303
Arafat, Yassar 7, 125, 157, 171, 242, 320
argument and advocacy 67–68
Armstrong, K. 5, 19, 35, 40
artistic strategies 94–95
arts: as beautiful resistance 91–101; peacemaking through 58–59
Ascherman, A. 4, 36, 37, 49, 57, 62, 65, 67, 86, 113–124, 223, 290
Ashrawi, H. 7, 8, 9, 23, 27, 28, 48, 49, 58, 62, 65, 71, 74, 75, 80, 125–132, 293
Ateek, N. 14, 25, 26, 34, 40, 47, 49, 53, 54, 55, 57, 58, 62, 68, 79, 83, 85, 133–144, 284
atomic bombs 60
Auden, W.H. 206
authentic dialogue 71, 72
Avishai, B. 78
Avnery, U. 4, 6, 7, 14, 24, 28, 33, 34, 35, 36, 38, 39, 40, 47, 49, 50, 62, 65, 66, 67, 73, 76, 145–157, 186, 187, 250, 266
Awad, A. 59, 235, 243
Awad, M. 54–55, 158–159, 237, 238
Awad, S. 48, 49, 54–55, 66, 80, 158–170, 222

Bachelet, M. 78
Bahour, S. 5, 24, 29, 48, 49, 77, 82, 171–181
Baker, J. 224, 287
Balfour, A. 6
Balfour Declaration 6, 25, 146
Bantustans 35, 73, 220
Barak, E. 185, 255, 304
Barghouti, O. 56
Bat Shalom 314
beautiful resistance: through arts 58–59; program of 21; through theatre 93
Begin, M. 184, 240
Beit Sahour 42, 64, 91
Beit Sahour Medical Center 107
Ben-Gurion, D. 6, 8, 34, 36, 39, 68, 120, 149–150
Bennis, P. 4, 8
Bethlehem University 91, 93
Bible 34, 36, 68, 100, 118, 139, 196, 255, 304
Biden, Joe 76, 274
bipartisan political support 8

Birzeit University 50, 64, 98, 102, 106, 110, 176, 179, 289, 292, 297
Blackhawk helicopters 304
Black Lives Matter (BLM) movement 29, 82, 274
Black September (1970) 103
Blood Brothers (Elias Chacour) 198
Bochner, A. P. 10
bombing of Gaza in 2014 26, 84
bombs 60, 237
Book of Genesis 51, 255
Boycott, Divestment, and Sanctions (BDS) campaign 46, 55–56, 60, 122, 211, 225, 229, 274
Breaking the Silence 98, 139
breakthrough peace agreement 7
breakthroughs 110, 166, 185, 198
Bridging the Divide: Peacebuilding in the Israeli-Palestinian Conflict 15
British 5–6, 146, 150, 160
British Emergency Defense Regulations 240
British Mandate over Palestine (1922–1947) 6
Bronstein, E. 9, 21, 33, 38, 46, 47, 48, 49, 52, 62, 69, 73, 182–191
Brueggemann, W. 32, 34, 79
B'Tselem 42, 51, 114, 253, 255, 261, 262, 314, 316
Bunton, M. 7, 15, 39, 43
Bureij refugee camp 208
Burgess, G. 27
Burgess, H. 27
Burnat, E. 49, 59, 83, 192
Bush, George W. 221
business of peacemaking 171–181
Butler, J. 82

Camp David (2000) 7, 247
Campt, D. 61, 63, 64, 69
Canada Park 187, 191, 307
cantons 35, 43, 135, 220
capitalism 82, 224, 274
Caplan, N. 78
Carey, R. 15, 41, 42
Carter, J. 181
Cassin, R. 216, 222
catastrophe of 1948 19, 39, 45
Center for Rapprochement in Beit Sahour 102
Chacour, E. 14, 32, 34, 46, 47, 48, 49, 58, 59, 80
Chomsky, N. 7, 8, 15, 43, 44, 79, 247
chosenness 34–36, 47
Christian Crusades 5, 40
Christian leaders 40, 57, 77, 79
Christian-Muslim program 136
Christian Peacemaker Teams (CPT) 237, 242
Christians 68, 100, 114, 137, 141, 161, 162, 196, 197, 200, 224, 239, 276, 284
Christian Zionists 34, 134, 141, 268
Christmas Lutheran Church 68–69, 231, 276, 283–284
civil disobedience 42, 95, 107, 108, 115, 165, 177, 180, 223
Civil Rights Movement 41, 48, 214, 216, 269
Coalition for Accountability and Integrity 130
Coalition of Women for Peace 314, 316
Cohen, R. 40
Cole, A. L. 10
collective mourning 79, 84
collective punishment 78, 111, 204, 207, 258
collective strategic thinking 81
colonialism 273, 274
colonial violence 82
Combatants for Peace 46, 48, 62, 69, 302
comedy 99
communal nonviolence 55
communication 3, 10, 15, 61–64, 70, 286
Composing Ethnography (Carolyn Ellis and Arthur Bochner) 10
comprehensive solution 203–213
conflict analyses 15, 75–76
conflict and peacemaking, models of 12–16
conflict management 12, 70, 224
conflict resolution 12, 13, 22, 30, 68, 84
conflict terminology 11
conflict transformation 3, 11–13, 16, 19, 23, 30, 40, 49, 52, 56, 60, 61, 74, 80, 85, 280
Congressional Research Service 8
Conquergood, D. 11
consensus definitions 84
contemporary dialogue 61
context transformation 13, 83
contextual theology 56, 57, 68, 138, 285
corpus separatum, Jerusalem as 40
Corrie, R. 132, 242
courageous leadership 249
Cowan, P. 42
critical ethnography 3, 10–12, 16, 18–19, 20, 30
critical peace movement 227
culture 59, 282–283
"culture-centered approach" of Dutta 62, 74

Dar al-Kalima University College of Arts and Culture 57, 59, 276
David, C. 247
Davis, W. T. 32, 34
"Deal of the Century" (2020) 7, 9, 76
debate, dialogue as 66–67
deception, "peace process" as 9–10
deceptive negotiations 72
de Certeau, M. 29, 73
decision-makers 57
De-Colonizer 182
demographics, ethnicity, and ethnocracy 33
dialogical communication 61
dialogic negotiation 62, 70

dialogue 61, 63; agonistic 63, 66, 70, 86; argument and advocacy 67–68; authentic 71, 72; between peacemakers 64–65; contemporary 61; and conversation 61; as debate 66–67; as difficult work 74; encounter programs 69; endless 72; ethnographic 18; exchange on 72–73; existential 70; false 72; Fatah and Hamas 67; with government officials and grassroots movements 65–66; in-depth 16, 28, 61, 62, 71, 74; interfaith 68, 286; inter-dialogue 00; interreligious 62, 68–69; intra-dialogue 68; intra-party 67; intrinsically positive 72; listening for understanding 63; living together as 70; meaningful 4, 22, 62, 74; multiple dialogical forms and issues 62; narratives as 73; and negotiation 70–72; Parents' Circle-Families Forum (PC-FF) 69–70; performative 11; professional 73; relationships, building 63–64; strategic 63, 80–82; unilateral 71; voice and transformational listening 62–63
dialogue, ethnography, and peacemaking 10–12
Diamond, L. 13, 15, 48, 49, 60
The Diary of Anne Frank 99
Dimona nuclear plant 60
diplomatic peace process 76
division of Palestine 6
domestic violence 207–209
Drayton, B. 97
Dutta, M. J. 20, 62, 74

Eastern European tribalism 33, 34
East Jerusalem 5, 7, 19, 40, 41, 91, 141, 229
education and peacemaking 58
11-day war of 2021 5
El-Farra, M. 21, 24, 26, 44, 47, 49, 51, 58, 62, 75, 77, 83, 84, 203–213, 290
Ellis, C. 10
encounter programs 63, 69
endless dialogues 72
endless negotiations 72
Erakat, S. 82
Eretz Israel 5, 40
ethical positionality 18
ethnic cleansing 6, 25, 33, 34, 75, 88, 148, 149, 154, 173, 207, 265, 266, 271, 274
The Ethnic Cleansing of Palestine (Ilan Pappe) 6, 207
ethnocracy 34, 45, 215, 269
ethnographic dialogues 18
ethnography 11, 18, 30
"An Exchange on Dialogue" (1988) 72, 74
existential dialogues 70
existential terms 17–18
Exodus 129
Ezer, G. 173

Facts (play) 98
failed projects 82, 87
faith 94
faith-based organizations 56
false dialogue 72
false negotiations 72
Farber, S. 15
Fatah 45, 67, 77, 208, 281
fellow travelers 24
Fine, M. 18
Finkelstein, N. 44
fire brigade issues 257
first *intifada* 41–43, 44, 47, 54, 58, 64, 68, 72, 83, 93, 185, 207
5 Broken Cameras (2011) 59, 83, 192–194
forgiveness and reconciliation 84, 85
forgotten Palestinians 40
Forum Against Unemployment 318
Fourth Geneva Convention 43, 56, 78, 175, 176, 225, 241, 243
Fox, S. 82
Freedom Charter 228, 229, 230
freedom fighters 145
Free Gaza movement 224
French 5, 91–92, 94, 98, 146, 150, 196
Friends of Sabeel North America (FOSNA) 233
Frisch, H. 40
From Gaza with Love (Mona el-Farra) 203, 206

Galilee 195, 196, 201, 269
Gandhi, Mahatma 160, 201, 237, 311
Gandhian liberation movement 168
Gaza 5, 9, 21, 35, 39, 44–45, 60, 67, 73, 77–78, 83, 84, 107, 122, 136, 143, 163, 171, 175, 179, 186, 199, 204, 205, 207, 208, 209, 210, 211, 212, 213, 226, 229, 243, 247, 255, 259, 290, 295, 309, 310, 311, 319, 320; Gaza Strip 7; Gaza War 291; humanitarian crisis in 44; Israeli attacks on 44; Israeli bombing of 26; three sails for 302–313
General Assembly 40, 180
generic transformers 83
Gene Sharp 165
Geneva Conventions 116, 256
Gerner, D. J. 5, 40
Godfrey-Goldstein, A. 8
Golan Heights 41, 315
government officials and grassroots movements, dialogue with 65–66
grassroots activists 14
grassroots community 164
grassroots interaction 126
grassroots movement 14, 46, 49, 63, 65–66, 107, 109
Great March of Return 44–45, 83, 213
Green Line 39, 150, 151

Greenstein, R. 31
grievability 83
Gush Shalom peace movement 145, 150, 151, 152

hafrada 31, 33, 47, 64
Halabi, R. 69
Hallward, M. C. 15
Halper, J. 4, 7, 8, 9, 14, 15, 18, 19, 22–24, 26, 27, 31, 33–37, 43, 45–51, 53, 55, 56, 58, 60, 62–66, 67–68, 70, 75–80, 82–83, 85, 86, 87, 102, 111, 120, 121, 134, 141, 143, 151, 163, 166, 168, 169, 174, 214–232, 258, 269, 275, 285, 286, 292, 299, 309, 317
Hamas 44–45, 55, 67, 77, 78, 208, 251, 281
Hamas-Fatah split 27, 48
Hammack, P. L. 31
Hammad, S. 42, 161
Handala 97, 101
Hardin-Simmons University 137
Hass, A. 309
healing function 84
Health and Wellness Center 277
Hebrew culture 33, 156
Hebrew Manifesto 150
Hertzberg, A. 114
Hezbollah 5, 250–251
Holocaust 18, 25, 37, 47, 73, 80, 241
Holocaust Memorial Day 306
Holy Land Trust 54, 55, 68, 158, 159, 162, 222
holy wars 5, 35, 161
Hostetter, R. 15, 42, 54
human dignity 51, 196, 222, 251, 254, 255
humanitarian crisis in Gaza 44
human rights 51–52; Jewish tradition and 113–124; mandate for 253–263
human-rights organizations 262–263
human-rights paradigm 78
human-rights work 51, 65
hydrogen bombs 60

iconic conflict 4
The Idea of Israel (Pappe) 25
identities, conflict of 31; constructing identities 31–33; demographics, ethnicity, and ethnocracy 33; land, "promised land," and illegal settlements 35–36; Palestinian identities and (dis)orientations 39–45; victimhood and war 36–38; Zionism and its discontents 33–35
identity change 47–48
identity formations 47–48
identity groups 81
illegal settlement-building 72
illegal settlements 19, 23, 30, 33, 35–36, 79
importance of Israel-Palestine conflict 4–5
in-depth dialogue 16, 28, 61, 62, 71, 74
indigenous peacemakers 13
informed listener 74
informed listening 10, 20–22, 63
"infrastructure of hope" 88, 276–288
injustice 18, 57, 63, 99–100, 140
interdisciplinary approaches 10
interfaith dialogue 68, 286
International Center of Bethlehem 276
International Criminal Court 180, 222, 242, 256, 258
International Criminal Court of Justice 258–259
international law 5, 15, 56, 174, 176, 177
international law and human rights 43, 48, 70, 78, 216, 225
International Solidarity Movement (ISM) 64, 102, 109, 226
interreligious dialogue 62, 68–69
intersectional dialogues and strategies 82
In the Fields of the Philistines 148
intifada 7, 23, 24, 42, 43, 44, 160, 177, 204, 227, 267, 298, 314
Intimate Brothers (play) 98
intra-dialogue 68
intra-party dialogue 67
"intrinsically positive" dialogue 72
Ionesco 95
Isaac, Munther 36
Islamic *jihad* 5, 40
Islamic Resistance Movement (Hamas) 41
Israel-Gaza wars 47, 225
Israeli-Arab citizens 153
Israeli Bar Association 52, 234
Israeli bombing of Gaza 26
Israeli bomb-making program 60
Israeli Committee Against Home Demolitions (ICAHD) 4, 22, 23, 56, 115, 132, 152, 214, 217, 218, 229
Israeli-Gaza war in 2014 64
Israeli-Hamas war of 2014 79, 289
The Israeli Information Center for Human Rights 314
Israeli-Jewish public 153
Israeli-Palestinian conflict 37
Israeli policy of *hafrada* 31, 64
Israeli Right 65, 226
Israeli-U.S. relationship 9
Israeli war (2006) 5, 38, 184, 345
issue transformation 13, 83

Jabareen, Y. 35
Jenin refugee camp 116, 236
Jeremiah 18, 57, 79
Jericho 139, 171, 179, 282
Jerusalem 5, 7, 9, 39–40, 76, 136, 138, 295
Jerusalem as *corpus separatum* 40
Jerusalem Center for Women 314
Jewish democracy 33, 53, 215, 240, 241
Jewish homeland 33

Jewish nationalism 215
Jewish tradition 254; and human rights 113–124
Jewish Voice for Peace (JVP) 82, 273
Jifna 294–295
jihad 5, 40, 239
Jordan 21, 94
Jordan/Egypt option 180
Judaism 36, 117, 254
Judaization 32, 229
Justice and Only Justice (Naim Ateek) 25, 68, 133, 138
justice and peace, journey for 133–144
justice workers 24, 46–47, 56, 58, 62

Kaba, M. 80
Kahanoff, M. 31, 33, 40
Kairos Palestine (2009) 10, 40, 57, 77, 79
Karyat Arba 98
Kaufman, E. 14, 15, 16, 23, 54, 72, 74
Keaten, J. 78
Kellett, P. M. 10, 62, 70, 81
Kelley, D. L. 84, 85
Kerry, John 7, 76, 226, 230
Kerry's POOF 76, 226, 230–231
Khalidi, R. 4, 5, 6, 7, 8, 15, 31, 32, 39, 40, 43, 45, 75
Khalidi, W. 6
Khan Younis 205
Kibbutzim 182, 183, 188
King, Martin Luther 160, 166, 201
Klein, M. 27
Klein, N. 82, 224
Knesset 28, 50, 65, 115, 150
Knowles, J. G. 10
Kuttab, D. 142
Kuttab, J. 5, 22, 36, 38, 47, 49, 51, 52, 53, 54, 72, 74, 78, 220, 233–244
Kuttab Holy Land Law Firm 233

Labour Party 190
laissez faire capitalism 224
land 35–36
land-for-peace paradigm 41, 78
land grabs 35, 126
la'ounf 164, 166
leadership 3, 27, 108, 109, 166, 249
Lederach, J. P. 4, 11, 12, 13, 14, 23, 24, 31, 45, 61, 62, 63, 66, 73, 75, 81, 83, 87, 88, 228, 232
Levy, G. 5, 9, 21, 24, 26, 31, 36, 38, 49, 52, 59, 63, 67, 71, 72, 79, 86, 181, 245–252, 265, 303, 309
LGBTQ 312
liberal Zionism 23, 33, 35, 47, 48
liberal Zionists 26, 35, 45
liberation 57, 85; 1947–1949 war of 85
liberation theology 53, 68, 140, 141
Likud party 187, 303
limbo 77–78
listening for understanding 63
The Longing (2001) 19, 39
Lutheran World Federation 284

Machsom Watch 139, 306
Madison, D. S. 10–11, 18–19
Madrid Conference (1991) 32
Malki, R. 27
Maltz, J. 86
marked knowledge 20
matrix of control 32, 216–219, 317
Mattar, P. 78
Mazen, A. 227, 320
McDonald, J. 13, 15, 48, 49, 60
meaningful dialogue 4, 22, 62, 74
mediation 13, 23
Melkite Catholic Church 195
Memorandum of Understanding (MOU) 8
Memorial Day 303, 306
Miall, H. 12
Middle East 5, 10, 25, 43, 53, 71, 153, 248, 318
Middle East Children's Alliance (MECA) 203, 208, 212
"middle out" approach 27
mid-level advocacy 67
mid-level peacemakers 3, 27, 30, 66, 74, 77, 79, 88
mid-level peacemaking 23, 30
military culture 38
military planning 250
Milner, A. 98
minimum basis for peace 77
Minister of Planning 292, 299
models of conflict and peacemaking 12–16
Monk, G. 10
Montell, J. 49, 51, 253
Montville, J. 13, 36–37, 45, 60, 63, 84
Moore, M. 192
Morris, B. 6, 21, 149, 265
Mount of Olives 291
Moustafa, M. 171
movement of direct action 15
multi-layered approach 27
multiple roles and goals 48–50
multi-track diplomacy 14, 16
multi-track peacemaking 27–28
Munayyer, Y. 26, 78
Muslims 68, 99–100, 102, 136, 137, 141, 161, 162, 199, 224
mythistory 32, 45

Naji Al-Ali, cartoons of 97
Nakba 17, 18, 19, 33, 47, 75, 80, 185, 187, 190–191, 304, 307
"naming and shaming," process of 51
narrative mediation 10

narrative of 1948 271
National Communication Association meeting in Atlanta (2003) 19
national identity, Palestinian 32
nationalism 31–34, 36, 67, 155, 244
National Reform Committee 130
nation building, peacemaking and 125–132
nation-states 32, 170
Navy Seals 312
Nazareth 133, 137, 138, 139
Nazi Germany 278
Nazi laws 240
negotiations 10, 13; deceptive 72; dialogic 62, 70; dialogue and 70–72; endless 72; false 72; Oslo 216
neutral objective body 241
Neve Shalom 69, 70, 306
New Horizons Wahat al-Salam for Children and Women 209
The New York Times 78
nongovernmental leaders 14, 26, 46
nongovernmental peacebuilders 26
nongovernmental peacemakers 3, 9, 14, 16, 27, 142, 143, 293
nonstate actors 15
nonviolence 53–55, 68, 122, 237, 238, 291; communal 55; strategic 82–83, 87
nonviolence movement 111, 131, 142, 159, 203, 272
nonviolent alternative 264–275
nonviolent civil disobedience 180
nonviolent conflict transformation 13
nonviolent movement 122, 136, 158–170, 237
nonviolent peacemaking 15
nonviolent social change 19
Norman, J. M. 15
Norwegian academics 7
nuclear weapons, international tensions over 5
Nusierat Camp of Gaza 209

Oasis of Peace 70
Obama, Barack 76, 141, 181
obsessive territoriality 35
occupation 131, 282
occupation-apartheid-warehousing complex 83
Occupied Palestinian Territories (OPT) 3, 29, 35, 43, 67, 69, 75, 77, 78, 84
Occupied Territories 7, 52, 78, 154, 225, 246, 320
One Democratic State (ODS) 86, 274
One Democratic State Campaign (ODSC) 87, 231
One Land, Two Peoples (Deborah Gerner) 5
one-state solution 77, 86, 122, 134–135, 142, 167, 211, 223, 225–229, 287, 291, 292, 317
Operation Cast Lead (2008–09) 5
Operation Pillar of Defense (2012) 5
Operation Protective Edge (2014) 5
oppression 11, 30, 53, 55–56, 77, 79, 85, 99, 100, 128, 135, 161, 164, 234–236, 240–241, 243, 244, 273, 282, 287, 307, 311
Orbis Books 138
orientations for understanding Israel-Palestine conflict 3; dialogue, ethnography, and peacemaking 10–12; failure of U.S. diplomacy 8–9; importance 4–5; interdisciplinary approaches 10; models of conflict and peacemaking 12–16; "peace process" as deception 9–10; Track One diplomacy, failure of 5–8
Oscars 192
Oslo Accords 7, 15, 18, 25, 43
Oslo II (1995) 7
Oslo process 7, 70, 72, 171, 216, 230, 244
Ottoman Empire 5
out-violencing 238
Oxford Research Group 180

Pacheco, A. 15, 43
Palestine Authority (PA) 27
The Palestine Centre for Rapprochement between People (PCR) 64
Palestine Center for the Study of Nonviolence 54
Palestine Liberation Organization (PLO) 40–41
Palestine National Council (PNC) 41
Palestine News Network (PNN) 162
Palestine Telecommunications Company 172
Palestinian Authority (PA) 9, 32, 50, 162, 181
Palestinian Centre for Rapprochement (PCR) 102
Palestinian citizens of Israel 33, 40, 56, 69, 70
Palestinian identities and (dis)orientations 39; failed "peace process" 43; First Intifada: 1987–1993 41–43; Gaza, Hamas, and the Great March of Return 44–45; Jerusalem 39–40; Palestine Liberation Organization (PLO) 40–41; Palestinian citizens of Israel 40; refugees 39; second *intifada* 44; six-day war and occupation 41
Palestinian Initiative for the Promotion of Global Dialogue and Democracy (MIFTAH) 23, 28, 49, 125
Palestinian land, loss of 29–30
Palestinian Liberation Organization (PLO) 9, 54, 181, 184
Palestinian liberation theology (1989) 53, 57, 140
Palestinian national identity 32, 40
Palestinian nationalism 41, 43, 87, 280
Palestinian Right 65, 78, 111, 131, 226
Palestinian Territories 41
pandemics 17, 82
Pappe, I. 6, 7, 8, 9, 17, 21, 23, 24, 25, 29, 31, 33, 34, 35, 37, 38, 40, 43, 44, 46, 47, 48, 49,

53, 55, 57, 58, 60, 62, 66, 70, 73, 79, 80, 82, 83, 87, 141, 155, 169, 207, 230, 231, 286
Parajuli, P. 20
Parents' Circle-Families Forum (PC-FF) 69–70
peace and justice workers 24, 46–47, 56, 58, 62
peacebuilders 23, 26, 27, 28, 30, 60, 86
peacebuilding 13, 14, 23–24, 316
peacemaker identities 46; arts, peacemaking through 58–59; education and peacemaking 58; human rights 51–52; identity formations 47–48; multiple roles and goals 48–50; nonviolence, popular resistance, and *sumud* 53–55; price of peacemaking 59–60; religion and peacemaking 56–58; South Africa and Boycott, Divestment, and Sanctions (BDS) campaign 55–56; truth and justice, perceptions of 52–53
peacemakers 31, 35, 36, 86; dialogues between 64–65; political definition of 24
peacemaking 11, 13, 15, 23–24; business of 171–181; education and 58; mid-level 23, 30; models of conflict and 12–16; multi-track 27–28; and nation building 125–132; nonviolent 15; and peacebuilding 23–24; price of 59–60; religion and 56–58; terms 22–27
Peace Now 23, 46, 150, 187, 267, 303
peace process 139, 237; as deception 9–10; diplomatic 76; failure of 43; Oslo Peace process 7; 2013–14 peace process 7
Pearlman, W. 15, 54, 83
Peleg, I. 39
People to People (P2P) programs 69, 117
Perez, S. 245
performative dialogue 11
personal and group transformations 13, 83–84
personal narratives 97, 129
Philpott, D. 23
Plan Dalet 6
platform for a just peace 75, 87; conflict analyses 75–76; forgiveness and reconciliation 85; "infrastructure of hope" 88; international law and human rights redux 78; liberation 85; limbo 77–78; minimum basis for peace 77; platform for a just peace 87–88; principles for a just peace 76–77; processes, structures, and scenarios 85–87; prophetic mourning and warning 79–80; restorative justice 84–85; security and safety 80; strategic dialogues 80–82; strategic nonviolence 82–83; transformations and restorations 83–85; trauma healing 84
Plaza Shopping Center 172
PLC (Palestinian Legislative Council) 130
"poetry of violence" 54, 237, 239
POOF 76, 226, 230–231
popular resistance 15, 42, 53–55, 93, 165, 311
positionality 11, 18–19, 30, 60
post-Zionism 35
post-Zionist 147
Powers, G. F. 23
price of peacemaking 59–60
principles for a just peace 76–77
"Principles for a Just Peace in Israel-Palestine" (2004) 53, 56
proactive movement 161
Proclamation of Independence for Israel 314, 319
professional dialoguers 73
pro-Israeli 18
promised land 34–36, 45
pro-Palestinian 18
prophetic mourning and warning 79–80
public opinion in Israel 145–157
pyramid of approaches to peacebuilding 14

Qaqun 182, 183, 187
Quartet 26, 126
Qumsiyeh, M. B. 15, 29, 42, 43, 54, 93
Qur'an 100

Rabbis for Human Rights 113, 114, 118, 132, 152, 174
Rabin, Y. 7, 42
Rabin Square 187
Raheb, M. 24, 32, 37, 45, 47, 48, 49, 57, 58, 59, 62, 67–69, 77, 82, 83, 84, 87, 88, 231
Ramsbotham, O. 12, 13, 14, 22, 63, 66, 67, 70, 81, 83, 86
Rapprochement Center 107, 108, 110
reconciliation 46, 57, 182–191
refugee experiences 47, 84
refugees 6, 39, 41, 91
Refusing to Be Enemies (2010) 15
relationships, building 20, 61, 63–64, 74
religion: multiple peacemaking roles for 68; and peacemaking 56–58
resistance 201; popular resistance 15, 42, 53–55, 93, 165, 311; tax resistance 107–108
Resolution 242 7, 41
restitution 48, 84, 85
restorations, transformations and 83; forgiveness and reconciliation 85; liberation 85; restorative justice 84–85; trauma healing 84
restorative justice 4, 17, 24, 84–85
right-wing Israeli policies 8
Roach, C. 20
Romero, O. 201
Rome Statute of the International Criminal Court 256
Rotberg, R. 73
Rouhana, N. N. 33, 35, 40

Roy, S. 44
Rubenberg, C. A. 7, 33
rule by law 241

Sabeel Center for Liberation Theology 25, 133
Sabeel Ecumenical Center for Liberation Theology 56
Sabeel Ecumenical Liberation Theology Center 68
Sabeel Liberation Theology Center 77
safety and security 37, 73, 80
Saffron, H. 314
Said, E. W. 7, 37, 43, 76, 220, 243, 270
Salameh, E. 27, 28, 34, 39, 42, 44, 47, 48, 49, 50, 58, 62, 63, 65, 72, 75, 83, 84, 88, 144, 289–301
Salem, W. 14, 15, 16, 23, 54, 72, 74
"sanctions" campaign 56
Sanders, B. 274
satyagraha 237
Schirch, L. 61, 63, 64, 69
schizophrenia 241, 254, 260
School for Peace 48, 69, 185, 187, 302, 304
second *intifada* 7, 15, 23, 44, 47, 55, 56, 64, 115, 177, 185, 186, 226, 245, 247, 267, 285, 298, 314
Second World War 5, 146
secure borders 7
security and safety 38, 45, 80, 88
Segev, T. 146
Selem Adam 222
self-consciousness 97
self-defense 117, 255, 279
self-determination 5, 214, 223, 225, 227, 252
self-empowerment 159
self-sufficiency 163
Semitic Action movement 150
Semitic union 148
"separation," policy of 64
Seraj 293
settlement-occupation-industrial complex 32
settler colonialism 65, 75, 273, 274
Shainin, J. 15
Shalhoub-Kevorkian, N. 36, 80
shalom
Shalom, G. 28, 50, 150–152, 239, 267
Shapira, Y. 21, 22, 44, 48, 49, 60, 62, 69, 85, 143, 302–313
Sharon, A. 71, 126–127, 250
Sharp, J. M. 8
Shehade, S. 305
The Shimon Peres Negev Nuclear Research Center 60
The Shock Doctrine (Naomi Klein) 224
Shomali, A. 42
The Silence of the Sea 101
Sinai 41, 315
Siniora, H. 15
situated knowledge 20–22, 24, 30
Six Day War 41, 150, 268, 303, 315
Smock, D. R. 68
social entrepreneurs 97
solution 86
South Africa 55–56, 227
South Lebanon 243
Soviet Jews for Justice 273
stakeholders 85
steadfastness 45, 55, 135, 285
strategic dialogues 63, 80–82
strategic engagement of discourses 63
strategic nonviolence 82–83, 87
strategic thinking 81, 141, 285
Stressinger, L. 101
structural transformation 13, 20, 83
struggle 18, 20; anti-apartheid 8, 55, 216; image of 46; for a just peace 214–232
Suleiman, C. 31
sumud 55, 135, 136, 139, 209, 285, 297
surreal discussions 75
Svirsky, G. 33, 35, 36, 41, 44, 48, 80, 186, 267, 272, 314–320
Sykes-Picot Agreement (1916) 5

Taba (2001) 7
Tales of the City by the Sea 101
Talmudic tradition of interpretation 234
Tamari, S. 80
taqwa, principle of 239
tawjihi 104
tax resistance 107–108
Tel al-Zaatar refugee camp 105
Tel Aviv 40, 76, 189, 247, 303, 304
telecommunications 171, 178
tension 11
terms 17; existential terms 17–18; informed listening 20–22; multi-track peacemaking 27–28; Palestinian land, loss of 29–30; peacemaking terms 22–27; positionality and critical ethnography 18–19; situated knowledge 20
terrorism 145
theology: contextual 56, 57, 68, 138, 285; liberation 53, 68, 140, 141
third-party intervention 128
third-party negotiators 8, 13
three-tiered peacemaker model 14
Tillich, P. 63
Torat Tzedek-Torah of Justice 113, 118
Track One diplomacy 5–8, 13, 14, 15, 16, 143
Track Two diplomacy 13, 14, 15, 16, 27, 28, 50, 218
Transformation: actor 13, 83; conflict 3, 11–13, 16, 19, 23, 30, 40, 49, 52, 56, 60, 61, 74, 80, 85, 280; context 13, 83; issue 13, 83; nonviolent conflict 13; personal and group transformations 13, 83–84; structural 13, 20, 83

transformational approach to conflict 12–13
transformational listening, voice and 62–63
transformational view approaches dialogue 62
transformations and restorations 83; forgiveness and reconciliation 85; liberation 85; restorative justice 84–85; trauma healing 84
Transjordan 6
trauma healing 84
tribalism 33–34
triple consciousness 19
Truman, Harry 8
Trump, D. 7, 9, 40, 76, 141
truth and justice 18, 24, 52–53
truth-telling 13, 25, 26, 52–53, 79, 88, 227, 237, 248
Twenty-One Positions (Abdelfattah Abusrour) 101
two-state solution 26, 86, 164, 167, 221, 222

UN agencies 300
unilateral dialogue 71
unitary state 216
United Nations (UN) 4, 5, 6, 7, 256
United Nations Security Council 8
Universal Declaration of Human Rights 51, 78, 216, 255
universal principles, international law 233–244
UN Office for the Coordination of Humanitarian Affairs (OCHA) 44
UN partition plan 6
UN peacekeepers 13
UN Relief and Works Agency (UNRWA) 41
UN Resolution 181 6, 25, 40, 177
UN Resolution 194 56, 87
UNRWA (The United Nations Refugee and Works Agency) 78, 91, 295
UN Security Council Resolution 242 7
UN Universal Declaration of Human Rights 222
U.S. diplomacy, failure of 8–9
U.S. Embassy 9, 40, 78
U.S.-Israel relationship 8

Vanunu, M. 60
Verhoeven, J. 14, 15, 16, 23, 54, 72, 74
victimhood 4, 21, 36–38, 45, 84, 216
"victims of victims" 37, 220
violence 160; colonial 82; domestic 207–209; "poetry of violence" 54, 237, 239
voice 62
voice and transformational listening 62–63

Wagner, D. E. 32, 34
Wahat al Salam 69, 70, 304, 313
Waldron, V. R. 84, 85
Wallace, N. 101
war: crimes 256; holy wars 5, 35, 161; Israel-Gaza wars 47, 225; 1947–1949 war of liberation 85; Six Day War 150, 268, 303, 315; victimhood and 36–38
warehousing 82, 83, 224
war of 1948 6, 39, 40, 73, 76, 148
war of 1967 7, 35, 41, 45, 47, 147, 150, 187, 214, 268
war of 2014 44, 64, 77, 78, 79, 117, 166, 212
War or Peace in the Semitic Region 147, 148
Warsaw Ghetto 268
Washington (2010) 7
Waxman, D. 39
We are the Children of the Camp 101
We Belong to the Land (Elias Chacour) 198, 199
Weizman, E. 73
West Bank 5, 7, 9, 19, 35, 39, 41, 43, 55, 73, 76, 77, 96, 120, 136, 138, 150, 175, 188, 208, 210, 212, 229, 247, 277, 290, 319, 320
Western European style democracy 33
West Jerusalem 141, 263
White House lawn 7
Wildangel, R. 7
Wink, W. 38, 250
Winslade. J. 10
win-win solutions 70, 81
Women for Peace 314, 318
Women Resist War and Occupation 320
women's empowerment 130
Wood, J. T. 11, 61
Woodhouse, T. 12
work for the common good 289–301

Yoder, C. 84
Yom Kippur War 38, 302, 249, 316

Zehr, H. 84, 85
zero-sum game 18
Zionism 23, 24, 33–37, 45, 48, 57, 60, 65, 98, 114, 146, 147, 154, 186, 188, 191, 214–215, 216, 234, 241, 266, 267, 268, 272, 273, 280, 318–319
The Zionist Idea (Arthur Hertzberg) 114
Zionist movement 7, 41, 146, 147, 175
Zionists 34, 240
Zochrot 183, 189–190